Award
Garden Merit
Plants
2003

Published in 2003 by
The Royal Horticultural Society,
80 Vincent Square, London SW1P 2PE

ISBN 0 1 902896 33 5

First published in 1993, second edition 1994, third edition 1998, fourth edition 2000.
fifth edition 2002, sixth edition 2003

Cover photographs:
Copyright RHS Herbarium
(front cover, top left) *Iris sibirica* 'Perfect Vision'
(front cover, bottom left) *Anemone blanda*
(front cover, right) Damson 'Farleigh's Damson', photographed by Graham Titchmarsh
(back cover, left) *Petunia* CONCHITA CRANBERRY FROST 'Concran', photographed by
Graham Titchmarsh
(back cover, right) *Eryngium planum* 'Bethlehem'

Printed by: Page Bros, Norfolk

visit the Royal Horticultural Society on the world wide web
www.rhs.org.uk

CONTENTS

INTRODUCTION   5
HARDY TREES, SHRUBS, CLIMBERS & BAMBOOS
    Trees & Shrubs   9
    Climbers   39
    Conifers   44
    Bamboos   47
HARDY HERBACEOUS PERENNIALS, GRASSES, BULBS & FERNS
    Herbaceous Perennials   48
    Grasses   73
    Bulbs, Corms & Tubers   74
    Ferns   89
HARDY ROCK AND ALPINE PLANTS   91
PLANTS FOR GLASS
    Heated Glass Protection:
        General   106
        Cacti & Succulents   116
        Climbers   121
        Summer Display   123
    Unheated Glass Protection:
        General   127
        Climbers   131
    Plants for the Alpine House   132
HARDY & HALF-HARDY ANNUALS
    Annuals for the Garden   134
    Annual Grasses for Drying   139
FRUIT AND VEGETABLES
    The Vegetable Garden   140
    The Fruit Garden   163
TRIALS IN 2003   166
INDEX TO ORNAMENTAL GENERA   168

INTRODUCTION

Changes in this edition

In this new edition of *AGM Plants*, the text of *AGM Plants 2002* has been fully updated to include all awards made to plants after trial in 2002. Plant names have been revised in the light of new taxonomic information, and notes and hardiness ratings have been modified where necessary. A number of plants that were omitted in error from the last edition have been reinstated.

The most noteworthy change however is the inclusion of detailed descriptions of AGM vegetables. These descriptions have been provided by members of the Vegetable Trials Sub-Committee, and reflect many years' collective experience both of overseeing vegetable trials for the Society, and of involvement in the horticultural trade itself. In accordance with the original purpose of the AGM, the descriptions are aimed at the ordinary gardener, and so concentrate on yield, flavour, appearance, best growing conditions, etc. It is hoped that these descriptions will prove to be of real practical use to gardeners when choosing between the many varieties of vegetable now available.

AGM Criteria

The AGM is intended to be of practical value to the ordinary gardener. It is awarded therefore only to a plant that meets the following criteria:

• it must be of outstanding excellence for ordinary garden decoration or use

• it must be available from nurseries, seed suppliers or specialist growers

• it must be of good constitution

• it must not require highly specialist growing conditions or care

• it must not be particularly susceptible to any pest or disease

• it must not be subject to an unreasonable degree of reversion in its vegetative or floral characteristics

Plants of all kinds can be considered for the AGM, including fruit and vegetables. An AGM plant may be cultivated for use or decoration. It can be hardy throughout the British Isles, or suitable only for cultivation under heated glass. It can range in size from *Sequoiadendron giganteum* to *Cornus canadensis*. Though growing conditions and plant types may vary, the purpose of the award is always the same: to highlight the best plants available to the ordinary gardener.

Committee assessment

The AGM is only awarded after a period of assessment by the Society's Standing and Joint Committees. Committees draw upon the knowledge and experience of a wide range of members, including nurserymen, specialist growers, and well-known horticulturists. Assessment for AGM takes place in one or more of the following ways:

• during trials at one of the Society's gardens or at some other venue

• during examination of specialist collections

• during round-table discussions by committee members, with contributions by specialists when necessary

Each Committee is responsible for recommending plants for the AGM from within its own particular area of interest. Round-table discussion necessarily played a large part in the first ten-yearly AGM review, the results of which appeared in the last edition, but trials continue to be the principal means of judging garden merit. This is especially the case in plant groups where large numbers of new cultivars are introduced each year.

There is no grading system within the AGM, and no attempt is made to distinguish the good from the very good. Committees are expected to set a particular standard against which each plant is to be judged: if a plant equals or exceeds the standard, it may be recommended for the award. No limit has been placed on the number of plants that may hold the award at any one time, but in groups that include many cultivars, standards have to be set especially high if the AGM is to offer helpful guidance to the gardener.

How to use this book

AGM Plants 2003 includes all confirmed awards as of January 2003.

To the left of each name there is a reference, in small type, to the year in which the plant received its award, e.g. 93 'Edward Goucher'.

The award lists are grouped into six sections:

1. Hardy trees and shrubs, including conifers, climbers and bamboos
2. Hardy herbaceous perennials, grasses, bulbs and ferns
3. Rock and alpine plants
4. Plants for glass, including heated and unheated protection, and plants
       for the alpine house
5. Hardy and half-hardy annuals
6. Fruit, vegetables and culinary herbs

Fruit and vegetables appear under their common names. All other plants are listed by botanical name. Common synonyms are cross-referred. In addition, an alphabetical index at the back of the book identifies the pages on which species and cultivars belonging to ornamental genera may be found. Some genera may be found in two or more categories, in which case a category description accompanies each page reference, e.g.

Lathyrus
        annuals 136
        as rock plants 98
        climbing 42
        hardy perennials 64

HARDINESS RATING
Every AGM plant has a hardiness rating. This is intended to serve as a general guide to growing conditions, and should be interpreted as follows:

H1	requires heated glass
H2	requires unheated glass
H3	hardy outside in some regions or particular situations or which, while usually grown outside in summer, needs frost-free protection in winter (e.g. dahlias)
H4	hardy throughout the British Isles
H1-2	intermediate between H1 and H2
H2-3	intermediate between H2 and H3
H3-4	intermediate between H3 and H4
H1+3	requiring heated glass; may be grown outside in summer

In the notes that follow entries for plants requiring heated glass, further guidance is given as follows:

Minimum temperature (°C)

15	hot glasshouse
10	warm glasshouse
2	cool glasshouse

The hardiness rating is an integral part of the AGM, and should be included in any citation of the award.

KEY TO ABBREVIATIONS
Certain groups of plants are preceded by a table of classification codes. For example, in
        Rosa 'Belle de Crécy' (G) (H4)
reference to the table at the head of *Rosa* indicates that (G) = a Gallica rose.

Other more general abbreviations are used throughout the book:
• between year and plant name:

A   annual
B   bulb, corm or tuber
C   climber
F   fern
G   suitable for cultivation under glass
H   herbaceous perennial
P   perennial grown as an annual
R   suitable for the rock garden or alpine house
T   tree or shrub

• after the plant name:
(v)   variegated
(d)   double-flowered
(f)   female
(m)   male
(F)   fruit
(C)   culinary
(D)   dessert

How to recognise the award
The trophy symbol ♀ is used throughout the horticultural trade. It appears on plant labels, in nursery catalogues, and in many books and magazines - including, of course, all the Society's own publications.

It is always worth checking that a plant labelled AGM or ♀ is included in *AGM Plants 2003*.

Orchids
All orchids other than those suitable for cultivation as rock garden or alpine house plants have been removed from the AGM list. The Orchid Committee is of the opinion that it cannot award AGMs to orchid cultivars, since these are generally only available for sale as tissue-cultured plants for periods of as little as six months.

Acknowledgements
The Society would like to thank all Committee members for the care and attention that has been given to the AGM assessment process during the past year. The Society is especially indebted to the members of the Vegetable Trials Sub-Committee for their hard work in compiling the descriptions of AGM vegetables. Janet Cook's valuable help in further developing the programming of the *AGM Plants 2003* database is also greatly appreciated.

HARDY TREES, SHRUBS, CLIMBERS & BAMBOOS

Trees & Shrubs

ABELIA (CAPRIFOLIACEAE)
  chinensis hort.
    ~ see *Abelia* × *grandiflora*
93 *floribunda* (H3)
93 × *grandiflora* (H4)
  rupestris hort.
    ~ see *Abelia* × *grandiflora*
02 *schumannii* (H4)

ABUTILON (MALVACEAE)
93 G *megapotamicum* (H3)
93 × *suntense* 'Jermyns' (H3)
93 *vitifolium* 'Tennant's White' (H3)
93 — 'Veronica Tennant' (H3)

ACER (ACERACEAE)
93 *campestre* (H4)
93 *capillipes* (H4)
93 *cappadocicum* 'Aureum' (H4)
93 — 'Rubrum' (H4)
93 *davidii* 'George Forrest' (H4)
93 — 'Serpentine' (H4)
93 *griseum* (H4)
93 *grosseri* var. *hersii* (H4)
93 *japonicum* 'Aconitifolium' (H4)
  — 'Aureum' ~ see *Acer shirasawanum*
    'Aureum'
  — 'Filicifolium' ~ see *Acer japonicum*
    'Aconitifolium'
  — 'Laciniatum'
    ~ see *Acer japonicum* 'Aconitifolium'
93 — 'Vitifolium' (H4)
93 *palmatum* 'Bloodgood' (H4)
93 — 'Burgundy Lace' (H4)
93 — 'Chitoseyama' (H4)
93 — var. *dissectum* (H4)
93 — — 'Crimson Queen' (H4)
93 — — 'Garnet' (H4)
93 — — 'Inaba-shidare' (H4)
93 — — 'Seiryû' (H4)
02 — 'Katsura' (H4)
02 — 'Nigrum' (H4)
93 — 'Ôsakazuki' (H4)
93 — 'Red Pygmy' (H4)

93 — 'Sango-kaku' (H4)
  — 'Senkaki' ~ see *Acer palmatum*
    'Sango-kaku'
02 — 'Trompenburg' (H4)
93 *pensylvanicum* (H4)
93 *platanoides* (H4)
93 — 'Crimson King' (H4)
93 — 'Schwedleri' (H4)
93 *pseudoplatanus* 'Brilliantissimum'
    (H4)
93 *rubrum* 'October Glory' (H4)
93 *rufinerve* (H4)
93 *shirasawanum* 'Aureum' (H4)
  tegmentosum subsp. *glaucorufinerve*
    ~ see *Acer rufinerve*
02 *triflorum* (H4)

AESCULUS (HIPPOCASTANACEAE)
93 × *carnea* 'Briotii' (H4)
93 *flava* (H4)
93 *hippocastanum* (H4)
93 — 'Baumannii' (d) (H4)
  — 'Flore Pleno' ~ see *Aesculus*
    hippocastanum 'Baumannii'
02 *indica* 'Sydney Pearce' (H4)
93 × *neglecta* 'Erythroblastos' (H4)
93 *parviflora* (H4)
93 *pavia* (H4)
  splendens ~ see *Aesculus pavia*

AETHIONEMA (BRASSICACEAE)
93 R *grandiflorum* (H4)
93 R — Pulchellum Group (H4)
93 R 'Warley Rose' (H4)

ALNUS (BETULACEAE)
93 *cordata* (H4)
93 *glutinosa* 'Imperialis' (H4)

ALYSSUM (BRASSICACEAE)
93 R *spinosum* 'Roseum' (H4)

AMELANCHIER (ROSACEAE)
93 × *grandiflora* 'Ballerina' (H4)

93 **lamarckii** (H4) ~ *often grown as* A. canadensis

ANDROMEDA (ERICACEAE)
93 R *polifolia* 'Compacta' (H4)
93 R — 'Compacta Alba' (H4)
93 R — 'Macrophylla' (H4)

ARALIA (ARALIACEAE)
chinensis hort. ~ see *Aralia elata*
93 *elata* (H4) ~ *may sucker; for wild garden*
— 'Albomarginata' ~ see *Aralia elata* 'Variegata'
93 — 'Variegata' (v) (H4)
sieboldii ~ see *Fatsia japonica*

ARBUTUS (ERICACEAE)
93 x *andrachnoides* (H4)*
93 *menziesii* (H3)*
93 *unedo* (H4)*
93 — f. *rubra* (H4)*
* *omitted in error from* AGM Plants 2002

ARTEMISIA (ASTERACEAE)
93 *abrotanum* (H4)
93 *alba* 'Canescens' (H4)
arborescens 'Brass Band' ~ see *Artemisia* 'Powis Castle'
canescens hort. ~ see *Artemisia alba* 'Canescens'
93 'Powis Castle' (H3)
procera Willd. ~ see *Artemisia abrotanum*
splendens hort. ~ see *Artemisia alba* 'Canescens'

AUCUBA (AUCUBACEAE)
93 *japonica* 'Crotonifolia' (f/v) (H4)
02 — 'Golden King' (m/v) (H4)
93 — f. *longifolia* (H4)
02 — 'Rozannie' (f/m) (H4)

AZARA (FLACOURTIACEAE)
93 *microphylla* (H3)
02 *serrata* (H3)

BALLOTA (LAMIACEAE)
02 *acetabulosa* (H3-4)
93 *pseudodictamnus* (H3-4)

BERBERIS (BERBERIDACEAE)
aquifolium 'Fascicularis' ~ see *Mahonia x wagneri* 'Pinnacle'

93 *darwinii* (H4)
93 *dictyophylla* (H4)
93 x *frikartii* 'Amstelveen' (H4)
02 'Georgei' (H4)
02 *julianae* (H4)
'Little Favourite' ~ see *Berberis thunbergii* 'Atropurpurea Nana'
93 x *lologensis* 'Apricot Queen' (H4)
93 x *media* 'Red Jewel' (H4)
93 x *ottawensis* f. *purpurea* 'Superba' (H4)
93 x *stenophylla* (H4)
93 R — 'Corallina Compacta' (H4)
02 *temolaica* (H4)
93 *thunbergii* f. *purpurea* (H4)
93 — — 'Atropurpurea Nana' (H4)
— — 'Atropurpurea Superba' ~ see *Berberis* x *ottawensis* f. *purpurea* 'Superba'
93 — — 'Bagatelle' (H4)
— — 'Crimson Pygmy' ~ see *Berberis thunbergii* f. *atropurpurea* 'Atropurpurea Nana'
02 — — 'Golden Ring' (H4)
93 — — 'Red Chief' (H4)
93 — — 'Rose Glow' (v) (H4)
93 *verruculosa* (H4)

BETULA (BETULACEAE)
alba L. ~ see *Betula pendula*
93 *albosinensis* (H4)
93 — var. *septentrionalis* (H4)
ermanii 'Blush' ~ see *Betula ermanii* 'Grayswood Hill'
93 — 'Grayswood Hill' (H4)
02 *nigra* 'Heritage' (H4)
93 *pendula* (H4)
— f. *crispa* ~ see *Betula pendula* 'Laciniata'
— 'Dalecarlica' hort. ~ see *Betula pendula* 'Laciniata'
93 — 'Laciniata' (H4)
93 — 'Tristis' (H4)
93 *utilis* var. *jacquemontii* 'Doorenbos' (H4) ~ *this plant may be available in the trade as* Betula utilis var. jacquemontii
02 — — 'Grayswood Ghost' (H4)
93 — — 'Jermyns' (H4)
93 — — 'Silver Shadow' (H4) ~ *this plant may be available in the trade as* Betula utilis var. jacquemontii
verrucosa ~ see *Betula pendula*

BRACHYGLOTTIS (ASTERACEAE)
    greyi misapplied   ~ see *Brachyglottis*
               'Sunshine' (Dunedin Group)
    laxifolia misapplied ~ see *Brachyglottis*
               'Sunshine' (Dunedin Group)
93   *monroi* (H4)
93   'Sunshine' (Dunedin Group) (H4)

BUDDLEJA (BUDDLEJACEAE)
93   *alternifolia* (H4)
93   *davidii* 'Black Knight' (H4)
93   — 'Dartmoor' (H4)
93   — 'Empire Blue' (H4)
02   — 'Nanho Blue' (H4)
02   — 'Nanho Purple' (H4)
93   — 'Royal Red' (H4)
93   — 'White Profusion' (H4)
93   *fallowiana* var. *alba* (H3)
93   *globosa* (H4)
93   'Lochinch' (H3-4)
93   'Pink Delight' (H4)
93   x *weyeriana* 'Sungold' (H4)

BUXUS (BUXACEAE)
02   *balearica* (H4)
93   *sempervirens* (H4)
93   — 'Elegantissima' (v) (H4)
    — 'Japonica Aurea'
            ~ see *Buxus sempervirens*
                'Latifolia Maculata'
93   — 'Latifolia Maculata' (v) (H4)
    — 'Silver Variegated'   ~ see *Buxus*
             sempervirens 'Elegantissima'
93   — 'Suffruticosa' (H4)

CALCEOLARIA (SCROPHULARIACEAE)
93   *integrifolia* (H3)
    rugosa   ~ see *Calceolaria*
                    integrifolia

CALLICARPA (VERBENACEAE)
93   *bodinieri* var. *giraldii* 'Profusion' (H4)

CALLISTEMON (MYRTACEAE)
93 G *citrinus* 'Splendens' (H3)
93 G *linearis* (H3)
93   *salignus* (H3)

CALLUNA (ERICACEAE)
    vulgaris 'Alba Elongata'~ see *Calluna*
               vulgaris 'Mair's Variety'
02   — 'Alexandra' PBR (H4)
02   — 'Alicia' PBR (H4)

93   — 'Allegro' (H4)
02   — 'Anette' PBR (H4)
93   — 'Annemarie' (d) (H4)
93   — 'Anthony Davis' (H4)
93   — 'Beoley Gold' (H4)
93   — 'County Wicklow' (d) (H4)
02   — 'Dark Beauty' PBR (d) (H4)
93   — 'Dark Star' (d) (H4)
93   — 'Darkness' (H4)
93   — 'Elsie Purnell' (d) (H4)
93   — 'Firefly' (H4)
93   — 'Gold Haze' (H4)
93   — 'J.H. Hamilton' (d) (H4)
93   — 'Joy Vanstone' (H4)
02   — 'Kerstin' (H4)
93   — 'Kinlochruel' (d) (H4)
93   — 'Mair's Variety' (H4)
93   — 'Mullion' (H4)
02   — 'My Dream' (d) (H4)
02   — 'Peter Sparkes' (d) (H4)
93   — 'Radnor' (d) (H4)
93   — 'Robert Chapman' (H4)
93   — 'Roland Haagen' (H4)
93   — 'Serlei Aurea' (H4)
93   — 'Silver Queen' (H4)
93   — 'Silver Rose' (H4)
93   — 'Sir John Charrington' (H4)
93   — 'Sister Anne' (H4)
    — 'Snowball'   ~ see *Calluna*
               vulgaris 'My Dream'
93   — 'Spring Cream' (H4)
93   — 'Sunset' (H4)
93   — 'Tib' (d) (H4)
02   — 'Velvet Fascination' (H4)
93   — 'White Lawn' (H4)
93   — 'Wickwar Flame' (H4)

CAMELLIA (THEACEAE)
02   'Black Lace' (*reticulata* x *williamsii*)
               (H4)
    'Contessa Lavinia Maggi'
           ~ see *Camellia japonica*
                  'Lavinia Maggi'
93   'Cornish Snow' (*cuspidata* x
             saluenensis) (H4)
93   'Cornish Spring' (*japonica* x *cuspidata*)
              (H4)
    'Donckelaeri'   ~ see *Camellia*
           japonica 'Masayoshi'
02   'Francie L' (*saluenensis* x
             reticulata) (H3-4)
96   'Freedom Bell' (hybrid) (H4)
02   *hiemalis* 'Sparkling Burgundy' (H3)

93   **'Inspiration'** (*reticulata* × *saluenensis*)
      (H4)

02   *japonica* **'Adelina Patti'** (H4)

93   — **'Adolphe Audusson'** (H4)

93   — **'Akashigata'** (H4)

02   — **'Alba Plena'** (H4)

93   — **'Alexander Hunter'** (H4)

02   — **'Annie Wylam'** (H4)

93   — **'Apple Blossom'** (H4)

02   — **'Australis'** (H4)

02   — **'Ave Maria'** (H4)

93   — **'Ballet Dancer'** (H4)

93   — **'Berenice Boddy'** (H4)

93   — **'Bob Hope'** (H4)

93   — **'Bob's Tinsie'** (H4)

02   — **'Bokuhan'** (H4)

02   — **'Brushfield's Yellow'** (H4)

93   — **'C.M. Hovey'** (H4)

93   — **'Carter's Sunburst'** (H4)

     — **'Chandleri Elegans'**
      ~ see *Camellia japonica* 'Elegans'

     — **'Colonel Firey'**   ~ see *Camellia*
      japonica 'C.M. Hovey'

02   — **'Commander Mulroy'** (H4)

93   — **'Coquettii'** (H4)

02   — **'Desire'** (H4)

93   — **'Doctor Tinsley'** (H4)

     — **'Donckelaeri'**   ~ see *Camellia*
      japonica 'Masayoshi'

93   — **'Elegans'** (H4)

     — **'Elegant Beauty'**   ~ see *Camellia*
      × *williamsii* 'Elegant Beauty'

02   — **'Fire Falls'** (H4)

     — **'Glen 40'**   ~ see *Camellia japonica*
      'Coquettii'

93   — **'Gloire de Nantes'** (H4)

93   — **'Grand Prix'** (H4)

93   — **'Guilio Nuccio'** (H4)

93   — **'Hagoromo'** (H4)

93   — **'Hakurakuten'** (H4)

02   — **'Joseph Pfingstl'** (H4)

     — **'Joy Sander'**   ~ see *Camellia*
      japonica 'Apple Blossom'

93   — **'Jupiter'** Paul (H4)

93   — **'Konronkoku'** (H4)

     — **'Kouron-jura'**   ~ see *Camellia*
      japonca 'Konronkoku'

     — **'Lady Clare'**   ~ see *Camellia*
      japonica 'Akashigata'

93   — **'Lavinia Maggi'** (H4)

02   — **'Lily Pons'** (H4)

02   — **'Lovelight'** (H4)

     — **'Magnoliiflora'**

      ~ see *Camellia japonica* 'Hagoromo'

02   — **'Margaret Davis Picotee'** (H4)

93   — **'Mars'** (H4)

93   — **'Masayoshi'** (H4)

93   — **'Mathotiana Alba'** (H4)

02   — **'Mathotiana Rosea'** (H4)

93   — **'Mercury'** (H4)

     — **'Nigra'**   ~ see *Camellia japonica*
      'Konronkoku'

93   — **'Nuccio's Gem'** (H4)

93   — **'Nuccio's Jewel'** (H4)

93   — **'R.L. Wheeler'** (H4)

93   — **'Rubescens Major'** (H4)

02   — **'San Dimas'** (H4)

93   — **'Scentsation'** (H4)

93   — **'Souvenir de Bahuaud-Litou'** (H4)

02   — **'Sylva'** (H4)

02   — **'Tom Thumb'** (H4)

93   — **'Tricolor'** (H4)

02   — **'Wilamina'** (H4)

     'Jury's Yellow'   ~ see *Camellia*
      × *williamsii* 'Jury's Yellow'

93   **'Leonard Messel'** (*reticulata* ×
      williamsii) (H4)

     'Pink Spangles'   ~ see *Camellia*
      japonica 'Mathotiana Rosea'

02   **'Royalty'** (*japonica* × *reticulata*) (H3)

93   *sasanqua* **'Crimson King'** (H3)

02   — **'Hugh Evans'** (H3)

02   — **'Jean May'** (H3)

     — **'Sparkling Burgundy'**   ~ see
     Camellia hiemalis 'Sparkling Burgundy'

93   **'Spring Festival'** (*cuspidata* hybrid)
      (H4)

     'Tinsie'   ~ see *Camellia japonica*
      'Bokuhan'

02   **'Tom Knudsen'** (*reticulata* × *japonica*)
      (H3)

     'Tricolor Sieboldii'
      ~ see *Camellia japonica* 'Tricolor'

99   **'Tristrem Carlyon'** (*reticulata* hybrid)
      (H4)

93   × *williamsii* **'Anticipation'** (H4)

93   — **'Bowen Bryant'** (H4)

93   — **'Brigadoon'** (H4)

93   — **'China Clay'** (H4)

93   — **'Daintiness'** (H4)

93   — **'Debbie'** (H4)

93   — **'Donation'** (H4)

93   — **'E.T.R. Carlyon'** (H4)

02   — **'Elegant Beauty'** (H4)

93   — **'Elsie Jury'** (H3)

93   — **'Galaxie'** (H4)

93 — 'George Blandford' (H4)
93 — 'Glenn's Orbit' (H4)
93 — 'J.C. Williams' (H4)
93 — 'Joan Trehane' (H4)
93 — 'Julia Hamiter' (H4)
02 — 'Jury's Yellow' (H4)
02 — 'Les Jury' (H4)
93 — 'Mary Christian' (H4)
02 — 'Mary Phoebe Taylor' (H4)
93 — 'Muskoka' (H4)
93 — 'Saint Ewe' (H4)
02 — 'Senorita' (H4)
93 — 'Water Lily' (H4)
02 — 'Wilber Foss' (H4)

CARPENTERIA (HYDRANGEACEAE)
93 *californica* (H3)

CARPINUS (CORYLACEAE)
93 *betulus* (H4)
93 — 'Fastigiata' (H4)
— 'Pyramidalis'   ~ see *Carpinus betulus* 'Fastigiata'
02 *japonica* (H4)
02 *turczaninowii* (H4)

CARYOPTERIS (VERBENACEAE)
02 x *clandonensis* 'Arthur Simmonds' (H4)
            ~ *often sold as 'Heavenly Blue'*
02 — 'First Choice' (H3-4)
02 — 'Worcester Gold' (H3-4)

CASSIOPE (ERICACEAE)
93 R 'Edinburgh' (H4)
93 R *lycopodioides* (H4)
93 R 'Muirhead' (H4)
93 R 'Randle Cooke' (H4)

CASTANEA (FAGACEAE)
93 *sativa* (H4)
02 — 'Albomarginata' (v) (H4)
— 'Argenteovariegata'
    ~ see *Castanea sativa* 'Albomarginata'

CATALPA (BIGNONIACEAE)
93 *bignonioides* (H4)
93 — 'Aurea' (H4)
— 'Purpurea'   ~ see *Catalpa* x *erubescens* 'Purpurea'
93 x *erubescens* 'Purpurea' (H4)

CEANOTHUS (RHAMNACEAE)
93 *arboreus* 'Trewithen Blue' (H3)

93 'Autumnal Blue' (H3)
93 'Blue Mound' (H3)
93 'Burkwoodii' (H3)
93 'Cascade' (H3)
02 'Concha' (H3)
02 'Dark Star' (H3)
93 x *delileanus* 'Gloire de Versailles' (H4)
93 — 'Topaze' (H4)
93 'Edinburgh' (H3)
93 'Italian Skies' (H3)
93 'Puget Blue' (H4)
repens   ~ see *Ceanothus thyrsiflorus* var. *repens*
93 'Southmead' (H3)
93 *thyrsiflorus* var. *repens* (H3)
02 — 'Skylark' (H3)

CERATOSTIGMA (PLUMBAGINACEAE)
93 *willmottianum* (H3-4)

CERCIDIPHYLLUM (CERCIDIPHYLLACEAE)
93 *japonicum* (H4)
02 — f. *pendulum* (H4)

CERCIS (CAESALPINIACEAE)
93 *canadensis* 'Forest Pansy' (H4)
93 *siliquastrum* (H4)

CESTRUM (SOLANACEAE)
93 *parqui* (H3)

CHAENOMELES (ROSACEAE)
speciosa 'Apple Blossom'
        ~ see *Chaenomeles speciosa* 'Moerloosei'
02 — 'Geisha Girl' (H4)
93 — 'Moerloosei' (H4)
93 x *superba* 'Crimson and Gold' (H4)
93 — 'Knap Hill Scarlet' (H4)
93 — 'Nicoline' (H4)
93 — 'Pink Lady' (H4)
93 — 'Rowallane' (H4)

CHAMAECYTISUS (PAPILIONACEAE)
93 *purpureus* 'Atropurpureus' (H4)
— 'Incarnatus'   ~ see *Chamaecytisus purpureus* 'Atropurpureus'

CHAMAEROPS (ARECACEAE)
excelsa hort.   ~ see *Trachycarpus fortunei*
93 *humilis* (H3)

CHIMONANTHUS (CALYCANTHACEAE)
93 *praecox* 'Grandiflorus' (H4)
93 — var. *luteus* (H4)

CHOISYA (RUTACEAE)
93 'Aztec Pearl' (H4)
93 *ternata* (H4)
93 — SUNDANCE 'Lich' PBR (H3)

CISTUS (CISTACEAE)
93 × *aguilarii* 'Maculatus' (H3)
algarvensis
~ see *Halimium ocymoides*
93 × *argenteus* 'Peggy Sammons' (H3)
'Barnsley Pink' ~ see *Cistus*
'Grayswood Pink'
'Chelsea Pink' ~ see *Cistus*
'Grayswood Pink'
crispus 'Sunset' ~ see *Cistus*
× *pulverulentus* 'Sunset'
93 × *cyprius* (H4)
93 — var. *ellipticus* 'Elma' (H3)
93 × *dansereaui* 'Decumbens' (H4)
'Elma' ~ see *Cistus* × *cyprius* var.
ellipticus 'Elma'
02 'Grayswood Pink' (H4)
93 *ladanifer* L. (H3)
— hort. ~ see *Cistus* × *cyprius*
lasianthus ~ see *Halimium lasianthum*
93 *laurifolius* (H4)
'Merrist Wood Cream'
~ see × *Halimiocistus wintonensis*
'Merrist Wood Cream'
ocymoides ~ see *Halimium ocymoides*
parviflorus hort. ~ see *Cistus*
'Grayswood Pink'
'Peggy Sammons' ~ see *Cistus*
× *argenteus* 'Peggy Sammons'
populifolius var. *lasiocalyx* ~ see *Cistus*
populifolius subsp. *major*
93 — subsp. *major* (H3) ~ awarded as
Cistus populifolius
var. *lasiocalyx*
02 × *pulverulentus* 'Sunset' (H3)
93 × *purpureus* (H3)
— 'Betty Taudevin' ~ see *Cistus*
× *purpureus*
sahucii ~ see × *Halimiocistus*
sahucii
'Silver Pink' misapplied ~ see *Cistus*
'Grayswood Pink'
93 × *skanbergii* (H3)
02 'Snow Fire' (H4)

wintonensis ~ see × *Halimiocistus*
wintonensis

CLEMATIS (RANUNCULACEAE)

(H) Heracleifolia Group

93 *tubulosa* 'Wyevale' (H) (H4)
~ previously listed under
C. heracleifolia
var. davidiana 'Wyevale'

CLERODENDRUM (VERBENACEAE)
93 *trichotomum* var. *fargesii* (H4)

CLETHRA (CLETHRACEAE)
93 *alnifolia* 'Paniculata' (H4)
93 *barbinervis* (H4)

CONVOLVULUS (CONVOLVULACEAE)
93 R *cneorum* (H3)

CORDYLINE (AGAVACEAE)
93 G *australis* (H3)
94 G — 'Albertii' (v) (H3)
02 G — 'Sundance' (H3)
02 G — 'Torbay Dazzler' (v) (H3)
02 G — 'Torbay Red' (H3)

CORNUS (CORNACEAE)
95 *alba* 'Aurea' (H4)
93 — 'Elegantissima' (v) (H4)
93 — 'Sibirica' (H4)
93 — 'Spaethii' (v) (H4)
— 'Westonbirt'
~ see *Cornus alba* 'Sibirica'
93 *alternifolia* 'Argentea' (v) (H4)
— 'Variegata' ~ see *Cornus*
alternifolia 'Argentea'
93 *controversa* 'Variegata'
(v) (H4)
93 'Eddie's White Wonder' (H4)
93 *florida* 'Cherokee Chief' (H4)
93 *kousa* var. *chinensis* (H4)
93 — 'Satomi' (H4)
02 *mas* 'Golden Glory' (H4)
93 — 'Variegata' (v) (H4)
93 'Norman Hadden' (H4)
93 'Porlock' (H4)
93 *stolonifera* 'Flaviramea' (H4)
02 — 'White Gold' (v) (H4)
— 'White Spot' ~ see *Cornus*
stolonifera 'White Gold'

CORONILLA (PAPILIONACEAE)
glauca ~ see *Coronilla valentina* subsp. *glauca*
93 G *valentina* subsp. *glauca* (H3)
93 G — subsp. *glauca* 'Citrina' (H3)

CORYLOPSIS (HAMAMELIDACEAE)
93 *pauciflora* (H4)
93 *sinensis* var. *calvescens* f. *veitchiana* (H4)
93 — var. *sinensis* (H4)
veitchiana ~ see *Corylopsis sinensis* var. *calvescens* f. *veitchiana*
willmottiae ~ see *Corylopsis sinensis* var. *sinensis*

CORYLUS (CORYLACEAE)
93 *colurna* (H4)
maxima 'Purple Filbert' ~ see *Corylus maxima* 'Purpurea'
93 — 'Purpurea' (F) (H4)

COTINUS (ANACARDIACEAE)
americanus ~ see *Cotinus obovatus*
93 *coggygria* (H4)
93 — 'Royal Purple' (H4)
93 'Flame' (H4)
93 *obovatus* (H4)

COTONEASTER (ROSACEAE)
93 R *adpressus* (H4)
93 *atropurpureus* 'Variegatus' (v) (H4)
93 *bullatus* (H4)
— f. *floribundus* ~ see *Cotoneaster bullatus*
93 R *cashmiriensis* (H4) ~ usually grown as C. cochleatus
93 R *conspicuus* 'Decorus' (H4) ~ as grown in gardens
93 *dammeri* (H4)
franchetii var. *sternianus* ~ see *Cotoneaster sternianus*
93 *frigidus* 'Cornubia' (H4)
93 *horizontalis* (H4)
— 'Variegatus' ~ see *Cotoneaster atropurpureus* 'Variegatus'
humifusus ~ see *Cotoneaster dammeri*
93 R *integrifolius* (H4) ~ often sold as C. microphyllus
93 *lacteus* (H4)
microphyllus var. *cochleatus* misapplied ~ see *Cotoneaster cashmiriensis*
— var. *thymifolius* (Lindl.) Koehne ~ see *Cotoneaster integrifolius*

'Rothschildianus' ~ see *Cotoneaster salicifolius* 'Rothschildianus'
93 *salicifolius* 'Rothschildianus' (H4)
93 *simonsii* (H4)
93 *sternianus* (H4)
× *watereri* 'Cornubia' ~ see *Cotoneaster frigidus* 'Cornubia'
93 — 'John Waterer' (H4)

CRATAEGUS (ROSACEAE)
crus-galli hort. ~ see *Crataegus persimilis* 'Prunifolia'
laevigata 'Coccinea Plena' ~ see *Crataegus laevigata* 'Paul's Scarlet'
93 — 'Paul's Scarlet' (d) (H4)
93 — 'Rosea Flore Pleno' (d) (H4)
93 × *lavalleei* 'Carrierei' (H4) ~ often listed as C. × lavalleei
93 *persimilis* 'Prunifolia' (H4)
prunifolia ~ see *Crataegus persimilis* 'Prunifolia'

CRINODENDRON (ELAEOCARPACEAE)
93 *hookerianum* (H3)

CYDONIA (ROSACEAE)
93 *oblonga* 'Vranja' Nenadovic (F) (H4)

CYTISUS (PAPILIONACEAE)
albus hort. ~ see *Cytisus multiflorus*
'Andreanus' ~ see *Cytisus scoparius* f. *andreanus*
93 R *ardoinoi* (H4)
93 *battandieri* (H4)
94 — 'Yellow Tail' (H4)
93 R × *beanii* (H4)
93 'Boskoop Ruby' (H4)
93 'Burkwoodii' (H4)
93 'Hollandia' (H4)
93 R × *kewensis* (H4) ~ only for the largest of rock gardens
93 'Lena' (H4)
93 *multiflorus* (H4)
'Porlock' ~ see *Genista* 'Porlock'
93 × *praecox* 'Allgold' (H4)
93 — 'Warminster' (H4)
purpureus 'Atropurpureus' ~ see *Chamaecytisus purpureus* 'Atropurpureus'
93 *scoparius* f. *andreanus* (H4)
93 'Zeelandia' (H4)

DABOECIA (ERICACEAE)
93 *cantabrica* 'Bicolor' (H4)

93   — f. *alba* 'David Moss' (H4)
93   — subsp. *scotica* 'Jack Drake' (H4)
93   — — 'Silverwells' (H4)
93   — — 'William Buchanan' (H4)
93   — 'Waley's Red' (H4)

DAPHNE (THYMELAEACEAE)
93 R *arbuscula* (H4)
93   *bholua* 'Jacqueline Postill' (H3)
93 R × *burkwoodii* (H4)
02   — 'G.K. Argles' (v) (H4)
93 R *cneorum* 'Eximia' (H4)
     japonica 'Striata'   ~ see *Daphne*
                        odora 'Aureomarginata'
93 R × *napolitana* (H4)
02   *odora* 'Aureomarginata' (v) (H3-4)
     — 'Marginata'   ~ see *Daphne odora*
                        'Aureomarginata'
93   *pontica* (H4)
     retusa   ~ see *Daphne tangutica*
                        Retusa Group
93 R *tangutica* (H4)
93 R — Retusa Group (H4)

DAVIDIA (DAVIDIACEAE)
93   *involucrata* (H4)
93   — var. *vilmoriniana* (H4)

DESFONTAINIA (LOGANIACEAE)
93   *spinosa* (H3)
     — *hookeri* ~ see *Desfontainia spinosa*

DESMODIUM (PAPILIONACEAE)
02   *elegans* (H4)
     tiliifolium   ~ see *Desmodium elegans*

DEUTZIA (HYDRANGEACEAE)
     chunii   ~ see *Deutzia ningpoensis*
93   × *elegantissima* 'Rosealind' (H4)
93   × *hybrida* 'Mont Rose' (H4)
93   *longifolia* 'Veitchii' (H4)
     × *magnifica* 'Rubra'   ~ see *Deutzia*
                        'Strawberry Fields'
02   *ningpoensis* (H4)
93   *setchuenensis* var. *corymbiflora* (H4)
94   'Strawberry Fields' (H4)

DIPELTA (CAPRIFOLIACEAE)
02   *floribunda* (H4)

DISANTHUS (HAMAMELIDACEAE)
93   *cercidifolius* (H4)

DRIMYS (WINTERACEAE)
02   *winteri* (H4)

DRYAS (ROSACEAE)
93 R *octopetala* (H4)
93 R — 'Minor' (H4)
93 R × *suendermannii* (H4)

ELAEAGNUS (ELAEAGNACEAE)
     angustifolia Caspica Group
                ~ see *Elaeagnus* 'Quicksilver'
93   × *ebbingei* 'Gilt Edge' (v) (H4)
02   *pungens* 'Goldrim' (v) (H4)
93   'Quicksilver' (H4)   ~ *usually*
     grown as E. angustifolia *var.* caspica

EMBOTHRIUM (PROTEACEAE)
93   *coccineum* (Lanceolatum Group)
                        'Ñorquinco' (H3)

ENKIANTHUS (ERICACEAE)
93   *campanulatus* (H4)
93   *cernuus* f. *rubens* (H4)
93   *perulatus* (H4)

ERICA (ERICACEAE)
93   *arborea* 'Albert's Gold' (H4)
93   — var. *alpina* (H4)
     — 'Arbora Gold'   ~ see *Erica*
                        arborea 'Albert's Gold'
     — 'Arnold's Gold'   ~ see *Erica*
                        arborea 'Albert's Gold'
93   — 'Estrella Gold' (H4)
93   *australis* (H4)
93   — 'Mr Robert' (H3)
93   — 'Riverslea' (H4)
94   *canaliculata* (H3)
93   *carnea* 'Adrienne Duncan' (H4)
93   — 'Ann Sparkes' (H4)
93   — 'Challenger' (H4)
93   — 'Foxhollow' (H4)
93   — 'Golden Starlet' (H4)
02   — 'Ice Princess' (H4)
02   — 'Isabell' (H4)
93   — 'Loughrigg' (H4)
93   — 'Myretoun Ruby' (H4)
02   — 'Nathalie' (H4)
93   — 'Pink Spangles' (H4)
93   — 'Praecox Rubra' (H4)
93   — 'R.B. Cooke' (H4)
02   — 'Rosalie' (H4)
93   — 'Springwood White' (H4)
93   — 'Sunshine Rambler' (H4)

	— 'Urville' ~ see *Erica carnea* 'Vivellii'
93	— 'Vivellii' (H4)
93	— 'Westwood Yellow' (H4)
93	*ciliaris* 'Mrs C.H. Gill' (H4)
93	— 'Stoborough' (H4)
93	*cinerea* f. *alba* 'Alba Minor' (H4)
93	— — 'Hookstone White' (H4)
93	— 'C.D. Eason' (H4)
93	— 'C.G. Best' (H4)
93	— 'Cindy' (H4)
93	— 'Eden Valley' (H4)
93	— 'Fiddler's Gold' (H4)
93	— 'Golden Hue' (H4)
	— 'Graham Thomas' ~ see *Erica cinerea* 'C.G. Best'
93	— 'Knap Hill Pink' (H4)
02	— 'Lime Soda' (H4)
93	— 'P.S. Patrick' (H4)
93	— 'Pentreath' (H4)
93	— 'Pink Ice' (H4)
93	— 'Stephen Davis' (H4)
93	— 'Velvet Night' (H4)
93	— 'Windlebrooke' (H4)
93	x *darleyensis* 'Arthur Johnson' (H4)
	— 'Cherry Stevens' ~ see *Erica* x *darleyensis* 'Furzey'
93	— 'Furzey' (H4)
93	— 'Ghost Hills' (H4)
93	— 'J.W. Porter' (H4)
93	— 'Jenny Porter' (H4)
93	— 'Kramer's Rote' (H4)
93	— 'White Perfection' (H4)
93	*erigena* 'Golden Lady' (H4)
93	— 'Irish Dusk' (H4)
93	— 'W.T. Rackliff' (H4)
93	*lusitanica* (H3)
93	x *stuartii* 'Irish Lemon' (H4)
93	*terminalis* (H4)
	— *stricta* ~ see *Erica terminalis*
93	*tetralix* 'Alba Mollis' (H4)
93	— 'Con Underwood' (H4)
93	— 'Pink Star' (H4)
93	*vagans* 'Birch Glow' (H4)
93	— 'Cornish Cream' (H4)
93	— 'Kevernensis Alba' (H4)
93	— 'Lyonesse' (H4)
93	— 'Mrs D.F. Maxwell' (H4)
93	— 'Valerie Proudley' (H4)
95	x *veitchii* 'Exeter' (H3)
93	— 'Gold Tips' (H4)
93	x *watsonii* 'Dawn' (H4)
93	x *williamsii* 'P.D. Williams' (H4)

ERINACEA (PAPILIONACEAE)

93 R	*anthyllis* (H4)
	pungens ~ see *Erinacea anthyllis*

ERIOBOTRYA (ROSACEAE)

93	*japonica* (F) (H3)

ESCALLONIA (ESCALLONIACEAE)

93	'Apple Blossom' (H4)
02	*bifida* (H3)
93	'Donard Radiance' (H4)
93	'Iveyi' (H3)
93	'Langleyensis' (H4)
	montevidensis ~ see *Escallonia bifida*
93	'Peach Blossom' (H4)
93	'Pride of Donard' (H4)
93	*rubra* 'Crimson Spire' (H4)

EUCALYPTUS (MYRTACEAE)

93	*dalrympleana* (H3)
93	*gunnii* (H3)
	niphophila ~ see *Eucalyptus pauciflora* subsp. *niphophila*
93	*parvifolia* (H4)
93	*pauciflora* subsp. *niphophila* (H4)

EUCRYPHIA (EUCRYPHIACEAE)

93	*glutinosa* (H4)
93	x *intermedia* 'Rostrevor' (H3)
93	x *nymansensis* 'Nymansay' (H3)

EUONYMUS (CELASTRACEAE)

93	*alatus* (H4)
	— 'Ciliodentatus' ~ see *Euonymus alatus* 'Compactus'
93	— 'Compactus' (H4)
93	*europaeus* 'Red Cascade' (H4)
93	*fortunei* 'Emerald Gaiety' (v) (H4)
	~ *reconfirmed after trial 2001*
93	— 'Emerald 'n' Gold' (v) (H4)
	~ *reconfirmed after trial 2001*
02	— 'Emerald Surprise' (v) (H4)
02	— 'Tustin' (H4)
	japonicus 'Aureovariegatus' ~ see *Euonymus japonicus* 'Ovatus Aureus'
02	— 'Chollipo' (H4)
	— 'Marieke' ~ see *Euonymus japonicus* 'Ovatus Aureus'
93	— 'Ovatus Aureus' (v) (H4)
99	*phellomanus* (H4)
93	*planipes* (H4)
	sachalinensis hort. ~ see *Euonymus planipes*

EUPHORBIA (EUPHORBIACEAE)
longifolia Lamarck
~ see *Euphorbia mellifera*
02 *mellifera* (H3)

EURYOPS (ASTERACEAE)
93 R *acraeus* (H4)
evansii ~ see *Euryops acraeus*

EXOCHORDA (ROSACEAE)
93 x *macrantha* 'The Bride' (H4)

FABIANA (SOLANACEAE)
93 *imbricata* f. *violacea* (H3)

FAGUS (FAGACEAE)
93 *sylvatica* (H4)
93 — 'Dawyck' (H4)
93 — 'Dawyck Gold' (H4)
93 — 'Dawyck Purple' (H4)
— 'Fastigiata' misapplied ~ see *Fagus sylvatica* 'Dawyck'
93 — var. *heterophylla* 'Aspleniifolia' (H4)
93 — 'Pendula' (H4)
93 — 'Purple Fountain' (H4)
93 — 'Riversii' (H4)

× FATSHEDERA (ARALIACEAE)
93 G *lizei* (H3)
93 G — 'Annemieke' (v) (H3)
— 'Lemon and Lime'
~ see × *Fatshedera lizei* 'Annemieke'
— 'Maculata' ~ see × *Fatshedera lizei* 'Annemieke'
93 G — 'Variegata' (v) (H3)

FATSIA (ARALIACEAE)
93 *japonica* (H4)
93 G — 'Variegata' (v) (H3)

FELICIA (ASTERACEAE)
93 G *amelloides* 'Santa Anita' (H3)
93 G — 'Santa Anita Variegated' (v) (H3)

FORSYTHIA (OLEACEAE)
93 x *intermedia* 'Lynwood' (H4)
96 — WEEK-END 'Courtalyn' PBR(H4)
02 MARÉE D'OR 'Courtasol' PBR(H4)

FOTHERGILLA (HAMAMELIDACEAE)
93 *major* (H4)

FRAXINUS (OLEACEAE)
93 *angustifolia* 'Raywood' (H4)
93 *excelsior* 'Jaspidea' (H4)
93 — 'Pendula' (H4)
93 — 'Westhof's Glorie' (H4)
93 *ornus* (H4)

FREMONTODENDRON (STERCULIACEAE)
93 'California Glory' (H3)

FUCHSIA (ONAGRACEAE)
93 'Achievement' (H4)
02 'Alice Hoffman' (d) (H3-4)
02 'Alison Patricia' (H3)
93 'Annabel' (d) (H3)
93 'Army Nurse' (d) (H4)
93 'Border Queen' (H3-4)
93 'Brutus' (H4)
93 'Celia Smedley' (H3)
93 'Checkerboard' (H3)
93 'Chillerton Beauty' (H3)
02 'Coachman' (H4)
93 'Dark Eyes' (d) (H4)
93 'Display' (H4)
02 'Doctor Foster' (H4)
93 'Dollar Princess' (d) (H4)
93 'Empress of Prussia' (H4)
93 'Flash' (H3-4)
02 'Foxgrove Wood' (H3-4)
93 'Garden News' (d) (H3-4)
93 'Genii' (H4)
93 'Golden Marinka' (v) (H3)
gracilis ~ see *Fuchsia magellanica* var. *gracilis*
02 'Hawkshead' (H3-4)
93 'Heidi Ann' (d) (H3)
93 'Herald' (H4)
93 'Jack Shahan' (H3)
02 'Jomam' (H3)
93 'La Campanella' (d) (H3)
93 'Lady Thumb' (d) (H3)
93 'Lena' (d) (H3)
02 'Liebriez' (d) (H3-4)
93 'Madame Cornélissen' (d) (H3)
93 *magellanica* var. *gracilis* (H3)
93 — — 'Variegata' (v) (H3)
— 'Riccartonii' ~ see *Fuchsia* 'Riccartonii'
93 'Margaret' (d) (H4)
93 'Margaret Brown' (H4)
93 'Marin Glow' (H3)
93 'Marinka' (H3)
02 'Monsieur Thibaut' (H4)

02	'Mrs Lovell Swisher' (H4)
93	'Mrs Popple' (H3)
93	'Mrs W.P. Wood' (H3)
93	'Nellie Nuttall' (H3)
93	'Phyllis' (d) (H4)
	'Princess Dollar' ~ see *Fuchsia* 'Dollar Princess'
93	'Prosperity' (d) (H3)
93	'Riccartonii' (H3)
02	'Rose of Castile Improved' (H4)
93	'Royal Velvet' (d) (H3)
02	'Rufus' (H3-4)
	'Rufus the Red' ~ see *Fuchsia* 'Rufus'
93	'Snowcap' (d) (H3-4)
93	'Son of Thumb' (H4)
93	'Swanley Gem' (H3)
93	'Swingtime' (d) (H3)
93	'Tennessee Waltz' (d) (H3)
93	'Tom Thumb' (H3)
	'Wendy' Catt ~ see *Fuchsia* 'Snowcap'
02	'White Pixie' (H3-4)
93	'Winston Churchill' (d) (H3)

GARRYA (GARRYACEAE)
93   *elliptica* 'James Roof' (m) (H4)

GAULTHERIA (ERICACEAE)
93 R *cuneata* (H4)
93   *mucronata* 'Bell's Seedling' (f/m) (H4)
   ~ hermaphrodite; male or several plants are required for the production of fruit in all the other cultivars listed
93   — 'Crimsonia' (f) (H4)
93   — 'Mulberry Wine' (f) (H4)
93   — 'Pink Pearl' (f) (H4)
93   — 'Sea Shell' (f) (H4)
93   — 'Wintertime' (f) (H4)
93 R *procumbens* (H4)

GENISTA (PAPILIONACEAE)
93   *aetnensis* (H4)
   delphinensis   ~ see *Genista sagittalis* subsp. *delphinensis*
93 R *lydia* (H4)
93   'Porlock' (H3)   *~ previously listed as* Cytisus *'Porlock'*
93 R *sagittalis* subsp. *delphinensis* (H4)
   — *minor*   ~ see *Genista sagittalis* subsp. *delphinensis*
93   *tinctoria* 'Flore Pleno' (d) (H4)
   — 'Plena'   ~ see *Genista tinctoria* 'Flore Pleno'

93	— 'Royal Gold' (H4)

GLEDITSIA (CAESALPINIACEAE)
93   *triacanthos* 'Sunburst' (H4)

GLOBULARIA (GLOBULARIACEAE)
93 R *cordifolia* (H4)

GREVILLEA (PROTEACEAE)
   banksii 'Canberra Hybrid'
      ~ see *Grevillea* 'Canberra Gem'
93   'Canberra Gem' (H3-4)
93   *rosmarinifolia* (H3)

GRISELINIA (GRISELINIACEAE)
93   *littoralis* (H3)
02   — 'Variegata' (v) (H3)

HALESIA (STYRACACEAE)
93   *monticola* var. *vestita* (H4)

× HALIMIOCISTUS (CISTACEAE)
   algarvensis
      ~ see *Halimium ocymoides*
   revolii hort.   ~ see × *Halimiocistus sahucii*
93   *sahucii* (H4)
   'Susan' ~ see *Halimium* 'Susan'
93   *wintonensis* (H3)
93   — 'Merrist Wood Cream' (H3)

HALIMIUM (CISTACEAE)
93   *lasianthum* (H3)
93   *ocymoides* (H3)
93   'Susan' (H3)
   wintonense   ~ see × *Halimiocistus wintonensis*

HAMAMELIS (HAMAMELIDACEAE)
93   × *intermedia* 'Arnold Promise' (H4)
97   — 'Barmstedt Gold' (H4)
   — 'Copper Beauty'
      ~ see *Hamamelis* × *intermedia* 'Jelena'
93   — 'Diane' (H4)
93   — 'Jelena' (H4)
93   — 'Pallida' (H4)
93   *mollis* (H4)   *~ grafted plants only*
93   *vernalis* 'Sandra' (H4)

HEBE (SCROPHULARIACEAE)
93 R *albicans* (H4)
   — 'Pewter Dome'   ~ see *Hebe* 'Pewter Dome'

— **'Red Edge'**
       ~ see *Hebe* 'Red Edge'

93 **'Blue Clouds'** (H3)   *~ of the trade*

  brachysiphon **'White Gem'**   ~ see
       Hebe 'White Gem'
       (*brachysiphon* hybrid)

02 **'Caledonia'** (H3)

  'Carl Teschner'   ~ see *Hebe*
       'Youngii'

  'E.B. Anderson'   ~ see *Hebe*
       'Caledonia'

  'Emerald Gem'   ~ see *Hebe* 'Emerald
       Green'

93 R **'Emerald Green'** (H3)

93 **'Great Orme'** (H3)

  'Green Globe'   ~ see *Hebe* 'Emerald
       Green'

93 *hulkeana* (H3)

  'James Stirling'   ~ see *Hebe ochracea*
       'James Stirling'

  'Knightshayes'   ~ see *Hebe*
       'Caledonia'

  mackenii   ~ see *Hebe* 'Emerald
       Green'

93 R *macrantha* (H3)

02 **'Margret'** PBR (H4)

93 **'Midsummer Beauty'** (H3)

  'Milmont Emerald'   ~ see *Hebe*
       'Emerald Green'

93 **'Mrs Winder'** (H4)

02 **'Neil's Choice'** (H4)

02 **'Nicola's Blush'** (H4)

93 R *ochracea* **'James Stirling'** (H4)

02 **'Oratia Beauty'** (H4)

02 **'Pascal'** (H4)

93 R **'Pewter Dome'** (H4)

93 R *pimeleoides* **'Quicksilver'** (H4)

93 R *pinguifolia* **'Pagei'** (H4)

02 **'Pink Elephant'** (v) (H3)

  'Porlock Purple'   ~ see *Parahebe*
       catarractae 'Delight'

  'Purple Emperor'
       ~ see *Hebe* 'Neil's Choice'

93 *rakaiensis* (H4)

93 R *recurva* **'Boughton Silver'** (H3)

93 **'Red Edge'** (H4)

02 **'Sapphire'** (H4)   *~ of the trade*

02 *topiaria* (H4)

02 *vernicosa* (H3)

  'Waikiki'   ~ see *Hebe* 'Mrs Winder'

  'Warleyensis'   ~ see *Hebe* 'Mrs
       Winder'

02 **'White Gem'** (*brachysiphon* hybrid) (H4)

02 **'Wingletye'** (H3)

02 **'Wiri Cloud'** (H3)

02 **'Wiri Dawn'** (H3)

02 **'Youngii'** (H3-4)

HELIANTHEMUM (CISTACEAE)

93 R **'Amy Baring'** (H4)

93 R **'Fire Dragon'** (H4)

  'Fireball'   ~ see *Helianthemum*
       'Mrs C.W. Earle'

93 R **'Henfield Brilliant'** (H4)

93 R **'Jubilee'** (d) (H4)

93 R **'Mrs C.W. Earle'** (d) (H4)

  'Mrs Clay'   ~ see *Helianthemum*
       'Fire Dragon'

93 R **'Rhodanthe Carneum'** (H4)

  'Snow Queen'   ~ see *Helianthemum*
       'The Bride'

93 R **'The Bride'** (H4)

  'Wisley Pink'   ~ see *Helianthemum*
       'Rhodanthe Carneum'

93 R **'Wisley Primrose'** (H4)

HELICHRYSUM (ASTERACEAE)

  alveolatum   ~ see *Helichrysum*
       splendidum

  angustifolium   ~ see *Helichrysum*
       italicum

93 *italicum* (H3)

  ledifolium ~ see *Ozothamnus ledifolius*

93 *splendidum* (H3)

  trilineatum   ~ see *Helichrysum*
       splendidum

HIBISCUS (MALVACEAE)

  syriacus BLUE BIRD   ~ see *Hibiscus*
       syriacus 'Oiseau Bleu'

02 — **'Bredon Springs'** (H4)

02 — **'Cicola'** (H4)

93 — **'Hamabo'** (H4)

02 — **'Lenny'** (H4)

02 — **'Meehanii'** (v) (H4)

93 — **'Oiseau Bleu'** (H4)

93 — **'Red Heart'** (H4)

02 — WHITE CHIFFON **'Notwoodtwo'** PBR
       (H4)

02 — **'William R. Smith'** (H4)

93 — **'Woodbridge'** (H4)

HIPPOPHAE (ELAEAGNACEAE)

93 *rhamnoides* (H4)   *~ male or several
       plants are required for the
       production of fruit*

HOHERIA (MALVACEAE)
93   **'Glory of Amlwch'** (H3)
93   *lyallii* (H4)
95   *sexstylosa* **'Stardust'** (H4)

HYDRANGEA (HYDRANGEACEAE)

(H)	Hortensia
(L)	Lacecap
(L/v)	Lacecap variegated

93   *arborescens* **'Annabelle'** (H4)
93   — **'Grandiflora'** (H4)
93   *aspera* **'Macrophylla'** (H3)
93   — subsp. *sargentiana* (H3)
93   — Villosa Group (H3)
93   *involucrata* **'Hortensis'** (d) (H3-4)
93   *macrophylla* **'Altona'** (H) (H3-4)
93   — **'Ami Pasquier'** (H) (H3-4)
        — **'Blue Wave'**   ~ see *Hydrangea*
            macrophylla 'Mariesii Perfecta'
        — **'Bluebird'** misapplied   ~ see
            Hydrangea serrata 'Bluebird'
93   — **'Europa'** (H) (H3-4)
93   — **'Générale Vicomtesse de Vibraye'**
            (H) (H3-4)
        — **'Geoffrey Chadbund'**
        ~ see *Hydrangea macrophylla* 'Möwe'
93   — **'Lanarth White'** (L) (H3-4)
99   — **'Lilacina'** (H3-4)
93   — **'Madame Emile Mouillère'**
            (H) (H3-4)
93   — **'Mariesii Perfecta'** (L) (H3-4)
93   — **'Möwe'** (L) (H3-4)
        ~ *previously listed as* H. macrophylla
            'Geoffrey Chadbund'
93   — **'Nigra'** (H) (H3-4)   ~ *valued in*
            particular for its stem effect
93   — **'Parzifal'** (H) (H3-4)
99   — **'Tokyo Delight'** (L) (H3-4)
93   — **'Veitchii'** (L) (H3-4)
        — **'Vicomte de Vibraye'**   ~ see
            Hydrangea macrophylla
            'Générale Vicomtesse de Vibraye'
93   — **'Westfalen'** (H) (H3-4)
93   — **'White Wave'** (H3-4)
93   *paniculata* **'Grandiflora'** (H4)
93   — **'Kyushu'** (H4)
02   — **PINK DIAMOND 'Interhydia'**
            (H4)
93   — **'Unique'** (H4)
93   **'Preziosa'** (H3-4)
93   *quercifolia* (H3-4)

sargentiana   ~ see *Hydrangea aspera*
            subsp. *sargentiana*
serrata **'Acuminata'**   ~ see
            Hydrangea serrata 'Bluebird'
93   — **'Bluebird'** (H3-4)
99   — **'Diadem'** (H3-4)
93   — **'Grayswood'** (H3-4)
99   — **'Miranda'** (L) (H3-4)
        — **'Preziosa'**   ~ see *Hydrangea*
            'Preziosa'
93   — **'Rosalba'** (H3-4)
99   — **'Tiara'** (H3-4)
villosa   ~ see *Hydrangea aspera*
            Villosa Group

HYPERICUM (CLUSIACEAE)
93   *forrestii* (H4)
        grandiflorum   ~ see *Hypericum*
            kouytchense
93   **'Hidcote'** (H4)
93   *kouytchense* (H4)
        leschenaultii hort. ~ see *Hypericum*
            'Rowallane'
93   x *moserianum* (H4)
93 R *olympicum* (H4)
93 R — f. *uniflorum* **'Citrinum'** (H4)
        patulum var. *forrestii*
            ~ see *Hypericum forrestii*
93   **'Rowallane'** (H3)
        'Sungold'   ~ see *Hypericum*
            kouytchense

IBERIS (BRASSICACEAE)
        commutata   ~ see *Iberis sempervirens*
93 R *sempervirens* (H4)
93 R — **'Schneeflocke'** (H4)
        — **SNOWFLAKE**   ~ see *Iberis*
            sempervirens 'Schneeflocke'

ILEX (AQUIFOLIACEAE)
93   x *altaclerensis* **'Belgica Aurea'** (f/v)
            (H4)
93   — **'Camelliifolia'** (f) (H4)
93   — **'Golden King'** (f/v) (H4)
93   — **'Hodginsii'** (m) (H4)
93   — **'Lawsoniana'** (f/v) (H4)
        — **'Silver Sentinel'**
        ~ see *Ilex* x *altaclerensis* 'Belgica Aurea'
93   *aquifolium* (H4)
95   — **'Amber'** (f) (H4)
93   — **'Argentea Marginata'** (f/v) (H4)
        — **'Argentea Variegata'**   ~ see *Ilex*
            aquifolium 'Argentea Marginata'

     — **'Aurea Regina'**   ~ see *Ilex*
         aquifolium 'Golden Queen'
93   — **'Ferox Argentea'** (m/v) (H4)
93   — **'Golden Queen'** (m/v) (H4)
93   — **'Handsworth New Silver'** (f/v)
       (H4)
93   — **'J.C. van Tol'** (f) (H4)
93   — **'Madame Briot'** (f/v) (H4)
93   — **'Myrtifolia Aurea Maculata'** (m/v)
       (H4)
     — **'Myrtifolia Aureovariegata'**
        ~ see *Ilex aquifolium* 'Myrtifolia
             Aurea Maculata'
93   — **'Pyramidalis'** (f) (H4)
93   — **'Pyramidalis Fructu Luteo'** (f)
       (H4)
     — **'Silver King'**   ~ see *Ilex aquifolium*
               'Silver Queen'
93   — **'Silver Queen'** (m/v) (H4)
     — **'Silver Sentinel'**
   ~ see *Ilex × altaclerensis* 'Belgica Aurea'
93   *crenata* **'Convexa'** (f) (H4)
93   — **'Golden Gem'** (f) (H4)
93   × *koehneana* **'Chestnut Leaf'** (f) (H4)
     'Pyramidalis'   ~ see *Ilex aquifolium*
                'Pyramidalis'

INDIGOFERA (PAPILIONACEAE)
93   *amblyantha* (H4)
     gerardiana ~ see *Indigofera heterantha*
93   *heterantha* (H4)

ITEA (ESCALLONIACEAE)
93   *ilicifolia* (H3)

JASMINUM (OLEACEAE)
93   *humile* **'Revolutum'** (H4)
93   *nudiflorum* (H4)
     reevesii hort.   ~ see *Jasminum humile*
                'Revolutum'
     sieboldianum   ~ see *Jasminum*
                nudiflorum

JOVELLANA (SCROPHULARIACEAE)
93   *violacea* (H3)

JUGLANS (JUGLANDACEAE)
93   *nigra* (F) (H4)
93   *regia* (F) (H4)

KALMIA (ERICACEAE)
93 R   *angustifolia* (H4)
02   — f. *rubra* (H4)

93   *latifolia* (H4)
02   — **'Freckles'** (H4)
02   — **'Little Linda'** (H4)
02   — **'Olympic Fire'** (H4)
02   — **'Pink Charm'** (H4)

KALMIOPSIS (ERICACEAE)
93 R   *leachiana* (H4)

KERRIA (ROSACEAE)
     japonica   ~ see *Kerria japonica*
                'Pleniflora'
93   — **'Golden Guinea'** (H4)
93   — **'Pleniflora'** (d) (H4)

KOELREUTERIA (SAPINDACEAE)
93   *paniculata* (H4)

KOLKWITZIA (CAPRIFOLIACEAE)
93   *amabilis* **'Pink Cloud'** (H4)

LABURNUM (PAPILIONACEAE)
93   × *watereri* **'Vossii'** (H4)

LAURUS (LAURACEAE)
93   *nobilis* (H4)
93   — **'Aurea'** (H4)

LAVANDULA (LAMIACEAE)
     angustifolia **'Alba Nana'**   ~ see
        Lavandula angustifolia 'Nana Alba'
02   — **'Beechwood Blue'** (H4)
93   — **'Hidcote'** (H4)   ~ *plants raised*
    from seed are not entitled to this cultivar
       name; reconfirmed after trial 2001
02   — **'Imperial Gem'** (H4)
02   — **LITTLE LOTTIE 'Clarmo'** (H4)
02   — **'Loddon Blue'** (H4)
02   — **'Loddon Pink'** (H4)
02   — **'Miss Katherine'** ᴾᴮᴿ (H4)
02   — **MISS MUFFET 'Scholmis'** (H4)
02   — **'Nana Alba'** (H4)
02   — **'Wendy Carlile'** (H4)
     'Cornard Blue'   ~ see *Lavandula*
                'Sawyers'
     'Hidcote Blue'   ~ see *Lavandula*
         angustifolia 'Hidcote'
02   × *intermedia* **'Alba'** (H4)
02   — **'Arabian Night'** (H4)
02   — **'Hidcote Giant'** (H4)
93   *lanata* (H3)
     'Loddon Pink'   ~ see *Lavandula*
        angustifolia 'Loddon Pink'

02 **'Richard Gray'** (H3-4)
02 **'Sawyers'** (H3-4)
spica **'Hidcote Purple'** ~ see
Lavandula angustifolia 'Hidcote'
93 *stoechas* (H3-4) ~ *reconfirmed after
trial 2001*
— **'Papillon'** ~ see *Lavandula
stoechas* subsp. *pedunculata*
93 — subsp. *pedunculata* (H3)
02 — **'Willow Vale'** (H3-4)

LAVATERA (MALVACEAE)
arborea **'Rosea'** ~ see *Lavatera*
'Rosea'
97 **'Bredon Springs'** (H3-4)
97 **'Burgundy Wine'** (H3-4)
97 **'Candy Floss'** (H3-4)
93 **'Rosea'** (H3-4)

× **LEDODENDRON (ERICACEAE)**
93 R **'Arctic Tern'** (H4)

LEIOPHYLLUM (ERICACEAE)
93 R *buxifolium* (H4)

LEPTOSPERMUM (MYRTACEAE)
humifusum ~ see *Leptospermum
rupestre*
lanigerum **'Silver Sheen'** ~ see
Leptospermum 'Silver Sheen'
prostratum ~ see *Leptospermum
rupestre*
93 *rupestre* (H4)
93 *scoparium* var. *incanum* **'Keatleyi'**
(H3)
93 R — **(Nanum Group) 'Kiwi'** (H3)
93 — **'Nichollsii'** (H3)
— var. *prostratum* hort. ~ see
Leptospermum rupestre
93 — **'Red Damask'** (d) (H3)
02 **'Silver Sheen'** (H3)

LESPEDEZA (PAPILIONACEAE)
93 *thunbergii* (H4)
tiliifolia ~ see *Desmodium elegans*

LEUCOTHOE (ERICACEAE)
93 *fontanesiana* (H4) ~ *previously
listed as* L. walteri
93 — **'Rollissonii'** (H4) ~ *previously
listed under* L. walteri
walteri ~ see *Leucothoe
fontanesiana*

LEYCESTERIA (CAPRIFOLIACEAE)
02 *formosa* (H4)

LIGUSTRUM (OLEACEAE)
93 *lucidum* (H4)
93 — **'Excelsum Superbum'** (v) (H4)
ovalifolium **'Aureomarginatum'**
~ see *Ligustrum ovalifolium* 'Aureum'
93 — **'Aureum'** (v) (H4)
93 *quihoui* (H4)

LINDERA (LAURACEAE)
93 *obtusiloba* (H4)

LINUM (LINACEAE)
93 R *arboreum* (H4)
93 R **'Gemmell's Hybrid'** (H4)

LIQUIDAMBAR (HAMAMELIDACEAE)
93 *styraciflua* **'Lane Roberts'** (H4)
93 — **'Worplesdon'** (H4)

LIRIODENDRON (MAGNOLIACEAE)
93 *tulipifera* (H4)
93 — **'Aureomarginatum'** (v) (H4)

LITHODORA (BORAGINACEAE)
93 R *diffusa* **'Grace Ward'** (H4)
93 R — **'Heavenly Blue'** (H4)
× *intermedia*
~ see *Moltkia* × *intermedia*
93 R *oleifolia* (H4)

LITHOSPERMUM (BORAGINACEAE)
'Grace Ward' ~ see *Lithodora
diffusa* 'Grace Ward'
'Heavenly Blue' ~ see *Lithodora
diffusa* 'Heavenly Blue'
oleifolium ~ see *Lithodora oleifolia*

LONICERA (CAPRIFOLIACEAE)
93 *nitida* **'Baggesen's Gold'** (H4)
93 × *purpusii* **'Winter Beauty'** (H4)

LOTUS (PAPILIONACEAE)
02 *hirsutus* (H3-4)

LUMA (MYRTACEAE)
93 *apiculata* (H3)
02 — **'Glanleam Gold'** (v) (H3)

LUPINUS (PAPILIONACEAE)
93 *arboreus* (H4)

MAGNOLIA (MAGNOLIACEAE)

93	'Ann' (H4)	~ *(De Vos hybrid)*
93	'Betty' (H4)	~ *(Kosar hybrid)*
93	*denudata* (H3-4)	
93	'Elizabeth' (H4)	
93	'Galaxy' (H4)	
93	*grandiflora* 'Exmouth' (H3-4)	
02	— 'Victoria' (H3-4)	
93	'Heaven Scent' (H4)	
		~ *(Gresham hybrid)*
	heptapeta	~ see *Magnolia denudata*
	hypoleuca	~ see *Magnolia obovata*
93	'Jane' (H4)	~ *(Kosar hybrid)*
93	*liliiflora* 'Nigra' (H4)	
93	x *loebneri* 'Leonard Messel' (H4)	
93	— 'Merrill' (H4)	
02	'Milky Way' (H4)	
93	*obovata* Thunb. (H4)	~ *awarded as* M. hypoleuca
93	'Pinkie' (H4)	~ *(Kosar hybrid)*
93	*salicifolia* (H3-4)	
93	*salicifolia* 'Wada's Memory' (H4)	
93	'Sayonara' (H4)	~ *(Gresham hybrid)*
93	*sieboldii* subsp. *sieboldii* (H4)	
93	x *soulangeana* 'Brozzonii' (H3-4)	
93	— 'Etienne Soulange-Bodin' (H3-4)	
	~ *usually grown as* M. x soulangeana	
93	— 'Lennei' (H3-4)	
93	— 'Lennei Alba' (H3-4)	
	— 'Nigra'	
	~ see *Magnolia liliiflora* 'Nigra'	
	— 'Rubra' misapplied	
	~ see *Magnolia* x *soulangeana* 'Rustica Rubra'	
93	— 'Rustica Rubra' (H3-4)	
02	'Star Wars' (H4)	
93	*stellata* (H4)	
93	— 'Waterlily' (H4)	
93	'Susan' (H4)	~ *(Kosar hybrid)*
93	*wilsonii* (H4)	

MAHONIA (BERBERIDACEAE)

93	*aquifolium* 'Apollo' (H4)	
	— 'Fascicularis'	
	~ see *Mahonia* x *wagneri* 'Pinnacle'	
93	*japonica* (H4)	
93	*lomariifolia* (H3)	
93	x *media* 'Buckland' (H4)	
93	— 'Lionel Fortescue' (H4)	
93	— 'Underway' (H4)	
93	— 'Winter Sun' (H4)	
93	x *wagneri* 'Pinnacle' (H4)	

MALUS (ROSACEAE)

93	'Evereste' (H4)	
93	*floribunda* (H4)	
	'Golden Hornet'	~ see *Malus* x *zumi* 'Golden Hornet'
93	*hupehensis* (H4)	
93	'John Downie' (C) (H4)	
	PERPETU	~ see *Malus* 'Evereste'
93	x *robusta* 'Red Sentinel' (H4)	
93	'Royal Beauty' (H4)	
93	*transitoria* (H4)	
93	*tschonoskii* (H4)	
93	x *zumi* 'Golden Hornet' (H4)	

MELIANTHUS (MELIANTHACEAE)

93 G *major* (H3)

MOLTKIA (BORAGINACEAE)

93 R x *intermedia* (H4)

MORUS (MORACEAE)

93 *nigra* (F) (H4)

MUSA (MUSACEAE)

02 *basjoo* (H3-4)

MYRTUS (MYRTACEAE)

	apiculata	~ see *Luma apiculata*
93	*communis* (H3)	
	— 'Jenny Reitenbach'	
	~ see *Myrtus communis* subsp. *tarentina*	
	— 'Microphylla'	~ see *Myrtus communis* subsp. *tarentina*
	— 'Nana'	~ see *Myrtus communis* subsp. *tarentina*
93	— subsp. *tarentina* (H3)	
	'Glanleam Gold'	~ see *Luma apiculata* 'Glanleam Gold'
	luma	~ see *Luma apiculata*

NANDINA (BERBERIDACEAE)

93	*domestica* (H3)
02	— 'Fire Power' (H3)

NYSSA (CORNACEAE)

93	*sinensis* (H4)
93	*sylvatica* (H4)

OLEARIA (ASTERACEAE)

93	*macrodonta* (H3)	
93	x *mollis* 'Zennorensis' (H3)	~ *valued in particular for its foliage effect*
93	x *scilloniensis* Dorrien-Smith (H3)	

OSMANTHUS (OLEACEAE)
93   x *burkwoodii* (H4)
93   *delavayi* (H4)
     heterophyllus **'Argenteomarginatus'**
     ~ see *Osmanthus heterophyllus* 'Variegatus'
93   — **'Gulftide'** (H4)
93   — **'Variegatus'** (v) (H4)

OSMAREA (OLEACEAE)
     burkwoodii   ~ see *Osmanthus*
                              x *burkwoodii*

OZOTHAMNUS (ASTERACEAE)
93   *ledifolius* (H4)
93   *rosmarinifolius* **'Silver Jubilee'** (H3)

PACHYSANDRA (BUXACEAE)
02   *terminalis* **'Green Carpet'** (H4)
93   — **'Variegata'** (v) (H4)

PAEONIA (PAEONIACEAE)

(S)	shrubby

93   *delavayi* (S) (H4)
93   — var. *ludlowii* (S) (H4)
     ludlowii   ~ see *Paeonia delavayi*
                              var. *ludlowii*
     lutea var. *ludlowii*   ~ see *Paeonia*
                              delavayi var. *ludlowii*

PARAHEBE (SCROPHULARIACEAE)
93 R *catarractae* **'Delight'** (H3)
     — **'Porlock Purple'**   ~ see *Parahebe*
                              catarractae 'Delight'
     'Greencourt'   ~ see *Parahebe*
                              catarractae 'Delight'
02   *lyallii* **'Julie-Anne'** (H3)

PARROTIA (HAMAMELIDACEAE)
93   *persica* (H4)

PAULOWNIA (SCROPHULARIACEAE)
93   *tomentosa* (H3)

PENSTEMON (SCROPHULARIACEAE)
93 R *davidsonii* var. *menziesii* (H4)
93 R *fruticosus* var. *scouleri* (H4)
93 R — — f. *albus* (H4)
     menziesii   ~ see *Penstemon*
                     davidsonii var. *menziesii*
93 R *newberryi* (H4)
93 R *pinifolius* (H4)
98 R — **'Wisley Flame'** (H4)

97 R *procerus* **'Roy Davidson'** (H4)
93 R *rupicola* (H4)
     scouleri   ~ see *Penstemon*
                         fruticosus var. *scouleri*

PERNETTYA (ERICACEAE)
     mucronata **'Bell's Seedling'**   ~ see
     Gaultheria mucronata 'Bell's Seedling'
     — **'Crimsonia'**   ~ see *Gaultheria*
                         mucronata 'Crimsonia'
     — **'Mulberry Wine'**   ~ see
     Gaultheria mucronata 'Mulberry Wine'
     — **'Pink Pearl'**   ~ see *Gaultheria*
                         mucronata 'Pink Pearl'
     — **'Sea Shell'**   ~ see *Gaultheria*
                         mucronata 'Sea Shell'
     — **'Wintertime'**   ~ see *Gaultheria*
                         mucronata 'Wintertime'

PEROVSKIA (LAMIACEAE)
93   **'Blue Spire'** (H4)   ~ *reconfirmed*
                              after trial 2001

PHILADELPHUS (HYDRANGEACEAE)
93   **'Beauclerk'** (H4)
93   **'Belle Etoile'** (H4)
93   *coronarius* **'Aureus'** (H4)
     — **'Bowles' Variety'**   ~ see
     Philadelphus coronarius 'Variegatus'
93   — **'Variegatus'** (v) (H4)
93   **'Manteau d'Hermine'** (d) (H4)
93   **'Sybille'** (H4)

PHLOMIS (LAMIACEAE)
93   *chrysophylla* (H3)
93   *fruticosa* (H4)
02   *lanata* (H3-4)

PHORMIUM (AGAVACEAE)
93   *cookianum* subsp. *hookeri* **'Cream
                    Delight'** (v) (H3-4)
93   — — **'Tricolor'** (H3-4)
93   **'Duet'** (v) (H3)
93   **'Sundowner'** (v) (H3)
93   *tenax* (H4)
     — **'Duet'**   ~ see *Phormium* 'Duet'
93   — **Purpureum Group** (H3-4)
93   — **'Variegatum'** (v) (H3-4)
93   **'Yellow Wave'** (v) (H3)

PHOTINIA (ROSACEAE)
93   x *fraseri* **'Red Robin'** (H4)
93   *villosa* (H4)

PHYGELIUS (SCROPHULARIACEAE)
    aequalis albus   ~ see *Phygelius*
          aequalis 'Yellow Trumpet'
    aequalis 'Aureus'   ~ see *Phygelius*
          aequalis 'Yellow Trumpet'
    — 'Cream Trumpet'   ~ see *Phygelius*
          aequalis 'Yellow Trumpet'
    — 'Indian Chief'   ~ see *Phygelius*
          × *rectus* 'African Queen'
02   — 'Trewidden Pink' (H4)
96   — 'Yellow Trumpet' (H3-4)
93   *capensis* (H3)   ~ *including plants*
          sold as P. capensis coccineus
    — *coccineus* ~ see *Phygelius capensis*
    'Golden Gate'   ~ see *Phygelius*
          aequalis 'Yellow Trumpet'
96   × *rectus* 'African Queen' (H3-4)
97   — 'Devil's Tears' (H4)
97   — 'Salmon Leap' (H4)

× PHYLLIOPSIS (ERICACEAE)
98 R 'Coppelia' (H4)

PHYLLODOCE (ERICACEAE)
93 R *caerulea* (H4)
    — *japonica*   ~ see *Phyllodoce*
          nipponica
93 R *nipponica* (H4)

PHYSOCARPUS (ROSACEAE)
93   *opulifolius* 'Dart's Gold' (H4)
02   — 'Diabolo' PBR(H4)

PIERIS (ERICACEAE)
93   'Firecrest' (H4)
93   'Flaming Silver' (v) (H4)
93   'Forest Flame' (H4)
93   *formosa* var. *forrestii* 'Wakehurst'
          (H3)
93   *japonica* 'Blush' (H4)
97   — 'Cavatine' (H4)
93   — 'Debutante' (H4)
93   — 'Grayswood' (H4)
93   — 'Little Heath' (v) (H4)
93   — 'Little Heath Green' (H4)
93   — 'Mountain Fire' (H4)
93   — 'Pink Delight' (H4)
96   — 'Prelude' (H4)
93   — 'Purity' (H4)
96   — 'Sarabande' (H4)
93   — 'Valley Valentine' (H4)
    — 'Variegata' hort.   ~ see *Pieris*
          japonica 'White Rim'

93   — 'White Rim' (v) (H4)   ~ *often*
          confused with 'Variegata'
          in the trade

PITTOSPORUM (PITTOSPORACEAE)
93   *eugenioides* 'Variegatum' (v) (H3)
93   'Garnettii' (v) (H3)
93   *tenuifolium* (H3)
93   — 'Irene Paterson' (v) (H3)
93   — 'Silver Queen' (f/v) (H3)
93   — 'Tom Thumb' (H3)
93   — 'Warnham Gold' (H3)
93   *tobira* (H3)

PLAGIANTHUS (MALVACEAE)
    lyallii   ~ see *Hoheria lyallii*

PLATANUS (PLATANACEAE)
    × *acerifolia*   ~ see *Platanus*
          × *hispanica*
93   × *hispanica* (H4)
93   *orientalis* (H4)
02   — f. *digitata* (H4)
    — 'Laciniata'   ~ see *Platanus*
          orientalis f. *digitata*

POLIOTHYRSIS (FLACOURTIACEAE)
02   *sinensis* (H4)

POLYGALA (POLYGALACEAE)
93 R *chamaebuxus* (H4)
93 R — var. *grandiflora* (H4)
    — 'Purpurea'   ~ see *Polygala*
          chamaebuxus var. *grandiflora*
    — 'Rhodoptera'   ~ see *Polygala*
          chamaebuxus var. *grandiflora*

POPULUS (SALICACEAE)
93   'Balsam Spire' (f) (H4)   ~ *also*
          grown as P. *'TT32'*
93   × *canadensis* 'Aurea'
          (H4)
93   *lasiocarpa* (H4)
93   *nigra* 'Italica' (m) (H4) ~ *awarded as*
          P. nigra *var.* italica
    — 'Pyramidalis' ~ see *Populus nigra*
          'Italica'
    'Serotina Aurea'   ~ see *Populus* ×
          canadensis 'Aurea'
    'Tacatricho 32'   ~ see *Populus*
          'Balsam Spire'
93   *tremula* (H4)

POTENTILLA (ROSACEAE)
davurica **'Abbotswood'** ~ see
Potentilla fruticosa 'Abbotswood'
93 *fruticosa* **'Abbotswood'** (H4)
~ *reconfirmed after trial 2001*
02 — **'Chelsea Star'** (H4)
02 — **'Groneland'** (H4)
02 — **'Hopleys Orange'** (H4)
02 — **'Jackman's Variety'** (H4)
02 — **'King Cup'** (H4)
02 — **'Limelight'** (H4)
02 — **LOVELY PINK 'Pink Beauty'** PBR (H4)
02 — **MARIAN RED ROBIN 'Marrob'** PBR
(H4)
02 — **'Medicine Wheel Mountain'** (H4)
02 — **'Penny White'** (H4)
93 — **'Primrose Beauty'** (H4)
~ *reconfirmed after trial 2001*
02 — **'Sommerflor'** (H4)
02 — **'Yellow Bird'** (H4)

PROSTANTHERA (LAMIACEAE)
93 *cuneata* (H4)

PRUNUS (ROSACEAE)
93 **'Accolade'** (H4)
93 **'Amanogawa'** (H4)
93 *avium* (H4)
— **'Grandiflora'** ~ see *Prunus avium*
'Plena'
93 — **'Plena'** (d) (H4)
'Blaze' ~ see *Prunus cerasifera*
'Nigra'
93 × *blireana* (d) (H4)
'Blushing Bride' ~ see *Prunus* 'Shôgetsu'
93 *cerasifera* **'Nigra'** (H4)
'Cheal's Weeping' ~ see *Prunus*
'Kiku-shidare-zakura'
93 × *cistena* (H4) ~ *valued in*
particular for its foliage effect
— **'Crimson Dwarf'** ~ see *Prunus*
× *cistina*
'Hillieri Spire' ~ see *Prunus* 'Spire'
93 **'Ichiyo'** (d) (H4) ~ *previously listed*
as P. *'Choshu-hizakura'*
93 *incisa* **'Praecox'** (H4)
93 **'Kanzan'** (H4)
93 **'Kiku-shidare-zakura'** (H4)
93 **'Kursar'** (H4)
93 *laurocerasus* (H4)
93 — **'Otto Luyken'** (H4)
93 *lusitanica* (H4)
'Mount Fuji' ~ see *Prunus* 'Shirotae'

93 **'Okame'** (H4)
93 *padus* **'Colorata'** (H4)
— **'Grandiflora'** ~ see *Prunus padus*
'Watereri'
93 — **'Watereri'** (H4)
93 **'Pandora'** (H4)
93 *pendula* **'Pendula Rosea'** (H4)
93 — **'Pendula Rubra'** (H4)
93 **'Pink Perfection'** (H4)
93 **'Pink Shell'** (H4)
'Pissardii Nigra' ~ see *Prunus*
cerasifera 'Nigra'
93 *sargentii* (H4)
'Sekiyama' ~ see *Prunus* 'Kanzan'
93 *serrula* (H4)
— var. *tibetica* ~ see *Prunus serrula*
serrulata **'Erecta'** ~ see *Prunus*
'Amanogawa'
— **'Grandiflora'** ~ see *Prunus* 'Ukon'
— **'Rosea'** ~ see *Prunus*
'Kiku-shidare-zakura'
'Shidare-zakura' ~ see *Prunus*
'Kiku-shidare-zakura'
93 **'Shirofugen'** (H4)
93 **'Shirotae'** (H4)
93 **'Shôgetsu'** (H4)
93 **'Spire'** (H4)
93 × *subhirtella* **'Autumnalis'** (H4)
93 — **'Autumnalis Rosea'** (H4)
— **'Pendula'** hort. ~ see *Prunus pendu-*
la 'Pendula Rosea'
— **'Pendula Rosea'** ~ see *Prunus*
pendula 'Pendula Rosea'
— **'Pendula Rubra'** ~ see *Prunus*
pendula 'Pendula Rubra'
93 **'Taihaku'** (H4)
tibetica ~ see *Prunus serrula*
93 **'Ukon'** (H4)
93 × *yedoensis* (H4)
'Yoshino' ~ see *Prunus* × *yedoensis*

PTELEA (RUTACEAE)
93 *trifoliata* **'Aurea'** (H4)

PTEROCARYA (JUGLANDACEAE)
93 *fraxinifolia* (H4)

PTEROSTYRAX (STYRACACEAE)
93 *hispida* (H4)

PTILOTRICHUM (BRASSICACEAE)
spinosum **'Roseum'** ~ see *Alyssum*
spinosum 'Roseum'

PUNICA (PUNICACEAE)
02 G *granatum* var. *nana* (H3)
93 — f. *plena* 'Rubrum Flore Pleno' (d) (H3)
~ *previously listed as* P. granatum
'Flore Pleno'

PYRACANTHA (ROSACEAE)
02 'Golden Charmer' (H4) ~ *often sold
as 'Orange Charmer'*
93 'Orange Glow' (H4)
93 *rogersiana* (H4)
93 — 'Flava' (H4)
02 SAPHYR ORANGE 'Cadange' PBR (H4)
02 SAPHYR ROUGE 'Cadrou' PBR (H4)
02 'Teton' (H4)

PYRUS (ROSACEAE)
93 *calleryana* 'Chanticleer' (H4)
93 *salicifolia* 'Pendula' (H4)

QUERCUS (FAGACEAE)
borealis ~ see *Quercus rubra*
93 *canariensis* (H4)
93 *castaneifolia* 'Green Spire' (H4)
93 *coccinea* 'Splendens' (H4)
93 *frainetto* 'Hungarian Crown' (H4)
93 x *hispanica* 'Lucombeana' (H4)
~ *awarded as* Quercus × lucombeana
'William Lucombe'
93 *ilex* (H4)
x *lucombeana* 'William Lucombe'
~ see *Quercus × hispanica*
'Lucombeana'
93 *palustris* (H4)
pedunculata ~ see *Quercus robur*
93 *petraea* (H4)
93 *robur* (H4)
93 — f. *fastigiata* 'Koster' (H4)
93 *rubra* (H4)
sessiliflora ~ see *Quercus petraea*

RHAMNUS (RHAMNACEAE)
93 *alaternus* 'Argenteovariegata' (v)
(H4)
— 'Variegata' ~ see *Rhamnus
alaternus* 'Argenteovariegata'

RHODODENDRON (ERICACEAE)
93 'Addy Wery' (EA) (H3-4) ~ *suitable
for small gardens*
02 'Albert Schweitzer' (H4)
02 'Alexander' (EA) (H4)
93 'Alice' (hybrid) (H4)

(A)	species or unclassified hybrid
(EA)	Evergreen Azalea
(G)	Ghent
(K)	Knap Hill or Exbury
(M)	Mollis
(O)	Occidentalis
(R)	Rustica
(V)	Vireya

93 'Annabella' (K) (H4) ~ *suitable
for small gardens*
'Arctic Tern' ~ see × *Ledodendron*
'Arctic Tern'
93 'Argosy' (H4) ~ *prefers light shade
and shelter*
93 *argyrophyllum* subsp. *nankingense*
'Chinese Silver' (H4)
93 *augustinii* 'Electra' (H3-4)
93 'Avalanche' (H4) ~ *the FCC clone;
prefers light shade and shelter*
93 'Bashful' (H4) ~ *reconfirmed after
trial 2001*
93 'Beethoven' (EA) (H3-4) ~ *suitable for
small gardens*
93 'Berryrose' (K) (H4) ~ *suitable for
small gardens*
93 'Blaauw's Pink' (EA) (H3-4) ~ *suitable
for small gardens*
BLAUE DONAU ~ see *Rhododendron*
'Blue Danube'
93 'Blewbury' (H4)
93 'Blue Danube' (EA) (H3-4)
~ *suitable for small gardens*
93 'Blue Peter' (H4)
'Blue Steel' ~ see *Rhododendron
fastigiatum* 'Blue Steel'
93 'Bouquet de Flore' (G) (H4)
~ *Verschaffelt's deciduous azalea;
suitable for small gardens*
93 'Bow Bells' (H4)
02 'Bruce Brechtbill' (H4) ~ *suitable
for small gardens*
93 *bureavii* (H4) ~ *valued especially
for its foliage; sometimes spelt* R. bureaui
93 *calophytum* (H4)
93 R *calostrotum* 'Gigha' (H4) ~ *suitable for
small gardens*
93 R — subsp. *keleticum* (H4) ~ *suitable for
small gardens*
02 *campylogynum* (H4) ~ *suitable for
small gardens*
02 'Cannon's Double' (K/d) (H4)
02 'Canzonetta' (EA) (H4) ~ *suitable
for small gardens*

93	**'Caroline Allbrook'** (H4)	
	~ reconfirmed after trial 2001	
93	**'Cecile'** (K) (H4)	*~ suitable for small gardens*
02	**'Cetewayo'** (H4)	
93	**'Champagne'** (H3-4)	*~ (Tortoiseshell Group)*
93	**'Chevalier Félix de Sauvage'** (H4)	
93	**'Choremia'** (H3)	*~ the FCC clone*
93 R	**'Cilpinense'** (H3-4)	*~ the FCC clone; suitable for small gardens*
93	**'Coccineum Speciosum'** (G) (H4)	*~ suitable for small gardens*
93	**'Corneille'** (G/d) (H4)	*~ suitable for small gardens*
02	**'Crane'** (H4)	*~ suitable for small gardens*
93	**'Crest'** (H3-4)	
93 R	**'Curlew'** (H4)	*~ suitable for small gardens; prefers cooler conditions*
93	**'Cynthia'** (H4)	
93	*dauricum* **'Midwinter'** (H4)	
93	**'David'** (H4)	*~ Rose's 'Hugh Koster' hybrid*
93	*davidsonianum* (H3-4)	
93	**'Daviesii'** (G) (H4)	*~ suitable for small gardens*
02	*decorum* (H4)	
	discolor	*~ see Rhododendron fortunei* subsp. *discolor*
93	**'Doctor M. Oosthoek'** (M) (H4)	*~ suitable for small gardens*
93	**'Dopey'** (H4)	*~ suitable for small gardens; reconfirmed after trial 2001*
93	**'Dora Amateis'** (H4)	*~ suitable for small gardens*
93	**'Double Damask'** (K/d) (H4)	*~ suitable for small gardens*
02	**'Dreamland'** (H4)	*~ suitable for small gardens*
93 R	**'Egret'** (H4)	*~ suitable for small gardens*
	'Electra'	*~ see Rhododendron augustinii* 'Electra'
93	**'Elisabeth Hobbie'** (H4)	*~ suitable for small gardens*
02	**'Elsie Lee'** (EA/d) (H3-4)	*~ suitable for small gardens*
93	**'Exquisitum'** (O) (H4)	*~ suitable for small gardens*
93	**'Fabia'** (H3)	*~ the FCC clone*
93	**'Faggetter's Favourite'** (H4)	
93	*falconeri* (H3-4)	*~ prefers light shade and shelter*
	'Fanny' *~ see Rhododendron* 'Pucella'	
02	**'Fantastica'** (H4)	*~ suitable for small gardens*
	fargesii	*~ see Rhododendron oreodoxa* var. *fargesii*
02	*fastigiatum* **'Blue Steel'** (H4)	*~ suitable for small gardens*
93	**'Fastuosum Flore Pleno'** (d) (H4)	
	fictolacteum	*~ see Rhododendron rex* subsp. *fictolacteum*
02	**'Fireball'** (K) (H4)	*~ suitable for small gardens*
93	**'Florida'** (EA/d) (H3-4)	*~ suitable for small gardens*
93	*fortunei* subsp. *discolor* (H4)	
93	**'Frank Galsworthy'** (H4)	
93	*fulvum* (H4)	
93	**'Furnivall's Daughter'** (H4)	
02	**'Gartendirektor Rieger'** (H4)	
02	**'Geisha Orange'** (EA) (H4)	*~ suitable for small gardens*
93	**'Gibraltar'** (K) (H4)	*~ suitable for small gardens*
93 R	**'Ginny Gee'** (H4)	*~ suitable for small gardens*
93	**'Golden Torch'** (H4)	*~ suitable for small gardens*
02	**'Goldkrone'** (H4)	
93	**'Gomer Waterer'** (H4)	
02	**'Gristede'** (H4)	*~ suitable for small gardens*
02	**'Hachmann's Marlis'** (H4)	*~ suitable for small gardens*
02	**'Hachmann's Polaris'** (H4)	*~ suitable for small gardens*
	(Hawk Group) 'Crest'	*~ see Rhododendron* 'Crest'
93	**'Helene Schiffner'** (H4)	
93	**'Hino-crimson'** (EA) (H3-4)	*~ suitable for small gardens*
93 R	**'Hinomayo'** (EA) (H3-4)	*~ suitable for small gardens*
	hippophaeoides **'Bei-ma-shan'**	*~ see Rhododendron hippophaeoides* 'Haba Shan'
93	— **'Haba Shan'** (H4)	*~ suitable for small gardens*
93	**'Homebush'** (K/d) (H4)	*~ suitable for small gardens*
02	**'Horizon Monarch'** (H3-4)	
93	**'Hotei'** (H4)	
93	**'Hotspur Red'** (K) (H4)	*~ suitable for small gardens*

93 **'Hydon Dawn'** (H4) ~ *suitable for small gardens*

93 **'Hydon Hunter'** (H4) ~ *reconfirmed after trial 2001*

'Iceberg' ~ see *Rhododendron* 'Lodauric Iceberg'

impeditum **'Blue Steel'** ~ see *Rhododendron fastigiatum* 'Blue Steel'

— **'Moerheim'** ~ see *Rhododendron* 'Moerheim'

93 *insigne* (H4)

93 **'Irene Koster'** (O) (H4) ~ *suitable for small gardens*

93 **'Irohayama'** (EA) (H3-4) ~ *suitable for small gardens*

'J.M. de Montague' ~ see *Rhododendron* 'The Hon. Jean Marie de Montague'

93 **'James Burchett'** (H4)

'Jean Marie Montague' ~ see *Rhododendron* 'The Hon. Jean Marie de Montague'

02 **'Johanna'** (EA) (H4) ~ *suitable for small gardens*

93 **'Kate Waterer'** (H4)

93 R *keiskei* var. *ozawae* **'Yaku Fairy'** (H4) ~ *suitable for small gardens*

keleticum ~ see *Rhododendron calostrotum* subsp. *keleticum*

'King George' Loder ~ see *Rhododendron* 'Loderi King George'

93 R *kiusianum* (EA) (H4) ~ *shows great variation but generally excellent; suitable for small gardens*

93 **'Klondyke'** (K) (H4) ~ *suitable for small gardens*

93 **'Kluis Sensation'** (H4)

'Koichiro Wada' ~ see *Rhododendron yakushimanum* 'Koichiro Wada'

93 **'Lady Clementine Mitford'** (H4)

93 **'Lavender Girl'** (H4)

93 **'Lem's Cameo'** (H3)

93 **'Lem's Monarch'** (H4)

02 **'Linda'** (H4) ~ *suitable for small gardens*

93 **'Lodauric Iceberg'** (H3-4) ~ *prefers light shade and shelter*

02 **'Loderi Game Chick'** (H3-4) ~ *prefers light shade and shelter*

93 **'Loderi King George'** (H3-4) ~ *prefers light shade and shelter*

93 **'Loderi Pink Diamond'** (H3-4) ~ *prefers light shade and shelter*

02 **'Loderi Pink Topaz'** (H3-4) ~ *prefers light shade and shelter*

93 **'Loderi Venus'** (H3-4) ~ *prefers light shade and shelter*

93 **'Loder's White'** (H3-4)

02 **'Lord Roberts'** (H4)

93 *lutescens* **'Bagshot Sands'** (H3-4)

93 *luteum* (A) (H4) ~ *suitable for small gardens*

93 *macabeanum* (H3-4) ~ *prefers light shade and shelter*

93 *makinoi* (H4)

93 **'Marion Street'** (H4) ~ *suitable for small gardens*

93 **'Markeeta's Prize'** (H4)

02 **'Martha Isaacson'** (A/d) (H4) ~ *suitable for small gardens*

93 **'May Day'** (H3-4) ~ *i.e. the AM clone; suitable for small gardens*

93 R **'Merganser'** (H4) ~ *suitable for small gardens*

93 R **'Moerheim'** (H4) ~ *suitable for small gardens*

93 **'Morning Cloud'** (H4) ~ *suitable for small gardens*

93 **'Mother's Day'** (EA) (H4) ~ *suitable for small gardens*

'Mount Seven Star' ~ see *Rhododendron nakaharae* 'Mount Seven Star'

93 **'Mrs A.T. de la Mare'** (H4)

93 **'Mrs Charles E. Pearson'** (H4)

93 **'Mrs Davies Evans'** (H4)

93 **'Mrs Furnivall'** (H4)

02 **'Mrs J.C. Williams'** (H4)

93 **'Mrs Lionel de Rothschild'** (H4) ~ *i.e. the AM clone*

93 **'Mrs R.S. Holford'** (H4)

93 **'Mrs T.H. Lowinsky'** (H4)

93 *mucronulatum* **'Cornell Pink'** (H4)

02 *nakaharae* **'Mount Seven Star'** (EA) (H4) ~ *suitable for small gardens*

02 **'Nancy Evans'** (H3-4)

93 **'Nancy Waterer'** (G) (H4) ~ *suitable for small gardens*

93 **'Narcissiflorum'** (G/d) (H4) ~ *suitable for small gardens*

93 **'Niagara'** (EA) (H3-4) ~ *suitable for small gardens*

93 *niveum* (H4)

93 **'Norma'** (R/d) (H4) ~ *suitable for small gardens*

93   *occidentale* (A) (H4)   ~ *extremely*
     variable; suitable for small gardens
02   'Old Port' (H4)
02   'Olga' (H4)
93   'Orange Beauty' (EA) (H3-4)
     ~ *suitable for small gardens*
02   *orbiculare* (H3-4)
93   *oreodoxa* var. *fargesii* (H4)
02   'Osmar' (H4)
     ~ *suitable for small gardens*
93   *pachysanthum* (H4)   ~ *valued*
     especially for its foliage
93   'Palestrina' (EA) (H3-4)
     ~ *suitable for small gardens*
02   'Panda' (EA) (H4)
     ~ *suitable for small gardens*
93   'Patty Bee' (H4)
     ~ *suitable for small gardens*
93   'Penheale Blue' (H4)
     ~ *suitable for small gardens*
93   'Percy Wiseman' (H4)   ~ *suitable*
     for small gardens; reconfirmed
     after trial 2001
93   'Persil' (K) (H4)
     ~ *suitable for small gardens*
     'Peter John Mezitt'
     ~ see *Rhododendron*
     (PJM Group) 'Peter John Mezitt'
93   'Pink Cherub' (H4)
~ *suitable for small gardens; reconfirmed*
     after trial 2001
02   'Pink Pancake' (EA) (H4)
     ~ *suitable for small gardens*
93   'Pink Pebble' (H3-4)
     ~ *suitable for small gardens*
93   (PJM Group) 'Peter John Mezitt' (H4)
     ~ *suitable for small gardens*
93   'Polar Bear' (H3-4)   ~ *the FCC*
     clone; prefers light shade and shelter
     'Polaris'   ~ see *Rhododendron*
     'Hachmann's Polaris'
93 R *polycladum* (Scintillans Group)'Policy
     (H4) ~ *the FCC clone of the Scintillans*
     Group; suitable
     for small gardens
93   'Praecox' (H4)
     ~ *suitable for small gardens*
93   'Princess Anne' (H4)
     ~ *suitable for small gardens*
93   'Professor Hugo de Vries' (H4)
93   *pseudochrysanthum* (H4)
93 R 'Ptarmigan' (H3-4)
     ~ *suitable for small gardens*

93   'Pucella' (G) (H4)
     ~ *suitable for small gardens*
93   'Purple Splendour' (H4)
02   'Purple Triumph' (EA) (H3)
02   'Purpurtraum' (EA) (H4)
     ~ *suitable for small gardens*
93   'Queen Elizabeth II' (H4)
02   *racemosum* (H4)
     ~ *suitable for small gardens*
93   — 'Rock Rose' (H3-4)
     ~ *suitable for small gardens*
02   'Racoon' (EA) (H4)
     ~ *suitable for small gardens*
93 R 'Ramapo' (H4)
     ~ *suitable for small gardens*
93   'Razorbill' (H4)
     ~ *suitable for small gardens*
02   'Rendezvous' (H4)
     ~ *suitable for small gardens*
93   'Renoir' (H4)   ~ *suitable for small*
     gardens; reconfirmed after trial 2001
02   *rex* subsp. *fictolacteum* (H3-4)
     ~ *prefers light shade and shelter*
02   — subsp. *rex* (H3-4)   ~ *prefers light*
     shade and shelter
02   'Rosata' (V/s) (H4)
93   'Rosebud' (EA/d) (H3-4)
     ~ *suitable for small gardens*
93   *roxieanum* var. *oreonastes* (H4)
     ~ *suitable for small gardens*
93 R *russatum* (H4)
     ~ *suitable for small gardens*
93 R 'Saint Merryn' (H4)
     ~ *suitable for small gardens*
93 R 'Sarled' (H4)   ~ *the AM clone;*
     suitable for small gardens
93   'Satan' (K) (H4)
     ~ *suitable for small gardens*
     'Satschiko'
     ~ see *Rhododendron* 'Geisha Orange'
93 R 'Scarlet Wonder' (H4)
     ~ *suitable for small gardens*
93   'Silver Slipper' (K) (H4)
     ~ *suitable for small gardens*
93   *sinogrande* (H3)
     ~ *prefers light shade and shelter*
93   'Sir Charles Lemon' (H3-4)
93   'Souvenir de Doctor S. Endtz' (H4)
93   'Souvenir of Anthony Waterer' (H4)
93   'Spek's Orange' (M) (H4)
     ~ *suitable for small gardens*
02   'Squirrel' (EA) (H4)
     ~ *suitable for small gardens*

stenophyllum
~ see *Rhododendron makinoi*
93 **'Strawberry Ice'** (K) (H4)
~ *suitable for small gardens*
93 **'Summer Fragrance'** (O) (H4)
~ *suitable for small gardens*
93 **'Sunte Nectarine'** (K) (H4)
~ *suitable for small gardens*
93 **'Susan'** (H4) ~ *Williams's*
R. campanulatum *hybrid*
02 **'Tatjana'** (H4)
~ *suitable for small gardens*
93 **'Taurus'** (H4)
93 **'Tessa Roza'** (H4)
~ *suitable for small gardens*
93 **'The Hon. Jean Marie de Montague'**
(H4)
93 **'The Master'** (H4)
~ *Slocock's 'China' hybrid*
02 **'Tibet'** (H3-4) ~ *suitable for small gardens*
02 **'Tidbit'** (H4)
~ *suitable for small gardens*
'Tortoiseshell Champagne'
~ see *Rhododendron* 'Champagne'
93 **'Tortoiseshell Orange'** (H3-4)
93 **'Tortoiseshell Wonder'** (H3-4)
02 *trichostomum* **(Ledoides Group)**
'Collingwood Ingram' (H4)
~ *suitable for small gardens*
93 **'Unique'** (H4)
~ *suitable for small gardens*
93 **'Vanessa Pastel'** (H3-4)
93 *vaseyi* (A) (H3-4)
~ *suitable for small gardens*
93 **'Vintage Rosé'** (H4) ~ *suitable for*
small gardens; reconfirmed after trial 2001
93 *viscosum* (A) (H4) ~ *variable, but*
good in all forms; suitable
for small gardens
02 **'Viscy'** (H4)
93 **'Vulcan'** (H4) ~ *Waterer's* R.
griersonianum *hybrid*
93 **'Vuyk's Rosyred'** (EA) (H4)
~ *suitable for small gardens*
93 **'Vuyk's Scarlet'** (EA) (H4)
~ *suitable for small gardens*
93 **'W.F.H.'** (H4) ~ *suitable for small gardens*
02 **'Wee Bee'** (H4)
~ *suitable for small gardens*
02 **'White Lights'** (A) (H4)
~ *suitable for small gardens*
93 **'Whitethroat'** (K/d) (H4)
~ *suitable for small gardens*

93 *williamsianum* (H4)
~ *suitable for small gardens*
02 *wiltonii* (H4)
93 **'Winsome' (hybrid)** (H3) ~ *the AM*
clone; suitable for
small gardens
02 **'Wombat'** (EA) (H4)
~ *suitable for small gardens*
yakushimanum **FCC form** ~ see
Rhododendron yakushimanum
'Koichiro Wada'
93 — **'Koichiro Wada'** (H4) ~ *suitable*
for small gardens; reconfirmed
after trial 2001
— subsp. *makinoi*
~ see *Rhododendron makinoi*
93 **'Yellow Hammer'** (H4)
93 *yunnanense* **'Openwood'** (H3-4)

RHUS (ANACARDIACEAE)
cotinus ~ see *Cotinus coggygria*
hirta ~ see *Rhus typhina*
93 × *pulvinata* **(Autumn Lace Group)**
'Red Autumn Lace' (H4)
93 *typhina* (H4) ~ *may sucker*
93 — **'Dissecta'** (H4) ~ *may sucker*
— **'Laciniata'** hort. ~ see *Rhus*
typhina 'Dissecta'

RIBES (GROSSULARIACEAE)
93 *sanguineum* **'Pulborough Scarlet'**
(H4)
02 — **WHITE ICICLE 'Ubric'** (H4)
93 *speciosum* (H3)

ROBINIA (PAPILIONACEAE)
93 *pseudoacacia* **'Frisia'** (H4)
93 × *slavinii* **'Hillieri'** (H4)

ROSA (ROSACEAE)
93 **ABBEYFIELD ROSE 'Cocbrose'** PBR(HT)
(H4)
02 **'Agnes'** (Ru) (H4)
93 × *alba* **'Alba Semiplena'** (A) (H4)
— **CELESTIAL** ~ see *Rosa* 'Céleste'
93 **ALEXANDER 'Harlex'** (HT) (H4)
93 **AMBER QUEEN 'Harroony'** PBR
(F) (H4)
93 **ANISLEY DICKSON 'Dickimono'** PBR(F)
(H4)
93 **ANNA FORD 'Harpiccolo'** PBR
(Min/Patio) (H4)
94 **ANNA LIVIA 'Kormetter'** PBR(F) (H4)

(A)	Alba
(Bb)	Bourbon
(Ce)	Centifolia
(Ch)	China
(Cl)	Climbing (in combination)
(D)	Damask
(Dpo)	Damask Portland
(G)	Gallica
(GC)	Ground Cover
(HP)	Hybrid Perpetual
(Min)	Miniature
(Mo)	Moss
(N)	Noisette
(Pat)	Patio
((PiH)	Pimpinellifolia Hybrid
(S)	Shrub

apothecary's rose ~ see *Rosa gallica*
var. *officinalis*
93 **'Arthur Bell'** (F) (H4)
02 **AVON 'Poulmulti'** PBR (GC) (H4)
02 **BABY LOVE 'Scrivluv'** PBR **(yellow)**
(Min/Patio) (H4)
93 **'Ballerina'** (HM/Poly) (H4)
93 **'Belle de Crécy'** (G) (H4)
02 **BERKSHIRE 'Korpinka'** PBR (GC) (H4)
93 **'Blairii Number Two'** (ClBb) (H4)
93 **'Blanche Double de Coubert'** (Ru)
(H4)
93 **'Blessings'** (HT) (H4)
93 **BONICA 'Meidomonac'** PBR (GC) (H4)
93 **'Buff Beauty'** (HM) (H4)
californica **'Plena'** ~ see *Rosa*
nutkana 'Plena'
'Canary Bird' ~ see *Rosa xanthina*
'Canary Bird'
94 **'Cantabrigiensis'** (S) (H4) ~ *more*
suitable for larger gardens
93 **'Capitaine John Ingram'** (CeMo)
(H4)
93 **'Cardinal de Richelieu'** (G) (H4)
94 **'Cécile Brünner'** (Poly) (H4)
93 **'Céleste'** (A) (H4) ~ *previously*
listed as R. *'Celestial'*
94 **'Céline Forestier'** (N) (H3)
02 **CENTENARY 'Koreledas'** PBR (F) (H4)
93 x *centifolia* **'Cristata'** (Ce) (H4)
93 **'Cerise Bouquet'** (S) (H4)
02 **CHAMPAGNE COCKTAIL 'Horflash'** PBR
(F) (H4)
Chapeau de Napoléon ~ see *Rosa*
x *centifolia* 'Cristata'
93 **'Charles de Mills'** (G) (H4)
02 **CHARLOTTE 'Auspoly'** PBR (S) (H4)
93 **'Chinatown'** (F/S) (H4)

chinensis **'Mutabilis'** ~ see *Rosa*
x *odorata* 'Mutabilis'
96 **CIDER CUP 'Dicladida'** PBR (Min/Patio)
(H4)
93 **'Complicata'** (G) (H4)
'Comte de Chambord' misapplied
~ see *Rosa* 'Madame Knorr'
93 **CONSTANCE SPRY 'Austance'** (Cl/S)
(H4)
93 **'Cornelia'** (HM) (H4)
crested moss ~ see *Rosa* x *centifolia*
'Cristata'
crimson damask ~ see *Rosa gallica*
var. *officinalis*
'Cristata' ~ see *Rosa* x *centifolia*
'Cristata'
02 **DAWN CHORUS 'Dicquasar'** PBR (HT)
(H4)
93 **'De Rescht'** (DPo) (H4)
02 **'Deep Secret'** (HT) (H4)
93 **'Duc de Guiche'** (G) (H4)
93 **'Duchesse de Montebello'** (G) (H4)
02 **EGLANTYNE 'Ausmak'** PBR (S) (H4)
93 **ELINA 'Dicjana'** PBR (HT) (H4)
'Empress Josephine' ~ see *Rosa*
x *francofurtana*
02 **'English Miss'** (F) (H4)
94 **ESCAPADE 'Harpade'** (F) (H4)
02 **EVELYN 'Aussaucer'** PBR (S) (H4)
'F.E. Lester' ~ see *Rosa*
'Francis E. Lester'
'Fairy Rose' ~ see *Rosa* 'The Fairy'
93 **'Fantin-Latour'** (*centifolia* **hybrid**)
(H4)
02 **FASCINATION 'Poulmax'** PBR (F) (H4)
93 **'Felicia'** (HM) (H4)
93 **'Félicité Parmentier'** (AxD) (H4)
02 **FELLOWSHIP 'Harwelcome'** PBR (F)
(H4)
93 **'Ferdinand Pichard'** (Bb) (H4)
ferruginea ~ see *Rosa glauca*
02 **FLOWER CARPET WHITE**
'Noaschnee' PBR (GC) (H4)
96 **'Fragrant Delight'** (F) (H4)
94 **'Francis E. Lester'** (HM/Ra) (H4)
93 x *francofurtana* (H4)
'Frau Dagmar Hartopp' ~ see *Rosa*
'Fru Dagmar Hastrup'
93 **'Fred Loads'** (F/S) (H4)
93 **FREEDOM 'Dicjem'** PBR (HT) (H4)
02 **FRIEND FOR LIFE 'Cocnanne'** PBR (F)
(H4)
93 **'Fritz Nobis'** (S) (H4)

93	'Fru Dagmar Hastrup' (Ru) (H4)
93	'Frühlingsgold' (PiH) (H4)
	gallica 'Complicata' ~ see *Rosa* 'Complicata'
93	— var. *officinalis* (G) (H4)
93	— 'Versicolor' (G) (H4)
93	'Geranium' (*moyesii* hybrid) (H4)
94	GERTRUDE JEKYLL 'Ausbord' PBR (S) (H4)
93	*glauca* Pourr. (S) (H4) ~ sometimes listed as R. ferruginea
02	GOLDEN CELEBRATION 'Ausgold' PBR (S) (H4)
93	'Golden Wings' (S) (H4)
02	GORDON'S COLLEGE 'Cocjabby' PBR (F) (H4)
93	GRAHAM THOMAS 'Ausmas' PBR (S) (H4)
02	GROUSE 'Korimro' PBR (S/GC) (H4)
02	'Hakuun' (F/Patio) (H4)
02	HERTFORDSHIRE 'Kortenay' PBR (GC) (H4)
02	HIGH HOPES 'Haryup' PBR (Cl) (H4)
	hugonis ~ see *Rosa xanthina* f. *hugonis*
	— 'Plenissima' ~ see *Rosa xanthina* f. *hugonis*
02	ICE CREAM 'Korzuri' PBR (HT) (H4)
93	ICEBERG 'Korbin' (F) (H4)
96	INDIAN SUMMER 'Peaperfume' PBR (HT) (H4)
93	INGRID BERGMAN 'Poulman' PBR (HT) (H4)
93	'Ispahan' (D) (H4)
94	JACQUELINE DU PRÉ 'Harwanna' PBR (S) (H4)
	'Jacques Cartier' hort. ~ see *Rosa* 'Marchesa Boccella'
	'Jenny Duval' misapplied ~ see *Rosa* 'Président de Sèze'
93	'Just Joey' (HT) (H4)
02	KENT 'Poulcov' PBR (S/GC) (H4)
93	'Königin von Dänemark' (A) (H4)
02	L.D. BRAITHWAITE 'Auscrim' PBR (S) (H4)
93	'La Ville de Bruxelles' (D) (H4)
02	'Lady Penzance' (RH) (H4)
02	L'AIMANT 'Harzola' PBR (F) (H4)
02	LANCASHIRE 'Korstesgli' PBR (GC) (H4)
93	'Lavender Lassie' (HM) (H4)
02	LITTLE BO-PEEP 'Poullen' PBR (Min/Patio) (H4)

	'Little White Pet' ~ see *Rosa* 'White Pet'
	longicuspis hort. ~ see *Rosa mulliganii*
93	LOVELY LADY 'Dicjubell' PBR (HT) (H4)
93	*macrophylla* 'Master Hugh' (H4)
93	'Madame Hardy' (ClD) (H4)
93	'Madame Isaac Pereire' (ClBb) (H4)
93	'Madame Knorr' (DPo) (H4)
02	MAGIC CARPET 'Jaclover' PBR (S/GC) (H4)
02	'Maiden's Blush' hort. (A) (H4)
	Maltese rose ~ see *Rosa* 'Cécile Brünner'
93	MANY HAPPY RETURNS 'Harwanted' PBR (S/F) (H4)
93	'Marchesa Boccella' (DPo) (H4)
93	MARGARET MERRIL 'Harkuly' (F/HT) (H4)
93	'Marguerite Hilling' (S) (H4)
02	MARJORIE FAIR 'Harhero' (Poly/S) (H4)
02	MARRY ME 'Dicwonder' PBR (Patio) (H4)
02	MARY ROSE 'Ausmary' PBR (S) (H4)
	'Master Hugh' ~ see *Rosa macrophylla* 'Master Hugh'
02	MATANGI 'Macman' (F) (H4)
02	MEMENTO 'Dicbar' PBR (F) (H4)
93	'Mevrouw Nathalie Nypels' (Poly) (H4)
02	MOLINEUX 'Ausmol' PBR (S) (H4)
93	MOUNTBATTEN 'Harmantelle' PBR (F) (H4)
	moyesii 'Geranium' ~ see *Rosa* 'Geranium' (*moyesii* hybrid)
93	*mulliganii* (Ra) (H4) ~ sometimes grown incorrectly as R. longicuspis
	mundi ~ see *Rosa gallica* 'Versicolor'
	— 'Versicolor' ~ see *Rosa gallica* 'Versicolor'
	'Mutabilis' ~ see *Rosa × odorata* 'Mutabilis'
	'Nathalie Nypels' ~ see *Rosa* 'Mevrouw Nathalie Nypels'
93	'Nevada' (S) (H4)
93	'Nozomi' (ClMin/GC) (H4)
02	'Nuits de Young' (CeMo) (H4)
93	*nutkana* 'Plena' (S) (H4) ~ usually grown as R. californica 'Plena'

93	× *odorata* 'Mutabilis' (Ch) (H3-4)
	officinalis ~ see *Rosa gallica* var.
	officinalis
	old velvet moss ~ see *Rosa* 'William Lobb'
02	Oxfordshire 'Korfullwind' PBR (GC) (H4)
02	Pat Austin 'Ausmum' PBR (S) (H4)
93	Paul Shirville 'Harqueterwife' PBR (HT) (H4)
93	Peace 'Madame A. Meilland' (HT) (H4)
93	'Penelope' (HM) (H4)
	× *penzanceana* ~ see *Rosa* 'Lady Penzance'
93	'Perle d'Or' (Poly) (H4)
93	*pimpinellifolia* 'Andrewsii' (H4)
93	Pink Flower Carpet 'Noatraum' PBR (GC) (H4)
93	'Pink Grootendorst' (Ru) (H4)
93	'Président de Sèze' (G) (H4)
02	Pretty Lady 'Scrivo' PBR (F) (H4)
02	Pretty Polly 'Meitonje' PBR (Min) (H4)
93	*primula* (S) (H3-4)
02	Princess of Wales 'Hardinkum' PBR (F) (H4)
	'Prolifera de Redouté' misapplied ~ see *Rosa* 'Duchesse de Montebello'
94	'Prosperity' (HM) (H4)
94	Queen Mother 'Korquemu' PBR (Patio) (H4)
	Queen of Denmark ~ see *Rosa* 'Königin von Dänemark'
	red rose of Lancaster ~ see *Rosa gallica* var. *officinalis*
93	Remember Me 'Cocdestin' PBR (HT) (H4)
02	Remembrance 'Harxampton' PBR (F) (H4)
	'Rescht' ~ see *Rosa* 'De Rescht'
93	'Rose d'Amour' (S) (H4) ~ *now considered to be a* R. virginiana *hybrid*
	'Rose de Rescht' ~ see *Rosa* 'De Rescht'
93	'Roseraie de l'Haÿ' (Ru) (H4)
93	Rosy Cushion 'Interall' PBR (S/GC) (H4)
93	Royal William 'Korzaun' PBR (HT) (H4)
	rubrifolia ~ see *Rosa glauca*
93	*rugosa* 'Alba' (Ru) (H4)

93	— 'Rubra' (Ru) (H4)
	— 'Scabrosa' ~ see *Rosa* 'Scabrosa'
	Saint Mark's rose ~ see *Rosa* 'Rose d'Amour'
93	'Sally Holmes' PBR (S) (H4)
93	Savoy Hotel 'Harvintage' PBR (HT) (H4)
93	'Scabrosa' (Ru) (H4)
	Scarlet Fire ~ see *Rosa* 'Scharlachglut'
	Scarlet Glow ~ see *Rosa* 'Scharlachglut'
02	Scepter'd Isle 'Ausland' PBR (S) (H4)
93	'Scharlachglut' (ClS) (H4)
93	'Schneezwerg' (Ru) (H4)
	'Semiplena' ~ see *Rosa* × *alba* 'Alba Semiplena'
93	Sexy Rexy 'Macrexy' PBR (F) (H4)
02	Shine On 'Dictalent' PBR (Patio) (H4)
02	Silver Anniversary 'Poulari' PBR (HT) (H4)
93	'Silver Jubilee' (HT) (H4)
	'Snow Dwarf' ~ see *Rosa* 'Schneezwerg'
93	*soulieana* (Ra/S) (H3-4) ~ *more suitable for larger gardens*
93	'Southampton' (F) (H4)
02	Sunset Boulevard 'Harbabble' PBR (F) (H4)
93	Surrey 'Korlanum' PBR (GC) (H4)
94	Swany 'Meiburenac' (Min/GC) (H4)
93	Sweet Dream 'Fryminicot' PBR (Patio) (H4)
93	Sweet Magic 'Dicmagic' PBR (Min/Patio) (H4)
93	Tall Story 'Dickooky' PBR (F) (H4)
93	Tequila Sunrise 'Dicobey' PBR (HT) (H4)
93	'The Fairy' (Poly) (H4)
93	The Lady 'Fryjingo' PBR (S) (H4)
93	The Times Rose 'Korpeahn' PBR (F) (H4)
	'Tipo Ideale' ~ see *Rosa* × *odorata* 'Mutabilis'
93	Troika 'Poumidor' (HT) (H4)
93	Trumpeter 'Mactru' (F) (H4)
93	'Tuscany Superb' (G) (H4)
02	Valencia 'Koreklia' PBR (HT) (H4)
02	Valentine Heart 'Dicogle' PBR (F) (H4)
	versicolor ~ see *Rosa gallica* 'Versicolor'

93 *virginiana* (H4)
— 'Plena'
~ see *Rosa* 'Rose d'Amour'
02 **WARM WISHES 'Fryxotic'** PBR (HT) (H4)
93 **WESTERLAND 'Korwest'** (F/S) (H4)
93 **'White Pet'** (Poly) (H4)
white rose of York
~ see *Rosa* × *alba* 'Alba Semiplena'
93 **'William Lobb'** (CeMo) (H4)
02 **WILTSHIRE 'Kormuse'** PBR (S/GC) (H4)
93 *xanthina* **'Canary Bird'** (S) (H4)
93 — f. *hugonis* (H4)
'Yellow Cécile Brünner'
~ see *Rosa* 'Perle d'Or'
93 **'Yesterday'** (Poly/F/S) (H4)
93 **'Yvonne Rabier'** (Poly) (H4)

ROSMARINUS (LAMIACEAE)
02 *officinalis* var. *angustissimus*
'Benenden Blue' (H4)
— 'Collingwood Ingram'
~ see *Rosmarinus officinalis* var.
angustissimus 'Benenden Blue'
— 'Fastigiatus' ~ see *Rosmarinus*
officinalis 'Miss
Jessopp's Upright'
02 — 'McConnell's Blue' (H4)
93 — 'Miss Jessopp's Upright' (H4)
— f. *pyramidalis* ~ see *Rosmarinus*
officinalis 'Miss
Jessopp's Upright'
93 — 'Severn Sea' (H4)
93 — 'Sissinghurst Blue' (H4)

RUBUS (ROSACEAE)
93 **'Benenden'** (H4)
02 *biflorus* (H4)
96 *cockburnianus* **'Goldenvale'** (H4)
93 *thibetanus* (H4)
— 'Silver Fern' ~ see *Rubus*
thibetanus
tridel **'Benenden'** ~ see *Rubus*
'Benenden'

SALIX (SALICACEAE)
93 *acutifolia* **'Blue Streak'** (m) (H4)
alba f. *argentea* ~ see *Salix alba* var.
sericea
— 'Chermesina' hort. ~ see *Salix alba*
subsp. *vitellina* 'Britzensis'
93 — var. *sericea* (H4)
— 'Splendens' ~ see *Salix alba* var.
sericea

93 — subsp. *vitellina* (H4)
93 — — 'Britzensis' (m) (H4)
93 *babylonica* var. *pekinensis* **'Tortuosa'**
(H4)
93 R **'Boydii'** (f) (H4)
02 *elaeagnos* subsp. *angustifolia* (H4)
93 *hastata* **'Wehrhahnii'** (m) (H4)
93 R *helvetica* (H4)
93 R *lanata* (H4)
93 *magnifica* (H4)
matsudana **'Tortuosa'** ~ see *Salix*
babylonica var.
pekinensis 'Tortuosa'
93 *purpurea* **'Pendula'** (H4)
93 R *reticulata* (H4)
rosmarinifolia hort. ~ see *Salix*
elaeagnos subsp. *angustifolia*

SALVIA (LAMIACEAE)
greggii **'Blush Pink'** ~ see *Salvia*
microphylla 'Pink Blush'
96 *microphylla* **'Kew Red'** (H3-4)
96 — var. *microphylla* **'Newby Hall'**
(H3-4)
96 — 'Pink Blush' (H3-4)
96 — 'Pleasant View' (H3-4)
93 *officinalis* **'Icterina'** (v) (H4)
93 — 'Purpurascens' (H4)
— 'Variegata' ~ see *Salvia*
officinalis 'Icterina'

SAMBUCUS (CAPRIFOLIACEAE)
93 *nigra* **'Aurea'** (H4)
02 — **BLACK BEAUTY 'Gerda'** (H4)
93 — f. *laciniata* (H4)
93 *racemosa* **'Sutherland Gold'**
(H4)

SANTOLINA (ASTERACEAE)
93 *chamaecyparissus* (H4)
— var. *corsica* ~ see *Santolina*
chamaecyparissus var. *nana*
93 R — var. *nana* (H4)
incana ~ see *Santolina*
chamaecyparissus
93 *pinnata* subsp. *neapolitana* (H4)
93 *rosmarinifolia* subsp. *rosmarinifolia*
'Primrose Gem' (H4)
tomentosa ~ see *Santolina pinnata*
subsp. *neapolitana*

SARCOCOCCA (BUXACEAE)
93 *confusa* (H4)

93   *hookeriana* (H4)
93   — var. *digyna* (H4)
93   *ruscifolia* var. *chinensis* (H4)
                ~ *often listed as* S. ruscifolia

SATUREJA (LAMIACEAE)
93 R   *coerulea* (H4)
        montana 'Coerulea'
                ~ see *Satureja coerulea*

SENECIO (ASTERACEAE)
        greyi hort.   ~ see *Brachyglottis*
                (Dunedin Group) 'Sunshine'
        laxifolius hort.   ~ see *Brachyglottis*
                (Dunedin Group) 'Sunshine'
        leucostachys   ~ see *Senecio viravira*
        monroi   ~ see *Brachyglottis*
                                      monroi
        'Sunshine'   ~ see *Brachyglottis*
                (Dunedin Group) 'Sunshine'
93 G   *viravira* (H3-4)

SKIMMIA (RUTACEAE)
93   × *confusa* 'Kew Green' (m) (H4)
93   *japonica* 'Fragrans' (m) (H4)
        — 'Fragrant Cloud'   ~ see *Skimmia*
                                japonica 'Fragrans'
93   — 'Nymans' (f) (H4)
93   — 'Rubella' (m) (H4)

SOPHORA (PAPILIONACEAE)
93   *japonica* (H4)
02   *microphylla* SUN KING 'Hilsop' ᴾᴮᴿ
                (H4)
93   *tetraptera* (H3)

SORBARIA (ROSACEAE)
        aitchisonii   ~ see *Sorbaria tomentosa*
                            var. *angustifolia*
93   *tomentosa* var. *angustifolia*
                (H4)

SORBUS (ROSACEAE)
        aria 'Decaisneana'   ~ see *Sorbus*
                            aria 'Majestica'
93   — 'Lutescens' (H4)
93   — 'Majestica' (H4)
        — 'Mitchellii'   ~ see *Sorbus*
                thibetica 'John Mitchell'
93   *aucuparia* 'Sheerwater Seedling'
                (H4)
        — 'Xanthocarpa'   ~ see *Sorbus*
                aucuparia var. *xanthocarpa*

93   — var. *xanthocarpa* (H4)
                ~ *previously listed as*
                S. aucuparia 'Fructu Luteo'
93   *cashmiriana* Hedl. (H4)
93   *commixta* 'Embley' (H4)
        fruticosa 'Koehneana'
                ~ see *Sorbus koehneana*
93   *hupehensis* C.K. Schneid. (H4)
93   — var. *obtusa* (H4)
        — 'Rosea'   ~ see *Sorbus hupehensis*
                                var. *obtusa*
93   *hybrida* L. 'Gibbsii' (H4)
93   *koehneana* C.K. Schneid. (H4)
                ~ *previously listed as*
                S. fruticosa 'Koehneana'
93 R   *reducta* (H4)
93   *sargentiana* (H4)
93   *thibetica* 'John Mitchell' (H4)
93   *vilmorinii* (H4)

SPARTIUM (PAPILIONACEAE)
93   *junceum* (H4)

SPIRAEA (ROSACEAE)
02   'Arguta' (H4)
        × *arguta* 'Bridal Wreath'   ~ see
                            Spiraea 'Arguta'
93   × *cinerea* 'Grefsheim' (H4)
        japonica 'Alpina'   ~ see *Spiraea*
                            japonica 'Nana'
02   — 'Candlelight' (H4)
02   — 'Dart's Red' (H4)
02   — GOLDEN PRINCESS 'Lisp' ᴾᴮᴿ (H4)
02   — MAGIC CARPET 'Walbuma' ᴾᴮᴿ
                (H4)
93 R   — 'Nana' (H4)
        — 'Nyewoods'   ~ see *Spiraea*
                            japonica 'Nana'
93   *nipponica* 'Snowmound' (H4)
        — Maxim. var. *tosaensis* hort.   ~ see
                Spiraea nipponica 'Snowmound'
93   *thunbergii* (H4)

STACHYURUS (STACHYURACEAE)
93   *praecox* (H4)

STEWARTIA (THEACEAE)
        'Korean Splendor'   ~ see *Stewartia*
                pseudocamellia Koreana Group
        koreana   ~ see *Stewartia*
                pseudocamellia Koreana Group
02   *malacodendron* (H4)
93   *pseudocamellia* (H4)

— var. *koreana* ~ see *Stewartia*
pseudo-camellia Koreana Group
93 — **Koreana Group** (H4)
93 *sinensis* (H4)

STYRAX (STYRACACEAE)
93 *hemsleyanus* (H4)
93 *japonicus* (H4)
02 — **Benibana Group** (H4)
— **'Roseus'** ~ see *Styrax japonicus*
Benibana Group
93 *obassia* (H4)

SYRINGA (OLEACEAE)
93 × *hyacinthiflora* **'Esther Staley'** (H4)
93 × *josiflexa* **'Bellicent'** (H4)
93 *meyeri* var. *spontanea* **'Palibin'** (H4)
microphylla **'Superba'**
~ see *Syringa pubescens*
subsp. *microphylla* 'Superba'
palibiniana ~ see *Syringa meyeri*
var. *spontanea* 'Palibin'
patula hort. ~ see *Syringa meyeri*
var. *spontanea* 'Palibin'
93 × *persica* (H4)
93 — **'Alba'** (H4)
93 — **'Elinor'** (H4)
93 *pubescens* subsp. *microphylla*
'Superba' (H4) ~ awarded as
S. microphylla *'Superba'*
93 — subsp. *patula* **'Miss Kim'** (H4)
93 *vulgaris* **'Andenken an Ludwig**
Späth' (H4)
93 — **'Charles Joly'** (d) (H4)
93 — **'Firmament'** (H4)
93 — **'Katherine Havemeyer'** (d) (H4)
93 — **'Madame Lemoine'** (d) (H4)
93 — **'Mrs Edward Harding'** (d) (H4)
— **'Souvenir de Louis Spaeth'**
~ see *Syringa vulgaris*
'Andenken an Ludwig Späth'
93 — **'Vestale'** (H4)

TAMARIX (TAMARICACEAE)
93 *ramosissima* **'Rubra'** (H4)
— **'Summer Glow'** ~ see *Tamarix*
ramosissima 'Rubra'
93 *tetrandra* (H4)

TEUCRIUM (LAMIACEAE)
93 *fruticans* **'Azureum'** (H3)

THYMUS (LAMIACEAE)
'Anderson's Gold'
~ see *Thymus pulegioides*
'Bertram Anderson'
× *citriodorus* **'Aureus'**
~ see *Thymus pulegioides* 'Aureus'
— **'Bertram Anderson'**
~ see *Thymus pulegioides*
'Bertram Anderson'
— **'Golden Lemon'** misapplied
~ see *Thymus pulegioides* 'Aureus'
93 R — **'Silver Queen'** (v) (H4)
93 R **'Coccineus'** (H4) ~ sometimes listed
incorrectly under T. serpyllum
'E.B. Anderson'
~ see *Thymus pulegioides*
'Bertram Anderson'
93 R *polytrichus* subsp. *britannicus*
'Thomas's White' (H4)
~ sometimes listed incorrectly under
T. serpyllum; previously listed as
T. polytrichus subsp. britannicus *'Albus'*
93 R *pulegioides* **'Aureus'** (H4)
~ awarded as T. ×
citriodorus *'Aureus'*
93 R — **'Bertram Anderson'** (H4)
~ awarded as T. ×
citriodorus *'Bertram Anderson'*
93 R *serpyllum* **'Pink Chintz'** (H4)

TILIA (TILIACEAE)
93 *cordata* (H4)
93 — **'Greenspire'** (H4)
93 × *euchlora* (H4)
93 × *europaea* **'Wratislaviensis'** (H4)
93 **'Petiolaris'** (H4)
platyphyllos **'Corallina'**
~ see *Tilia platyphyllos* 'Rubra'
93 — **'Rubra'** (H4)
93 *tomentosa* **'Brabant'** (H4)
— **'Petiolaris'**
~ see *Tilia* 'Petiolaris'

TRACHYCARPUS (ARECACEAE)
93 *fortunei* (H3-4)

ULEX (PAPILIONACEAE)
93 *europaeus* **'Flore Pleno'** (d) (H4)
— **'Plenus'** ~ see *Ulex europaeus*
'Flore Pleno'

VACCINIUM (ERICACEAE)
93 *corymbosum* (F) (H4)

93   *cylindraceum* (H4)
93   *glaucoalbum* (H3-4)
93 R *vitis-idaea* **Koralle Group** (H4)

VERBASCUM (SCROPHULARIACEAE)
93 R 'Letitia' (H3)

VIBURNUM (CAPRIFOLIACEAE)
93   x *bodnantense* 'Charles Lamont' (H4)
93   — 'Dawn' (H4)
93   — 'Deben' (H4)
93   x *burkwoodii* 'Anne Russell' (H4)
93   — 'Fulbrook' (H4)
93   — 'Park Farm Hybrid' (H4)
93   x *carlcephalum* (H4)
93   *carlesii* 'Aurora' (H4)
93   *cinnamomifolium* (H3)
93   *davidii* (H4)   ~ *male or several plants are required for the production of fruit*
93   *farreri* (H4)
     fragrans Bunge   ~ see *Viburnum farreri*
93   *furcatum* (H4)
93   x *hillieri* 'Winton' (H4)
93   x *juddii* (H4)
     mariesii   ~ see *Viburnum plicatum* 'Mariesii'
93   *opulus* 'Compactum' (H4)
93   — 'Notcutt's Variety' (H4)
93   — 'Roseum' (H4)
     — 'Sterile'   ~ see *Viburnum opulus* 'Roseum'
93   — 'Xanthocarpum' (H4)
93   *plicatum* 'Mariesii' (H4)

93   — 'Pink Beauty' (H4)
93   'Pragense' (H4)
93   *sargentii* 'Onondaga' (H4)
93   *tinus* 'Eve Price' (H4)
02   — 'French White' (H4)
93   — 'Gwenllian' (H4)

WEIGELA (CAPRIFOLIACEAE)
93   *florida* 'Foliis Purpureis' (H4)
93   'Florida Variegata' (v) (H4)
93   'Praecox Variegata' (v) (H4)
02   'Red Prince' (H4)

XANTHOCERAS (SAPINDACEAE)
93   *sorbifolium* (H3-4)

YUCCA (AGAVACEAE)
93   *filamentosa* (H4)
93   — 'Bright Edge' (v) (H3)
93   — 'Variegata' (v) (H3)
93   *flaccida* 'Golden Sword' (v) (H3)
93   — 'Ivory' (H3-4)
93   *gloriosa* (H4)
     — 'Aureovariegata'   ~ see *Yucca gloriosa* 'Variegata'
93   — 'Variegata' (v) (H4)
93   *recurvifolia* (H4)

ZAUSCHNERIA (ONAGRACEAE)
93 R *californica* 'Dublin' (H3)
     — 'Glasnevin'   ~ see *Zauschneria californica* 'Dublin'
02   — 'Western Hills' (H4)

ZELKOVA (ULMACEAE)
93   *serrata* (H4)

Climbers

ACTINIDIA (ACTINIDIACEAE)
93   *kolomikta* (H4)

AMPELOPSIS (VITACEAE)
     henryana   ~ see *Parthenocissus henryana*

CAMPSIS (BIGNONIACEAE)
93   *radicans* f. *flava* (H4)
     — 'Yellow Trumpet'   ~ see *Campsis radicans* f. *flava*

93   x *tagliabuana* 'Madame Galen' (H4)

CELASTRUS (CELASTRACEAE)
93   *orbiculatus* **Hermaphrodite Group** (H4)

CLEMATIS (RANUNCULACEAE)
see p.40 for list of classification codes
02   'Abundance' (Vt) (H4)
02   **ALABAST** 'Poulala' PBR (Fl) (H4)
93   'Alba Luxurians' (Vt) (H4)
02   'Alionushka' (D) (H4)

(A)	Alpina Group (Section Atragene)
(D)	Diversifolia Group
(Fl)	Florida Group (double-flowered)
(Fo)	Forsteri Group
(J)	Jackmanii Group
(L)	Lanuginosa Group
(P)	Patens Group
(T)	Texensis Group
(Ta)	Tangutica Group
(Vt)	Viticella Group

93 R *alpina* (A) (H4)
— 'Columbine White'
~ see *Clematis alpina* 'White Columbine'
02 — 'Constance' (A) (H4)
02 — 'Foxy' (A) (H4)
93 — 'Frances Rivis' (A) (H4)
02 — 'Frankie' (A) (H4)
02 — 'Jacqueline du Pré' (A) (H4)
02 — 'Pink Flamingo' (A) (H4)
93 — 'White Columbine' (A) (H4)
02 ANNA LOUISE 'Evithree' PBR (P) (H4)
02 'Arabella' (D) (H4)
02 ARCTIC QUEEN 'Evitwo' PBR (Fl) (H4)
02 *armandii* 'Apple Blossom' (H4)
02 'Betty Corning' (Vt × T) (H4)
93 'Bill MacKenzie' (Ta) (H4)   ~ *plants*
raised from seed are not entitled
to this cultivar name
02 'Blekitny Aniol' (J/Vt) (H4)
BLUE ANGEL
~ see *Clematis* 'Blekitny Aniol'
buchananiana Finet & Gagnep.   ~ see
Clematis rehderiana
02 x *cartmanii* hort. 'Avalanche' PBR (Fo)
(H3)
— hort. 'Blaaval'   ~ see *Clematis* ×
cartmanii 'Avalanche' PBR
93 *cirrhosa* 'Freckles' (H3)
02 — 'Wisley Cream' (H3)
93 'Comtesse de Bouchaud' (J) (H4)
93 'Daniel Deronda' (P) (H4)
93 x *durandii* (D) (H4)
93 'Edith' (L) (H4)
93 'Ernest Markham' (J/Vt) (H4)
93 'Etoile Violette' (Vt) (H4)
x *fargesioides*
~ see *Clematis* 'Paul Farges'
flammula 'Rubra Marginata'
~ see *Clematis* × *triternata*
'Rubromarginata'
02 'Fuji-musume' (L) (H4)
93 'Gillian Blades' (P) (H4)
93 'Gipsy Queen' (J) (H4)

02 GOLDEN TIARA 'Kugotia' PBR (Ta) (H4)
93 'Helsingborg' (A) (H4)
93 'Henryi' (P) (H4)
02 'Huldine' (Vt) (H4)
93 'Jackmanii' (J) (H4)
02 'John Huxtable' (J) (H4)
02 JOSEPHINE 'Evijohill' PBR (H4)
93 x *jouiniana* 'Praecox' (H4)
93 'Ken Donson' (L) (H4)
02 'Kermesina' (Vt) (H4)
93 'Lasurstern' (P) (H4)
02 *macropetala* 'Lagoon' (A/d) Jackman 1959
(H4)
93 — 'Markham's Pink' (A/d) (H4)
93 'Madame Grangé' (J) (H4)
93 'Madame Julia Correvon'
(Vt) (H4)
'Madame le Coultre'
~ see *Clematis* 'Marie Boisselot'
93 'Marie Boisselot' (L) (H4)
93 'Minuet' (Vt) (H4)
93 'Miss Bateman' (P) (H4)
93 *montana* f. *grandiflora* (H4)
02 — var. *rubens* 'Broughton Star' (d) (H4)
93 — — 'Elizabeth' (H4)
93 — — 'Freda' (H4)
02 — — 'Mayleen' (H4)
93 — — 'Tetrarose' (H4)
93 'Mrs Cholmondeley' (L) (H4)
93 'Mrs George Jackman' (P) (H4)
93 'Nelly Moser' (L/P) (H4)
93 'Niobe' (J) (H4)
orientalis 'Bill MacKenzie'
~ see *Clematis* 'Bill MacKenzie'
02 'Pagoda' (P×Vt) (H4)
02 'Paul Farges' (H4)
02 PETIT FAUCON 'Evisix' PBR (H4)
93 'Polish Spirit' (Vt) (H4)
potaninii 'Summer Snow'
~ see *Clematis* 'Paul Farges'
02 'Prince Charles' (J) (H4)
02 'Princess Diana' (T) (H4)
93 *rehderiana* (H4)
02 'Rhapsody' F.Watkinson (P) (H4)
93 'Richard Pennell' (P) (H4)
02 'Rosy O'Grady' (A) (H4)
93 'Royal Velours' (Vt) (H4)
93 'Royalty' (L×P) (H4)
'Snowdrift'
~ see *Clematis* 'Paul Farges'
SUMMER SNOW
~ see *Clematis* 'Paul Farges'
02 'Sunset' (J) (H4)

tangutica 'Bill MacKenzie'
　　　　～ see *Clematis* 'Bill MacKenzie'
02　— 'Lambton Park' (H4)
texensis 'The Princess of Wales'
　　　　～ see *Clematis* 'Princess Diana'
93　'The President' (P) (H4)
'The Princess of Wales'
　　　　～ see *Clematis* 'Princess Diana'
93　x *triternata* 'Rubromarginata'
　　　　(H4)
93　'Venosa Violacea' (Vt) (H4)
02　'Victoria' (J) (H4)
02　*viticella* (H4)
93　— 'Purpurea Plena Elegans'
　　　　(d) (H4)
02　'Warszawska Nike' (H4)
93　'Will Goodwin' (L) (H4)

CODONOPSIS (CAMPANULACEAE)
convolvulacea hort.
　　　　～ see *Codonopsis grey-wilsonii*
forrestii hort.
　　　　～ see *Codonopsis grey-wilsonii*
93 R *grey-wilsonii* (H4)　　～ *previously*
　　　　listed as C. convolvulacea, *under*
　　　　which name the plant is
　　　　widely cultivated
nepalensis Grey-Wilson
　　　　～ see *Codonopsis grey-wilsonii*

HEDERA (ARALIACEAE)
algeriensis 'Gloire de Marengo'
　　　　～ see *Hedera canariensis*
　　　　'Gloire de Marengo'
93 G *canariensis* 'Gloire de Marengo' (v) (H3)
93 G — 'Marginomaculata' (H3)
93 G — 'Ravensholst' (H3)　　～ *previously*
　　　　listed as H. colchica
　　　　'Ravensholst'
　　— 'Variegata'　　～ see *Hedera*
　　　　canariensis 'Gloire de Marengo'
93　*colchica* (H4)
93　— 'Dentata' (H4)
　　— 'Dentata Aurea'　　～ see *Hedera*
　　　　colchica 'Dentata Variegata'
　　— 'Dentata Variegata' (v) (H4)
　　— 'My Heart'
　　　　～ see *Hedera colchica*
　　— 'Paddy's Pride'　　～ see *Hedera*
　　　　colchica 'Sulphur Heart'
93　— 'Sulphur Heart' (v) (H4)
　　— 'Variegata'　　～ see *Hedera*
　　　　colchica 'Dentata Variegata'

cristata　　　　～ see *Hedera helix*
　　　　'Parsley Crested'
93　*helix* 'Angularis Aurea' (H4)
02　— 'Caecilia' (v) (H4)
02　— 'Ceridwen' (v) (H4)
　　— 'Clotted Cream'
　　　　～ see *Hedera helix* 'Caecilia'
93　— 'Congesta' (H4)
　　— 'Cristata'
　　　　～ see *Hedera helix* 'Parsley Crested'
　　— 'Cristata Melanie'
　　　　～ see *Hedera helix* 'Melanie'
　　— 'Curleylocks'
　　　　～ see *Hedera helix* 'Manda's Crested'
　　— 'Deltoidea'
　　　　～ see *Hedera hibernica* 'Deltoidea'
　　— 'Discolor'
　　　　～ see *Hedera helix* 'Minor Marmorata'
02　— 'Duckfoot' (H4)
93　— 'Erecta' (H4)
93　— 'Glacier' (v) (H4)
　　— 'Gold Harald'
　　　　～ see *Hedera helix* 'Goldchild'
93　— 'Goldchild' (v) (H3-4)
　　— 'Golden Ann'
　　　　～ see *Hedera helix* 'Ceridwen'
　　— 'Golden Ester'
　　　　～ see *Hedera helix* 'Ceridwen'
02　— 'Golden Ingot' (v) (H4)
　　— 'Golden Kolibri'
　　　　～ see *Hedera helix* 'Midas Touch'
　　— 'Helvig'
　　　　～ see *Hedera helix* 'White Knight'
　　— subsp. *hibernica*
　　　　～ see *Hedera hibernica*
　　— 'Holly'　　～ see *Hedera helix*
　　　　'Parsley Crested'
93　— 'Ivalace' (H4)
　　— 'Maculata'　　～ see *Hedera helix*
　　　　'Minor Marmorata'
93　— 'Manda's Crested' (H4)
02　— 'Maple Leaf' (H4)
02　— 'Melanie' (H4)
93　— 'Midas Touch' (v) (H3-4)
02　— 'Minor Marmorata' (v) (H4)
02　— 'Parsley Crested' (H4)
　　— 'Salt and Pepper'　　～ see *Hedera*
　　　　helix 'Minor Marmorata'
93　— 'Spetchley' (H4)
02　— 'White Knight' (v) (H4)
93　*hibernica* (H4)
　　　　～ *especially for large gardens*
02　— 'Deltoidea' (H4)

HUMULUS (CANNABACEAE)
93   *lupulus* **'Aureus'** (H4)

HYDRANGEA (HYDRANGEACEAE)
93   *anomala* **subsp.** *petiolaris* (H4)
     tiliifolia   ~ see *Hydrangea anomala*
                    subsp. *petiolaris*

JASMINUM (OLEACEAE)
93   *officinale* (H4)
93   — **'Argenteovariegatum'** (v) (H4)
02   — **'Inverleith'** (H4)
     — **'Variegatum'**   ~ see *Jasminum*
          officinale 'Argenteovariegatum'

LAPAGERIA (PHILESIACEAE)
93 G *rosea* (H3)

LATHYRUS (PAPILIONACEAE)
93   *latifolius* (H4)
98   — **'Albus'** (H4)   ~ *perennial, tall,*
                              old-fashioned
     — **PINK PEARL**   ~ see *Lathyrus*
                   latifolius 'Rosa Perle'
97   — **'Rosa Perle'** (H4)
     — **WEISSE PERLE**
        ~ see *Lathyrus latifolius* 'White Pearl'
93   — **'White Pearl'** (H4)   ~ *most plants*
                              now sold under this
                              name are 'Albus'
     — **'White Pearl'** misapplied
          ~ see *Lathyrus latifolius* 'Albus'
02   *rotundifolius* (H4)

LONICERA (CAPRIFOLIACEAE)
     x *americana* hort.
                   ~ see *Lonicera* × *italica*
93   *caprifolium* (H4)
     — **f.** *pauciflora*
                   ~ see *Lonicera* × *italica*
     'Early Cream'
                   ~ see *Lonicera caprifolium*
97   *etrusca* **'Donald Waterer'** (H4)
97   — **'Superba'** (H4)
     flexuosa   ~ see *Lonicera japonica*
                            var. *repens*
93   x *italica* (H4)   ~ *often available in*
          trade as L. × americana; *the true*
          L. × americana *is much less common*
93   *japonica* **'Halliana'** (H4)
97   — **var.** *repens* (H4)
     periclymenum **'Belgica'** misapplied
          ~ see *Lonicera* × *italica*

     — **'Florida'**   ~ see *Lonicera*
                    periclymenum 'Serotina'
93   — **'Graham Thomas'** (H4)
93   — **'Serotina'** (H4)   ~ *the plant*
          selected at East Malling (EM85)
                    is the more vigorous
93   *sempervirens* (H4)
02   *similis* **var.** *delavayi* (H4)
93   *tragophylla* (H4)

PARTHENOCISSUS (VITACEAE)
93   *henryana* (H4)
93   *quinquefolia* (H4)
93   *tricuspidata* (H4)

PASSIFLORA (PASSIFLORACEAE)
93   *caerulea* (H3)
     chinensis   ~ see *Passiflora caerulea*
     mayana   ~ see *Passiflora caerulea*

PILEOSTEGIA (HYDRANGEACEAE)
93   *viburnoides* (H4)

ROSA (ROSACEAE)

(Cl)	Climbing (in combination)
(F)	Floribunda or Cluster-flowered
(HT)	Hybrid Tea or Large-flowered
(Min)	Miniature
(N)	Noisette
(Poly)	Polyantha
(PiH)	Pimpinellifolia hybrid (Hybrid Scots Briar)
(Ra)	Rambler
(S)	Shrub
(T)	Tea

93   **'Adélaïde d'Orléans'** (Ra) (H4)
93   **'Albéric Barbier'** (Ra) (H4)
93   **'Albertine'** (Ra) (H4)
02   **'Aloha'** (ClHT) (H4)
93   *banksiae* **'Lutea'** (Ra/d) (H3)
94   **'Bleu Magenta'** (Ra) (H4)
93   **'Bobbie James'** (Ra) (H4)
          ~ *more suitable for larger gardens*
02   **'Climbing Arthur Bell'** PBR (ClF) (H4)
93   **'Climbing Cécile Brünner'** (ClPoly)
                    (H4)
93   **'Climbing Etoile de Hollande'**
                    (ClHT) (H4)
93   **'Climbing Iceberg'** (ClF) (H4)
93   **'Climbing Lady Hillingdon'** (ClT)
                    (H3)
     'Climbing Little White Pet'
          ~ see *Rosa* 'Félicité Perpétue'

93 'Climbing Mrs Sam McGredy'
   (ClHT) (H4)
93 'Climbing Shot Silk' (ClHT) (H4)
93 'Compassion' (ClHT) (H4)
93 'Crimson Shower' (Ra) (H4)
02 'Dortmund' (ClHScB) (H4)
93 DUBLIN BAY 'Macdub' (Cl) (H4)
02 'Easlea's Golden Rambler'
   (Ra) (H4)
93 'Félicité Perpétue' (Ra) (H4)
93 *filipes* 'Kiftsgate' (Ra) (H4)
   ~ *more suitable for larger gardens*
93 'François Juranville' (Ra) (H4)
93 'Golden Showers' (Cl) (H4)
93 HANDEL 'Macha' (Cl) (H4)
   'Kiftsgate'
   ~ see *Rosa filipes* 'Kiftsgate'
   'Lady Hillingdon'
   ~ see *Rosa* 'Climbing
   Lady Hillingdon'
93 LAURA FORD 'Chewarvel' PBR (ClMin)
   (H4)
96 LAWINIA 'Tanklewi' PBR (ClHT) (H4)
02 'Leverkusen' (Cl) (H4)
02 LITTLE RAMBLER 'Chewramb' PBR
   (MinRa) (H4)
93 'Madame Alfred Carrière' (N) (H4)
93 'Madame Grégoire Staechelin'
   (ClHT) (H4)
93 'Maigold' (ClPiH) (H4)
93 'Mermaid' (Cl) (H3-4)
93 'Morning Jewel' (ClF) (H4)
93 'New Dawn' (Cl) (H4)
02 NICE DAY 'Chewsea' PBR (ClMin) (H4)
02 OPEN ARMS 'Chewpixcel' PBR
   (ClMin) (H4)
93 'Parade' (Cl) (H4)
93 'Paul Transon' (Ra) (H4)
93 'Paul's Himalayan Musk' (Ra) (H3-4)
   ~ *more suitable for larger gardens*
02 PENNY LANE 'Hardwell' PBR (Cl) (H4)
93 'Phyllis Bide' (Ra) (H4)
93 'Rambling Rector' (Ra) (H4)   ~ *more*
   suitable for larger gardens
93 'Sander's White Rambler' (Ra) (H4)
93 'Seagull' (Ra) (H4)
   'Spanish Beauty'   ~ see *Rosa*
   'Madame Grégoire Staechelin'
93 SUMMER WINE 'Korizont' PBR (Cl) (H4)
02 SUPER ELFIN 'Helkleger' PBR (Ra) (H4)
93 'The Garland' (Ra) (H4)
   'The New Dawn'
   ~ see *Rosa* 'New Dawn'

02 TRADITION '95 'Korkeltin' PBR (Cl) (H4)
93 'Veilchenblau' (Ra) (H4)
93 WARM WELCOME 'Chewizz' PBR
   (ClMin) (H4)
02 WHITE CLOUD 'Korstacha' PBR
   (S/ClHT) (H4)

SCHIZOPHRAGMA (HYDRANGEACEAE)
02 *hydrangeoides* 'Roseum' (H4)
93 *integrifolium* (H4)

SOLANUM (SOLANACEAE)
   crispum 'Autumnale'   ~ see *Solanum*
   crispum 'Glasnevin'
93 — 'Glasnevin' (H3)
93 *laxum* 'Album' (H3)   ~ *awarded as*
   S. jasminoides *'Album'*

TROPAEOLUM (TROPAEOLACEAE)
02 *majus* 'Darjeeling Double' (d) (H4)
93 *speciosum* (H4)
93 *tuberosum* var. *lineamaculatum*
   'Ken Aslet' (H3)

VITIS (VITACEAE)

| (B) | Black |
| (O) | Outdoor |

93 'Brant' (O/B) (H4)
93 *coignetiae* (H4)
   henryana
   ~ see *Parthenocissus henryana*
   inconstans
   ~ see *Parthenocissus tricuspidata*
   quinquefolia
   ~ see *Parthenocissus quinquefolia*
93 *vinifera* 'Purpurea' (O/B) (H4)

WISTERIA (PAPILIONACEAE)
93 *floribunda* 'Alba' (H4)
   — 'Hon-beni'   ~ see *Wisteria floribun-*
   da 'Rosea'
   — 'Honey Bee Pink'   ~ see *Wisteria*
   floribunda 'Rosea'
   — 'Honko'   ~ see *Wisteria floribunda*
   'Rosea'
   — 'Longissima'   ~ see *Wisteria*
   floribunda 'Multijuga'
   — 'Longissima Alba'   ~ see
   Wisteria floribunda 'Alba'
   — 'Macrobotrys'   ~ see *Wisteria*
   floribunda 'Multijuga'
93 — 'Multijuga' (H4)

— **'Pink Ice'** ~ see *Wisteria floribunda* 'Rosea'

93 — **'Rosea'** (H4)
— **'Shiro-naga'** ~ see *Wisteria floribunda* 'Alba'
— **'Shiro-noda'** ~ see *Wisteria floribunda* 'Alba'

— **'Snow Showers'** ~ see *Wisteria floribunda* 'Alba'
multijuga **'Alba'** ~ see *Wisteria floribunda* 'Alba'
93 *sinensis* (H4)
93 — **'Alba'** (H4)

Conifers

Large & Medium

ABIES (PINACEAE)
93 *concolor* (H4)
93 *koreana* **'Silberlocke'** (H4)
nobilis ~ see *Abies procera*
93 *nordmanniana* (H4)
93 *pinsapo* **'Glauca'** (H4)
93 *procera* (H4)

CALOCEDRUS (CUPRESSACEAE)
93 *decurrens* (H4)

CEDRUS (PINACEAE)
93 *atlantica* **Glauca Group** (H4)
~ *previously listed as* C. libani *subsp.* atlantica Glauca Group
93 *deodara* (H4)
93 — **'Aurea'** (H4)
93 *libani* (H4) ~ *previously listed as* C. libani *subsp.* libani

CHAMAECYPARIS (CUPRESSACEAE)
93 *lawsoniana* **'Chilworth Silver'** (H4)
93 — **'Ellwoodii'** (H4)
93 — **'Ellwood's Gold'** (H4)
93 — **'Fletcheri'** (H4)
93 — **'Grayswood Pillar'** (H4)
93 — **'Green Hedger'** (H4)
93 — **'Intertexta'** (H4)
— **'Jackman's Green Hedger'** ~ see *Chamaecyparis lawsoniana* 'Green Hedger'
93 — **'Kilmacurragh'** (H4)
— **'Lane'** hort. ~ see *Chamaecyparis lawsoniana* 'Lanei Aurea'
93 — **'Lanei Aurea'** (H4) ~ *awarded as* C. lawsoniana *'Lane'* hort.
— **'Lanei'** hort. ~ see *Chamaecyparis lawsoniana* 'Lanei Aurea'
02 — **'Little Spire'** (H4)

93 — **'Lutea'** (H4)
— **'Nyewoods'** ~ see *Chamaecyparis lawsoniana* 'Chilworth Silver'
93 — **'Pelt's Blue'** (H4)
93 — **'Pembury Blue'** (H4)
93 — **'Stardust'** (H4)
— **'Van Pelt'** ~ see *Chamaecyparis lawsoniana* 'Pelt's Blue'
— **'Van Pelt's Blue'** ~ see *Chamaecyparis lawsoniana* 'Pelt's Blue'
93 — **'Wisselii'** (H4)
leylandii ~ see × *Cupressocyparis leylandii*
93 *nootkatensis* **'Pendula'** (H4)
93 *obtusa* **'Crippsii'** (H4)
— **'Crippsii Aurea'** ~ see *Chamaecyparis obtusa* 'Crippsii'
93 — **'Nana Gracilis'** (H4)
93 *pisifera* **'Boulevard'** (H4)
93 — **'Filifera Aurea'** (H4)
93 *thyoides* **'Ericoides'** (H4)

CRYPTOMERIA (CUPRESSACEAE)
93 *japonica* (H4)
93 — **'Bandai-sugi'** (H4)
93 — **'Elegans Compacta'** (H4)

× CUPRESSOCYPARIS (CUPRESSACEAE)
02 *leylandii* (H4)
93 — **'Gold Rider'** (H4)
93 — **'Robinson's Gold'** (H4)

CUPRESSUS (CUPRESSACEAE)
02 *arizonica* var. *glabra* **'Blue Ice'** (H3)
93 — **'Pyramidalis'** (H3)
93 *macrocarpa* **'Goldcrest'** (H3)
02 — **'Golden Pillar'** (H3)
sempervirens **'Pyramidalis'** ~ see *Cupressus sempervirens* Stricta Group

— var. *sempervirens* ~ see *Cupressus sempervirens* Stricta Group
93 — **Stricta Group** (H3) ~ *previously listed as* C. sempervirens *'Stricta'*

GINKGO (GINKGOACEAE)
93 *biloba* (H4)

JUNIPERUS (CUPRESSACEAE)
93 *chinensis* **'Aurea'** (H4)
93 — **'Blaauw'** (H4)
93 — **'Kaizuka'** (H4)
93 — **'Obelisk'** (H4)
93 — **'Plumosa Aurea'** (H4)
93 — **'Pyramidalis'** (H4)
— **'Sulphur Spray'** ~ see *Juniperus* × *pfitzeriana* 'Sulphur Spray'
93 *communis* **'Green Carpet'** (H4)
93 — **'Hibernica'** (H4)
× *gracilis* **'Blaauw'**
~ see *Juniperus chinensis* 'Blaauw'
× *media* **'Plumosa Aurea'**
~ see *Juniperus chinensis* 'Plumosa Aurea'
× *pfitzeriana* **'Blaauw'**
~ see *Juniperus chinensis* 'Blaauw'
93 — **'Old Gold'** (H4)
93 — **'Pfitzeriana Compacta'** (H4)
93 — **'Sulphur Spray'** (H4)
~ *previously listed as* J. virginiana *'Sulphur Spray'*
93 *squamata* **'Blue Carpet'** (H4)
93 — **'Blue Star'** (H4)
93 — **'Holger'** (H4)
93 *virginiana* **'Grey Owl'** (H4)
— **'Sulphur Spray'** ~ see *Juniperus* × *pfitzeriana* 'Sulphur Spray'

LARIX (PINACEAE)
93 *decidua* (H4)
93 *kaempferi* (H4)
leptolepis ~ see *Larix kaempferi*

LIBOCEDRUS (CUPRESSACEAE)
decurrens
~ see *Calocedrus decurrens*

METASEQUOIA (CUPRESSACEAE)
93 *glyptostroboides* (H4)

PICEA (PINACEAE)
93 *breweriana* (H4)

kosteri **'Glauca'** ~ see *Picea pungens* 'Koster'
93 *omorika* (H4)
93 — **'Pendula'** (H4)
93 *orientalis* (H4)
93 — **'Aurea'** (v) (H4)
93 *pungens* **'Globosa'** (H4)
93 — **'Hoopsii'** (H4)
93 — **'Koster'** (H4)

PINUS (PINACEAE)
93 *coulteri* (H4)
griffithii ~ see *Pinus wallichiana*
93 *heldreichii* (H4) ~ *previously listed as* P. heldreichii *var.* leucodermis
— var. *leucodermis*
~ see *Pinus heldreichii*
93 *jeffreyi* (H4)
leucodermis ~ see *Pinus heldreichii*
93 *muricata* (H4)
93 *nigra* (H4)
— var. *corsicana* ~ see *Pinus nigra* subsp. *laricio*
93 — subsp. *laricio* (H4)
— subsp. *maritima* ~ see *Pinus nigra* subsp. *laricio*
93 *pinaster* (H4)
93 *pinea* (H4)
93 *ponderosa* (H4)
93 *pumila* **'Glauca'** (H4)
93 *radiata* (H3-4)
93 *sylvestris* (H4)
93 — **Aurea Group** (H4) ~ *previously listed as* P. sylvestris *'Aurea'*
93 *wallichiana* (H4)

PLATYCLADUS (CUPRESSACEAE)
93 *orientalis* **'Elegantissima'** (H4)
~ *previously listed as* Thuja orientalis *'Elegantissima'*

PODOCARPUS (PODOCARPACEAE)
chilinus ~ see *Podocarpus salignus*
93 *salignus* (H3)

PSEUDOLARIX (PINACEAE)
93 *amabilis* (H4)
kaempferi
~ see *Pseudolarix amabilis*

PSEUDOTSUGA (PINACEAE)
93 *menziesii* (H4)

taxifolia
					~ see *Pseudotsuga menziesii*

SCIADOPITYS (SCIADOPITYACEAE)
93	*verticillata* (H4)

SEQUOIA (CUPRESSACEAE)
93	*sempervirens* (H4)

SEQUOIADENDRON (CUPRESSACEAE)
93	*giganteum* (H4)

TAXODIUM (CUPRESSACEAE)
	ascendens **'Nutans'**		~ see *Taxodium*
			distichum var. *imbricatum* 'Nutans'
93	*distichum* (H4)
93	— var. *imbricatum* **'Nutans'** (H4)

TAXUS (TAXACEAE)
93	*baccata* (H4)		~ *male and female*
					flowers are usually borne
					on separate plants
93	— **'Adpressa Variegata'** (m/v) (H4)
93	— **'Dovastoniana' (f)** (H4)
93	— **'Dovastonii Aurea'** (m/v) (H4)
93	— **'Fastigiata'** (f) (H4)
93	— **'Fastigiata Aureomarginata'**
			(m/v) (H4)
	— **'Hibernica'**	~ see *Taxus baccata*
					'Fastigiata'
93	— **'Repandens'** (f) (H4)
93	— **'Repens Aurea'** (v) (H4)
93	— **'Semperaurea'** (m) (H4)
93	— **'Standishii' (f)** (H4)
93	x *media* **'Hicksii' (f)** (H4)

THUJA (CUPRESSACEAE)
	'Extra Gold'		~ see *Thuja plicata*
					'Irish Gold'
93	*occidentalis* **'Danica'** (H4)
	— **'Emerald'**	~ see *Thuja occidentalis*
					'Smaragd'
93	— **'Holmstrup'** (H4)
93	— **'Rheingold'** (H4)
93	— **'Smaragd'** (H4)
	orientalis **'Elegantissima'**		~ see
					Platycladus orientalis
					'Elegantissima'
93	*plicata* **'Atrovirens'** (H4)
93	— **'Aurea'** (H4)
93	— **'Fastigiata'** (H4)
93	— **'Irish Gold'** (v) (H4)
93	— **'Stoneham Gold'** (H4)

THUJOPSIS (CUPRESSACEAE)
93	*dolabrata* (H4)

TSUGA (PINACEAE)
93	*canadensis* **'Jeddeloh'** (H4)
93	— **'Pendula'** (H4)
93	*heterophylla* (H4)
	menziesii		~ see *Pseudotsuga*
					menziesii

Dwarf

ABIES (PINACEAE)
93	*balsamea* **Hudsonia Group** (H4)
				~ *previously listed as*
				A. balsamea *f.* hudsonia
93	*concolor* **'Compacta'** (H4)
	— **'Glauca Compacta'**
		~ see *Abies concolor* 'Compacta'
93	*lasiocarpa* var. *arizonica* **'Compacta'**
				(H4)
93	*nordmanniana* **'Golden Spreader'**
				(H4)

CHAMAECYPARIS (CUPRESSACEAE)
93	*lawsoniana* **'Aurea Densa'** (H4)
93	— **'Gimbornii'** (H4)
93	— **'Lutea Nana'** (H4)
93	— **'Minima Aurea'** (H4)
93	— **'Minima Glauca'** (H4)
	— **'Nana Lutea'** ~ see *Chamaecyparis*
					lawsoniana 'Lutea Nana'
93	— **'Pygmaea Argentea'** (v) (H4)
93	*obtusa* **'Nana'** (H4)
93	— **'Nana Aurea'** (H4)
	pisifera **'Filifera Nana Aurea'**	~ see
					Chamaecyparis pisifera
					'Golden Mop'
93	— **'Golden Mop'** (H4)

CRYPTOMERIA (CUPRESSACEAE)
98	*japonica* **'Globosa Nana'** (H4)
93	— **'Vilmoriniana'** (H4)

JUNIPERUS (CUPRESSACEAE)
93	*communis* **'Compressa'** (H4)
93	— **'Hornibrookii'** (H4)
93	— **'Repanda'** (H4)
	horizontalis **'Blue Rug'** ~ see *Juniperus*
					horizontalis 'Wiltonii'
93	— **'Wiltonii'** (H4)
93	*procumbens* **'Nana'** (H4)

MICROBIOTA (CUPRESSACEAE)
93   *decussata* (H4)

PICEA (PINACEAE)
93   *abies* **'Little Gem'** (H4)
93   — **'Nidiformis'** (H4)
93   *glauca* **'Echiniformis'** (H4)
93   *mariana* **'Nana'** (H4)
98   *omorika* **'Nana'** (H4)

PINUS (PINACEAE)
93   *heldreichii* **'Smidtii'** (H4)
93   *mugo* **'Mops'** (H4)
93   — **Pumilio Group** (H4)   ~ *previously*
       *listed as*P. mugo *var.* pumilio

93   *parviflora* **'Adcock's Dwarf'** (H4)
93   *sylvestris* **'Beuvronensis'** (H4)

PLATYCLADUS (CUPRESSACEAE)
93   *orientalis* **'Aurea Nana'** (H4)
                    ~ *previously listed as*
       Thuja orientalis *'Aurea Nana'*

THUJA (CUPRESSACEAE)
93   *occidentalis* **'Lutea Nana'** (H4)
       orientalis **'Aurea Nana'**   ~ see
                    Platycladus orientalis
                    'Aurea Nana'
       — **'Miller's Gold'**   ~ see *Platycladus*
                    orientalis 'Aurea Nana'

Bamboos

ARUNDINARIA (POACEAE)
auricoma   ~ see *Pleioblastus*
                    auricomus
fastuosa   ~ see *Semiarundinaria*
                    fastuosa
fortunei   ~ see *Pleioblastus variegatus*
japonica   ~ see *Pseudosasa japonica*
murieliae   ~ see *Fargesia murielae*
variegata ~ see *Pleioblastus variegatus*
viridistriata   ~ see *Pleioblastus*
                    auricomus

CHUSQUEA (POACEAE)
93   *culeou* (H4)

FARGESIA (POACEAE)
93   *murielae* (H4)
02   — **'Simba'** (H4)
02   *nitida* **'Nymphenburg'** (H4)
       spathacea hort.   ~ see *Fargesia*
                    murielae

× **HIBANOBAMBUSA (POACEAE)**
02   *tranquillans* **'Shiroshima'** (v) (H4)

INDOCALAMUS (POACEAE)
02   *tessellatus* (H4)

PHYLLOSTACHYS (POACEAE)
93   *aurea* (H4)
       aureocaulis   ~ see *Phyllostachys*
                    aureosulcata'Aureocaulis'

02   *aureosulcata* **'Aureocaulis'** (H4)
02   — **'Spectabilis'** (H4)
93   *nigra* (H4)
93   — **f. henonis** (H4)
02   *vivax* **'Aureocaulis'** (H4)

PLEIOBLASTUS (POACEAE)
93   *auricomus* (v) (H4)
       fortunei   ~ see *Pleioblastus*
                    variegatus
93   *variegatus* (v) (H4)
       viridistriatus   ~ see *Pleioblastus*
                    auricomus

PSEUDOSASA (POACEAE)
93   *japonica* (H4)

SASA (POACEAE)
       tessellata   ~ see *Indocalamus*
                    tessellatus

SEMIARUNDINARIA (POACEAE)
93   *fastuosa* (H4)

SINARUNDINARIA (POACEAE)
       murieliae   ~ see *Fargesia murielae*

THAMNOCALAMUS (POACEAE)
       spathaceus hort.   ~ see *Fargesia*
                    murielae

48

HARDY HERBACEOUS PERENNIALS, GRASSES, BULBS AND FERNS

ACAENA (ROSACEAE)
93 R *microphylla* (H4)

ACANTHUS (ACANTHACEAE)
93 *spinosus* (H4)

ACHILLEA (ASTERACEAE)
93 R *ageratifolia* (H4)
99 'Belle Epoque' (H4)
99 'Christine's Pink' (H4)
93 'Coronation Gold' (H4)
       ~ *reconfirmed 1999 after trial*
99 'Credo' (H4)
99 *filipendulina* 'Cloth of Gold' (H4)
93 — 'Gold Plate' (H4)
       ~ *reconfirmed 1999 after trial*
99 — 'Parker's Variety' (H4)
99 'Heidi' (H4)
99 'Helios' (H4)
99 'Hella Glashoff' (H4)
99 'Lachsschönheit' (H4)
93 R × *lewisii* 'King Edward' (H4)
99 'Lucky Break' (H4)
99 'Martina' (H4)
99 *millefolium* 'Kelwayi' (H4)
99 — 'Lansdorferglut' (H4)
99 'Mondpagode' (H4)
93 'Moonshine' (H3)
99 *ptarmica* 'Aunt Stientje' (H4)
      SALMON BEAUTY   ~ *see Achillea*
                       'Lachsschönheit'
99 'Summerwine' (H4)
99 — 'The Pearl' (The Pearl Group)
          (clonal) (d) (H4)
93 R *tomentosa* (H4)

ACONITUM (RANUNCULACEAE)
      × *bicolor* ~ see A. × *cammarum* 'Bicolor'
93 'Bressingham Spire' (H4)
              ~ *likes moist soil*
93 × *cammarum* 'Bicolor' (H4)
              ~ *likes moist soil*
02 *carmichaelii* 'Arendsii' (H4)
93 *carmichaelii* (Wilsonii Group)
      'Kelmscott' (H4) ~ *likes moist soil*
      hyemale ~ see *Eranthis hyemalis*
93 'Spark's Variety' (H4) ~ *likes moist soil*

ACTAEA (RANUNCULACEAE)
      alba   ~ see *Actaea pachypoda*
      erythrocarpa   ~ see *Actaea rubra*
93 *matsumurae* 'Elstead' (H4)
      ~ *previously listed as* Cimicifuga simplex
          var. matsumurae *'Elstead'; dislikes lime*
93 *pachypoda* (H4)   ~ *awarded as A.*
                         alba; *dislikes lime*
93 *racemosa* (H4) ~ *previously listed as*
          Cimicifuga racemosa; *dislikes lime*
93 *rubra* (H4)   ~ *dislikes lime*
02 *simplex* (Atropurpurea Group)
          'Brunette' (H4)   ~ *dislikes lime*
      spicata var. *rubra* ~ see *Actaea rubra*

AGROSTEMMA (CARYOPHYLLACEAE)
      coronaria ~ see *Lychnis coronaria*

AJUGA (LAMIACEAE)
93 *reptans* 'Catlin's Giant' (H4)
      — 'Macrophylla'   ~ *see Ajuga*
                      reptans 'Catlin's Giant'

ALCHEMILLA (ROSACEAE)
93 R *erythropoda* (H4)
93 *mollis* (H4)

ALYSSUM (BRASSICACEAE)
      saxatile   ~ see *Aurinia saxatilis*
      — 'Citrinum' ~ see *Aurinia saxatilis*
                         'Citrina'

ANAPHALIS (ASTERACEAE)
93 *margaritacea* var. *yedoensis* (H4)
93 *triplinervis* (H4)
93 — 'Sommerschnee' (H4)
      — SUMMER SNOW   ~ see *Anaphalis*
              triplinervis 'Sommerschnee'

ANCHUSA (BORAGINACEAE)
93 *azurea* 'Loddon Royalist' (H4)
      myosotidiflora ~ see *Brunnera macrophylla*

ANDROSACE (PRIMULACEAE)
      carnea var. *halleri*   ~ see *Androsace*
                      carnea subsp. *rosea*
93 R — subsp. *laggeri* (H4)

93 R — subsp. *rosea* (H4)
halleri   ~ see *Androsace carnea*
                      subsp. *rosea*
93 R *lanuginosa* (H4)
mucronifolia hort.   ~ see *Androsace*
                      sempervivoides
primuloides ~ see *Androsace studiosorum*
sarmentosa misapplied
          ~ see *Androsace studiosorum*
— var. *yunnanensis* misapplied
          ~ see *Androsace studiosorum*
93 R *sempervivoides* (H4)
93 R *studiosorum* (H4)   ~ *awarded as* A.
          sarmentosa, *a misapplied name*

ANEMONE (RANUNCULACEAE)
93 R *apennina* (H4)
93 R *blanda* (H4)
93 R — 'Radar' (H4)
93 R — var. *rosea* (H4)
93 R — 'White Splendour' (H4)
hepatica   ~ see *Hepatica nobilis*
97 *hupehensis* 'Bowles' Pink' (H4)
93 — 'Hadspen Abundance' (H4)
97 — var. *japonica* 'Pamina' (H4)
— — PRINCE HENRY   ~ see *Anemone*
          hupehensis var. *japonica*
          'Prinz Heinrich'
93 — — 'Prinz Heinrich' (H4)
— 'September Charm'   ~ see *Anemone* ×
          hybrida 'September Charm'
× *hybrida* 'Alba' hort. (UK)   ~ see
          Anemone × *hybrida*
          'Honorine Jobert'
— 'Bowles' Pink'   ~ see *Anemone*
          hupehensis 'Bowles' Pink'
97 — 'Elegans' (H4)
93 — 'Honorine Jobert' (H4)
93 — 'Königin Charlotte' (H4)
— 'Pamina'   ~ see *Anemone hupehensis*
          var. *japonica* 'Pamina'
— PRINCE HENRY   ~ see *Anemone*
          hupehensis var. *japonica*
          'Prinz Heinrich'
— 'Prinz Heinrich'   ~ see *Anemone*
          hupehensis var. *japonica*
          'Prinz Heinrich'
— QUEEN CHARLOTTE   ~ see *Anemone*
          × *hybrida* 'Königin Charlotte'
93 — 'September Charm' (H4)
          ~ *previously listed as* A. hupehensis
          'September Charm'
97 R × *lipsiensis* 'Pallida' (H4)

93 R *nemorosa* (H4)
93 R — 'Allenii' (H4)
93 R — 'Robinsoniana' (H4)
93 R — 'Vestal' (d) (H4)
97 R — 'Virescens' (H4)
pulsatilla   ~ see *Pulsatilla vulgaris*
93 R *ranunculoides* (H4)
sulphurea   ~ see *Pulsatilla alpina*
          subsp. *apiifolia*

ANTENNARIA (ASTERACEAE)
dioica var. *rosea*   ~ see *Antennaria rosea*
93 R *rosea* (H4)

ANTHEMIS (ASTERACEAE)
93 R *punctata* subsp. *cupaniana* (H3-4)

ANTHYLLIS (PAPILIONACEAE)
93 R *montana* 'Rubra' (H4)

AQUILEGIA (RANUNCULACEAE)
akitensis hort.   ~ see *Aquilegia*
          flabellata var. *pumila*
alpina 'Hensol Harebell'
          ~ see *Aquilegia* 'Hensol Harebell'
93 R *bertolonii* (H4)
93 *canadensis* (H4)
93 *coerulea* (H4)
93 R *flabellata* (H4)
— 'Nana Alba'   ~ see *Aquilegia*
          flabellata var. *pumila* f. *alba*
93 R — var. *pumila* (H4)
93 R — — f. *alba* (H4)
93 'Hensol Harebell' (H4)
japonica   ~ see *Aquilegia flabellata*
          var. *pumila*
98 *longissima* (H4)
vulgaris MUNSTEAD WHITE
          ~ see *Aquilegia vulgaris* 'Nivea'
93 — 'Nivea' (H4)
93 — var. *stellata* 'Nora Barlow'
          (Barlow Series) (d) (H4)

ARABIS (BRASSICACEAE)
93 R *alpina* subsp. *caucasica* 'Flore Pleno'
          (d) (H4)
caucasica 'Plena'   ~ see *Arabis alpina*
          subsp. *caucasica* 'Flore Pleno'
ferdinandi-coburgi 'Variegata'
          ~ see *Arabis procurrens* 'Variegata'
93 R *procurrens* 'Variegata' (v) (H4)
          ~ *probably correctly treated as*
          a form of A. × suendermannii

ARENARIA (CARYOPHYLLACEAE)
93 R   *montana* (H4)

ARMERIA (PLUMBAGINACEAE)
    caespitosa   ~ see *Armeria juniperifolia*
    — 'Bevan's Variety'   ~ see *Armeria*
      juniperifolia 'Bevan's Variety'
93 R   *juniperifolia* (H4)
93 R   — 'Bevan's Variety' (H4)
93 R   *maritima* 'Vindictive' (H4)

ARTEMISIA (ASTERACEAE)
93   *absinthium* 'Lambrook Mist' (H3-4)
02   *arborescens* (H3)
93   — 'Lambrook Silver' (H4)
    assoana   ~ see *Artemisia caucasica*
93   *caucasica* (H3-4)
    douglasiana 'Valerie Finnis'   ~ see
      Artemisia ludoviciana 'Valerie Finnis'
93 R   *frigida* (H3-4)
93   *lactiflora* (H4)
    lanata Willd. non Lam.   ~ see *Artemisia*
      caucasica
93   *ludoviciana* subsp. *ludoviciana* (H4)
      ~ *previously listed as*
      A. ludoviciana *var.* ludoviciana
93   — 'Silver Queen' (H4)
93   — 'Valerie Finnis' (H4)
    pedemontana   ~ see *Artemisia caucasica*
93   *schmidtiana* (H4)
93 R   — 'Nana' (H4)
    vallesiaca ~ see *Seriphidium vallesiacum*

ARUNCUS (ROSACEAE)
02   *aethusifolius* (H4)
93   *dioicus* (m) (H4)
    plumosus   ~ see *Aruncus dioicus* (m)
    sylvestris   ~ see *Aruncus dioicus* (m)

ASPERULA (RUBIACEAE)
93 R   *arcadiensis* (H3)   ~ *widely grown as*
      A. suberosa, *another quite*
      distinct species
    suberosa hort.   ~ see *Asperula arcadiensis*

ASTELIA (ASTELIACEAE)
94   *chathamica* (H3)
    — 'Silver Spear' ~ see *Astelia chathamica*

ASTER (ASTERACEAE)
93 R   *alpinus* (H4)
93   *amellus* 'Framfieldii' (H4)
93   — 'Jacqueline Genebrier' (H4)

93   — 'King George' (H4)
93   — 'Veilchenkönigin' (H4)
    — VIOLET QUEEN   ~ see *Aster amellus*
      'Veilchenkönigin'
93   'Coombe Fishacre' (H4)
93   *cordifolius* 'Chieftain' (H4)
    — 'Little Carlow'   ~ see *Aster* 'Little
      Carlow' (*cordifolius* hybrid)
    — 'Photograph'   ~ see *Aster*
      'Photograph'
93   — 'Sweet Lavender' (H4)
93   *ericoides* 'Blue Star' (H4)
93   — 'Brimstone' (H4)
93   — 'Golden Spray' (H4)
    — 'Monte Cassino'   ~ see *Aster*
      pringlei 'Monte Cassino'
93   — 'Pink Cloud' (H4)
98   — f. *prostratus* 'Snow Flurry' (H4)
93   x *frikartii* 'Mönch' (H4)
    — WONDER OF STAFA   ~ see *Aster* x
      frikartii 'Wunder von Stäfa'
93   — 'Wunder von Stäfa' (H4)
93   'Kylie' (H4)
93   *lateriflorus* 'Horizontalis' (H4)
93   'Little Carlow' (*cordifolius* hybrid) (H4)
93   *novae-angliae* 'Harrington's Pink' (H4)
02   *novae-angliae* 'Rosa Sieger' (H4)
93   'Ochtendgloren' (*pringlei* hybrid)
      (H4)
93   'Photograph' (H4)
93   *pilosus* var. *demotus* (H4)
93   *pringlei* 'Monte Cassino' (H4)
93   'Ringdove' (*ericoides* hybrid) (H4)
    sedifolius 'Snow Flurries'
      ~ see *Aster ericoides*
      f. *prostratus* 'Snow Flurry'
    tradescantii hort.   ~ see *Aster pilosus*
      var. *demotus*
93   *turbinellus* hort. (H4)

ASTILBE (SAXIFRAGACEAE)
93   x *arendsii* 'Brautschleier' (H4)
    — BRIDAL VEIL   ~ see *Astilbe*
      x *arendsii* 'Brautschleier'
93   — 'Fanal' (H4)
93   'Bronce Elegans' (*simplicifolia*
      hybrid) (H4)
93 R   *chinensis* var. *pumila* (H4)
93   — var. *taquetii* 'Superba' (H4)
93 R   x *crispa* 'Perkeo' (H4)
    — 'Peter Pan'
      ~ see *Astilbe* x *crispa* 'Perkeo'
93 R   *glaberrima* var. *saxatilis* (H4)

OSTRICH PLUME ~ see *Astilbe*
'Straussenfeder' (*thunbergii* hybrid)
pumila
~ see *Astilbe chinensis* var. *pumila*
93 'Rheinland' (*japonica* hybrid) (H4)
93 R *simplicifolia* (H4)
— BRONZE ELEGANCE
~ see *Astilbe* 'Bronce Elegans'
(*simplicifolia* hybrid)
93 'Sprite' (*simplicifolia* hybrid) (H4)
93 'Straussenfeder' (*thunbergii* hybrid)
(H4)
'Superba' ~ see *Astilbe chinensis*
var. *taquetii* 'Superba'

ASTRANTIA (APIACEAE)
carniolica 'Variegata'
~ see *Astrantia major*
'Sunningdale Variegated'
helleborifolia hort.
~ see *Astrantia maxima*
major subsp. *involucrata* 'Margery
Fish' ~ see *Astrantia major*
subsp. *involucrata* 'Shaggy'
93 — subsp. *involucrata* 'Shaggy' (H4)
93 — 'Sunningdale Variegated' (v) (H4)
— 'Variegata' ~ see *Astrantia major*
'Sunningdale Variegated'
93 *maxima* (H4)

AUBRIETA (BRASSICACEAE)
albomarginata
~ see *Aubrieta* 'Argenteovariegata'
02 R 'Argenteovariegata' (v) (H4)
02 R 'Aureovariegata' (v) (H4)
02 R 'Bressingham Pink' (d) (H4)
93 R 'Doctor Mules' (H4)
'Golden King'
~ see *Aubrieta* 'Aureovariegata'
02 R 'Greencourt Purple' (H4)
02 R 'Mrs Rodewald' (H4)
02 R 'Red Cascade' (Cascade Series) (H4)

AURINIA (BRASSICACEAE)
93 R *saxatilis* (H4)
93 R — 'Citrina' (H4)

BAPTISIA (PAPILIONACEAE)
93 *australis* (H4)

BERGENIA (SAXIFRAGACEAE)
97 'Ballawley' (H4) ~ *previously listed
under* B. purpurascens

beesiana
~ see *Bergenia purpurascens*
93 'Bressingham White' (H4)
ciliata × *Bergenia crassifolia*
~ see *Bergenia* × *schmidtii*
93 *cordifolia* 'Purpurea' (H4)
crassifolia 'Orbicularis'
~ see *Bergenia* × *schmidtii*
delavayi
~ see *Bergenia purpurascens*
var. *delavayi*
'Delbees'
~ see *Bergenia* 'Ballawley'
93 'Morgenröte' (H4)
MORNING RED
~ see *Bergenia* 'Morgenröte'
93 *purpurascens* (H4)
— 'Ballawley'
~ see *Bergenia* 'Ballawley'
98 — var. *delavayi* (H4)
93 × *schmidtii* (H4)
93 'Silberlicht' (H4)
SILVERLIGHT ~ see Bergenia 'Silberlicht'

BESCHORNERIA (AGAVACEAE)
93 *yuccoides* (H3)

BILLARDIERA (PITTOSPORACEAE)
94 *longiflora* (H3)

BOCCONIA (PAPAVERACEAE)
cordata ~ see *Macleaya cordata*

BRUNNERA (BORAGINACEAE)
93 *macrophylla* (H4)
93 — 'Hadspen Cream' (v) (H4)

BUTOMUS (BUTOMACEAE)
93 *umbellatus* (H4)

CALTHA (RANUNCULACEAE)
93 *palustris* (H4) ~ *needs boggy soil*
93 — 'Flore Pleno' (d) (H4)
~ *needs boggy soil*

CAMPANULA (CAMPANULACEAE)
93 R *betulifolia* (H4)
93 R 'Birch Hybrid' (H4)
93 'Burghaltii' (H4)
93 R *carpatica* (H4)
93 R *chamissonis* 'Superba' (H4)
93 R *cochleariifolia* (H4)
finitima ~ see *Campanula betulifolia*

93 R **'G.F. Wilson'** (H4)
93 R *garganica* (H4)
93 R — **'W.H. Paine'** (H4)
93   *glomerata* **'Superba'** (H4)
02   **'Kent Belle'** (H4)
93   *lactiflora* **'Alba'** (H4)   ~ *applies to a selected pure white clone*
93   — **'Loddon Anna'** (H4)
93   — **'Prichard's Variety'** (H4)
93   — **'Superba'** (H4)
93   *latiloba* **'Alba'** (H4)
93   — **'Hidcote Amethyst'** (H4)
93   — **'Highcliffe Variety'** (H4)
93   — **'Percy Piper'** (H4)
      muralis
          ~ see *Campanula portenschlagiana*
02   *persicifolia* **'Chettle Charm'** PBR (H4)
93   — **'Fleur de Neige'** (d) (H4)
      — **'George Chiswell'**
          ~ see *Campanula persicifolia* 'Chettle Charm' PBR
      — subsp. *sessiliflora* **'Alba'**
          ~ see *Campanula latiloba* 'Alba'
      — — **'Highcliffe'**   ~ see *Campanula latiloba* 'Highcliffe Variety'
      — — **'Percy Piper'**
          ~ see *Campanula latiloba* 'Percy Piper'
      pilosa **'Superba'**   ~ see *Campanula chamissonis* 'Superba'
93 R *portenschlagiana* (H4)
94 R *poscharskyana* **'Stella'** (H4)
      pusilla
          ~ see *Campanula cochleariifolia*
93 R *raineri* (H4)
97 R *tommasiniana* (H4)

CANNA (CANNACEAE)
02   **'Alaska'** (H3)
02   **'Amundsen'** (H3)
02   **'Annaeei'** (H3)
02   **'Aphrodite'** van Klaveren (H3)
02   x *ehemanii* (H3)
02   **'Erebus'** (H3)
02   **'General Eisenhower'** (H3)
02   **'Ingeborg'** (H3)
02   **'Louis Cayeux'** (H3)
02   **'Musifolia'** (H3)
02   **'Mystique'** (H3)
02   **'Picasso'** (H3)
02   **'Ra'** (H3)
02   **'Roi Soleil'** (H3)
02   **'Russian Red'** (H3)

02   **'Schwäbische Heimat'** (H3)
02   **'Shenandoah'** (H3)
02   TROPICANNA **'Phasion'** PBR (v) (H3)
02   **'Verdi'** (H3)
02   **'Whithelm Pride'** (H3)
02   **'Wyoming'** (H3)

CARDAMINE (BRASSICACEAE)
00 R *pentaphylla* (H4)

CAREX (CYPERACEAE)
02   *buchananii* (H4)
93   *elata* **'Aurea'** (v) (H4)
      — **'Bowles' Golden'**
          ~ see *Carex elata* 'Aurea'
98   — **'Knightshayes'** (H4)
      'Evergold'
          ~ see *Carex oshimensis* 'Evergold'
      hachijoensis **'Evergold'**
          ~ see *Carex oshimensis* 'Evergold'
      morrowii **'Evergold'**
          ~ see *Carex oshimensis* 'Evergold'
93   *oshimensis* **'Evergold'** (v) (H4)
      riparia **'Bowles' Golden'**
          ~ see *Carex elata* 'Aurea'
      stricta **'Bowles' Golden'**
          ~ see *Carex elata* 'Aurea'

CATANANCHE (ASTERACEAE)
93   *caerulea* **'Major'** (H4)

CERATOSTIGMA (PLUMBAGINACEAE)
93   *plumbaginoides* (H3-4)

CHIASTOPHYLLUM (CRASSULACEAE)
93 R *oppositifolium* (H4)
      simplicifolium
          ~ see *Chiastophyllum oppositifolium*

CHRYSANTHEMOPSIS (ASTERACEAE)
      hosmariense
          ~ see *Rhodanthemum hosmariense*

CHRYSANTHEMUM (ASTERACEAE)
93   **'Allouise'** (25b) (H3)
          ~ *disbudded, in the open*
97   **'Amber Enbee Wedding'** (29d) (H3)
          ~ *spray, in the open*
95   **'Amber Yvonne Arnaud'** (24b) (H3)
          ~ *disbudded, in the open*
97   **'Angora'** (25b) (H3)
          ~ *disbudded, in the open*

(18a)	October-flowering Pompon: True Pompon
(18b)	October-flowering Pompon: Semi-pompon
(19a)	October-flowering Spray: Anemone
(19b)	October-flowering Spray: Pompon
(19c)	October-flowering Spray: Reflexed
(19d)	October-flowering Spray: Single
(19e)	October-flowering Spray: Intermediate
(19f)	October-flowering Spray: Spider, Quill, Spoon or Any Other Type
(22a)	Charm: Anemone
(22b)	Charm: Pompon
(22c)	Charm: Reflexed
(22d)	Charm: Single
(22e)	Charm: Intermediate
(22f)	Charm: Spider, Quill, Spoon or Any Other Type
(23a)	Early-flowering Outdoor Incurved: Large-flowered
(23b)	Early-flowering Outdoor Incurved: Medium-flowered
(23c)	Early-flowering Outdoor Reflexed: Small-flowered
(24a)	Early-flowering Outdoor Reflexed: Large-flowered
(24b)	Early-flowering Outdoor Reflexed: Medium-flowered
(24c)	Early-flowering Outdoor Reflexed: Small-flowered
(25a)	Early-flowering Outdoor Intermediate: Large-flowered
(25b)	Early-flowering Outdoor Intermediate: Medium-flowered
(25c)	Early-flowering Outdoor Intermediate: Small-flowered
(28a)	Early-flowering Outdoor Pompon: True Pompon
(28b)	Early-flowering Outdoor Pompon: Semi-pompon
(29a)	Early-flowering Outdoor Spray: Anemone
(29b)	Early-flowering Outdoor Spray: Pompon
(29c)	Early-flowering Outdoor Spray: Reflexed
(29d)	Early-flowering Outdoor Spray: Single
(29e)	Early-flowering Outdoor Spray: Intermediate
(29f)	Early-flowering Outdoor Spray: Spider, Quill, Spoon or Any Other Type
(29K)	Early-flowering Outdoor Spray: Korean
(29Rub)	Early-flowering Outdoor Spray: Rubellum

93 **'Anna Marie'** (19c) (H3)
~ *spray, in the open*
'Apricot Enbee Wedding'
~ see *Chrysanthemum*
'Bronze Enbee Wedding'
94 **'Apricot Margaret'** (29c) (H3)
~ *spray, in the open*
95 **BRAVO 'Yobra'** PBR (22c) (H3)
~ *spray, in the open*
00 **'Brietner'** (24b) (H3)
93 **'Bronze Enbee Wedding'** (29d) (H3)
~ *spray, in the open*
95 **'Bronze Fairie'** (28b) (H3)
~ *spray, in the open*
93 **'Bronze Margaret'** (29c) (H3)
~ *spray, in the open*
01 **'Bronze Max Riley'** (23b) (H3)
93 **'Bronze Pennine Wine'** (29c) (H3)
~ *spray, in the open*
99 **'Bronze Talbot Parade'** (29c) (H3)
93 **'Cameo'** (28a) (H3)
~ *spray, in the open*
98 **'Candlewick Limelight'** (29d) (H3)
96 **'Cherry Nathalie'** (19c) (H3)
~ *spray, in the open*
93 **'Chestnut Talbot Parade'** (29c) (H3)
~ *spray, in the open*
93 **'Cream Margaret'** (29c) (H3)
~ *spray, in the open*
93 **'Creamist'** (25b) (H3)
~ *disbudded, in the open*
93 **'Crimson Yvonne Arnaud'** (24b) (H3)
~ *disbudded, in the open*
93 **DANA 'Yodana'** (25b) (H3)
~ *disbudded, in the open*
93 **DEBONAIR 'Yodebo'** PBR (22c) (H3)
~ *spray, in the open*
93 **'Dee Gem'** (29c) (H3)
~ *spray, in the open*
93 **'Denise'** (28b) (H3)
~ *spray, in the open*
98 **'Dowches Patricia'** (29d) (H3)
96 **'Eastleigh'** (24b) (H3)
~ *disbudded, in the open*
94 **EMILY 'Yoemily'** (22) (H3)
~ *spray, in the open*
93 **'Enbee Wedding'** (29d) (H3)
~ *spray, in the open*
95 **'Fairie'** (28a) (H3)
~ *spray, in the open*
93 **'Fleet Margaret'** (29c) (H3)
~ *spray, in the open*

94   'George Griffiths' (24b) (H3)
    ~ *disbudded, in the open*

94   'Gold Enbee Wedding' (29d) (H3)
    ~ *spray, in the open*

    'Gold Margaret'~ see *Chrysanthemum*
    'Golden Margaret'

93   'Golden Creamist' (25b) (H3)
    ~ *disbudded, in the open*

93   'Golden Margaret' (29c) (H3)
    ~ *spray, in the open*

93   GOLDMINE 'Yogol' (22c) (H3)
    ~ *spray, in the open*

94   'Goodlife Sombrero' (29a) (H3)
    ~ *spray, in the open*

93   GRENADINE 'Yogrena' (22c) (H3)
    ~ *spray, in the open*

93   'Heide' (29c) (H3)   ~ *spray, in the open*

93   HOLLY 'Yoholly' (22b) (H3)
    ~ *spray, in the open*

hosmariense
    ~ see *Rhodanthemum hosmariense*

02   'Lautrec' (H3)   ~ *cushion*

93   'Lemon Margaret' (29c) (H3)
    ~ *spray, in the open*

01   LISA 'Yolisa' [PBR] (22c) (H3)

99   LYNN 'Yolynn' [PBR] (22c) (H3)

93   'Madeleine' (29c) (H3)
    ~ *spray, in the open*

95   'Mancetta Bride' (29a) (H3)
    ~ *spray, in the open*

98   'Mancetta Jupiter' (29a) (H3)

maresii ~ see *Rhodanthemum hosmariense*

93   'Margaret' (29c) (H3)
    ~ *spray, in the open*

95   'Mavis' (28a) (H3) ~ *spray, in the open*

93   'Max Riley' (23b) (H3)
    ~ *disbudded, in the open*

maximum 'Aglaia'~ see *Leucanthemum*
    × *superbum* 'Aglaia'

— 'T.E. Killin'   ~ see *Leucanthemum*
    × *superbum* 'T.E. Killin'

— 'Wirral Supreme'
    ~ see *Leucanthemum*
    superbum 'Wirral Supreme'

93   MIRAGE 'Yomira' (22b) (H3)
    ~ *spray, in the open*

93   'Myss Angie' (29c) (H3)
    ~ *spray, in the open*

97   'Myss Madi' (29c) (H3)
    ~ *spray, in the open*

96   'Nantyderry Sunshine' (28b) (H4)

94   'Nathalie' (19c) (H3) ~ *spray, in the open*

99   NICOLE 'Yonicole' [PBR] (22c) (H3)

93   'Nora Brook' (25b) (H3)
    ~ *disbudded, in the open*

93   'Nuflair' (24b) (H3)
    ~ *disbudded, in the open*

93   'Orno' (29b) (H3) ~ *spray, in the open*

93   'Payton Dale' (29c) (H3)
    ~ *spray, in the open*

93   'Payton Prince' (29c) (H3)
    ~ *spray, in the open*

93   'Peach Allouise' (25b) (H3)
    ~ *disbudded, in the open*

93   'Peach Enbee Wedding'
    (29d) (H3)
    ~ *spray, in the open*

00   'Peak Glow' (H3)

96   'Pennine Alfie' (29f) (H3)
    ~ *spray, in the open*

93   'Pennine Calypso' (29b) (H3)
    ~ *spray, in the open*

93   'Pennine Canary' (29c) (H3)
    ~ *spray, in the open*

94   'Pennine Club' (29d) (H3)
    ~ *spray, in the open*

93   'Pennine Flute' (29f) (H3)
    ~ *spray, in the open*

93   'Pennine Gambol' (29a) (H3)
    ~ *spray, in the open*

94   'Pennine Ginger' (29c) (H3)
    ~ *spray, in the open*

98   'Pennine Glory' (29c) (H3)

94   'Pennine Goal' (29c) (H3)
    ~ *spray, in the open*

93   'Pennine Jade' (29d) (H3)
    ~ *spray, in the open*

93   'Pennine Jude' (29a) (H3)
    ~ *spray, in the open*

96   'Pennine Lace' (29f) (H3)
    ~ *spray, in the open*

94   'Pennine Lotus' (29c) (H3)
    ~ *spray, in the open*

93   'Pennine Magic' (29c) (H3)
    ~ *spray, in the open*

94   'Pennine Magnet' (29a) (H3)
    ~ *spray, in the open*

97   'Pennine Marie' (29a) (H3)
    ~ *spray, in the open*

93   'Pennine Oriel' (29a) (H3)
    ~ *spray, in the open*

93   'Pennine Phyllis' (29b) (H3)
    ~ *spray, in the open*

99   'Pennine Polo' (29d) (H3)

93   'Pennine Signal' (29d) (H3)
    ~ *spray, in the open*

93	**'Pennine Silver'** (29c) (H3)
	~ *spray, in the open*
93	**'Pennine Soldier'** (29d) (H3)
	~ *spray, in the open*
93	**'Pennine Sweetheart'** (29c) (H3)
	~ *spray, in the open*
93	**'Pennine Tango'** (29d) (H3)
	~ *spray, in the open*
93	**'Pennine Twinkle'** (29a) (H3)
	~ *spray, in the open*
93	**'Pennine Whistle'** (29f) (H3)
	~ *spray, in the open*
94	**'Pink Julie Ann'** (24b) (H3)
	~ *disbudded, in the open*
93	**'Pink Margaret'** (29c) (H3)
	~ *spray, in the open*
98	**'Pinocchio'** (29c) (H3)
93	**'Poppet'** (28a) (H3) ~ *spray, in the open*
97	**'Primrose Allouise'** (24b) (H3)
	~ *disbudded, in the open*
00	**'Primrose Enbee Wedding'** (29d) (H3)
93	**'Purple Pennine Wine'** (29c) (H3)
	~ *spray, in the open*
02	**'Purple Talbot Parade'** (29c) (H3)
	~ *spray*
93	**'Red Wendy'** (29c) (H3)
	~ *spray, in the open*
93	**'Regalia'** (24b) (H3)
	~ *disbudded, in the open*
93	**'Rosedew'** (25a) (H3)
	~ *disbudded, in the open*
96	**'Royal Knight'** (22c) (H3)
	~ *spray, in the open*
98	**'Ruby Enbee Wedding'** (29d) (H3)
93	**'Rylands Gem'** (24b) (H3)
	~ *disbudded, in the open*
94	**'Salmon Enbee Wedding'** (29d) (H3)
	~ *spray, in the open*
96	**'Salmon Fairie'** (28a) (H3)
	~ *spray, in the open*
94	**'Salmon Pennine Rose'** (29b) (H3)
	~ *spray, in the open*
93	**'Salmon Pennine Wine'** (29c) (H3)
	~ *spray, in the open*
93	**'Salmon Talbot Parade'** (29c) (H3)
	~ *spray, in the open*
93	**'Solley'** (29c) (H3) ~ *spray, in the open*
93	**'Southway Sure'** (29d) (H3)
	~ *spray, in the open*
97	**'Southway Swan'** (29d) (H3)
	~ *spray, in the open*
02	SUNNY LINDA **'Sunny Lindayo'** (H3)
	~ *cushion*

01	**'Susan's Bonnet'** (29a) (H3)
93	**'Swalwell'** (25b) (H3)
	~ *disbudded, in the open*
93	**'Talbot Bouquet'** (29a) (H3)
	~ *spray, in the open*
93	**'Talbot Imp'** (29c) (H3)
	~ *spray, in the open*
93	**'Talbot Parade'** (29c) (H3)
	~ *spray, in the open*
02	**'Tightrope'** (H3) ~ *cushion*
02	**'Turner'** (H3) ~ *cushion*
	uliginosum
	~ see *Leucanthemella serotina*
93	**'Wendy'** (29c) (H3)
	~ *spray, in the open*
92	**'Wessex Shell'** (29d) (H3)
	~ *spray, in the open*
95	**'Wessex Tang'** (29d) (H3)
	~ *spray, in the open*
93	**'White Allouise'** (25b) (H3)
	~ *disbudded, in the open*
93	**'White Margaret'** (29c) (H3)
	~ *spray, in the open*
93	**'Yellow Fairie'** (28b) (H3)
	~ *spray, in the open*
93	**'Yellow Heide'** (29c) (H3)
	~ *spray, in the open*
02	**'Yellow Mancetta Bride'** (29a) (H3)
	~ *spray*
93	**'Yellow Margaret'** (29c) (H3)
	~ *spray, in the open*
94	**'Yellow Pennine Oriel'** (29a) (H3)
	~ *spray, in the open*
98	**'Yellow Rio'** (22d) (H3)
93	***yezoense*** (H4)
93	**'Yvonne Arnaud'** (24b) (H3)
	~ *disbudded, in the open*

CIMICIFUGA (RANUNCULACEAE)
racemosa ~ see *Actaea racemosa*
simplex **'Elstead Variety'** ~ see *Actaea matsumurae* 'Elstead'
— **var. *matsumurae* 'Elstead'**
~ see *Actaea matsumurae* 'Elstead'

CLEMATIS (RANUNCULACEAE)
02	***integrifolia*** **'Pangbourne Pink'** (H4)
93	— **'Rosea'** (H4)

CONVOLVULUS (CONVOLVULACEAE)
mauritanicus ~ see *Convolvulus sabatius*
93 R ***sabatius*** (H3)

COREOPSIS (ASTERACEAE)
verticillata 'Golden Shower'
~ see *Coreopsis verticillata* 'Grandiflora'
93 — 'Grandiflora' (H4)
~ *re-confirmed after trial 2001*
01 — 'Moonbeam' (H4)
01 — 'Old Timer' (H4)
01 — 'Zagreb' (H4)

CORNUS (CORNACEAE)
93 R *canadensis* (H4)

CORYDALIS (PAPAVERACEAE)
caucasica var. *alba* misapplied
~ see *Corydalis malkensis*
00 R *decipiens* hort. (H4)
— Schott, Nyman & Kotschy
~ see *Corydalis solida* subsp. *incisa*
02 R *flexuosa* (H4)
93 R *malkensis* (H4)
~ *reconfirmed after trial 2000*
00 R *solida* subsp. *incisa* (H4)
00 R — subsp. *solida* 'Dieter Schacht' (H4)
~ *previously listed under f.* transsylvanica
93 R — subsp. *solida* 'George Baker' (H4)
~ *reconfirmed after trial 2000;*
previously listed under
f. transsylvanica
00 R *triternata* (H4)

COTYLEDON (CRASSULACEAE)
oppositifolia
~ see *Chiastophyllum oppositifolium*
simplicifolia
~ see *Chiastophyllum oppositifolium*

CRAMBE (BRASSICACEAE)
93 *cordifolia* (H4)
02 *maritima* (H4)

CREPIS (ASTERACEAE)
93 R *incana* (H4)

CRINUM (AMARYLLIDACEAE)
93 × *powellii* (H3)
97 — 'Album' (H3)
— 'Roseum' ~ see *Crinum* × *powellii*

CYANANTHUS (CAMPANULACEAE)
integer hort.
~ see *Cyananthus microphyllus*
93 R *lobatus* (H4)
93 R *microphyllus* (H4)

CYNARA (ASTERACEAE)
93 *cardunculus* (H3-4)

DACTYLORHIZA (ORCHIDACEAE)
93 R *elata* (H4)
93 R *foliosa* (H4)
maderensis ~ see *Dactylorhiza foliosa*

DAHLIA (ASTERACEAE)

(Sin)	1 Single
(Anem)	2 Anemone-flowered
(Col)	3 Collerette
(SWL)	4D Waterlily, Small
(MinWL)	4E Waterlily, Miniature
(GD)	5A Decorative, Giant
(SD)	5D Decorative, Small
(MinD)	5E Decorative, Miniature
(MinBa)	6B Miniature Ball
(Pom)	7 Pompon
((MC)	8C Cactus, Medium
(SC)	8D Cactus, Small
(MinC)	8E Cactus, Miniature
(LS-c)	9B Semi-cactus, Large
(MS-c)	9C Semi-cactus, Medium
(SS-c)	9D Semi-cactus, Small
(MinS-c)	9E Semi-cactus, Miniature
(Misc)	10 Miscellaneous
(DwB)	Dwarf Bedding (in combination)
(Lil)	Lilliput (in combination)

96 'Allan Sparkes' (SWL) (H3)
94 'Almand's Climax' (GD) (H3)
93 'Alva's Doris' (SS-c) (H3)
99 'Alva's Supreme' (GD) (H3)
96 'Andrew Magson' (SS-c) (H3)
00 'Asahi Chohje' (Anem) (H3)
94 'Autumn Lustre' (SWL) (H3)
97 'Aylett's Gaiety' (MinD/DwB) (H3)
98 'Bednall Beauty' (Misc/DwB) (H3)
95 'Bishop of Llandaff' (Misc) (H3)
96 'Bridge View Aloha' (MS-c) (H3)
99 'Brookfield Delight' (Sin/Lil) (H3)
95 'Candy Cupid' (MinBa) (H3)
02 'Catherine Bateson' (MinD) (H3)
02 'Chessy' (Sin/Lil) (H3)
95 'Clair de Lune' (Col) (H3)
95 'Cream Alva's' (GD) (H3)
96 'Dark Stranger' (MC) (H3)
95 'Davar Donna' (MS-c) (H3)
95 'David Howard' (MinD) (H3)
93 'Ellen Huston' (Sin/DwB) (H3)
94 'Fascination' (SWL/DwB) (H3)
95 'Figurine' (SWL) (H3)
95 'Finchcocks' (SWL) (H3)

00	'Freya's Paso Doble' (Anem) (H3)	94	'Pink Pastelle' (MS-c) (H3)
96	'Freya's Thalia' (Sin/Lil) (H3)	00	'Pink Sensation' (SC) (H3)
99	'Gallery Art Deco' PBR (SD) (H3)	95	'Porcelain' (SWL) (H3)
99	'Gallery Art Nouveau' PBR (MinD) (H3)	94	'Preston Park' (Sin/DwB) (H3)
02	'Gallery Cobra' PBR (SD/DwB) (H3)		'Samantha'
00	'Gallery Degas' PBR (MinD) (H3)		~ see *Dahlia* 'Harvest Samantha'
00	'Gallery Leonardo' PBR (SD) (H3)	98	'Small World' (Pom) (H3)
00	'Gallery Pablo' PBR (SD) (H3)	93	'So Dainty' (MinS-c) (H3)
01	'Gallery Renoir' PBR (SD) (H3)	02	'Tally Ho' (Misc) (H3)
99	'Gallery Vincent' PBR (MinD) (H3)		'Taratahi Lilac'
93	'Garden Party' (MC/DwB) (H3)		~ see *Dahlia* 'Lilac Taratahi'
93	'Geerlings' Indian Summer' (MS-c) (H3)	00	'Taratahi Ruby' (SWL) (H3)
00	'Geoffrey Kent' (MinD) (H3)		'Tiny Tot' ~ see *Dahlia* 'Harvest Tiny Tot'
93	'Glorie van Heemstede' (SWL) (H3)	99	'Tu Jays Nicola' (Misc) (H3)
94	'Hamari Accord' (LS-c) (H3)	93	'Wandy' (Pom) (H3)
93	'Hamari Bride' (MS-c) (H3)	99	'Weston Pirate' (MinC) (H3)
93	'Hamari Gold' (GD) (H3)	99	'Weston Spanish Dancer' (MinC) (H3)
96	'Hamari Rosé' (MinBa) (H3)	97	'White Alva's' (GD) (H3)
97	'Hamari Sunshine' (LD) (H3)	93	'White Ballet' (SD) (H3)
93	'Hamilton Lillian' (SD) (H3)	93	'Wittemans Superba' (SS-c) (H3)
97	'Harvest Amanda' (Sin/Lil) (H3)	93	'Wootton Cupid' (MinBa) (H3)
96	'Harvest Inflammation' (Sin/Lil) (H3)	94	'Wootton Impact' (MS-c) (H3)
96	'Harvest Samantha' (Sin/Lil) (H3)	94	'Yellow Hammer' (Sin/DwB) (H3)
96	'Harvest Tiny Tot' (Sin/Lil) (H3)	94	'Yelno Harmony' (SD) (H3)
95	'Hillcrest Desire' (SC) (H3)	95	'Zorro' (GD) (H3)
93	'Hillcrest Royal' (MC) (H3)		
00	'Honka' (Misc) (H3)		**DARMERA (SAXIFRAGACEAE)**
94	'Ice Cream Beauty' (SWL) (H3)	93	*peltata* (H4) ~ *can be invasive*
	'Inflammation'		
	~ see *Dahlia* 'Harvest Inflammation'		**DELPHINIUM (RANUNCULACEAE)**
94	'Jeanette Carter' (MinD) (H3)	01	'Atholl' (H4)
94	'John Street' (SWL) (H3)	01	'Atlantis' (Belladonna Group) (H4)
98	'Jomanda' (MinBa) (H3)	93	'Blue Dawn' (H4)
94	'Karenglen' (MinD) (H3)	93	'Blue Nile' (H4)
93	'Kathleen's Alliance' (SC) (H3)	93	'Bruce' (H4)
95	'Kathryn's Cupid' (MinBa) (H3)	99	'Can-can' (H4)
01	'Kenora Sunset' (MS-c) (H3)	96	'Cassius' (H4)
96	'Kenora Valentine' (LD) (H3)	01	'Cherub' (H4)
95	'Kidd's Climax' (GD) (H3)	98	'Claire' (H4)
95	'Lemon Elegans' (SS-c) (H3)	99	'Clifford Sky' (H4)
01	'Lilac Taratahi' (SC) (H3)	93	'Conspicuous' (H4)
98	'Lismore Willie' (SWL) (H3)	98	'Constance Rivett' (H4)
96	'Little Dorrit' (Sin/Lil) (H3)	00	'Elizabeth Cook' (H4)
00	'Marie Schnugg' (Misc) (H3)	93	'Emily Hawkins' (H4)
98	'Minley Carol' (Pom) (H3)	93	'Faust' (H4)
00	'Moonfire' (Misc/Dw) (H3)	93	'Fenella' (H4)
98	'Nicola Jane' (Pom) (H3)	02	'Galileo' (H4)
98	'NZ's Robert' (MinWL/Lil) (H3)	93	'Gillian Dallas' (H4)
96	'Omo' (Sin/Lil) (H3)	93	'Giotto' (H4)
95	'Peach Cupid' (MinBa) (H3)	93	'Langdon's Royal Flush' (H4)
96	'Peachette' (Misc/Lil) (H3)	95	'Lilian Bassett' (H4)
93	'Pearl of Heemstede' (SD) (H3)	93	'Loch Leven' (H4)
95	'Phill's Pink' (SD) (H3)	93	'Lord Butler' (H4)

01	'Lucia Sahin' (H4)
98	'Michael Ayres' (H4)
94	'Min' (H4)
00	'Olive Poppleton' (H4)
98	'Oliver' (H4)
96	'Our Deb' (H4)
93	'Rosemary Brock' (H4)
	'Royal Flush' ~ see *Delphinium* 'Langdon's Royal Flush'
93	'Sandpiper' (H4)
93	'Spindrift' (H4)
93	'Summerfield Miranda' (H4)
93	'Sungleam' (H4)
00	'Sunkissed' (H4)
93	'Tiddles' (H4)
96	'Walton Gemstone' (H4)

DIANTHUS (CARYOPHYLLACEAE)

(p)	Pink
(pf)	Perpetual-flowering Carnation
(b)	Border Carnation
(M)	Malmaison Carnation

94	'Alfriston' (b) (H4)
93 R	*alpinus* (H4)
93 R	— 'Joan's Blood' (H4)
02	'Ander's Kath Phillips' (pf) (H4)
93 R	× *arvernensis* (p) (H4)
	'Auvergne' ~ see *Dianthus* × *arvernensis*
93	'Becky Robinson' (p) (H4)
98	'Betty Morton' (p) (H4)
02	'Betty's Pink' (b) (H4)
	'Bourboule' ~ see *Dianthus* 'La Bourboule'
94	'Bovey Belle' (p) (H4)
02	'Brilliant Star' (p) (H4)
94	'Bryony Lisa' (b) (H4)
	caesius ~ see *Dianthus gratianopolitanus*
02	'Calypso Star' (p) (H4)
98	CARMINE VALDA 'Devon Louise' (p) (H4)
	'Catherine's Choice' ~ see *Dianthus* 'Rhian's Choice'
	Cheddar pink ~ see *Dianthus gratianopolitanus*
	'Cheryl' ~ see *Dianthus* 'Houndspool Cheryl'
98	'Chesswood Sandilands' (p) (H4)
99	'Chetwyn Doris' (p) (H4)
94	'Chris Crew' (b) (H4)
02	'Christine Dickinson' (pf) (H4)
96	'Claire Tautz' (b) (H4)
95	'Claret Joy' (p) (H4)
94	'Coronation Ruby' (p) (H4)

94	'Cranmere Pool' (p) (H4)
01	'Crimson Joy' (p) (H4)
98	CRIMSON VALDA 'Devon Kitty' (p) (H4)
00	'Dainty Dame' (p) (H4)
97	'David Russell' (b) (H4)
94	'David Saunders' (b) (H4)
93 R	*deltoides* (H4)
96	'Devon Carla' (p) (H4)
93	'Devon Dove' PBR (p) (H4)
93	'Devon Glow' PBR (p) (H4)
93	'Devon Maid' PBR (p) (H4)
96	'Devon Pride' (p) (H4)
95	'Devon Wizard' PBR (p) (H4)
96	'Diane' (p) (H4)
93	'Doris' (p) (H4)
	'Doris Ruby' ~ see *Dianthus* 'Houndspool Ruby'
97	'Eileen Neal' (b) (H4)
93	'Eileen O'Connor' (b) (H4)
94	'Flanders' (b) (H4)
95	'Golden Cross' (b) (H4)
93	'Golden Sceptre' (b) (H4)
93	'Gran's Favourite' (p) (H4)
93 R	*gratianopolitanus* (H4)
97	'Grey Dove' (p) (H4)
95	'Hannah Louise' (b) (H4)
	'Haytor' ~ see *Dianthus* 'Haytor White'
95	'Haytor Rock' (p) (H4)
93	'Haytor White' (p) (H4)
94	'Hazel Ruth' (b) (H4)
01	HOT SPICE 'Redstart' (p) (H4)
94	'Houndspool Cheryl' (p) (H4)
93	'Houndspool Ruby' (p) (H4)
94	'Howard Hitchcock' (b) (H4)
02	'India Star' PBR (p) (H4)
93 R	'Inshriach Dazzler' (p) (H4)
93	'Irene Della-Torré' (b) (H4)
98	'Irene's Choice' (p) (H4)
94	'Jean Knight' (b) (H4)
98	'Jenny Gascoigne' (p) (H4)
	'Joan's Blood' ~ see *Dianthus alpinus* 'Joan's Blood'
02	'John Sandall' (b) (H4)
95	'Joy' (p) (H4)
97	'Kathleen Hitchcock' (b) (H4)
93	'Kesteven Kirkstead' (p) (H4)
93 R	'La Bourboule' (p) (H4)
98	'Lemsii' (p) (H4)
02	'Leon Tautz' (b) (H4)
95	'Letitia Wyatt' (p) (H4)
99	'Linfield Dorothy Perry' (p) (H4)
94	'Louise's Choice' (p) (H4)
94	'Maisie Neal' (b) (H4)

99	'Mambo' (pf) (H4)
93	'Marg's Choice' (p) (H4)
99	'Marion Robinson' (b) (H4)
01	'Mendlesham Belle' (p) (H4)
00	'Mendlesham Maid' (p) (H4)
97	'Michael Saunders' (b) (H4)
93	'Monica Wyatt' (p) (H4)
96	'Natalie Saunders' (b) (H4)
	neglectus ~ see *Dianthus pavonius*
96	'Nichola Ann' (b) (H4)
02	'Night Star' (p) (H4)
96	'Oakwood Gillian Garforth' (p) (H4)
96	'Oakwood Romance' (p) (H4)
97	'Oakwood Splendour' (p) (H4)
93 R	*pavonius* (H4)
93	'Peter Wood' (b) (H4)
93 R	'Pike's Pink' (p) (H4)
99	PINK VALDA 'Devon Judith' (p) (H4)
02	'Pixie Star' PBR (p) (H4)
99	'Prado' (pf) (H4)
93	'Rhian's Choice' (p) (H4)
94	'Riccardo' (b) (H4)
94	'Rose Joy' (p) (H4)
98	'Rose Monica Wyatt' PBR (p) (H4)
	'Ruby'
	~ see *Dianthus* 'Houndspool Ruby'
	'Ruby Doris'
	~ see *Dianthus* 'Houndspool Ruby'
97	'Ruth White' (b) (H4)
93	'Sandra Neal' (b) (H4)
94	'Sheila's Choice' (p) (H4)
94	'Spinfield Bridesmaid' (b) (H4)
95	'Spinfield Happiness' (b) (H4)
96	'Spinfield Lane' (b) (H4)
01	'Spinfield Strawberry Crush' (b) (H4)
01	'Spinfield Verona' (b) (H4)
97	'Spinfield Wizard' (b) (H4)
97	'Suffolk Pride' (p) (H4)
93	'Suffolk Summer' (p) (H4)
94	'Tamsin' (p) (H4)
94	'Tamsin Fifield' (b) (H4)
96	'Trisha's Choice' (p) (H4)
94	'Uncle Teddy' (b) (H4)
93	'Valda Wyatt' (p) (H4)
99	'Whatfield Can-can' (H4)
00	'Whatfield Magenta' (p) (H4)
96	'White Joy' PBR (p) (H4)
01	WHITE VALDA 'Devon Isolde' (p) (H4)
93 R	'Whitehill' (p) (H4)
93	'Whitesmith' (b) (H4)
95	'Widecombe Fair' (p) (H4)
96	'Zoe's Choice' (p) (H4)

DIASCIA (SCROPHULARIACEAE)

95	*barberae* 'Blackthorn Apricot' (H3-4)
95	— 'Fisher's Flora' (H3-4)
93 R	— 'Ruby Field' (H3-4)
02	CORAL BELLE 'Hecbel' PBR (H3-4)
	cordata hort.
	~ see *Diascia barberae* 'Fisher's Flora'
	cordifolia ~ see *Diascia barberae*
	'Fisher's Flora'
95	'Dark Eyes' (H3-4)
	elegans ~ see *Diascia vigilis*
95	'Elizabeth' (H3-4)
95	'Frilly' (H3-4)
95	'Hector's Hardy' (H3-4)
95	*integerrima* (H3-4)
	integrifolia ~ see *Diascia integerrima*
95	'Joyce's Choice' (H3-4)
95	'Lady Valerie' (H3-4)
95	'Lilac Belle' (H3-4)
95	'Lilac Mist' (H3-4)
93	*rigescens* (H3)
	'Ruby Field'
	~ see *Diascia barberae* 'Ruby Field'
95	'Rupert Lambert' (H3-4)
95	'Twinkle' (H3-4)
93	*vigilis* (H3)

DICENTRA (PAPAVERACEAE)

02	'Bacchanal' (H4)
	'Boothman's Variety'
	~ see *Dicentra* 'Stuart Boothman'
93	'Langtrees' (H4)
93	'Luxuriant' (H4)
93	*spectabilis* (H4)
93	— 'Alba' (H4)
93 R	'Stuart Boothman' (H4)

DICTAMNUS (RUTACEAE)

93	*albus* var. *albus* (H4)
93	— var. *purpureus* (H4)
	fraxinella ~ see *Dictamnus albus*
	var. *purpureus*

DIGITALIS (SCROPHULARIACEAE)

	ambigua ~ see *Digitalis grandiflora*
02	*ferruginea* (H4)
93	*grandiflora* (H4)
93	× *mertonensis* (H4)
	orientalis ~ see *Digitalis grandiflora*

DODECATHEON (PRIMULACEAE)

	amethystinum
	~ see *Dodecatheon pulchellum*

94 R *dentatum* (H4)
93 R *hendersonii* (H4)
   integrifolium
      ~ see *Dodecatheon hendersonii*
93 R *meadia* (H4)
93 R — **f. *album*** (H4)
   pauciflorum (Dur.) E.Greene
      ~ see *Dodecatheon meadia*
   — hort. ~ see *Dodecatheon pulchellum*
93 R *pulchellum* (H4)
   — *radicatum*
      ~ see *Dodecatheon pulchellum*
   radicatum ~ see *Dodecatheon pulchellum*

DORONICUM (ASTERACEAE)
93   **'Miss Mason'** (H4)

ECHINOPS (ASTERACEAE)
93   *bannaticus* **'Taplow Blue'** (H4)
93   *ritro* **L.** (H4)
96   — subsp. *ruthenicus* (H4)
   — **'Veitch's Blue'** misapplied
      ~ see *Echinops ritro*

EDRAIANTHUS (CAMPANULACEAE)
93 R *pumilio* (H4)

EPIMEDIUM (BERBERIDACEAE)
93 R *grandiflorum* (H4)
93 R — **'Nanum'** (H4)
93 R — **'Rose Queen'** (H4)
93 R — **'White Queen'** (H4)
   macranthum
      ~ see *Epimedium grandiflorum*
93   × *perralchicum* (H4)
93   *pinnatum* subsp. *colchicum* (H4)
   — *elegans* ~ see *Epimedium pinnatum*
      subsp. *colchicum*
93   × *rubrum* (H4)
93   × *versicolor* **'Sulphureum'** (H4)
93 R × *youngianum* **'Niveum'** (H4)

ERANTHIS (RANUNCULACEAE)
93 R *hyemalis* (H4)
93 R — **(Tubergenii Group) 'Guinea
      Gold'** (H4)

EREMURUS (ASPHODELACEAE)
98   *robustus* (H4)
98   *stenophyllus* (H4)

ERIGERON (ASTERACEAE)
94 R *aureus* **'Canary Bird'** (H4)

DARKEST OF ALL
      ~ see *Erigeron* 'Dunkelste Aller'
93   **'Dunkelste Aller'** (H3)
93   **'Foersters Liebling'** (H4)
93   *karvinskianus* (H3)
   mucronatus
      ~ see *Erigeron karvinskianus*
   'Profusion' ~ see *Erigeron karvinskianus*

ERINUS (SCROPHULARIACEAE)
93 R *alpinus* (H4)

ERODIUM (GERANIACEAE)
   chamaedryoides **'Roseum'** hort.
      ~ see *Erodium* × *variabile* 'Roseum'
93 R *glandulosum* (H4)
   macradenum ~ see *Erodium glandulosum*
   petraeum subsp. *glandulosum*
      ~ see *Erodium glandulosum*
93 R × *variabile* **'Roseum'** (H4)

ERYNGIUM (APIACEAE)
93   *alpinum* (H4)
93   *bourgatii* **'Oxford Blue'** (H4)
93   × *oliverianum* (H4)
99   *planum* **'Bethlehem'** (H4)
93   × *tripartitum* (H4) ~ re-confirmed 1999

ERYSIMUM (BRASSICACEAE)
93   **'Bowles' Mauve'** (H3)
93   **'Bredon'** (H3)

EUPATORIUM (ASTERACEAE)
96   *ligustrinum* (H3)
   micranthum ~ see *Eupatorium ligustrinum*
93   *purpureum* subsp. *maculatum*
      'Atropurpureum' (H4)
02   *rugosum* **'Chocolate'** (H4)
   weinmannianum
      ~ see *Eupatorium ligustrinum*

EUPHORBIA (EUPHORBIACEAE)
93   *amygdaloides* var. *robbiae* (H4)
98   *characias* **'Portuguese Velvet'** (H4)
93   — subsp. *wulfenii* (H3-4)*
93   — — **'John Tomlinson'** (H3-4)*
93   — — **'Lambrook Gold'** (H3-4)*
02   *cornigera* (H4)
   epithymoides ~ see *Euphorbia polychroma*
02   **EXCALIBUR 'Froeup'** PBR (H4)
93   *griffithii* **'Dixter'** (H4)
   longifolia hort. ~ see *Euphorbia cornigera*
93   × *martini* (H3)

93 R *myrsinites* (H4)
93 *palustris* (H4)
  pilosa 'Major' ~ see *Euphorbia polychroma* 'Major'
93 *polychroma* (H4)
96 — 'Major' (H4)
02 REDWING 'Charam' ᴾᴮᴿ (H4)
  robbiae ~ see *Euphorbia amygdaloides* var. *robbiae*
93 *schillingii* (H4)
02 *sikkimensis* (H4)
  wallichii Kohli ~ see *Euphorbia cornigera*
* omitted in error from AGM Plants 2002

FILIPENDULA (ROSACEAE)
  palmata purpurea
    ~ see *Filipendula purpurea*
93 *purpurea* (H4)
93 *rubra* 'Venusta' (H4)
  — 'Venusta Magnifica' ~ see *Filipendula rubra* 'Venusta'

GALEGA (PAPILIONACEAE)
93 × *hartlandii* 'Alba' (H4)
02 — 'Lady Wilson' (H4)
02 *officinalis* 'Alba' (H4)

GAURA (ONAGRACEAE)
93 *lindheimeri* (H4)

GENTIANA (GENTIANACEAE)
93 R *acaulis* (H4)
  angulosa hort. ~ see *Gentiana verna* 'Angulosa'
93 R *asclepiadea* (H4)
93 R 'Inverleith' (H4)
  kochiana ~ see *Gentiana acaulis*
  lagodechiana ~ see *Gentiana septemfida* var. *lagodechiana*
93 R × *macaulayi* (H4)
93 R — 'Edinburgh' (H4)
93 R *septemfida* (H4)
93 R — var. *lagodechiana* (H4)
93 R *sino-ornata* (H4)
93 R × *stevenagensis* (H4)
94 R 'Strathmore' (H4)
02 R *verna* 'Angulosa' hort. (H4)

GERANIUM (GERANIACEAE)
  aconitifolium misapplied
    ~ see *Geranium palmatum*
  anemonifolium
    ~ see *Geranium palmatum*

96 'Ann Folkard' (H4)
  armenum ~ see *Geranium psilostemon*
93 R 'Ballerina' (Cinereum Group) (H4)
  'Buxton's Blue' ~ see *Geranium wallichianum* 'Buxton's Variety'
93 R *cinereum* subsp. *subcaulescens* var. *subcaulescens* (H4) ~ *previously listed as* G. cinereum *var.* subcaulescens
96 *clarkei* 'Kashmir White' (H4)
93 R *dalmaticum* (H4)
93 *endressii* (H4)
  — 'Wargrave Pink' ~ see *Geranium* × *oxonianum* 'Wargrave Pink'
  grandiflorum var. *alpinum*
    ~ see *Geranium himalayense* 'Gravetye'
  himalayense alpinum ~ see *Geranium himalayense* 'Gravetye'
93 — 'Gravetye' (H4)
  ibericum misapplied
    ~ see *Geranium* × *magnificum*
  — var. *platypetalum* hort.
    ~ see *Geranium* × *magnificum*
93 'Johnson's Blue' (H4)
93 *macrorrhizum* 'Album' (H4)
93 — 'Ingwersen's Variety' (H4)
93 × *magnificum* (H4)
93 × *oxonianum* 'A.T. Johnson' (H4)
93 — 'Wargrave Pink' (H4)
93 *palmatum* (H3)
  platypetalum misapplied
    ~ see *Geranium* × *magnificum*
  pratense 'Flore Pleno' ~ see *Geranium pratense* 'Plenum Violaceum'
93 — 'Mrs Kendall Clark' (H4)
  — 'Plenum Purpureum'
    ~ see *Geranium pratense* 'Plenum Violaceum'
93 — 'Plenum Violaceum' (d) (H4)
  — 'Rectum Album' ~ see *Geranium clarkei* 'Kashmir White'
93 *psilostemon* (H4)
  rectum 'Album' ~ see *Geranium clarkei* 'Kashmir White'
93 R *renardii* (H4)
93 R × *riversleaianum* 'Russell Prichard' (H4)
93 R *sanguineum* 'Album' (H4)
  — var. *lancastrense* ~ see *Geranium sanguineum* var. *striatum*
  — var. *prostratum* (Cav.) Pers.
    ~ see *Geranium sanguineum* var. *striatum*

93 R — 'Shepherd's Warning' (H4)
93 R — var. *striatum* (H4)
93 R *subcaulescens* 'Splendens' (H4)
93 *sylvaticum* 'Album' (H4)
93 — 'Mayflower' (H4)
93 *wallichianum* 'Buxton's Variety' (H4)

GEUM (ROSACEAE)
  alpinum   ~ see *Geum montanum*
93 'Fire Opal' (H4)
93 'Lady Stratheden' (H4)
93 R *montanum* (H4)
93 'Mrs J. Bradshaw' (H4)

GILLENIA (ROSACEAE)
93 *trifoliata* (H4)

GLAUCIDIUM (GLAUCIDIACEAE)
93 R *palmatum* (H4)

GUNNERA (GUNNERACEAE)
93 *manicata* (H3-4)

GYPSOPHILA (CARYOPHYLLACEAE)
93 *paniculata* 'Bristol Fairy' (d) (H4)
93 R *repens* (H4)
93 'Rosenschleier' (d) (H4)
  'Rosy Veil'
       ~ see *Gypsophila* 'Rosenschleier'
  VEIL OF ROSES
       ~ see *Gypsophila* 'Rosenschleier'

HABERLEA (GESNERIACEAE)
93 R *rhodopensis* (H4)

HACQUETIA (APIACEAE)
93 R *epipactis* (H4)

HEBE (SCROPHULARIACEAE)
  perfoliata   ~ see *Parahebe perfoliata*

HEDYCHIUM (ZINGIBERACEAE)
93 *coccineum* 'Tara' (H3)

HELENIUM (ASTERACEAE)
01 'Baudirektor Linne' (H4)
01 'Blütentisch' (H4)
01 'Butterpat' (H4)
01 'Feuersiegel' (H4)
01 'Gartensonne' (H4)
01 'Karneol' (H4)
01 'Moerheim Beauty' (H4)
01 'Ring of Fire' (H4)

01 'Rubinzwerg' (H4)
01 'Sahin's Early Flowerer' (H4)
01 'Summer Circle' (H4)
01 'Waldtraut' (H4)
01 'Wesergold' (H4)

HELIANTHUS (ASTERACEAE)
93 'Capenoch Star' (H4)
01 'Gullick's Variety' (H4)
01 x *laetiflorus* 'Miss Mellish' (H4)
01 'Lemon Queen' (H4)
93 'Loddon Gold' (H4)   ~ reconfirmed
                              after trial 2001
93 'Monarch' (H4)   ~ reconfirmed after
                              trial 2001

HELIOPSIS (ASTERACEAE)
  GOLDEN PLUME   ~ see *Heliopsis*
  helianthoides var. *scabra* 'Goldgefieder'
01 *helianthoides* var. *scabra*
              'Benzinggold' (H4)
93 — — 'Goldgefieder' (H4)
01 — — 'Light of Loddon' (H4)
01 — — 'Sonnenglut' (H4)
01 — — 'Spitzentänzerin' (H4)
01 — — 'Waterperry Gold' (H4)

HELLEBORUS (RANUNCULACEAE)
93 *argutifolius* (H4)
  corsicus ~ see *Helleborus argutifolius*
93 *foetidus* (H4)
  lividus subsp. *corsicus*
          ~ see *Helleborus argutifolius*
93 *niger* (H4)
93 x *nigercors* (H4) ~ seedlings variable;
                      clones may be virused
93 x *sternii* Blackthorn Group (H3-4)

HEPATICA (RANUNCULACEAE)
  angulosa ~ see *Hepatica transsilvanica*
93 R *nobilis* (H4)
93 R *transsilvanica* (H4)
  triloba   ~ see *Hepatica nobilis*

HEUCHERA (SAXIFRAGACEAE)
01 'Blackbird' (H4)
01 'Burgundy Frost' (H4)
01 'Can-can' (H4)
01 'Chocolate Veil' (H4)
01 'Fireworks' PBR (H4)
01 'Magic Wand' PBR (H4)
01 'Molly Bush' (H4)
01 'Purple Petticoats' (H4)

01	**'Quilter's Joy'** (H4)
01	**'Raspberry Regal'** (H4)
01	**'Regina'** (H4)
01	*sanguinea* **'Alba'** (H4)
01	**'Sashay'** (H4)
93	**'Scintillation'** (H4)
01	**'Smokey Rose'** (H4)

x **HEUCHERELLA (SAXIFRAGACEAE)**

01	**'Kimono'** (H4)
93	*tiarelloides* (H4)

HOSTA (HOSTACEAE)

albomarginata ~ see *Hosta* 'Paxton's Original' *(sieboldii)*

'Argentea Variegata' *(undulata)* ~ see *Hosta undulata* var. *undulata*

'Aureomaculata' *(fortunei)* ~ see *Hosta fortunei* var. *albopicta*

93 **'Aureomarginata'** *(ventricosa)* (v) (H4)

'Blue Angel' misapplied ~ see *Hosta sieboldiana* var. *elegans*

93 **'Blue Angel'** *(sieboldiana)* (H4)

'Cream Delight' *(undulata)* ~ see *Hosta undulata* var. *undulata*

93 *crispula* (v) (H4)

'Eldorado' ~ see *Hosta* 'Frances Williams' *(sieboldiana)*

'Elegans' ~ see *Hosta sieboldiana* var. *elegans*

'Fortis' ~ see *Hosta undulata* var. *erromena*

93 *fortunei* var. *albopicta* (H4)

93 — — f. *aurea* (H4)

93 — var. *aureomarginata* (H4)

93 — var. *hyacinthina* (H4)

93 **'Francee'** *(fortunei)* (v) (H4)

93 **'Frances Williams'** *(sieboldiana)* (v) (H4)

glauca ~ see *Hosta sieboldiana* var. *elegans*

'Golden Circles' ~ see *Hosta* 'Frances Williams' *(sieboldiana)*

93 **'Golden Tiara'** (v) (H4)

93 **'Halcyon'** (Tardiana Group) (H4)

'Holstein' ~ see *Hosta* 'Halcyon' (Tardiana Group)

93 **'Honeybells'** (H4)

93 **'Krossa Regal'** (H4)

93 *lancifolia* (H4)

93 **'Love Pat'** *(tokudama)* (H4)

'Mediovariegata' *(undulata)* ~ see *Hosta undulata* var. *undulata*

'Obscura Marginata' *(fortunei)* ~ see *Hosta fortunei* var. *aureomarginata*

93 **'Paxton's Original'** *(sieboldii)* (v) (H4)

'Picta' *(fortunei)* ~ see *Hosta fortunei* var. *albopicta*

plantaginea var. *grandiflora* ~ see *Hosta plantaginea* var. *japonica*

93 — var. *japonica* (H4) ~ awarded as *Hosta plantaginea* var. grandiflora

'Robusta' *(fortunei)* ~ see *Hosta sieboldiana* var. *elegans*

93 **'Royal Standard'** (H4)

93 **'Sagae'** (v) (H3-4)

'Sazanami' *(crispula)* ~ see *Hosta crispula*

93 **'Shade Fanfare'** (v) (H4)

93 *sieboldiana* var. *elegans* (H4)

93 **'Sum and Substance'** (H4)

93 *undulata* var. *erromena* (H4)

93 — var. *undulata* (v) (H4)

93 — var. *univittata* (v) (H4)

'Variegata' *(undulata)* ~ see *Hosta undulata* var. *undulata*

'Variegata' *(ventricosa)* ~ see *Hosta* 'Aureomarginata' *(ventricosa)*

'Variegated' *(fluctuans)* ~ see *Hosta* 'Sagae'

93 *ventricosa* (H4)

— **'Aureomarginata'** ~ see *Hosta* 'Aureomarginata' *(ventricosa)*

93 *venusta* (H4)

'Wayside Perfection' ~ see *Hosta* 'Royal Standard'

93 **'Wide Brim'** (v) (H4)

'Yellow Edge' *(fortunei)* ~ see *Hosta fortunei* var. *aureomarginata*

'Yellow Edge' *(sieboldiana)* ~ see *Hosta* 'Frances Williams' *(sieboldiana)*

INULA (ASTERACEAE)

02 *magnifica* **'Sonnenstrahl'** (H4)

IPHEION (ALLIACEAE)

93 R *uniflorum* **'Froyle Mill'** (H4)

93 R — **'Wisley Blue'** (H4)

KIRENGESHOMA (HYDRANGEACEAE)

93 *palmata* (H4)

LAMIUM (LAMIACEAE)

93 *maculatum* **'White Nancy'** (H4)

LATHYRUS (PAPILIONACEAE)
    cyaneus hort.   ~ *see Lathyrus vernus*
93 R *vernus* (H4)
97 R — **'Alboroseus'** (H4)

LEUCANTHEMELLA (ASTERACEAE)
93   *serotina (H4)*

LEUCANTHEMOPSIS (ASTERACEAE)
    hosmariensis ~ *see Rhodanthemum*
                   hosmariense

LEUCANTHEMUM (ASTERACEAE)
    hosmariense ~ see *Rhodanthemum*
                   hosmariense
    maximum uliginosum
            ~ see *Leucanthemella*
                     serotina
93   *superbum* **'Aglaia'** (d) (H4)
93   — **'T.E. Killin'** (d) (H4)
93   — **'Wirral Supreme'** (d) (H4)

LEWISIA (PORTULACACEAE)
93 R *cotyledon* (H4)
93 R — var. *heckneri* (H4)
93 R — **Sunset Group** (H4)

LIBERTIA (IRIDACEAE)
98   *grandiflora* (H4)

LIGULARIA (ASTERACEAE)
93   *dentata* **'Desdemona'** (H4)
93   **'Gregynog Gold'** (H4)
98   *przewalskii* (H4)
93   **'The Rocket'** (H4)

LOBELIA (CAMPANULACEAE)
93   *cardinalis* (H3)
97   **'Pink Elephant'** (H4)
93   **'Queen Victoria'** (H3)

LYCHNIS (CARYOPHYLLACEAE)
93   *chalcedonica* (H4)
98   *coronaria* (H4)
    — **'Abbotswood Rose'**
         ~ see *Lychnis* x *walkeri*
               'Abbotswood Rose'
93   — **'Alba'** (H4)
02 R *flos-jovis* (H4)
93 R *viscaria* **'Splendens Plena'** (d) (H4)
93   x *walkeri* **'Abbotswood Rose'** (H4)

LYSICHITON (ARACEAE)
93   *americanus* (H4)
93   *camtschatcensis* (H4)

LYSIMACHIA (PRIMULACEAE)
96   *ciliata* **'Firecracker'** (H4)
    — **'Purpurea'** ~ see *Lysimachia*
                ciliata 'Firecracker'
93   *clethroides* (H4)
93 R *nummularia* **'Aurea'** (H4)

LYTHRUM (LYTHRACEAE)
02   *salicaria* **'Blush'** (H4)
93   — **'Feuerkerze'** (H4)
    — **FIRECANDLE** ~ see *Lythrum*
             salicaria 'Feuerkerze'

MACLEAYA (PAPAVERACEAE)
93   *cordata* (Willd.) R. Br. (H4)
02   x *kewensis* **'Flamingo'** (H4)
93   *microcarpa* **'Kelway's Coral Plume'**
        (H4)

MALVA (MALVACEAE)
93   *moschata* f. *alba* (H4)

MECONOPSIS (PAPAVERACEAE)
    baileyi ~ see *Meconopsis betonicifolia*
93   *betonicifolia* (H4)
93   *grandis* (H4)
93 R *quintuplinervia* (H4)
93   x *sheldonii* (H4)
93 R **'Slieve Donard' (Infertile Blue**
        Group) (H4)

MERTENSIA (BORAGINACEAE)
93   *pulmonarioides* (H4)
    virginica
        ~ see *Mertensia pulmonarioides*

MIMULUS (SCROPHULARIACEAE)
    'Andean Nymph'
        ~ see *Mimulus naiandinus*
93 R *cupreus* **'Whitecroft Scarlet'** (H4)
93 R **'Highland Red'** (H4)
93 R *naiandinus* (H3) ~ *previously listed*
        as M. *'Andean Nymph'*

MONARDA (LAMIACEAE)
93   **'Beauty of Cobham'** (H4)
93   **'Cambridge Scarlet'** (H4)
93   **'Croftway Pink'** (H4)

NEMESIA (SCROPHULARIACEAE)
99   **BLUE CLOUD 'Penblu'** (H3)
   ~ *previously listed as* N. *'Blue Cloud'*
   'Bluebird'
     ~ see *Nemesia* 'Fleurie Bluebird'
99   *caerulea* **'Sea Mist'** (H3)
99   *denticulata* (H3-4)
   — **'Confetti'**
     ~ see *Nemesia denticulata*
99   **'Fleurie Bluebird'** (H3)
   ~ *distinct from* N. BLUEBIRD *'Hubbird'*
99   **'Innocence'** (H3)
99   **MELANIE 'Fleuron'** PBR (H3)

NEPETA (LAMIACEAE)
02   × *faassenii* (H4)
   mussinii Spreng.
     ~ see *Nepeta racemosa*
   — hort.   ~ see *Nepeta* × *faassenii*
02   *racemosa* (H4)
   reichenbachiana
     ~ see *Nepeta racemosa*

NYMPHAEA (NYMPHAEACEAE)

(H)	Hardy

93   **'Escarboucle'** (H) (H4)
93   **'Gladstoneana'** (H) (H4)
93   **'Gonnère'** (H) (H4)
   × *helvola*   ~ see *Nymphaea* 'Pygmaea
     Helvola'
93   **'James Brydon'** (H) (H4)
93   **'Marliacea Chromatella'** (H) (H4)
93   **'Pygmaea Helvola'** (H) (H4)
   'Tuberosa Flavescens'
     ~ see *Nymphaea*
     'Marliacea Chromatella'

OENOTHERA (ONAGRACEAE)
   cinaeus   ~ see *Oenothera fruticosa*
     subsp. *glauca*
   fruticosa **FIREWORKS** ~ see *Oenothera*
     fruticosa 'Fyrverkeri'
93   — **'Fyrverkeri'** (H4)
93   — subsp. *glauca* (H4)
93 R *macrocarpa* (H4)
   missouriensis
     ~ see *Oenothera macrocarpa*
   tetragona   ~ see *Oenothera fruticosa*
     subsp. *glauca*
   — var. *fraseri*   ~ see *Oenothera*
     fruticosa subsp. *glauca*

OLSYNIUM (IRIDACEAE)
93 R *douglasii* (H4)

OMPHALODES (BORAGINACEAE)
93 R *cappadocica* (H4)
96 R — **'Cherry Ingram'** (H4)

ONOPORDUM (ASTERACEAE)
   arabicum ~ see *Onopordum nervosum*
93   *nervosum* (H4)

ONOSMA (BORAGINACEAE)
93 R *taurica* (H4)

OPHIOPOGON (CONVALLARIACEAE)
   'Black Dragon'   ~ see *Ophiopogon*
     planiscapus 'Nigrescens'
93 R *planiscapus* **'Nigrescens'** (H4)
   ~ *also valued as a pot plant under glass*

ORCHIS (ORCHIDACEAE)
   elata   ~ see *Dactylorhiza elata*
   foliosa ~ see *Dactylorhiza foliosa*
   maderensis ~ see *Dactylorhiza foliosa*

ORIGANUM (LAMIACEAE)
93   *laevigatum* (H3)
93   — **'Herrenhausen'** (H4)
93 R *rotundifolium* (H4)
93   *vulgare* **'Aureum'** (H4)

OSTEOSPERMUM (ASTERACEAE)
   barberae hort. ~ see *Osteospermum*
     jucundum
   'Blackthorn Seedling'   ~ see
     Osteospermum jucundum
     'Blackthorn Seedling'
   caulescens hort. ~ see *Osteospermum*
     'White Pim'
   ecklonis var. *prostratum*
     ~ see *Osteospermum*
     'White Pim'
95   **'Hopleys'** (H3-4)
93   *jucundum* (H3-4)
95   — **'Blackthorn Seedling'** (H3-4)
95   — **'Langtrees'** (H3-4)
95   — **'Merriments Joy'** (H3-4)
95   **'Lady Leitrim'** (H3-4)
   'Langtrees'   ~ see *Osteospermum*
     jucundum 'Langtrees'
   'Merriments Joy'
     ~ see *Osteospermum*
     jucundum 'Merriments Joy'

'Pale Face'	~ see *Osteospermum*
'Lady Leitrim'
95	**'Weetwood'** (H3-4)
93	**'White Pim'** (H3-4)

OURISIA (SCROPHULARIACEAE)
93 R	**'Snowflake'** (H4)

PAEONIA (PAEONIACEAE)
93	*lactiflora* **'Bowl of Beauty'** (H4)
02	— **'Cheddar Gold'** (H4)
93	— **'Duchesse de Nemours'** (H4)
93	— **'Félix Crousse'** (H4)
93	— **'Festiva Maxima'** (H4)
93	— **'Lady Alexandra Duff'** (H4)
93	— **'Laura Dessert'** (H4)
93	— **'Monsieur Jules Elie'** (H4)
93	— **'Sarah Bernhardt'** (H4)
93	— **'Whitleyi Major'** (H4)
93	*mlokosewitschii* (H4)
93 R	*obovata* (H4)
93 R	— var. *alba* (H4)
93	*officinalis* **'Anemoniflora Rosea'** (H4)
93	— **'Rosea Plena'** (H4)
93	— **'Rubra Plena'** (H4)
93	*peregrina* **'Otto Froebel'** (H4)
	— **'Sunshine'**
~ see *Paeonia peregrina*
'Otto Froebel'
'Sunshine'	~ see *Paeonia peregrina*
'Otto Froebel'

PAPAVER (PAPAVERACEAE)
bracteatum	~ see *Papaver orientale*
var. *bracteatum*
97	*orientale* **'Aglaja'** (H4)
93	— **'Black and White'** (H4)
93	— var. *bracteatum* (H4)
93	— **'Cedric Morris'** (H4)
97	— **'Effendi'** (H4)
97	— **'John III'** (H4)
97	— **'Karine'** (H4)
97	— **'Khedive'** (H4)	~ *reconfirmed*
2001 after trial
97	— **'Leuchtfeuer'** (H4)
97	— **'Lighthouse'** (H4)

PARAHEBE (SCROPHULARIACEAE)
93 R	*perfoliata* (H3-4)

PELTIPHYLLUM (SAXIFRAGACEAE)
peltatum	~ see *Darmera peltata*

PENSTEMON (SCROPHULARIACEAE)
93	**'Alice Hindley'** (H3)
93	**'Andenken an Friedrich Hahn'** (H4)
93	**'Apple Blossom'** (H3-4)
	'Barbara Barker'
~ see *Penstemon* 'Beech Park'
93	**'Beech Park'** (H3)
	'Bisham Seedling'
~ see *Penstemon* 'White Bedder'
	'Burford White'
~ see *Penstemon* 'White Bedder'
	'Catherine de la Mare'
~ see *Penstemon heterophyllus*
'Catherine de la Mare'
93	**'Cherry'** (H3)
	'Cherry Ripe' misapplied
~ see *Penstemon* 'Cherry'
93	**'Chester Scarlet'** (H3)
93	**'Connie's Pink'** (H3)
93	**'Evelyn'** (H4)
	'Firebird'
~ see *Penstemon* 'Schoenholzeri'
	'Garnet'
~ see *Penstemon* 'Andenken an
Friedrich Hahn'
93	**'George Home'** (H3)
93	*hartwegii* (H3-4)
93	*heterophyllus* **'Catherine de la Mare'**
(H4)
93	**'Hewell Pink Bedder'** (H3)
93	**'Hidcote Pink'** (H3-4)
93	*isophyllus* (H3-4)
	'John Nash' misapplied
~ see *Penstemon*
'Alice Hindley'
	'June'	~ see *Penstemon*
'Pennington Gem'
	'Lord Home'	~ see *Penstemon*
'George Home'
93	**'Margery Fish'** (H3)
93	**'Maurice Gibbs'** (H3)
	'Mrs Morse'	~ see *Penstemon*
'Chester Scarlet'
93	**'Osprey'** (H3)
93	**'Pennington Gem'** (H3)
	'Phyllis'	~ see *Penstemon* 'Evelyn'
93	**'Port Wine'** (H3)
93	**'Raven'** (H3)
	'Royal White'	~ see *Penstemon*
'White Bedder'
93	**'Rubicundus'** (H3)
	'Ruby'	~ see *Penstemon*
'Schoenholzeri'

93	**'Schoenholzeri'** (H4)
	'Sissinghurst Pink'
	~ see *Penstemon* 'Evelyn'
	'Snow Storm' ~ see *Penstemon*
	'White Bedder'
	'Snowflake' ~ see *Penstemon*
	'White Bedder'
02	**'Sour Grapes'** (H3-4)
	'Sour Grapes' hort. ~ see *Penstemon*
	'Stapleford Gem'
	'Souvenir d'André Torres'
	misapplied ~ see *Penstemon*
	'Chester Scarlet'
93	**'Stapleford Gem'** (H3)
	'True Sour Grapes' ~ see *Penstemon*
	'Sour Grapes'
93	**'White Bedder'** (H3)

PERSICARIA (POLYGONACEAE)
93 R *affinis* **'Darjeeling Red'** (H4)
— **'Dimity'** ~ see *Persicaria affinis*
'Superba'
93 R — **'Donald Lowndes'** (H4)
93 R — **'Superba'** (H4)
93 *amplexicaulis* **'Firetail'** (H4)
93 *bistorta* **'Superba'** (H4)
93 R *vacciniifolia* (H4)

PETRORHAGIA (CARYOPHYLLACEAE)
93 R *saxifraga* (H4)

PHLOMIS (LAMIACEAE)
93 *russeliana* (H4)
samia Boissier ~ see *Phlomis russeliana*
viscosa misapplied ~ see *Phlomis russeliana*

PHLOX (POLEMONIACEAE)
93 R *adsurgens* (H4)
canadensis ~ see *Phlox divaricata*
02 *carolina* **'Bill Baker'** (H4)
93 — **'Miss Lingard'** (H4)
'Chattahoochee' ~ see *Phlox*
divaricata subsp. *laphamii*
'Chattahoochee'
'Daniel's Cushion'
~ see *Phlox subulata*
'McDaniel's Cushion'
93 R *divaricata* (H4)
93 R — subsp. *laphamii* **'Chattahoochee'**
(H4)
93 R *douglasii* **'Boothman's Variety'** (H4)
93 R — **'Crackerjack'** (H4)
93 R — **'Iceberg'** (H4)

93 R — **'Red Admiral'** (H4)
93 R **'Kelly's Eye'** (H4)
93 *maculata* **'Alpha'** (H4)
93 — **'Omega'** (H4)
02 — **'Princess Sturdza'** (H4)
'Millstream'
~ see *Phlox* × *procumbens* 'Millstream'
93 *paniculata* **'Alba Grandiflora'** (H4)
93 — **'Albert Leo Schlageter'** (H4)
93 — **'Blue Ice'** (H4)
93 — **'Brigadier'** (H4)
93 — **'Bright Eyes'** (H4)
93 — **'Dodo Hanbury-Forbes'** (H4)
93 — **'Eventide'** (H4)
93 — **'Fujiyama'** (H4)
93 — **'Le Mahdi'** (H4)
93 — **'Mother of Pearl'** (H4)
— **'Mount Fujiyama'** ~ see *Phlox*
paniculata 'Fujiyama'
93 — **'Prince of Orange'** (H4)
93 — **'Prospero'** (H4)
02 — **'Starfire'** (H4)
93 — **'White Admiral'** (H4)
93 — **'Windsor'** (H4)
93 R × *procumbens* **'Millstream'** (H4)
93 R *stolonifera* **'Blue Ridge'** (H4)
93 R *subulata* **'McDaniel's Cushion'** (H4)
93 R — **'Red Wings'** (H4)

PHYSALIS (SOLANACEAE)
93 *alkekengi* (H4)

PHYSOSTEGIA (LAMIACEAE)
virginiana **'Snow Queen'**
~ see *Physostegia virginiana*
'Summer Snow'
93 — **'Summer Snow'** (H4)
93 — **'Vivid'** (H4)

PLATYCODON (CAMPANULACEAE)
93 R *grandiflorus* (H4)
93 R — **'Apoyama'** (H4)
93 R — **'Mariesii'** (H4)

PLUMBAGO (PLUMBAGINACEAE)
larpentiae ~ see *Ceratostigma*
plumbaginoides

POLEMONIUM (POLEMONIACEAE)
02 *archibaldiae* (H4)
foliosissimum hort. ~ see *Polemonium*
archibaldiae
93 **'Lambrook Mauve'** (H4)

reptans **'Lambrook Manor'**
~ see *Polemonium* 'Lambrook Mauve'

POLYGALA (POLYGALACEAE)
93 R   *calcarea* **'Lillet'** (H4)

POLYGONATUM (CONVALLARIACEAE)
93   × *hybridum* (H4)
      japonicum
            ~ see *Polygonatum odoratum*
      multiflorum hort.
            ~ see *Polygonatum* × *hybridum*
02   *odoratum* (H4)
93   — **'Flore Pleno'** (d) (H4)
02   — var. *pluriflorum* **'Variegatum'** (v)
      (H4)
      officinale
            ~ see *Polygonatum odoratum*

POLYGONUM (POLYGONACEAE)
      affine **'Darjeeling Red'**
            ~ see *Persicaria affinis*
                  'Darjeeling Red'
      — **'Donald Lowndes'** ~ see *Persicaria*
            affinis 'Donald Lowndes'
      — **'Superbum'**
            ~ see *Persicaria affinis* 'Superba'
      bistorta **'Superbum'**
            ~ see *Persicaria bistorta* 'Superba'
      vacciniifolium
            ~ see *Persicaria vacciniifolia*

PONTEDERIA (PONTEDERIACEAE)
93   *cordata* (H4)

POTENTILLA (ROSACEAE)
      ambigua   ~ see *Potentilla cuneata*
93 R   *cuneata* (H4)
      fragariiformis
            ~ see *Potentilla megalantha*
93   **'Gibson's Scarlet'** (H4)
93 R   *megalantha* (H4)
93   *nepalensis* **'Miss Willmott'** (H4)
93 R   × *tonguei* (H4)
93   **'William Rollison'** (H4)
      willmottiae   ~ see *Potentilla*
            nepalensis 'Miss Willmott'

PRIMULA (PRIMULACEAE)
      acaulis   ~ see *Primula vulgaris*
02   *alpicola* (H4)
      × *arctotis*   ~ see *Primula* × *pubescens*
93 R   *auricula* L. (2) (H4)

(2)	Auricula
(4)	Candelabra
(7)	Cortusoides
(9)	Denticulata
(11)	Farinosae
(17)	Muscarioides
(18)	Nivales
(26)	Sikkimensis
(30)	Vernales
(Poly)	Polyanthus
(Prim)	Primrose

98   **Barnhaven Blues Group** (Prim)(30) (H4)
            ~ *a hardy overwintering type;*
                  from seed in the open ground
93   *bulleyana* (4) (H4)
93   *chionantha* (18) (H4)
02   *cockburniana* (4) (H4)
97   **'Crescendo Blue Shades' (Crescendo**
            Series) (Poly)(30) (H4)
97   **'Crescendo Bright Red' (Crescendo**
            Series) (Poly)(30) (H4)
97   **'Crescendo Golden' (Crescendo**
            Series) (Poly)(30) (H4)
97   **'Crescendo Pink and Rose Shades'**
            (Crescendo Series) (Poly)(30) (H4)
93 R   *denticulata* (9) (H4)
93 R   *elatior* (30) (H4)
93   *florindae* (26) (H4)
93 R   *frondosa* (H4)
      'Garryard Guinevere'
            ~ see *Primula* 'Guinevere'
93 R   **'Guinevere'** (Poly)(30) (H4)
      helodoxa   ~ see *Primula prolifera*
      ianthina   ~ see *Primula prolifera*
93 R   **'Inverewe'** (4) (H4)
02   *japonica* **'Miller's Crimson'**
      (4) (H4)
02   — **'Postford White'** (4) (H4)
93 R   **'Lady Greer'** (Poly)(30) (H4)
      littoniana   ~ see *Primula vialii*
93 R   *marginata* (2) (H4)
98 R   — **'Beamish'** (2) (H4) ~ *a hardy plant,*
      but in the south of England recommended
      for cultivation in alpine house conditions
93 R   — **'Linda Pope'** (2) (H4)
98 R   — **'Prichard's Variety'** (2) (H4)   ~ *a*
      hardy plant, but in the south of England
            recommended for cultivation in
                  alpine house conditions
      nivalis Pallas ~ see *Primula chionantha*
93   *prolifera* (4) (H4)
93 R   × *pubescens* (2) (H4)
93   *pulverulenta* (4) (H4)

93 — **Bartley hybrids** (4) (H4)
97 **'Rainbow Blue Shades' (Rainbow Series)** (Poly)(30) (H4)
97 **'Rainbow Cream Shades' (Rainbow Series)** (Poly)(30) (H4)
97 **'Rainbow Scarlet Shades' (Rainbow Series)** (Poly)(30) (H4)
'Ravenglass Vermilion'
~ see *Primula* 'Inverewe'
93 R *rosea* (11) (H4)
sibthorpii ~ see *Primula vulgaris* subsp. *sibthorpii*
93 R *sieboldii* (7) (H4)
02 *sikkimensis* (26) (H4)
smithiana ~ see *Primula prolifera*
93 R *veris* (30) (H4)
vernalis ~ see *Primula vulgaris*
93 R *vialii* (17) (H4)
98 *vulgaris* (Prim)(30) (H4)
93 R — subsp. *sibthorpii* (Prim)(30) (H4)
93 R — subsp. *vulgaris* (Prim)(30) (H4)
93 R **'Wanda'** (Prim)(30) (H4)

PRUNELLA (LAMIACEAE)
93 *grandiflora* **'Loveliness'** (H4)

PULMONARIA (BORAGINACEAE)
93 *angustifolia* (H4)
— **'Rubra'** ~ see *Pulmonaria rubra*
'Highdown' ~ see *Pulmonaria* 'Lewis Palmer'
93 **'Lewis Palmer'** (H4)
93 **'Margery Fish'** (H4)
officinalis rubra
~ see *Pulmonaria rubra*
93 *rubra* (H4)
93 *saccharata* **Argentea Group** (H4)
~ *awarded as* P. saccharata *'Argentea'*
93 **'Sissinghurst White'** (H4) ~ *previously ascribed to* P. officinalis
vallarsae **'Margery Fish'**
~ see *Pulmonaria* 'Margery Fish'

PULSATILLA (RANUNCULACEAE)
93 R *alpina* subsp. *apiifolia* (H4)
— subsp. *sulphurea* ~ see *Pulsatilla alpina* subsp. *apiifolia*
93 R *halleri* (H4)
93 R — subsp. *slavica* (H4)
lutea ~ see *Pulsatilla alpina* subsp. *apiifolia*
93 R *vulgaris* (H4)
93 R — **'Alba'** (H4)

PYRETHROPSIS (ASTERACEAE)
hosmariense ~ see *Rhodanthemum hosmariense*

RAMONDA (GESNERIACEAE)
93 R *myconi* (H4)
93 R *nathaliae* (H4)
pyrenaica ~ see *Ramonda myconi*

RANUNCULUS (RANUNCULACEAE)
93 *aconitifolius* **'Flore Pleno'** (d) (H4)
02 *acris* **'Flore Pleno'** (d) (H4)
93 R *gramineus* (H4)
93 R *montanus* **'Molten Gold'** (H4)

REHMANNIA (SCROPHULARIACEAE)
93 *glutinosa* (H3)

RHEUM (POLYGONACEAE)
palmatum **'Atropurpureum'** ~ see *Rheum palmatum* 'Atrosanguineum'
02 — **'Atrosanguineum'** (H4)

RHODANTHEMUM (ASTERACEAE)
93 R *hosmariense* (H4)

RHODOHYPOXIS (HYPOXIDACEAE)
93 R *baurii* (H4)

RODGERSIA (SAXIFRAGACEAE)
93 *aesculifolia* (H4)
98 **'Irish Bronze'** (H4)
93 *pinnata* **'Superba'** (H4)
93 *podophylla* (H4)

ROMNEYA (PAPAVERACEAE)
93 *coulteri* (H4)
02 — **'White Cloud'** (H4)
× *hybrida* ~ see *Romneya coulteri* 'White Cloud'

ROSCOEA (ZINGIBERACEAE)
93 R *cautleyoides* (H4)
98 — **'Kew Beauty'** (H4)
93 R *humeana* (H4) ~ *name often misapplied*

RUDBECKIA (ASTERACEAE)
deamii
~ see *Rudbeckia fulgida* var. *deamii*
93 *fulgida* var. *deamii* (H4) ~ *reconfirmed after trial 2002*
93 — var. *sullivantii* **'Goldsturm'** (H4)
02 — var. *speciosa* (H4)

93 **'Goldquelle'** (d) (H4) *~ reconfirmed after trial 2002*

02 **'Herbstsonne'** (H4)
02 *laciniata* **'Goldkugel'** (d) (H4)

SALVIA (LAMIACEAE)
 acetabulosa ~ see *Salvia multicaulis*
 ambigens ~ see *Salvia guaranitica* 'Blue Enigma'
93 *candelabrum* (H3-4) *~ min. 2C*
 cardinalis ~ see *Salvia fulgens*
93 *fulgens* (H3)
 greggii **'Raspberry Royal'** ~ see *Salvia* 'Raspberry Royale'
96 *guaranitica* **'Blue Enigma'** (H3-4)
 haematodes ~ see *Salvia pratensis* Haematodes Group
93 *involucrata* (H3)
02 — **'Bethellii'** (H3-4)
96 G — **'Boutin'** (H3)
96 × *jamensis* **'Los Lirios'** (H3-4)
96 *multicaulis* (H4)
96 *nemorosa* **'Amethyst'** (H4)
 — **EAST FRIESLAND** ~ see *Salvia nemorosa* 'Ostfriesland'
96 — **'Lubecca'** (H4)
96 — **'Ostfriesland'** (H4)
 — **'Plumosa'** ~ see *Salvia nemorosa* 'Pusztaflamme'
96 — **'Porzellan'** (H4)
96 — **'Pusztaflamme'** (H4) *~ awarded as S. nemorosa 'Plumosa'*
93 *patens* (H3)
94 — **'Cambridge Blue'** (H3)
 — **'Oxford Blue'** ~ see *Salvia patens*
 — **'Royal Blue'** ~ see *Salvia patens*
93 *pratensis* Haematodes Group (H4)
96 — **'Indigo'** (H4)
96 **'Raspberry Royale'** (H3-4)
96 G *roemeriana* (H3)
96 *spathacea* (H3-4)
96 G *splendens* **'Van-Houttei'** (H3)
93 × *superba* (H4)
96 — **'Rubin'** (H4)
96 × *sylvestris* **'Blauhügel'** (H4)
96 — **'Mainacht'** (H4)
 — **MAY NIGHT** ~ see *Salvia* × *sylvestris* 'Mainacht'
96 — **'Tänzerin'** (H4)
93 *uliginosa* (H3-4)
 'Van-Houttei' ~ see *Salvia splendens* 'Van-Houttei'

SANGUINARIA (PAPAVERACEAE)
93 R *canadensis* f. *multiplex* **'Plena'** (d) (H4)

SAPONARIA (CARYOPHYLLACEAE)
93 R **'Bressingham'** (H4)
93 R *ocymoides* (H4)
93 R — **'Rubra Compacta'** (H4)
93 R × *olivana* (H4)

SAXIFRAGA (SAXIFRAGACEAE)

(5)	Irregulares
(7)	Porphyrion
(8)	Ligulatae
(11)	Gymnopera
(15)	Saxifraga

 × *apiculata* sensu stricto hort. ~ see *Saxifraga* 'Gregor Mendel'
93 R *callosa* (8) (H4)
 — var. *bellardii* ~ see *Saxifraga callosa*
 — *lingulata* ~ see *Saxifraga callosa*
93 R **'Clarence Elliott'** (*umbrosa*) (11) (H4)
 cortusifolia var. *fortunei* ~ see *Saxifraga fortunei*
93 R **'Cranbourne'** (× *anglica*) (7) (H4)
 'Crimson Rose' (*paniculata*) ~ see *Saxifraga* 'Rosea'
98 R **'Cumulus'** (*iranica* hybrid) (7) (H4)
96 R **'Duncan Lowe'** (*andersonii*) (7) (H4)
93 R **'Faldonside'** (× *boydii*) (7) (H4)
93 R *ferdinandi-coburgi* (7) (H4)
 'Flavescens' misapplied ~ see *Saxifraga* 'Lutea'
 florulenta Schott, Nyman & Kotschy ~ see *Saxifraga callosa*
93 R *fortunei* (5) (H4)
93 R **'Gloria'** (*burseriana*) (7) (H4)
93 R **'Gregor Mendel'** (× *apiculata*) (7) (H4)
93 R **'Jenkinsiae'** (× *irvingii*) (7) (H4)
93 R **'Kathleen Pinsent'** (8) (H4)
 lingulata ~ see *Saxifraga callosa*
 'Lutea' (*aizoon*) ~ see *Saxifraga* 'Lutea'
93 R **'Lutea'** (*paniculata*) (8) (H4)
93 R **'Luteola'** (× *boydii*) (7) (H4)
93 R **'Major'** (*cochlearis*) (8) (H4)
 'Major Lutea' ~ see *Saxifraga* 'Luteola'
93 R **'Minor'** (*cochlearis*) (8) (H4)
94 R **'Peter Burrow'** (× *poluanglica*) (7) (H4)
 primuloides ~ see *Saxifraga* 'Primuloides'
93 R **'Primuloides'** (*umbrosa*) (11) (H4)
93 R **'Rosea'** (*paniculata*) (8) (H4)
 'Rubra' (*aizoon*) ~ see *Saxifraga* 'Rosea'

93 R **'Sanguinea Superba'** (× *arendsii*)
(15) (H4)
93 R **'Southside Seedling'** (8) (H4)
93 R **'Splendens'** (*oppositifolia*) (7) (H4)
93 R **'Theoden'** (*oppositifolia*) (7) (H4)
93 R **'Tumbling Waters'** (8) (H4)
umbrosa var. *primuloides*
~ see *Saxifraga* 'Primuloides'
93 R × *urbium* (11) (H4)
urbium primuloides **'Elliott's Variety'**
~ see *Saxifraga* 'Clarence Elliott'
'Valborg' ~ see *Saxifraga* 'Cranbourne'
'Valentine' ~ see *Saxifraga* 'Cranbourne'

SCABIOSA (DIPSACACEAE)
93 *caucasica* **'Clive Greaves'** (H4)
93 — **'Miss Willmott'** (H4)

SEDUM (CRASSULACEAE)
AUTUMN JOY ~ see *Sedum* 'Herbstfreude'
96 **'Bertram Anderson'** (H4)
93 R *cauticola* (H4)
ellacombeanum ~ see *Sedum*
kamtschaticum var. *ellacombeanum*
floriferum ~ see *Sedum kamtschaticum*
93 **'Herbstfreude'** (H4)
93 R *kamtschaticum* (H4)
93 R — var. *ellacombeanum* (H4)
93 R — var. *kamtschaticum* **'Variegatum'**
(v) (H4)
93 R **'Ruby Glow'** (H4)
93 R *spathulifolium* **'Cape Blanco'** (H4)
93 R — **'Purpureum'** (H4)
93 *spectabile* (H4)
93 — **'Brilliant'** (H4)
spurium DRAGON'S BLOOD ~ see
Sedum spurium 'Schorbuser Blut'
93 R — **'Schorbuser Blut'** (H4)
93 *telephium* subsp. *maximum*
'Atropurpureum' (H4)
93 R **'Vera Jameson'** (H4)

SEMPERVIVUM (CRASSULACEAE)
93 R *arachnoideum* (H4)
— **'Laggeri'** ~ see *Sempervivum*
arachnoideum subsp.
tomentosum
93 R — subsp. *tomentosum* (H4)
arvernense ~ see *Sempervivum tectorum*
93 R *ciliosum* (H4)
93 R **'Commander Hay'** (H4)
densum ~ see *Sempervivum tectorum*
93 R *tectorum* (H4)

webbianum ~ see *Sempervivum*
arachnoideum subsp. *tomentosum*

SENECIO (ASTERACEAE)
'Gregynog Gold'
~ see *Ligularia* 'Gregynog Gold'
przewalski ~ see *Ligularia przewalskii*

SERIPHIDIUM (ASTERACEAE)
93 *vallesiacum* (H4)

SIDALCEA (MALVACEAE)
02 **'Elsie Heugh'** (H4)
93 **'William Smith'** (H4)

SILENE (CARYOPHYLLACEAE)
93 R *alpestris* **'Flore Pleno'**
(d) (H4)
93 R *schafta* (H4)
— **'Abbotswood'** ~ see *Lychnis* × *walkeri*
'Abbotswood Rose'

SILPHIUM (ASTERACEAE)
02 *perfoliatum* (H4)

SISYRINCHIUM (IRIDACEAE)
douglasii ~ see *Olsynium douglasii*
grandiflorum ~ see *Olsynium douglasii*
02 R *idahoense* **'Album'** (H4)
'May Snow' ~ see *Sisyrinchium*
idahoense 'Album'

SOLIDAGO (ASTERACEAE)
02 **'Gardone'** (H4)
93 **'Goldenmosa'** (H4)
'Lemore' ~ see × *Solidaster luteus*
'Lemore'

× SOLIDASTER (ASTERACEAE)
93 *luteus* **'Lemore'** (H4)

SPIRAEA (ROSACEAE)
venusta **'Magnifica'**
~ see *Filipendula rubra* 'Venusta'

STACHYS (LAMIACEAE)
93 *macrantha* **'Robusta'** (H4) ~ *will*
grow in total shade

SYMPHYTUM (BORAGINACEAE)
02 *caucasicum* (H4)
93 × *uplandicum* **'Variegatum'** (v) (H4)

TANACETUM (ASTERACEAE)
93   coccineum 'Eileen May Robinson' (H4)
93   — 'James Kelway' (H4)
02   ptarmiciflorum (H3-4)

THALICTRUM (RANUNCULACEAE)
      aquilegiifolium PURPLE CLOUD
            ~ see Thalictrum aquilegiifolium
                              'Thundercloud'
93   — 'Thundercloud' (H4)
93   delavayi (H4)
93   — 'Hewitt's Double' (d) (H4)
      dipterocarpum hort.
            ~ see Thalictrum delavayi
93   flavum subsp. glaucum (H4)
      speciosissimum   ~ see Thalictrum
                        flavum subsp. glaucum

TIARELLA (SAXIFRAGACEAE)
      collina   ~ see Tiarella wherryi
93 R cordifolia (H4)
93 R wherryi (H4)

TOLMIEA (SAXIFRAGACEAE)
      menziesii 'Goldsplash'   ~ see Tolmiea
                     menziesii 'Taff's Gold'
      — 'Maculata'   ~ see Tolmiea menziesii
                              'Taff's Gold'
93   — 'Taff's Gold' (v) (H4)   ~ valued in
                        particular as a pot plant
                              under glass
      — 'Variegata' ~ see Tolmiea menziesii
                              'Taff's Gold'

TRADESCANTIA (COMMELINACEAE)
93   (Andersoniana Group) 'Isis' (H4)
93   — 'J.C. Weguelin' (H4)
93   — 'Osprey' (H4)

TRICYRTIS (CONVALLARIACEAE)
93   formosana (H4)

TROLLIUS (RANUNCULACEAE)
93   chinensis 'Golden Queen' (H4)
93   × cultorum 'Goldquelle' (H4)
93   — 'Orange Princess' (H4)
93   — 'Superbus' (H4)
      europaeus 'Superbus'   ~ see Trollius
                        × cultorum 'Superbus'

VERATRUM (MELANTHIACEAE)
93   nigrum (H4)

VERBASCUM (SCROPHULARIACEAE)
02   chaixii 'Album' (H4)
93   (Cotswold Group) 'Cotswold Beauty'
           (H4)
93   — 'Gainsborough' (H4)
93   — 'Pink Domino' (H4)

VERBENA (VERBENACEAE)
02   bonariensis (H3-4)
93   'Lawrence Johnston' (H3)
      patagonica   ~ see Verbena bonariensis
      'Pink Bouquet' ~ see V. 'Silver Anne'
93   'Silver Anne' (H3)

VERONICA (SCROPHULARIACEAE)
      austriaca var. dubia
            ~ see Veronica prostrata
93   — subsp. teucrium 'Crater Lake
           Blue' (H4)
93   — — 'Royal Blue' (H4)
      — — 'Shirley Blue'
            ~ see Veronica 'Shirley Blue'
93 R cinerea (H4)
93   gentianoides (H4)
      perfoliata   ~ see Parahebe perfoliata
93 R prostrata (H4)
97 R — 'Spode Blue' (H4)
      rupestris   ~ see Veronica prostrata
93   'Shirley Blue' (H4)

VINCA (APOCYNACEAE)
02   difformis (H3-4)
      major 'Elegantissima'
            ~ see Vinca major 'Variegata'
93   — 'Variegata' (v) (H4)
02   minor f. alba (H4)
93   — — 'Gertrude Jekyll' (H4)
93   — 'Argenteovariegata' (v) (H4)
93   — 'Atropurpurea' (H4)
93   — 'Azurea Flore Pleno' (d) (H4)
      — 'Bowles' Blue'   ~ see Vinca minor
                              'La Grave'
      — 'Bowles' Variety'   ~ see Vinca
                        minor 'La Grave'
      — 'Caerulea Plena' ~ see Vinca minor
                        'Azurea Flore Pleno'
93   — 'La Grave' (H4)
      — 'Purpurea'   ~ see Vinca minor
                        'Atropurpurea'
      — 'Rubra'   ~ see Vinca minor
                        'Atropurpurea'
      — 'Variegata'   ~ see Vinca minor
                        'Argenteovariegata'

VIOLA (VIOLACEAE)

(Va)	Viola
(Vt)	Violet
(Vtta)	Violetta

93   **Aspasia'** (Va) (H4)
93   **'Beshlie'** (Va) (H4)
93   **'Clementina'** (Va) (H4)
93 R *cornuta* (H4)
93 R — **Alba Group** (H4)
93 R — **'Minor'** (H4)
93 R *cucullata* (H4)
    'Haslemere' ~ see *Viola* 'Nellie Britton'
93   **'Huntercombe Purple'** (Va) (H4)

93   **'Inverurie Beauty'** (Va) (H4)
93 R **'Jackanapes'** (Va) (H4)
93   **'Little David'** (Vtta) (H4)
93   **'Lorna'** (Va) (H4)
93   **'Maggie Mott'** (Va) (H4)
93   **'Martin'** (Va) (H4)
93 R **'Molly Sanderson'** (Va) (H4)
93   **'Moonlight'** (Va) (H4)
93   **'Nellie Britton'** (Va) (H4)
    obliqua   ~ see *Viola cucullata*
93   *odorata* **'Wellsiana'** (Vt) (H4)
02   *sororia* **'Albiflora'** (H4)

WAHLENBERGIA (CAMPANULACEAE)
  pumilio   ~ see *Edraianthus pumilio*

Grasses

AVENA (POACEAE)
  candida ~ see *Helictotrichon sempervirens*

CORTADERIA (POACEAE)
02   *richardii* (Endl.) Zotov (H3-4)
93   *selloana* **'Aureolineata'** (v) (H3)
    — **'Gold Band'**   ~ see *Cortaderia selloana* 'Aureolineata'
93   — **'Pumila'** (H4)
93   — **'Sunningdale Silver'** (H3)
    Toe Toe ~   see *Cortaderia richardii*

FESTUCA (POACEAE)
93 R *glauca* **'Blaufuchs'** (H4)
    — **BLUE FOX** ~ see *Festuca glauca* 'Blaufuchs'

HAKONECHLOA (POACEAE)
02   *macra* **'Alboaurea'** (H4)
93   — **'Aureola'** (H4)
    — **'Variegata'** ~ see *Hakonechloa macra* 'Alboaurea'

HELICTOTRICHON (POACEAE)
93   *sempervirens* (H4)

MILIUM (POACEAE)
98   *effusum* **'Aureum'** (H4)

MISCANTHUS (POACEAE)
01   *sinensis* var. *condensatus* **'Cosmopolitan'** (v) (H4)
01   — **'Flamingo'** (H4)

01   — **'Gewitterwolke'** (H4)
01   — **'Ghana'** (H4)
01   — **'Gold und Silber'** (H4)
01   — **'Grosse Fontäne'** (H4)
01   — **'Kaskade'** (H4)
01   — **'Kleine Fontäne'** (H4)
01   — **'Kleine Silberspinne'** (H4)
01   — **'Morning Light'** (v) (H4)
01   — **'Septemberrot'** (H4)
01   — **'Silberfeder'** (H4)   ~ awarded as 'Silver Feather'
01   — **'Strictus'** (H4)
01   — **'Undine'** (H4)
01   — **'Variegatus'** (v) (H4)
01   — **'Zebrinus'** (v) (H4)

MOLINIA (POACEAE)
93   *caerulea* subsp. *caerulea* **'Variegata'** (v) (H4)

PENNISETUM (POACEAE)
  longistylum hort. ~ see *P. villosum*
93   *orientale* (H3)
02   *villosum* (H3)

PHALARIS (POACEAE)
  arundinacea **'Elegantissima'** ~ see *P. arundinacea* var. *picta* 'Picta'
93   — var. *picta* **'Picta'** (v) (H4)   ~ *can be invasive*

STIPA (POACEAE)
93   *gigantea* (H4)

Bulbs, Corms & Tubers

AGAPANTHUS (ALLIACEAE)
93 *campanulatus* subsp. *patens* (H3)
93 'Loch Hope' (H3)

ALLIUM (ALLIACEAE)
aflatunense hort.
~ see *Allium hollandicum*
albopilosum ~ see *Allium cristophii*
azureum ~ see *Allium caeruleum*
95 'Beau Regard' (H4)
beesianum hort.
~ see *Allium cyaneum*
93 R *caeruleum* (H4)
— *azureum* ~ see *Allium caeruleum*
02 R *caesium* (H4)
93 R *carinatum* subsp. *pulchellum* (H4)
02 R — subsp. *pulchellum* f. *album* (H4)
93 R *cernuum* 'Hidcote' (H4)
— 'Major'
~ see *Allium cernuum* 'Hidcote'
cirrhosum ~ see *Allium carinatum*
subsp. *pulchellum*
93 *cristophii* (H4)
93 R *cyaneum* (H4)
93 R *flavum* (H4)
95 *giganteum* (H4)
95 'Gladiator' (H4)
95 'Globemaster' (H4)
95 *hollandicum* (H4)
93 — 'Purple Sensation' (H4)
02 — 'Purple Surprise' (H4)
93 R *insubricum* (H4) ~ *most plants sold as* A. narcissiflorum *are this species*
93 R *karataviense* (H3)
93 R *moly* 'Jeannine' (H4)
murrayanum misapplied
~ see *Allium unifolium*
narcissiflorum hort.
~ see *Allium insubricum*
93 R *oreophilum* 'Zwanenburg' (H4)
ostrowskianum 'Zwanenburg'
~ see *Allium oreophilum* 'Zwanenburg'
pulchellum ~ see *Allium carinatum* subsp. *pulchellum*
02 R *thunbergii* (H4)
02 R *unifolium* (H4)

ALSTROEMERIA (ALSTROEMERIACEAE)
94 'Apollo' (H4) ~ *recommended for cultivation in the open ground*
94 'Coronet' (H4) ~ *recommended for cultivation in the open ground*
94 'Friendship' (H4) ~ *recommended for cultivation in the open ground*
94 'Orange Gem' (H4) ~ *recommended for cultivation in the open ground*
94 'Orange Glory' (H4) ~ *recommended for cultivation in the open ground*
94 'Yellow Friendship' (H4)
~ *recommended for cultivation in the open ground*

ANTHERICUM (ANTHERICACEAE)
algeriense
~ see *Anthericum liliago* var. *major*
93 R *liliago* var. *major* (H4)

ARISAEMA (ARACEAE)
93 R *candidissimum* (H4)

ARUM (ARACEAE)
93 *italicum* subsp. *italicum* 'Marmoratum' (H4)
— 'Pictum'
~ see *Arum italicum* subsp. *italicum* 'Marmoratum'

BEGONIA (BEGONIACEAE)
02 *grandis* subsp. *evansiana* (H3-4)

CALLA (ARACEAE)
aethiopica
~ see *Zantedeschia aethiopica*

CAMASSIA (HYACINTHACEAE)
leichtlinii 'Alba' hort.
~ see *Camassia leichtlinii* subsp. *leichtlinii*
93 — subsp. *leichtlinii* (H4)

CHIONODOXA (HYACINTHACEAE)
93 R *forbesii* Siehei Group (H4)
93 R *luciliae* Boissier (H4)
93 R *sardensis* (H4)
siehei ~ see *Chionodoxa forbesii* Siehei Group

COLCHICUM (COLCHICACEAE)
93 R *agrippinum* (H4)
    autumnale var. *major*
        ~ see *Colchicum byzantinum*
97 R — **'Nancy Lindsay'** (H4)
93 R *byzantinum* (H4)
97 R **'Pink Goblet'** (H4)
97 R **'Rosy Dawn'** (H4)
93 R *speciosum* (H4)
93 R — **'Album'** (H4)
97 R — **'Cedric Morris'** (H4)
97 R *tenorei* (H4)
97 R **'Waterlily'** (d) (H4)

CONVALLARIA (CONVALLARIACEAE)
93   *majalis* (H4)

CROCOSMIA (IRIDACEAE)
02   x *crocosmiiflora* **'Carmin Brillant'**
        (H3-4)
93   — **'Solfatare'** (H3)
02   — **'Star of the East'** (H3)
93   **'Lucifer'** (H4)
93   *masoniorum* (H3)
02   — **'Rowallane Yellow'** (H3-4)
02   **'Severn Sunrise'** (H3-4)

CROCUS (IRIDACEAE)
93 R *angustifolius* (H4)
    aureus
       ~ see *Crocus flavus* subsp. *flavus*
93 R *banaticus* (H4)
93 R *cartwrightianus* (H4)
94 R — **'Albus'** Tubergeh (H4)
93 R *chrysanthus* (H4)
93 R — **'Blue Pearl'** (H4)
93 R — **'Cream Beauty'** (H4)
93 R — **'E.A. Bowles'** (H4)
93 R — **'Ladykiller'** (H4)
93 R — **'Snow Bunting'** (H4)
93 R — **'Zwanenburg Bronze'** (H4)
93 R *cilicium* (H2-4)
    'Cloth of Gold'
       ~ see *Crocus angustifolius*
93 R *corsicus* (H4)
    'Dutch Yellow'   ~ see *Crocus luteus*
       'Golden Yellow'
93 R *etruscus* (H4)
    flavus
       ~ see *Crocus flavus* subsp. *flavus*
93 R — subsp. *flavus* (H4)
    'Golden Mammoth' ~ see *Crocus* x
       luteus 'Golden Yellow'

93 R *goulimyi* subsp. *goulimyi* (H4)
    — **'Albus'**   ~ see *Crocus goulimyi*
       'Mani White'
94 R — **'Mani White'** (H4)
94 R *hadriaticus* (H4)
    — var. *chrysobelonicus*
       ~ see *Crocus hadriaticus*
93 R *imperati* (H4)
93 R *kotschyanus* (H4)
94 R *laevigatus* (H4)
    'Large Yellow'   ~ see *Crocus* x *luteus*
       'Golden Yellow'
94 R *longiflorus* (H4)
93 R x *luteus* **'Golden Yellow'** (H4)
93 R *malyi* (H2-4)
    'Mammoth Yellow'   ~ see *Crocus* x
       luteus 'Golden Yellow'
93 R *medius* (H4)
94 R *ochroleucus* (H4)
93 R *pulchellus* (H4)
    sativus var. *cartwrightianus*
       ~ see *Crocus cartwrightianus*
    sibiricus   ~ see *Crocus sieberi*
93 R *sieberi* (H4)
93 R — **'Albus'** (H4)
    — **'Bowles' White'**
       ~ see *Crocus sieberi* 'Albus'
93 R — **'Hubert Edelsten'** (H4)
93 R — subsp. *sublimis* **'Tricolor'** (H4)
93 R *speciosus* (H4)
94 R — **'Albus'** (H4)
    x *stellaris* **'Golden Yellow'**
       ~ see *Crocus* x *luteus*
       'Golden Yellow'
    susianus   ~ see *Crocus angustfolius*
93 R *tommasinianus* (H4)
93 R *tournefortii* (H2-4)
    'Yellow Mammoth'   ~ see *Crocus* x
       luteus 'Golden Yellow'
94 R **'Zephyr'** (H4)
    ~ *awarded as* C. pulchellus *'Zephyr'*

CYCLAMEN (PRIMULACEAE)
93 R *coum* (H4)
93 R — subsp. *coum* f. *coum* **Pewter Group**
    europaeum
       ~ see *Cyclamen purpurascens*
93 R *hederifolium* (H4)
    neapolitanum
       ~ see *Cyclamen hederifolium*
    orbiculatum   ~ see *Cyclamen coum*
93 R *purpurascens* (H4)
93 R *repandum* subsp. *repandum* (H3)

ERYTHRONIUM (LILIACEAE)
94 R *californicum* (H4)
93 R — **'White Beauty'** (H4)
93 R *dens-canis* (H4)
93 R **'Pagoda'** (H4)
93 R *revolutum* (H4)
— **'White Beauty'** ~ see
Erythronium californicum
'White Beauty'
93 R *tuolumnense* (H4)

EUCOMIS (HYACINTHACEAE)
98 *pallidiflora* (H4)

FRITILLARIA (LILIACEAE)
93 R *acmopetala* (H4)
97 R *hermonis* subsp. *amana* **'Cambridge'**
(H4)
imperialis **'Lutea Maxima'** ~ see
Fritillaria imperialis
'Maxima Lutea'
93 — **'Maxima Lutea'** (H4)
93 R *meleagris* var. *unicolor* subvar. *alba*
(H4)
nigra hort. ~ see *Fritillaria*
pyrenaica
93 R *pallidiflora* (H4)
96 R *persica* **'Adiyaman'** (H4)
93 R *pyrenaica* (H4)

GALANTHUS (AMARYLLIDACEAE)
93 R **'Atkinsii'** (H4)
caucasicus hort. (H4)
~ see *Galanthus elwesii*
var. *monostictus*
93 R *elwesii* (H4)
93 R — var. *monostictus* (H4)
graecus Orph. ex Boiss.
~ see *Galanthus elwesii*
93 R **'Magnet'** (H4)
93 R *nivalis* (H4)
93 R — f. *pleniflorus* **'Flore Pleno'** (d) (H4)
93 R *plicatus* (H4)
~ *including both subsp.* plicatus
and subsp. byzantinus
02 R *reginae-olgae* subsp. *reginae-olgae*
(H2-4)
93 R **'S. Arnott'** (H4)
02 R *woronowii* (H4)

GALTONIA (HYACINTHACEAE)
02 *candicans* (H4)

GLADIOLUS (IRIDACEAE)
byzantinus ~ see *Gladiolus communis*
subsp. *byzantinus*
93 *callianthus* **'Murielae'** (H3)
93 *communis* subsp. *byzantinus* (H4)
'Murieliae' ~ see *Gladiolus*
callianthus 'Murielae'
93 **'Robinetta'** (*recurvus* hybrid) (H3)
93 **'The Bride'** (x *colvillei*) (H3)

HEMEROCALLIS (HEMEROCALLIDACEAE)
93 **'Beloved Returns'** (H4)
93 **'Berlin Lemon'** (H4)
93 **'Berlin Red'** (H4)
93 **'Berlin Red Velvet'** (H4)
93 **'Burning Daylight'** (H4)
93 **'Cartwheels'** (H4)
93 **'Chief Sarcoxie'** (H4)
93 **'Corky'** (H4)
flava ~ see *Hemerocallis lilioasphodelus*
93 **'Golden Chimes'** (H4)
93 **'Green Flutter'** (H4)
93 **'Helle Berlinerin'** (H4)
93 **'Lemon Bells'** (H4)
93 *lilioasphodelus* (H4)
93 **'Marion Vaughn'** (H4)
93 **'Missenden'** (H4)
93 **'Neyron Rose'** (H4)
93 **'Nova'** (H4)
93 **'Pink Damask'** (H4)
93 **'Red Precious'** (H4)
94 **'Royal Mountie'** (H4)
93 **'Stoke Poges'** (H4)
94 **'Tetrina's Daughter'** (H4)
93 **'Whichford'** (H4)

HYACINTHUS (HYACINTHACEAE)
azureus ~ see *Muscari azureum*
93 *orientalis* **'Anna Marie'** (H4)
93 — **'Blue Jacket'** (H4)
93 — **'Borah'** (H4)
93 — **'City of Haarlem'** (H4)
93 — **'Delft Blue'** (H4)
93 — **'Gipsy Queen'** (H4)
93 — **'L'Innocence'** (H4)
93 — **'Ostara'** (H4)
93 — **'Pink Pearl'** (H4)

IRIS (IRIDACEAE)
98 **'Acstede Nine Hundred'** (IB) (H4)
02 **'Adoring Glances'** (SDB) (H4)
93 **'Adrienne Taylor'** (SDB) (H4)
93 **'Agnes James'** (CH) (H3)

(AB)	Arilbred
(BB)	Border Bearded
(Cal-Sib)	Series Californicae x Series Sibiricae
(CH)	Californian Hybrid
(DB)	Dwarf Bearded (not assigned)
(Dut)	Dutch
(IB)	Intermediate Bearded
(La)	Louisiana Hybrid
(MDB)	Miniature Dwarf Bearded
(MTB)	Miniature Tall Bearded
(SDB)	Standard Dwarf Bearded
(Sino-Sib)	Series Sibiricae, chromosome number 2n=40
(SpecHybrid)	Interspecific Hybrid
(Spuria)	Spuria
(TB)	Tall Bearded

94 *albicans* (H4)
98 'Alison Taylor' (IB) (H4)
00 'Alizes' (TB) (H4)
   anglica   ~ see *Iris latifolia*
93 'Annikins' (IB) (H4)
96 'Apricorange' (TB) (H4)
93 'Arctic Fancy' (IB) (H4)
93 'Arnold Sunrise' (CH) (H3)
02 'Ballet Lesson' (SDB) (H4)
93 'Banbury Beauty' (CH) (H3)
02 'Bedford Lilac' (SDB) (H4)
94 'Belise' (Spuria) (H4)
02 'Berlin Tiger' (H4)
98 'Bewdley' (IB) (H4)
93 'Bibury' (SDB) (H4)
94 'Big Money' (CH) (H3)
   biglumis   ~ see *Iris lactea*
98 'Blackbeard' (BB) (H4)
00 'Black Sergeant' (TB (H4)
93 'Blue Ballerina' (CH) (H3)
99 'Blue Line' (SDB) (H4)
93 'Blue Luster' (TB) (H4)
00 'Bob Nichol' (TB (H4)
02 'Bold Stroke' (IB) (H4)
96 'Breakers' (TB) (H4)
94 'Broadleigh Carolyn' (CH) (H3)
94 'Bromyard' (SDB) (H4)
94 'Bronzaire' (IB) (H4)
93 'Brown Lasso' (BB) (H4)
94 R *bucharica* Foster (H3-4)
02 'Bumblebee Deelite' (MTB) (H4)
96 'Cardew' (TB) (H4)
99 'Carolyn Rose' (MTB) (H4)
02 'Cee Jay' (IB) (H4)
   chamaeiris   ~ see *Iris lutescens*
02 'Chickee' (MTB) (H4)
93 'Chiltern Gold' (IB) (H4)
94 *chrysographes* (H4)

95 'Clara Garland' (IB) (H4)
98 'Clarke Cosgrove' (Spuria) (H4)
00 'Clear Morning Sky' (TB) (H4)
94 *confusa* (H3)
02 'Cool Treat' (BB) (H4)
02 'Cranapple' (BB) (H4)
96 'Cream Soda' (TB) (H4)
94 R *cristata* (H4)
94 *crocea* (H4)
93 'Dark Rosaleen' (TB) (H4)
94 *delavayi* (H4)
02 'Delicate Lady' (IB) (H4)
93 'Designer's Choice' (TB) (H4)
98 'Destination' (Spuria) (H4)
95 'Diligence' (SDB) (H4)
94 *douglasiana* (H4)
93 'Dovedale' (TB) (H4)
02 'Driftwood' (Spuria) (H4)
00 'Dwight Enys' (TB) (H4)
95 'Eardisland' (IB) (H4)
93 'Early Light' (TB) (H4)
00 'Eileen Louise' (TB) (H4)
99 'Eleanor Clare' (IB) (H4)
94 *ensata* (H4)
99 — 'Aldridge Snow Maiden' (H4)
99 — 'Aldridge Visitor' (H4)
99 — 'Barr Purple East' (H4)
99 — 'Caprician Butterfly' (H4)
02 — 'Chance Beauty' (SpecHybrid) (H4)
95 — 'Continuing Pleasure' (H4)
95 — 'Flying Tiger' (H4)
96 — 'Fringed Cloud' (H4)
96 — 'Give-me-Patience' (H4)
96 — 'Hue and Cry' (H4)
95 — 'Imperial Magic' (H4)
95 — 'Katy Mendez' (H4)
96 — 'Lasting Pleasure' (H4)
96 — 'Magic Opal' (H4)
96 — 'Mancunian' (H4)
96 — 'Ol' Man River' (H4)
96 — 'Returning Tide' (H4)
95 — 'Rose Queen' (H4)
95 — 'Southern Son' (H4)
96 — 'Summer Storm' (H4)
96 — 'The Great Mogul' (H4)
95 — 'Variegata' (v) (H4)
96 — 'Vintage Festival' (H4)
94 'Eye Magic' (IB) (H4)
93 'Eyebright' (SDB) (H4)
00 'Fern Oakley' (TB) (H4)
94 'Fierce Fire' (IB) (H4)
97 'Fine Line' (Cal-Sib) (H3)
00 'Floating World' (CH) (H3)

94	**'Florentina'** (IB/TB) (H4)
94	*foetidissima* (H4)
94	— **'Variegata'** (v) (H4)
94	*forrestii* (H4)
99	**'Fritillary Flight'** (IB) (H4)
94	x *fulvala* (H4)
00	**'Garlanda'** (TB) (H4)
02	**'George'** (Reticulata) (H4)
	'Gerald Darby' ~ see *Iris* x *robusta*
	'Gerald Darby'
94	*germanica* (H4)
	— var. *florentina* ~ see *Iris* 'Florentina'
94	**'Golden Waves'** (Cal-Sib) (H3)
96	**'Goring Ace'** (CH) (H3)
00	**'Goring Passion'** (CH) (H3)
00	**'Goring Steeple'** (CH) (H3)
94	*graminea* (H4)
	graminifolia ~ see *Iris kerneriana*
93	**'Green Spot'** (SDB) (H4)
99	**'Gwyneth Evans'** (BB) (H4)
93	**'Happy Mood'** (IB) (H4)
93	**'Holden Clough'** (SpecHybrid) (H4)
02	**'Honeyplic'** (IB) (H4)
94	*hoogiana* (H3)
93	**'Ice Dancer'** (TB) (H4)
98	**'Ila Crawford'** (Spuria) (H4)
02	**'Impetuous'** (BB) (H4)
95	**'Innocent Heart'** (IB) (H4)
93	**'Jane Phillips'** (TB) (H4)
00	**'Janine Louise'** (TB) (H4)
94	*japonica* (H3)
94	— **'Variegata'** (v) (H3)
93	**'Jeremy Brian'** (SDB) (H4)
	kaempferi ~ see *Iris ensata*
96	**'Katharine Hodgkin'** (Reticulata) (H4)
94	**'Katie-Koo'** (IB) (H4)
00	**'Ken's Choice'** (TB) (H4)
94	*kerneriana* (H4)
02	**'Kitt Peak'** (Spuria) (H4)
94	*lactea* (H4)
94 R	*lacustris* (H4)
99	**'Lady Belle'** (MTB) (H4)
93	*laevigata* (H4)
	— **'Rose Queen'** ~ see *Iris ensata*
	'Rose Queen'
94	— **'Variegata'** (v) (H4)
99	**'Langport Wren'** (IB) (H4)
00	**'Lark Rise'** (TB) (H4)
93	*latifolia* (H4)
94	*lazica* (H4)
94	**'Lincoln Imp'** (CH) (H3)
99	**'Lisa Jane'** (SDB) (H4)
94	**'Little Tilgates'** (CH) (H3)

02	**'Loose Valley'** (MTB) (H4)
02	**'Love for Leila'** (Spuria) (H4)
99	**'Luli-Ann'** (SDB) (H4)
94 R	*lutescens* (H4)
96	**'Lydia Jane'** (Spuria) (H4)
99	**'Madeleine Spring'** (BB) (H4)
02	**'Magic Bubbles'** (IB) (H4)
94 R	*magnifica* (H3-4)
99	**'Mary Constance'** (IB) (H4)
93	**'Mary McIlroy'** (SDB) (H4)
94	**'Maui Moonlight'** (IB) (H4)
96	**'Meg's Mantle'** (TB) (H4)
99	**'Michael Paul'** (SDB) (H4)
00	**'Midnight Web'** (TB) (H4)
94	*milesii* (H4)
99	**'Mini Might'** (SDB) (H4)
94	*missouriensis* (H4)
00	**'Mister Matthew'** (TB) (H4)
02	**'Monspur Cambridge Blue'** (Spuria) (H4)
02	**'Morning's Blush'** (SDB) (H4)
96	**'Morwenna'** (TB) (H4)
	nertschinskia ~ see *Iris sanguinea*
96	**'Nicola Jane'** (TB) (H4)
93	**'No Name'** (CH) (H3)
98	**'Norton Sunlight'** (Spuria) (H4)
	ochroleuca ~ see *Iris orientalis*
93	**'Orange Dawn'** (TB) (H4)
	orchioides Hort. ~ see *Iris bucharica*
94	*orientalis* Mill. (H4)
95	**'Orinoco Flow'** (BB) (H4)
93	**'Ouija'** (BB) (H4)
94	**'Pajaro Dunes'** (CH) (H3)
94	**'Pale Shades'** (IB) (H4)
	pallida **'Aurea'**
	~ see *Iris pallida* 'Variegata'
	— **'Aurea Variegata'**
	~ see *Iris pallida* 'Variegata'
	— var. *dalmatica*
	~ see *Iris pallida* subsp *pallida*
94	— subsp. *pallida* (H4)
94	— **'Variegata'** Hort. (v) (H4)
93	**'Paradise Bird'** (TB) (H4)
93	**'Pascoe'** (TB) (H4)
00	**'Peacock Pavane'** (CH) (H3)
94	**'Peggy Chambers'** (IB) (H4)
02	**'Phil Edinger'** (H4)
96	**'Phil Keen'** (TB) (H4)
95	**'Pink Parchment'** (BB) (H4)
96	**'Precious Heather'** (TB) (H4)
02	**'Prince of Burgundy'** (IB) (H4)
	'Princess Beatrice'
	~ see *Iris pallida* subsp. *pallida*
96	**'Princess Sabra'** (TB) (H4)

94	**'Professor Blaauw'** (Dut) (H4)
98	**'Protégé'** (Spuria) (H4)
99	**'Prudy'** (BB) (H4)
94	*pseudacorus* (H4)
02	— **'Roy Davidson'** (H4)
94	— **'Variegata'** (v) (H4)
94	**'Purple Landscape'** (SDB) (H4)
95	**'Rain Dance'** (SDB) (H4)
94	**'Raspberry Blush'** (IB) (H4)
93 R	*reticulata* (H4)
94	**'Ring o' Roses'** (CH) (H3)
00	**'River Avon'** (TB) (H4)
97	**'Robin Goodfellow'** (MTB) (H4)
93	x *robusta* 'Gerald Darby' (H4)
	'Rose Queen'
	~ see *Iris ensata* 'Rose Queen'
93	**'Royal Contrast'** (SDB) (H4)
	rudskyi ~ see *Iris variegata*
94	*sanguinea* (H4)
94	**'Sarah Taylor'** (SDB) (H4)
93	**'Scintilla'** (IB) (H4)
94	*setosa* (H4)
96	**'Severn Side'** (TB) (H4)
94	**'Shelford Giant'** (Spuria) (H4)
95	**'Sherbet Lemon'** (IB) (H4)
96	**'Sherwood Primrose'** (TB) (H4)
94	**'Short Order'** (CH) (H3)
94	*sibirica* (H4)
96	— **'Annemarie Troeger'** (H4)
95	— **'Berlin Ruffles'** (H4)
02	— **'Blaue Milchstrasse'** (H4)
02	— **'Bournemouth Beauty'** (H4)
95	— **'Butter and Sugar'** (H4)
93	— **'Cambridge'** (H4)
99	— **'Cleedownton'** (H4)
95	— **'Cleeton Double Chance'**
	(Sino-Sib) (H4)
96	— **'Crème Chantilly'** (H4)
93	— **'Dreaming Spires'** (H4)
96	— **'Dreaming Yellow'** (H4)
02	— **'Exuberant Encore'** (H4)
96	— **'Glanusk'** (H4)
95	— **'Glaslyn'** (H4)
02	— **'Granny Jean'** (H4)
96	— **'Harpswell Happiness'** (H4)
96	— **'Isla Serle'** (H4)
99	— **'Kathleen Mary'** (H4)
02	— **'Lavendelwein'** (H4)
96	— **'Mikiko'** (H4)
95	— **'Oban'** (H4)
96	— **'Perfect Vision'** (H4)
99	— **'Plissee'** (H4)
99	— **'Prussian Blue'** (H4)

96	— **'Regency Belle'** (H4)
96	— **'Reprise'** (H4)
96	— **'Roisin'** (H4)
96	— **'Rosselline'** (H4)
93	— **'Ruffled Velvet'** (H4)
99	— **'Shall We Dance'** (H4)
95	— **'Shirley Pope'** (H4)
95	— **'Silver Edge'** (H4)
02	— **'Siobhan'** (H4)
96	— **'Smudger's Gift'** (H4)
95	— **'Soft Blue'** (H4)
02	— **'Trim the Velvet'** (H4)
95	— **'Welfenprinz'** (H4)
95	— **'White Swirl'** (H4)
95	— **'Zakopane'** (H4)
	sieboldii ~ see *Iris sanguinea*
96	**'Sindpers'** (Juno) (H3)
94	*sintenisii* (H4)
93	**'Snowy Owl'** (TB) (H4)
00	**'Somerset Blue'** (TB) (H4)
02	**'Sonoran Señorita'** (Spuria) (H4)
95	**'Sparkling Lemonade'** (BB) (H4)
	spuria subsp. *ochroleuca*
	~ see *Iris orientalis*
93	**'Stepping Out'** (TB) (H4)
02	**'Stinger'** (SDB) (H4)
99	**'Strawberry Love'** (IB) (H4)
	stylosa ~ see *Iris unguicularis*
99	**'Sun Doll'** (SDB) (H4)
95	**'Sunny Dawn'** (IB) (H4)
02	**'Sunrise in Sonora'** (Spuria) (H4)
02	**'Sunset Colors'** (Spuria) (H4)
93	**'Superstition'** (TB) (H4)
95	**'Susan Gillespie'** (IB) (H4)
94	**'Sweet Kate'** (SDB) (H4)
94	**'Tarot'** (BB) (H4)
95	**'Templecloud'** (IB) (H4)
00	**'Thornbird'** (TB) (H4)
	thunbergii ~ see *Iris sanguinea*
93	**'Tintinara'** (TB) (H4)
93	**'Tirra Lirra'** (SDB) (H4)
93	**'Titan's Glory'** (TB) (H4)
02	**'Tol-long'** (H4)
93	*unguicularis* (H4)
	— var. *lazica* ~ see *Iris lazica*
02	— **'Mary Barnard'** (H4)
93	**'Vanity'** (TB) (H4)
94	*variegata* (H4)
94	*versicolor* (H4)
94	**'Vinho Verde'** (IB) (H4)
93	**'Violet Icing'** (TB) (H4)
93	**'Warleggan'** (TB) (H4)
99	**'Welch's Reward'** (MTB) (H4)

93   'Wensleydale' (TB) (H4)
99   'Westar' (SDB) (H4)
93   'Wharfedale' (TB) (H4)
93   'Whiteladies' (IB) (H4)
94   *wilsonii* (H4)
94 R *winogradowii* (H4)
00   'Wise Gift' (Cal-Sib) (H3)
02   'Wyoming Cowboys' (Spuria) (H4)
      xiphioides   ~ see *Iris latifolia*
02   'Zero' (SDB) (H4)

KNIPHOFIA (ASPHODELACEAE)
93   'Bees' Sunset' (H4)
93   'Brimstone' (H4)
93   'Buttercup' (H4)
93   *caulescens* (H3-4)
93   'David' (H4)
93   *galpinii* Baker (H4)
                  ~ *name often misapplied*
      'Nobilis' ~ see *Kniphofia uvaria* 'Nobilis'
93   'Royal Standard' (H4)
93   'Samuel's Sensation' (H4)
93   'Sunningdale Yellow' (H4)
93   'Toffee Nosed' (H4)
93   *uvaria* 'Nobilis' (H4)

LEUCOJUM (AMARYLLIDACEAE)
93   *aestivum* 'Gravetye Giant' (H4)
93 R *autumnale* (H4)
93 R *vernum* (H4)

LILIUM (LILIACEAE)

(Ia)	Upright flowers, borne singly or in an umbel
(Ib)	Outward-facing flowers
(VIa)	Plants with trumpet-shaped flowers
(IX)	All species and their varieties and forms
(VII)	Hybrids of Far Eastern species as L. auratum, L. japonicum, L. rubellum and L. speciosum (Oriental Hybrids)
(VIIb)	Plants with bowl-shaped flowers

02   **African Queen Group** (VIa) (H4)
02   'Apollo' (Ia) (H4)
93   *candidum* (IX) (H4)
93   'Casa Blanca' (VIIb) (H4)
02   'Fata Morgana' (Ia/d) (H4)
02   'Garden Party' (VII) (H4)
02   'Golden Splendour' (H4)
02   'Grand Cru' (Ia) (H4)
93   *henryi* (IX) (H4)
02   'Joy' (VIIb) (H4)
02   'King Pete' (Ib) (H4)

02   *lancifolium* var. *splendens* (IX) (H4)
      'Le Rêve'   ~ see *Lilium* 'Joy'
02   'Lennox' (H4)
02   *martagon* (IX) (H4)
93   — var. *album* (IX) (H4)
02   'Medaillon' (Ia) (H4)
02   'Novo Cento' (H4)
02   *pardalinum* (IX) (H4)
93   **Pink Perfection Group** (VIa) (H4)
93   *pumilum* (IX) (H4)
93   *regale* (IX) (H4)
02   'Sam' (VII) (H4)
      tenuifolium   ~ see *Lilium pumilum*
93   x *testaceum* (IX) (H4)

LIRIOPE (CONVALLARIACEAE)
      graminifolia hort. ~ see *Liriope muscari*
93   *muscari* (H4)
      platyphylla   ~ see *Liriope muscari*

MAIANTHEMUM (CONVALLARIACEAE)
      racemosum   ~ see *Smilacina racemosa*

MUSCARI (HYACINTHACEAE)
93 R *armeniacum* (H4)
93 R *aucheri* (H4)
93 R *azureum* (H4)
      chalusicum ~ see *Muscari pseudomuscari*
93 R *pseudomuscari* (H4)

NARCISSUS (AMARYLLIDACEAE)

(1)	Trumpet
(2)	Large-cupped
(3)	Small-cupped
(4)	Double
(5)	Triandrus
(6)	Cyclamineus
(7)	Jonquilla and Apodanthus
(8)	Tazetta
(9)	Poeticus
(10)	Bulbocodium
(11a)	Split-corona: Collar
(11b)	Split-corona: Papillon
(12)	Miscellaneous
(13)	Species

*Miniature and smaller daffodils are marked *.
See also **Hardy Rock Plants** and **Plants for the
Alpine House.***
01   'Aberfoyle' (2) (H4)   ~ *bright yellow
                    with a deep orange-red corona;
                    free-flowering and very early*
95   'Accent' (2) (H4)   ~ *a sturdy flower
                    with a wonderfully deep pink corona*

93 **'Actaea'** (9) (H4) *~ an old and reliable poeticus daffodil, fragrant and with a deep red rim*

96 **'April Tears'** (5) (H4) *~ a deep lemon-yellow daffodil of great charm, with several neatly formed pendent flowers per stem**

93 **'Arctic Gold'** (1) (H4) *~ a vigorous and free-flowering trumpet daffodil of the deepest golden yellow*

01 **'Arkle'** (1) (H4) *~ a deep yellow trumpet daffodil of immense size and vigour*

93 **'Armada'** (2) (H4) *~ a strong and vigorous plant with vivid yellow petals and orange corona*

94 R *asturiensis* (13) (H3-4) *~ miniature yellow trumpet daffodil, hugging the ground; requiring acid soil and flowering from late winter to early spring**

95 **'Avalanche'** (8) (H3) *~ a plant of amazing vigour, with strong stems bearing up to a dozen beautifully formed yellow and white flowers*

98 **'Badbury Rings'** (3) (H4) *~ a wonderful yellow small-cupped daffodil with an orange rim; a leader on the show bench as well as a good garden plant*

93 **'Bantam'** (2) (H4) *~ a bright and perky intermediate-sized daffodil with golden petals and an orange corona often sharply rimmed with red **

98 **'Barnum'** (1) (H4) *~ large and robust; deep golden yellow with very wide petals; a long-lasting flower of great substance and proud stance*

93 **'Bawnboy'** (1) (H4) *~ a deep yellow trumpet daffodil; strong-growing and reliable*

01 **'Ben Hee'** (2) (H4) *~ a pristine white daffodil of beautiful form*

93 **'Biscayne'** (1) (H4) *~ a most reliable and vigorous yellow trumpet daffodil of excellent pose*

01 **'Border Beauty'** (2) (H4) *~ a very large and showy bright red and yellow flower of excellent pose*

02 **'Boslowick'** (11a) (H4) *~ an excellent, early season flower with spreading orange corona*

01 **'Boulder Bay'** (2) (H4) *~ a large yellow flower with trumpet-like corona and flared orange rim; distinct*

93 **'Brabazon'** (1) (H4) *~ a deep golden yellow trumpet daffodil; tall, strong and free-flowering*

98 **'Bram Warnaar'** (1) (H4) *~ a sturdy and long-lasting yellow flower with a bold trumpet*

93 **'Bravoure'** (1) (H4) *~ an extremely large flower with wonderful contrast between white petals and bold yellow trumpet*

95 **'Broomhill'** (2) (H4) *~ sparkling white; wonderfully reliable for both show and garden*

98 **'Bryanston'** (2) (H4) *~ a tall, strong and early-flowering plant of "look you in the eye" pose, with well formed and long-lasting flowers of deep golden yellow*

94 R *bulbocodium* (13) (H3-4) *~ hoop petticoat; miniature yellow flowers with narrow petals and large corona; best in a wet position on acid soil**

98 **'Bunting'** (7) (H4) *~ fragrant, and one of the brightest of the orange and yellow jonquils*

95 **'Camelot'** (2) (H4) *~ large round mid-yellow flower; robust and vigorous*

96 **'Cantabile'** (9) (H4) *~ the poeticus daffodil by which all others are judged; reliable and well-formed*

98 **'Carib Gipsy'** (2) (H4) *~ strong and vigorous plant; pale yellow petals and a well-contrasted white corona with broad golden yellow rim*

95 **'Carlton'** (2) (H4) *~ famously reliable for large-scale planting*

95 **'Ceylon'** (2) (H4) *~ one of the best orange and yellow daffodils for sun resistance and a striking pose*

93 **'Charity May'** (6) (H4) *~ a free-flowering daffodil of shy pose and swept-back petals**

93 **'Charter'** (2) (H4) *~ a large flower with petals and corona rim of luminous lemon-yellow*

95 **'Cheerfulness'** (4) (H4) ~ *sturdy and fragrant, with several neat semi-double flowers per stem*

99 **'Chesterton'** (9) (H4) ~ *a* poeticus *daffodil of good foliage, form and colour which stands up well to the weather*

96 **'Chit Chat'** (7) (H4) ~ *dainty and bright yellow, with two to four nicely formed round flowers per stem**

01 **'Chromacolor'** (2) (H4) ~ *eye-catching large flower with pure white petals and bright pink trumpet-shaped corona*

98 **'Crackington'** (4) (H4) ~ *reliable orange and yellow double daffodil of rapid increase; standing well in all weathers*

93 R *cyclamineus* (13) (H4) ~ *miniature yellow trumpet daffodil with strongly reflexed petals; flowering in early spring in a wet position on acid soil; very durable**

95 **'Daydream'** (2) (H3) ~ *a beautifully formed flower with the petals bright lemon-yellow and the corona gradually turning white*

01 **'Desdemona'** (2) (H4) ~ *a tall and reliable all-white daffodil*

02 **'Dickcissel'** (7) (H4) ~ *very free flowering with heads held well above the foliage; good for show, flower arranging and cutting as well as the garden*

99 **'Dispatch Box'** (1) (H4) ~ *an out-standing yellow trumpet daffodil; free-flowering, with the blooms held well above the foliage*

01 **'Doctor Hugh'** (3) (H4) ~ *a large bold flower of great impact, with pure white petals and bright orange cup; a leading show variety too*

93 **'Double Event'** (4) (H4) ~ *well formed double daffodil with yellow and white petals intermingled*

93 **'Dove Wings'** (6) (H4) ~ *sister seedling to 'Charity May', with all the same qualities but dressed in yellow and white**

02 **'Drumlin'** (1) (H4) ~ *large and strong, with yellow and white flowers of great impact over a long period*

95 **'Dutch Master'** (1) (H4) ~ *a very large traditional yellow trumpet of great vigour*

01 **'Eaton Song'** (12) (H4) ~ *a short-stemmed, twin-headed, yellow and orange daffodil with a very long flowering period*

93 **'Empress of Ireland'** (1) (H4) ~ *stately and imposing white daffodil with a beautifully flanged trumpet*

01 **'Exception'** (1) (H4) ~ *a sturdy trumpet daffodil of deep golden yellow; free-flowering in early spring*

98 **'Falconet'** (8) (H4) ~ *multi-headed, brightly coloured and fragrant*

93 **'February Gold'** (6) (H4) ~ *distinct profile with swept-back petals and long trumpet; ideal for naturalising*

93 **'Feeling Lucky'** (2) (H4) ~ *a colourful flower of rapid increase*

95 **'Foundling'** (6) (H4) ~ *a sturdy and prolific plant of intermediate size with reflexed white petals and a neat corona of bright pink**

95 **'Gay Kybo'** (4) (H4) ~ *a large and imposing double daffodil of neat form on a strong stem*

95 **'Geranium'** (8) (H4) ~ *multi-headed, reliable and fragrant; and good for cutting*

98 **'Gin and Lime'** (1) (H4) ~ *lime-yellow trumpet daffodil of immense size and vigour*

98 **'Glenfarclas'** (1) (H4) ~ *one of the few orange trumpet daffodils; very bright and cheerful*

95 **'Gold Convention'** (2) (H4) ~ *smooth flower of beautiful form and deepest yellow; strong constitution and good pose*

95 **'Golden Aura'** (2) (H4) ~ *well rounded flowers of perfect form and polished golden yellow*

93 **'Golden Dawn'** (8) (H3) ~ *reliable tazetta daffodil of attractive colouring; several scented flowers per stem*

95 **'Golden Jewel'** (2) (H4) ~ *deep golden yellow flower with jewel-smooth texture; excellent stem and pose*

93 **'Golden Rapture'** (1) (H4) ~ *a massive golden yellow trumpet daffodil of great impact*

95 **'Golden Vale'** (1) (H4) *~ a sturdy yellow trumpet daffodil with broad and spreading petals*

01 **'Goldfinger'** (1) (H4) *~ a deep yellow trumpet daffodil; free-flowering, long-lasting and consistent*

98 **'Grasmere'** (1) (H4) *~ a large and formal yellow flower with neatly frilled trumpet*

01 **'Hambledon'** (2) (H4) *~ a strong and vigorous plant, with the corona of the large lemon-yellow flower becoming a subtle buff pink*

95 **'Hawera'** (5) (H4) *~ a vigorous and free-flowering* triandrus *daffodil with a number of neatly nodding flowers per stem*

01 **'High Society'** (2) (H4) *~ lives up to its name; beautiful white flowers with pink-rimmed yellow corona*

99 **'Highfield Beauty'** (8) (H4) *~ tall weather-resistant flowers of strong constitution and very good pose*

02 **'Hoopoe'** (8) (H4) *~ durable yellow and orange flowers produced in great quantity over a long period*

93 **'Ice Follies'** (2) (H4) *~ creamy white flowers, frilled and highly ornate; robust and reliable in all climates; ideal for naturalising*

01 **'Ice Wings'** (5) (H4) *~ small clusters of nodding pure white flowers on 9-inch stems; vigorous and reliable*

01 **'Intrigue'** (7) (H4) *~ hauntingly luminous yellow flowers, with the small corona becoming white*

93 **'Irish Minstrel'** (2) (H4) *~ a big round flower with white petals and contrasting deep yellow cup; strong and vigorous*

95 **'Itzim'** (6) (H4) *~ a bright little flower with swept-back petals and long red trumpet*

95 **'Jack Snipe'** (6) (H4) *~ a cyclamineus daffodil with creamy white petals typically reflexed and the cylindrical corona in vividly contrasting yellow*

93 **'Jenny'** (6) (H4) *~ the white sibling of 'Charity May' and 'Dove Wings'*

95 **'Jetfire'** (6) (H4) *~ a cyclamineus daffodil with orange corona; vigorous and free-flowering; early season*

94 R ***jonquilla*** (13) (H4) *~ jonquil; up to six strongly scented yellow flowers on a round stem*

95 **'Jumblie'** (12) (H4) *~ two to three orange and yellow flowers per stem with reflexed petals; a small neat plant ideal for the rock garden*

98 **'Kaydee'** (6) (H4) *~ sparkling white reflexed petals and a lightly flared trumpet of vivid pink*

01 **'King's Grove'** (1) (H4) *~ a bold flower with yellow petals and orange trumpet; tall and of excellent pose*

93 **'Kingscourt'** (1) (H4) *~ a mid-yellow trumpet daffodil of classic form and smoothest texture*

93 **'Larkwhistle'** (6) (H4) *~ reliable all-yellow* cyclamineus *daffodil*

02 **'Lemon Drops'** (5) (H4) *~ very free flowering, over a long period*

00 **'Lingerie'** (4) (H4) *~ a floriferous double daffodil on a strong stem, holding its head up well; petals of lemon-yellow and white intermingled*

01 **'Little Beauty'** (1) (H4) *~ well-named dwarf daffodil with lovely contrast between the white petals and yellow trumpet*

97 **'Little Gem'** (1) (H4) *~ a well-formed miniature trumpet daffodil of great vigour; ideal for the rock garden*

93 **'Loch Owskeich'** (2) (H4) *~ a sturdy and rather short-stemmed plant, with robust orange and yellow flowers holding their colour well in full sun*

02 **'Manly'** (4) (H4) *~ a large double flower of great impact, standing up well on a strong stem*

01 **'Menehay'** (11a) (H4) *~ excellent example in orange and yellow of the modern split-corona daffodil*

93 **'Merlin'** (3) (H4) *~ petals of purest white and the brilliant yellow corona rimmed with true red*

minimus hort. *~ see Narcissus asturiensis*

98 **'Minnow'** (8) (H3) *~ beautifully formed miniature flowers, better for a milder climate*

94 R   *minor* (13) (H4) ~ *small yellow trumpet daffodil with forward-facing petals**

01   **'Mission Bells'** (5) (H4)   ~ *several icy-white bell-like flowers per stem; ideal* for smaller gardens*

95   **'Misty Glen'** (2) (H4) ~ *an impeccably formed white flower enhanced by the deep green in the eye of the corona*

01   **'Mite'** (6) (H4)   ~ *strongly swept-back petals on a light-weight little flower ideal for the rock garden**

01   *moschatus* (13) (H4)   ~ *a creamy white trumpet daffodil of medium size with forward-facing petals**

95   **'Mount Hood'** (1) (H4)   ~ *a most reliable white trumpet daffodil*

  'Nimrod'   ~ *see* 'Carlton'

99   **'Notre Dame'** (2) (H4)   ~ *floriferous and late-season, with sun-resistant pink rim*

93   *obvallaris* (13) (H4)   ~ *the Tenby daffodil; sturdy yellow trumpet daffodil of medium size with spreading petals; early spring flowering**

93   **'Ormeau'** (2) (H4)   ~ *a beautifully smooth flower, greenish yellow and well proportioned*

98   **'Oryx'** (7) (H4)   ~ *three or four perfectly formed light yellow flowers on each tall stem*

93   **'Papua'** (4) (H4) ~ *a strong all-yellow double daffodil which stands well in the garden*

93   **'Passionale'** (2) (H4)   ~ *a refined daffodil of great vigour, with pastel-pink corona*

95   **'Peeping Tom'** (6) (H4)   ~ *a deep golden yellow trumpet daffodil, strong-growing and reliable, with slightly reflexed and nicely twisted petals*

01   **'Pimpernel'** (2) (H4)   ~ *a large flower with yellow petals and a small corona of sun-resistant orange*

93   **'Pinza'** (2) (H4)   ~ *a colourful sun-resistant flower of excellent pose and great impact*

01   **'Pipit'** (7) (H4)   ~ *up to four neatly formed flowers of luminous lemon-yellow per stem*

96   **'Pixie's Sister'** (7) (H4)   ~ *a number of well-formed scented flowers gracefully held on a short stem; needs dry summer dormancy**

  poeticus **pheasant's eye**

   ~ see *Narcissus poeticus* var. *recurvus*

93   **— var. *recurvus*** (13) (H4)

   ~ *pheasant's eye; strongly scented flowers with pure white reflexed and twisted petals and a short green or yellow corona with crimson rim; flowering in late spring*

01   **'Precocious'** (2) (H4)   ~ *a distinctive white-petalled flower of great impact, with frilled corona of startling reddish pink*

94 R   *pseudonarcissus* (13) (H4) ~ *Lent lily; medium-size trumpet daffodil with down-ward-facing flowers, straw coloured forward-facing petals and a darker yellow corona with little flange*

  — subsp. *moschatus* ~ see *Narcissus moschatus*

01   **'Purbeck'** (3) (H4)   ~ *an immaculately formed flower, with white petals and a small orange-banded corona*

98   **'Quail'** (7) (H4)   ~ *a multi-headed jonquil of deep golden yellow; vigorous, free-flowering and fragrant**

01   **'Rainbow'** (2) (H4)   ~ *a reliable white flower with a well-defined rim of salmon pink; good for mass planting*

01   **'Rapture'** (6) (H4)   ~ *one of the most perfectly formed of all the golden yellow daffodils with swept-back petals**

93   **'Red Devon'** (2) (H4)   ~ *a very good orange and yellow flower of rounded form**

98   **'Reggae'** (6) (H4)   ~ *a dainty pink and white flower with fly-away petals; very free-flowering, with blooms held well above the foliage*

93   **'Rijnveld's Early Sensation'** (1) (H4)

   ~ *earliest to flower of all the larger daffodils; a strong and robust yellow trumpet with-standing the winter weather and lasting a long time in the garden*

95   **'Rippling Waters'** (5) (H4)   ~ *several pure white pendulous flowers per stem*

95   **'Romance'** (2) (H4)   ~ *a wonderfully strong round flower, with white petals and deep pink lobed corona*

93   **'Rugulosus'** (7) (H4)   ~ *a multi-headed and fragrant jonquil; very vigorous and strong growing; good for cutting*

93   **'Saint Keverne'** (2) (H4)   ~ *deep golden yellow daffodil; tall, straight and regimentally formal*

01 **'Salome'** (2) (H4) ~ *very consistent; with the corona opening yellow and turning to warm pink*

96 **'Segovia'** (3) (H4) ~ *a most attractive little flower in yellow and white; for the rock garden*

99 **'Serena Lodge'** (4) (H4) ~ *a long-lasting and showy double daffodil standing on strong stems*

02 **'Silent Valley'** (1) (H4) ~ *a strong plant with plenty of flowers both for show bench and garden*

98 **'Sir Winston Churchill'** (4) (H4) ~ *several scented double flowers per stem in orange and white*

98 **'Special Envoy'** (2) (H4) ~ *a sturdy and reliable all-yellow daffodil*

93 **'Spellbinder'** (1) (H4) ~ *an entrancing sulphur-yellow flower, with the trumpet turning white at maturity*

96 **'Sun Disc'** (7) (H4) ~ *flowers like gleaming little gold discs; ideal for the rock garden*

98 **'Surfside'** (6) (H4) ~ *an imposing yellow and white flower with beautifully reflexed petals*

93 **'Suzy'** (7) (H4) ~ *several fragrant yellow flowers per stem, with small coronas of bright orange*

93 **'Sweetness'** (7) (H4) ~ *wonderfully fragrant flowers shining like golden stars*

01 **'Swift Arrow'** (6) (H4) ~ *flower well named for its fly-away golden yellow petals and long trumpet*

95 **'Tahiti'** (4) (H4) ~ *sturdy and prolific double daffodil with neat orange and yellow flowers*

98 **'Tamar Fire'** (4) (H4) ~ *one of the brightest double daffodils in its colour range; standing well in the garden*

93 R **'Tête-à-tête'** (12) (H4) ~ *a magnificent free-flowering little daffodil for pots, rock garden or naturalising*

01 R **'Topolino'** (1) (H4) ~ *a very reliable plant for the rockery, with creamy white petals and a brightly contrasted yellow trumpet*

97 **'Toto'** (12) (H4) ~ *a graceful flower, with the narrow corona opening yellow and becoming white; of excellent increase*

01 **'Tracey'** (6) (H4) ~ *a charming little white daffodil with swept-back petals*

01 **'Trena'** (6) (H4) ~ *classic form combined with a wonderful contrast between white petals and yellow trumpet make this a much coveted variety*

95 **'Trevithian'** (7) (H4) ~ *two to three soft yellow fragrant flowers per stem*

94 R ***triandrus*** (13) (H3) ~ *Angel's tears; two to six small white pendent flowers per stem, with sharply reflexed petals; flowering on acid soil*

01 **'Tripartite'** (11a) (H4) ~ *several small mid-yellow flowers per stem with the corona neatly split; exceptionally free-flowering and vigorous*

98 **'Triple Crown'** (3) (H4) ~ *a golden yellow flower with deep red rim; free-flowering and quick to increase*

95 **'Tuesday's Child'** (5) (H4) ~ *one to three yellow and white weather-resistant flowers per stem, standing up well in the flower border*

98 **'Tyrone Gold'** (1) (H4) ~ *large deep golden trumpet daffodil; a strong plant with 'look you in the eye' pose*

93 **'Ulster Prince'** (1) (H4) ~ *a golden yellow flower with large pointed petals and bold trumpet*

02 **'Unique'** (4) (H4) ~ *a robust double flower holding its colour well and flowering fairly early in the season*

01 **'Vernal Prince'** (3) (H4) ~ *a vigorous and beautiful daffodil, with smooth white petals and deep greenish-lemon cup*

93 **'Verona'** (3) (H4) ~ *completely round, all-white flower with a small disc-like corona*

93 **'Vigil'** (1) (H4) ~ *a strong and vigorous trumpet daffodil of distinctively angular form in icy white*

95 **'Viking'** (1) (H4) ~ *a trumpet daffodil of beautiful form in deep golden yellow*

93 **'Vulcan'** (2) (H4) ~ *a tall flower with sun-resistant bright orange corona*

01 **'Wheal Coates'** (7) (H4) ~ *a distinctive orange and yellow flower with a very long flowering season*

93   **'White Lion'** (4) (H4)   *~ a many-petalled double daffodil of nice form, well posed on a strong stem*

98   **'Willy Dunlop'** (2) (H4)   *~ a flower of great size and substance with a good contrast between pure white petals and deep yellow corona*

95   **'Yellow Cheerfulness'** (4) (H4)   *~ an all-yellow sport of 'Cheerfulness', with the same admirable attributes*

NERINE (AMARYLLIDACEAE)
93   *bowdenii* (H3-4)
98   **'Zeal Giant'** (H3-4)

OPHIOPOGON (CONVALLARIACEAE)
    graminifolius   ~ see *Liriope muscari*

ORNITHOGALUM (HYACINTHACEAE)
93   *nutans* (H4)

OXALIS (OXALIDACEAE)
93 R   *adenophylla* (H4)
93 R   *enneaphylla* (H4)
93 R   **'Ione Hecker'** (H4)

PARADISEA (ASPHODELACEAE)
93 R   *liliastrum* (H4)

PSEUDOMUSCARI (HYACINTHACEAE)
    azureum   ~ see *Muscari azureum*

SCHIZOSTYLIS (IRIDACEAE)
    coccinea **'Gigantea'** ~ see *Schizostylis coccinea* 'Major'
    — **'Grandiflora'** ~ see *Schizostylis coccinea* 'Major'
93   — **'Jennifer'** (H4)
93   — **'Major'** (H4)
93   — **'Sunrise'** (H4)
    — **'Sunset'**   ~ see *Schizostylis coccinea* 'Sunrise'

SCILLA (HYACINTHACEAE)
93 R   *bifolia* (H4)
93 R   *mischtschenkoana* **'Tubergeniana'** (H4)
93 R   *siberica* (H4)

SMILACINA (CONVALLARIACEAE)
93   *racemosa* (H4)   *~ previously listed as* Maianthemum racemosum

TRILLIUM (TRILLIACEAE)
93 R   *chloropetalum* var. *giganteum* (H4)
    — var. *rubrum*   ~ see *Trillium chloropetalum* var. *giganteum*
93 R   *erectum* (H4)
93 R   *grandiflorum* (H4)
93 R   — **'Flore Pleno'** (d) (H4)
93 R   *luteum* (H4)
93 R   *rivale* (H3)
    sessile var. *luteum*   ~ see *Trillium luteum*
    — **'Rubrum'**   ~ see *Trillium chloropetalum* var. *giganteum*

TULIPA (LILIACEAE)

(1)	Single Early Group
(2)	Double Early Group
(3)	Triumph Group
(4)	Darwinhybrid Group
(5)	Single Late Group (including Darwin Group and Cottage Group)
(6)	Lily-flowered Group
(7)	Fringed Group
(8)	Viridiflora Group
(9)	Rembrandt Group
(10)	Parrot Group
(11)	Double Late Group
(12)	Kaufmanniana Group
(13)	Fosteriana Group
(14)	Greigii Group
(15)	Miscellaneous

97   **'Addis'** (14) (H4)
93   **'Alfred Cortot'** (12) (H4)
97   **'Ali Baba'** (14) (H4)
97   *altaica* (15) (H4)
93   **'Ancilla'** (12) (H4)
99   **'Angélique'** (11) (H4)
95   **'Antonio Moro'** (3) (H4)
93   **'Apeldoorn's Elite'** (4) (H4)
99   **'Apricot Beauty'** (1) (H4)
93   **'Apricot Parrot'** (10) (H4)
93   **'Aristocrat'** (5) (H4)
97   **'Arma'** (7) (H4)
95   **'Artist'** (8) (H4)
95   **'Astarte'** (3) (H4)
93 R   *aucheriana* (15) (H4)
95   **'Baby Doll'** (2) (H4)
    bakeri ~ see *Tulipa saxatilis* (Bakeri Group)
93   **'Ballade'** (6) (H4)
95   **'Ballerina'** (6) (H4)
99   **'Barcelona'** (3) (H4)
    batalinii   ~ see *Tulipa linifolia* Batalinii Group

97	'Bella Vista' (14) (H4)
97	'Ben van Zanten' (3) (H4)
93	'Big Chief' (4) (H4)
95	'Black Diamond' (5) (H4)
95	'Black Parrot' (10) (H4)
99	'Blue Bell' (3) (H4)
95	'Blue Heron' (7) (H4)
	'Bright Gem' ~ see *Tulipa linifolia*
	(Batalinii Group) 'Bright Gem'
97	'Buttercup' (14) (H4)
95	'Calgary' (3) (H4)
97	'Calypso' (14) (H4)
97	'Candela' (13) (H4)
93	'Capri' (4) (H4)
99	'Carnaval de Nice' (11/v) (H4)
93	'China Lady' (14) (H4)
95	'China Pink' (6) (H4)
95	'China Town' (8) (H4)
93 R	*clusiana* var. *chrysantha* (15) (H4)
99	— 'Cynthia' (15) (H4)
95	'Companion' (3) (H4)
93	'Corsage' (14) (H4)
95	'Cruquius' (3) (H4)
99	'Crystal Beauty' (7) (H4)
97	'Czaar Peter' (H4)
97	'Daydream' (4) (H4)
93	'Demeter' (3) (H4)
95	'Don Quichotte' (3) (H4)
97	'Donald Duck' (14) (H4)
93	'Donna Bella' (14) (H4)
93	'Dover' (4) (H4)
95	'Dreamland' (5) (H4)
95	'Dynamite' (3) (H4)
93	'Early Harvest' (12) (H4)
97	'Early Star' (14) (H4)
97	'Easter Moon' (13) (H4)
97	'Easter Surprise' (14) (H4)
93	'Engadin' (14) (H4)
99	'Esperanto' (8/v) (H4)
99	'Etude' (3) (H4)
95	'Fancy Frills' (7) (H4)
93	'Fantasy' (10) (H4)
93	'Fidelio' (3) (H4)
97	'Fire Queen' (3) (H4)
93	'First Lady' (3) (H4)
99	'Flaming Youth' (13) (H4)
99	'Fringed Beauty' (7) (H4)
99	'Fringed Elegance' (7) (H4)
99	'Friso' (3) (H4)
97	'Garden Party' (3) (H4)
99	'Gerbrand Kieft' (11) (H4)
97	'Glück' (12) (H4)
99	'Grand Prestige' (14) (H4)
95	'Grand Style' (5) (H4)
93	'Halcro' (5) (H4)
95	'Hamilton' (7) (H4)
95	'Heart's Desire' (3) (H4)
99	'Holberg' (3) (H4)
93	'Hollands Glorie' (4) (H4)
97	'Ivory Floradale' (4) (H4)
93	'Jeantine' (12) (H4)
93	'Jewel of Spring' (4) (H4)
97	'Juan' (13) (H4)
97	'Julius Caesar' (14) (H4)
93	'Keizerskroon' (1) (H4)
93	'Kingsblood' (5) (H4)
93	*kolpakowskiana* (15) (H4)
93	'Koningin Wilhelmina' (4) (H4)
95	'Lambada' (7) (H4)
93	'Landseadel's Supreme' (5) (H4)
	'Lilac Wonder' ~ see *Tulipa saxatilis*
	(Bakeri Group) 'Lilac Wonder'
99	'Lily Schreyer' (3) (H4)
93 R	*linifolia* (15) (H4)
93 R	— **Batalinii Group** (15) (H4)
95 R	—— 'Bright Gem' (15) (H4)
97	'Little Beauty' (15) (H4)
97	'Longfellow' (14) (H4)
97	'Marina' (14) (H4)
97	'Marit' (4) (H4)
93	'Marjolein' (6) (H4)
93	'Maureen' (5) (H4)
99	'Maywonder' (11) (H4)
95	'Mieke Bos' (3) (H4)
93	'Mirella' (3) (H4)
93	'Monte Carlo' (2/d) (H4)
99	'Monte Rosa' (3) (H4)
93	'Most Miles' (3) (H4)
93	'Mrs John T. Scheepers' (5) (H4)
99	'Musical' (3) (H4)
93	'My Lady' (4) (H4)
97	'Odia' (14) (H4)
99	'Ollioules' (4) (H4)
97	'Olympic Flame' (4) (H4)
93	'Orange Bouquet' (3) (H4)
97	'Orange Emperor' (13) (H4)
97	'Orange Princess' (11) (H4)
	'Orange Sun'
	~ see *Tulipa* 'Oranjezon'
95	'Orange Surprise' (3) (H4)
93	'Oranje Nassau' (2) (H4)
95	'Oranjezon' (4) (H4)
97	'Oratorio' (14) (H4)
97	'Oriental Beauty' (14) (H4)
93	'Oriental Splendour' (14) (H4)
99	'Orleans' (3) (H4)

99	*orphanidea* **Whittallii Group** (15) (H4)
93	**'Oxford'** (4) (H4)
95	**'Parabole'** (7) (H4)
93	**'Parade'** (4) (H4)
97	**'Perfectionist'** (14) (H4)
95	**'Picture'** (5) (H4)
97	**'Pink Impression'** (4) (H4)
97	**'Pink Sensation'** (14) (H4)
93	**'Plaisir'** (14) (H4)
93	*praestans* **'Fusilier'** (15) (H4)
93	**'President Kennedy'** (4) (H4)
95	**'Prince Charles'** (3) (H4)
95	**'Princess Victoria'** (3) (H4)
97	**'Princesse Charmante'** (14) (H4)
97	**'Prins Carnaval'** (1) (H4)
93	**'Prinses Irene'** (3) (H4)
97	**'Purissima'** (13) (H4)
95	**'Queen of Bartigons'** (5) (H4)
95	**'Queen of Sheba'** (6) (H4)
93	**'Red Georgette'** (5) (H4)
97	**'Red Impression'** [PBR] (4) (H4)
97	**'Red Paradise'** (1) (H4)
93	**'Red Riding Hood'** (14) (H4)
95	**'Red Shine'** (6) (H4)
93	**'Red Surprise'** (14) (H4)
95	**'Red Wing'** (7) (H4)
97	**'Rosanna'** (14) (H4)
95	*saxatilis* **(Bakeri Group) 'Lilac Wonder'** (15) (H4)
99	**'Sevilla'** (3) (H4)
93	**'Showwinner'** (12) (H4)
99	**'Smyrna'** (14) (H4)
93	**'Sorbet'** (5) (H4)
93	*sprengeri* (15) (H4)
93	**'Spring Green'** (8) (H4)
93	**'Stockholm'** (2) (H4)
93	**'Stresa'** (12) (H4)

99	**'Strong Gold'** (3) (H4)
93	**'Sweet Harmony'** (5) (H4)
99	**'Synaeda King'** (6) (H4)
93 R	*tarda* (15) (H4)
99	**'Ted Turner'** (H4)
95	**'Telecom'** (3) (H4)
93	**'Temple of Beauty'** (5) (H4)
99	**'Tender Beauty'** (4) (H4)
93	**'Toronto'** (14) (H4)
97	**'Toulon'** (13) (H4)
97	**'Trinket'** (14) (H4)
93 R	*turkestanica* (15) (H4)
95	**'Union Jack'** (5) (H4)
93 R	*urumiensis* (15) (H4)
99	**'Valentine'** (3) (H4)
99	**'Vivex'** (4) (H4)
97	*vvedenskyi* **'Tangerine Beauty'** (15) (H4)
95	**'West Point'** (6) (H4)
	'White Emperor' ~ see *Tulipa* 'Purissima'
95	**'White Triumphator'** (6) (H4)
	whittallii ~ see *Tulipa orphanidea* Whittallii Group
95	**'Wildhof'** (3) (H4)
95	**'Wirosa'** (11) (H4)
99	**'World Expression'** (5) (H4)
97	**'Yellow Dover'** (4) (H4)
97	**'Yellow Purissima'** (13) (H4)
93	**'Zampa'** (14) (H4)

UVULARIA (CONVALLARIACEAE)
93 R	*grandiflora* (H4)

ZANTEDESCHIA (ARACEAE)
93	*aethiopica* (H3)
97	— **'Crowborough'** (H3)
93	— **'Green Goddess'** (H3)

Ferns

ADIANTUM (ADIANTACEAE)
97   *aleuticum* (H4)
97 R — **'Subpumilum'** (H4)   *~ previously listed as* A. aleuticum *var.* subpumilum
   capillus-veneris **'Mairisii'**   *~ see Adiantum × mairisii*
97   × *mairisii* (H3)   *~ sterile, needs vegetative propagation*
93   *pedatum* (H4)
   — **var.** *aleuticum*   *~ see Adiantum aleuticum*
   — **var.** *subpumilum*   *~ see Adiantum aleuticum* 'Subpumilum'
93   *venustum* (H4)

ASPLENIUM (ASPLENIACEAE)
93   *scolopendrium* (H4)
97   — **'Crispum Bolton's Nobile'** (H4)
97 R — **'Kaye's Lacerated'** (H4)
   ~ comes true from spores
97   *trichomanes* (H4)

ATHYRIUM (WOODSIACEAE)
93   *filix-femina* (H4)
97   — **'Frizelliae'** (H4)
97   — **'Vernoniae'** (H4)
   goeringianum **'Pictum'**
   ~ see Athyrium niponicum var. pictum
   niponicum **f.** *metallicum*
   ~ see Athyrium niponicum var. pictum
93 G — **var.** *pictum* (H3)   *~ also valued for cultivation under glass*
97   *otophorum* (H4)

BLECHNUM (BLECHNACEAE)
97   *chilense* (H3)   *~ often found under the name* B. tabulare
   magellanicum misapplied
   ~ see Blechnum chilense
97 R *penna-marina* (H4)
93   *spicant* (H4)
   tabulare misapplied
   ~ see Blechnum chilense

CYRTOMIUM (DRYOPTERIDACEAE)
93 G *falcatum* (H3)   *~ min. 2C*
97   *fortunei* (H4)

DAVALLIA (DAVALLIACEAE)
93 G *mariesii* (H3)   *~ min. 2C*

DICKSONIA (DICKSONIACEAE)
93 G *antarctica* (H3)
97 G *fibrosa* (H3)

DRYOPTERIS (DRYOPTERIDACEAE)
93   *affinis* (H4)
97   — **'Crispa Gracilis'** (H4)
   ~ including cultivated stock of D. *'Crispa Congesta', which is almost certainly the same*
97   — **'Cristata'** (H4)
97   — **'Cristata Angustata'** (H4)
   — **'Cristata The King'**
   ~ see Dryopteris affinis 'Cristata'
97   — **'Polydactyla Mapplebeck'** (H4)
   atrata hort.   *~ see Dryopteris cycadina*
   austriaca hort.
   ~ see Dryopteris dilatata
97   *cycadina* (H4)
97   *dilatata* (H4)
97   — **'Crispa Whiteside'** (H4)
97   — **'Lepidota Cristata'** (H4)
93   *erythrosora* (H4)
93   — **var.** *prolifera* (H4)   *~ previously listed as Dryopteris erythrosora* 'Prolifera'
93   *filix-mas* (H4)
   — **'Crispa Congesta'**
   ~ see Dryopteris affinis 'Crispa Gracilis'
97   — **'Cristata'** (H4)
97   — **'Grandiceps Wills'** (H4)
   hirtipes   *~ see Dryopteris cycadina*
   pseudomas   *~ see Dryopteris affinis*
93   *wallichiana* (H4)   *~ there is a lot of variation within this species, depending upon the country of origin*

GYMNOCARPIUM (WOODSIACEAE)
93 R *dryopteris* (H4)
97   — **'Plumosum'** (H4)
   ~ comes true from spores

MATTEUCCIA (WOODSIACEAE)
93   *struthiopteris* (H4)

ONOCLEA (WOODSIACEAE)
93   *sensibilis* (H4)

OSMUNDA (OSMUNDACEAE)
97   *cinnamomea* (H4)
97   *claytoniana* (H4)
93   *regalis* (H4)
97   — **'Cristata'** (H4)

PHANEROPHLEBIA (DRYOPTERIDACEAE)
   falcata   ~ see *Cyrtomium falcatum*
   fortunei   ~ see *Cyrtomium fortunei*

PHYLLITIS (ASPLENIACEAE)
   scolopendrium   ~ see *Asplenium scolopendrium*

POLYPODIUM (POLYPODIACEAE)
97   *cambricum* **'Cambricum'** (H4)
97   — **'Grandiceps Fox' (Cristatum Group)** (H4)
97   — **'Whilharris'** (H4)

97   *glycyrrhiza* **'Longicaudatum'** (H4)
97   *interjectum* **'Cornubiense'** (H4)

POLYSTICHUM (DRYOPTERIDACEAE)
93   *aculeatum* (H4)
   falcatum   ~ see *Cyrtomium falcatum*
   fortunei   ~ see *Cyrtomium fortunei*
97   *munitum* (H4)
97   *polyblepharum* (H4)
93   *setiferum* (H4)
97   — **'Divisilobum Densum'** (H4)
97   — **'Divisilobum Iveryanum'** (H4)
     ~ not available spore grown
97   — **'Pulcherrimum Bevis'** (H4)
97   *tsussimense* (H4)

WOODSIA (WOODSIACEAE)
97   *polystichoides* (H4)

WOODWARDIA (BLECHNACEAE)
93   *radicans* (H3)   ~ min. 2C

HARDY ROCK PLANTS

For plants for the alpine house, see **Plants for Glass**.
For dwarf conifers, see **Hardy Trees, Shrubs, Climbers & Bamboos**.

ACAENA (ROSACEAE)
93 H *microphylla* (H4)

ACHILLEA (ASTERACEAE)
93 H *ageratifolia* (H4)
93 H x *lewisii* 'King Edward' (H4)
93 H *tomentosa* (H4)

ACONITUM (RANUNCULACEAE)
    hyemale   ~ see *Eranthis hyemalis*

ADIANTUM (ADIANTACEAE)
97 F *aleuticum* 'Subpumilum' (H4)
            ~ *previously listed as* A.
            aleuticum *var.* subpumilum
    pedatum var. *subpumilum*
            ~ see *Adiantum aleuticum*
            'Subpumilum'

AETHIONEMA (BRASSICACEAE)
93 T *grandiflorum* (H4)
93 T — Pulchellum Group (H4)
93 T 'Warley Rose' (H4)

ALCHEMILLA (ROSACEAE)
93 H *erythropoda* (H4)

ALLIUM (ALLIACEAE)
    azureum   ~ see *Allium caeruleum*
    beesianum hort.   ~ see *Allium cyaneum*
93 B *caeruleum* (H4)
    — *azureum*   ~ see *Allium caeruleum*
02 B *caesium* (H4)
93 B *carinatum* subsp. *pulchellum*
            (H4)
02 B — — f. *album* (H4)
93 B *cernuum* 'Hidcote' (H4)
    — 'Major'
            ~ see *Allium cernuum* 'Hidcote'
    cirrhosum   ~ see *Allium carinatum*
            subsp. *pulchellum*

93 B *cyaneum* (H4)
93 B *flavum* (H4)
93 B *insubricum* (H4)   ~ *most plants sold*
            as A. narcissiflorum *are*
            this species
93 B *karataviense* (H3)
93 B *moly* 'Jeannine' (H4)
    murrayanum misapplied
            ~ see *Allium unifolium*
    narcissiflorum hort.
            ~ see *Allium insubricum*
93 B *oreophilum* 'Zwanenburg' (H4)
    ostrowskianum 'Zwanenburg'
            ~ see *Allium oreophilum*
            'Zwanenburg'
    pulchellum   ~ see *Allium carinatum*
            subsp. *pulchellum*
02 B *thunbergii* (H4)
02 B *unifolium* (H4)

ALYSSUM (BRASSICACEAE)
    saxatile   ~ see *Aurinia saxatilis*
    — 'Citrinum'
            ~ see *Aurinia saxatilis* 'Citrina'
93 T *spinosum* 'Roseum' (H4)

ANDROMEDA (ERICACEAE)
93 T *polifolia* 'Compacta' (H4)
93 T — 'Compacta Alba' (H4)
93 T — 'Macrophylla' (H4)

ANDROSACE (PRIMULACEAE)
    carnea var. *halleri*   ~ see *Androsace*
            carnea subsp. *rosea*
93 H — subsp. *laggeri* (H4)
93 H — subsp. *rosea* (H4)
    halleri   ~ see *Androsace carnea*
            subsp. *rosea*
93 H *lanuginosa* (H4)
    mucronifolia hort.
            ~ see *Androsace sempervivoides*

primuloides
   ~ see *Androsace studiosorum*
sarmentosa misapplied
   ~ see *Androsace studiosorum*
— var. *yunnanensis* misapplied
   ~ see *Androsace studiosorum*
93 H **sempervivoides** (H4)
93 H **studiosorum** (H4)
   ~ awarded as A. sarmentosa,
   a misapplied name

ANEMONE (RANUNCULACEAE)
93 H ***apennina*** (H4)
93 H ***blanda*** (H4)
93 H **— 'Radar'** (H4)
93 H **— var. *rosea*** (H4)
93 H **— 'White Splendour'** (H4)
  hepatica ~ see *Hepatica nobilis*
97 H **x *lipsiensis* 'Pallida'** (H4)
93 H ***nemorosa*** (H4)
93 H **— 'Allenii'** (H4)
93 H **— 'Robinsoniana'** (H4)
93 H **— 'Vestal'** (d) (H4)
97 H **— 'Virescens'** (H4)
  pulsatilla ~ see *Pulsatilla vulgaris*
93 H ***ranunculoides*** (H4)
  sulphurea ~ see *Pulsatilla alpina*
   subsp. *apiifolia*

ANTENNARIA (ASTERACEAE)
  dioica* var. *rosea
   ~ see *Antennaria rosea*
93 H ***rosea*** (H4)

ANTHEMIS (ASTERACEAE)
93 H ***punctata* subsp. *cupaniana*** (H3-4)

ANTHERICUM (ANTHERICACEAE)
  algeriense ~ see *Anthericum liliago*
   var. *major*
93 B ***liliago* var. *major*** (H4)

ANTHYLLIS (PAPILIONACEAE)
93 H ***montana* 'Rubra'** (H4)

AQUILEGIA (RANUNCULACEAE)
  akitensis hort.
   ~ see *Aquilegia flabellata* var. *pumila*
93 H ***bertolonii*** (H4)
93 H ***flabellata*** (H4)
  — 'Nana Alba'
   ~ see *Aquilegia flabellata*
   var. *pumila* f. *alba*

93 H **— var. *pumila*** (H4)
93 H **— — f. *alba*** (H4)
  japonica ~ see *Aquilegia flabellata*
   var. *pumila*

ARABIS (BRASSICACEAE)
93 H ***alpina* subsp. *caucasica* 'Flore Pleno'**
   (d) (H4)
  ***caucasica* 'Plena'**
   ~ see *Arabis alpina*
   subsp. *caucasica* 'Flore Pleno'
  ***ferdinandi-coburgi* 'Variegata'**
   ~ see *Arabis procurrens* 'Variegata'
93 H ***procurrens* 'Variegata'** (v) (H4)
   ~ probably correctly treated
   as a form of A. x suendermannii

ARENARIA (CARYOPHYLLACEAE)
93 H ***montana*** (H4)

ARISAEMA (ARACEAE)
93 B ***candidissimum*** (H4)

ARMERIA (PLUMBAGINACEAE)
  caespitosa
   ~ see *Armeria juniperifolia*
  — 'Bevan's Variety'
   ~ see *Armeria juniperifolia*
   'Bevan's Variety'
93 H ***juniperifolia*** (H4)
93 H **— 'Bevan's Variety'** (H4)
93 H ***maritima* 'Vindictive'** (H4)

ARTEMISIA (ASTERACEAE)
93 H ***frigida*** (H3-4)
93 H ***schmidtiana* 'Nana'** (H4)

ASPERULA (RUBIACEAE)
93 H ***arcadiensis*** (H3) ~ widely grown as
   A. suberosa, *another quite*
   distinct species
  suberosa hort.
   ~ see *Asperula arcadiensis*

ASPLENIUM (ASPLENIACEAE)
97 F ***scolopendrium* 'Kaye's Lacerated'**
   (H4)
   ~ comes true from spores

ASTER (ASTERACEAE)
93 H ***alpinus*** (H4)

ASTILBE (SAXIFRAGACEAE)
93 H *chinensis* var. *pumila* (H4)
93 H × *crispa* 'Perkeo' (H4)
— 'Peter Pan'   ~ see *Astilbe* × *crispa*
'Perkeo'
93 H *glaberrima* var. *saxatilis* (H4)
pumila
~ see *Astilbe chinensis* var. *pumila*
93 H *simplicifolia* (H4)

AUBRIETA (BRASSICACEAE)
albomarginata
~ see *Aubrieta* 'Argenteovariegata'
02 H 'Argenteovariegata' (v) (H4)
02 H 'Aureovariegata' (v) (H4)
02 H 'Bressingham Pink' (d) (H4)
93 H 'Doctor Mules' (H4)
'Golden King'
~ see *Aubrieta* 'Aureovariegata'
02 H 'Greencourt Purple' (H4)
02 H 'Mrs Rodewald' (H4)
02 H 'Red Cascade' (H4)

AURINIA (BRASSICACEAE)
93 H *saxatilis* (H4)
93 H — 'Citrina' (H4)

BERBERIS (BERBERIDACEAE)
93 T × *stenophylla* 'Corallina Compacta'
(H4)

BLECHNUM (BLECHNACEAE)
97 F *penna-marina* (H4)

CAMPANULA (CAMPANULACEAE)
93 H *betulifolia* (H4)
93 H 'Birch Hybrid' (H4)
93 H *carpatica* (H4)
93 H *chamissonis* 'Superba' (H4)
93 H *cochleariifolia* (H4)
finitima
~ see *Campanula betulifolia*
93 H 'G.F. Wilson' (H4)
93 H *garganica* (H4)
93 H — 'W.H. Paine' (H4)
muralis   ~ see *Campanula*
portenschlagiana
pilosa 'Superba'   ~ see *Campanula*
chamissonis 'Superba'
93 H *portenschlagiana* (H4)
94 H *poscharskyana* 'Stella' (H4)
pusilla
~ see *Campanula cochleariifolia*

93 H *raineri* (H4)
97 H *tommasiniana* (H4)

CARDAMINE (BRASSICACEAE)
00 H *pentaphylla* (H4)

CASSIOPE (ERICACEAE)
93 T 'Edinburgh' (H4)
93 T *lycopodioides* (H4)
93 T 'Muirhead' (H4)
93 T 'Randle Cooke' (H4)

CHIASTOPHYLLUM (CRASSULACEAE)
93 H *oppositifolium* (H4)
simplicifolium
~ see *Chiastophyllum oppositifolium*

CHIONODOXA (HYACINTHACEAE)
93 B *forbesii* Siehei Group (H4)
93 B *luciliae* Boissier (H4)
93 B *sardensis* (H4)
siehei   ~ see *Chionodoxa forbesii*
Siehei Group

CHRYSANTHEMOPSIS (ASTERACEAE)
hosmariense
~ see *Rhodanthemum hosmariense*

CHRYSANTHEMUM (ASTERACEAE)
hosmariense
~ see *Rhodanthemum hosmariense*
maresii
~ see *Rhodanthemum hosmariense*

CLEMATIS (RANUNCULACEAE)

(A)   Alpina Group (Section Atragene)

93 C *alpina* (A) (H4)

CODONOPSIS (CAMPANULACEAE)
convolvulacea hort.
~ see *Codonopsis grey-wilsonii*
forrestii hort.
~ see *Codonopsis grey-wilsonii*
93 C *grey-wilsonii* (H4)
~ *previously listed as*
C. convolvulacea, *under*
which name the plant is
widely cultivated
nepalensis Grey-Wilson
~ see *Codonopsis grey-wilsonii*

COLCHICUM (COLCHICACEAE)
93 B *agrippinum* (H4)
    autumnale var. *major*
        ~ see *Colchicum byzantinum*
97 B — **'Nancy Lindsay'** (H4)
93 B *byzantinum* (H4)
97 B **'Pink Goblet'** (H4)
97 B **'Rosy Dawn'** (H4)
93 B *speciosum* (H4)
93 B — **'Album'** (H4)
97 B — **'Cedric Morris'** (H4)
97 B *tenorei* (H4)
97 B **'Waterlily'** (d) (H4)

CONVOLVULUS (CONVOLVULACEAE)
93 T *cneorum* (H3)
    mauritanicus
        ~ see *Convolvulus sabatius*
93 H *sabatius* (H3)

CORNUS (CORNACEAE)
93 H *canadensis* (H4)

CORYDALIS (PAPAVERACEAE)
    caucasica var. *alba* misapplied
        ~ see *Corydalis malkensis*
00 H *decipiens* hort. (H4)
    — Schott, Nyman & Kotschy
        ~ see *Corydalis solida*
        subsp. *incisa*
02 H *flexuosa* (H4)
93 H *malkensis* (H4)   ~ *reconfirmed after trial 2000*
00 H *solida* subsp. *incisa* (H4)
00 H — subsp. *solida* **'Dieter Schacht'**
    (H4)   ~ *previously listed under f.* transsylvanica
93 H — subsp. *solida* **'George Baker'** (H4)
    ~ *reconfirmed after trial 2000; previously listed under f.* transsylvanica
00 H *triternata* (H4)

COTONEASTER (ROSACEAE)
93 T *adpressus* (H4)
93 T *cashmiriensis* (H4) ~ *usually grown as C. cochleatus*
93 T *conspicuus* **'Decorus'** (H4)
    ~ *as grown in gardens*
93 T *integrifolius* (H4)   ~ *often sold as C. microphyllus*
    microphyllus var. *cochleatus*
    misapplied
    ~ see *Cotoneaster cashmiriensis*

— var. *thymifolius* (Lindl.) Koehne
    ~ see *Cotoneaster integrifolius*

COTYLEDON (CRASSULACEAE)
    oppositifolia
        ~ see *Chiastophyllum oppositifolium*
    simplicifolia
        ~ see *Chiastophyllum oppositifolium*

CREPIS (ASTERACEAE)
93 H *incana* (H4)

CROCUS (IRIDACEAE)
93 B *angustifolius* (H4)
    aureus
        ~ see *Crocus flavus* subsp. *flavus*
93 B *banaticus* (H4)
93 B *cartwrightianus* (H4)
94 B — **'Albus'** (H4)
93 B *chrysanthus* (H4)
93 B — **'Blue Pearl'** (H4)
93 B — **'Cream Beauty'** (H4)
93 B — **'E.A. Bowles'** (H4)
93 B — **'Ladykiller'** (H4)
93 B — **'Snow Bunting'** (H4)
93 B — **'Zwanenburg Bronze'** (H4)
93 B *cilicium* (H2-4)
    'Cloth of Gold'
        ~ see *Crocus angustifolius*
93 B *corsicus* (H4)
    'Dutch Yellow' ~ see *Crocus* × *luteus* **'Golden Yellow'**
93 B *etruscus* (H4)
    flavus   ~ see *Crocus flavus* subsp. *flavus*
93 B — subsp. *flavus* (H4)
    'Golden Mammoth'
        ~ see *Crocus* × *luteus* **'Golden Yellow'**
93 B *goulimyi* (H4)
    — **'Albus'** ~ see *Crocus goulimyi* **'Mani White'**
94 B — **'Mani White'** (H4)
94 B *hadriaticus* (H4)
    — var. *chrysobelonicus*
        ~ see *Crocus hadriaticus*
93 B *imperati* (H4)
93 B *kotschyanus* (H4)
94 B *laevigatus* (H4)
    'Large Yellow' ~ see *Crocus* × *luteus* **'Golden Yellow'**
94 B *longiflorus* (H4)
93 B × *luteus* **'Golden Yellow'** (H4)

93 B *malyi* (H2-4)
'Mammoth Yellow'   ~ see *Crocus*
                  × *luteus* 'Golden Yellow'
93 B *medius* (H4)
94 B *ochroleucus* (H4)
93 B *pulchellus* (H4)
      sativus var. *cartwrightianus*
                  ~ see *Crocus cartwrightianus*
      sibiricus   ~ see *Crocus sieberi*
93 B *sieberi* (H4)
93 B — **'Albus'** (H4)
      — **'Bowles' White'**   ~ see *Crocus*
                        sieberi 'Albus'
93 B — **'Hubert Edelsten'** (H4)
93 B — subsp. *sublimis* **'Tricolor'** (H4)
93 B *speciosus* (H4)
94 B — **'Albus'** (H4)
      × *stellaris* **'Golden Yellow'**
                  ~ see *Crocus* × *luteus*
                        'Golden Yellow'
      susianus   ~ see *Crocus angustifolius*
93 B *tommasinianus* (H4)
93 B *tournefortii* (H2-4)
      'Yellow Mammoth'   ~ see *Crocus*
                  × *luteus* 'Golden Yellow'
94 B **'Zephyr'** (H4)   ~ *awarded as C.*
                  pulchellus *'Zephyr'*

CYANANTHUS (CAMPANULACEAE)
      integer hort.   ~ see *Cyananthus*
                        microphyllus
93 H *lobatus* (H4)
93 H *microphyllus* (H4)

CYCLAMEN (PRIMULACEAE)
93 B *coum* (H4)
93 B — subsp. *coum* f. *coum* **Pewter**
            Group (H2-4)
      europaeum   ~ see *Cyclamen*
                        purpurascens
93 B *hederifolium* (H4)
      neapolitanum   ~ see *Cyclamen*
                        hederifolium
      orbiculatum   ~ see *Cyclamen coum*
93 B *purpurascens* (H4)
93 B *repandum* subsp. *repandum* (H3)

CYTISUS (PAPILIONACEAE)
93 T *ardoinoi* (H4)
93 T × *beanii* (H4)
93 T × *kewensis* (H4)   ~ *only for the largest*
                        of rock gardens

DACTYLORHIZA (ORCHIDACEAE)
93 H *elata* (H4)
93 H *foliosa* (H4)
      maderensis
            ~ see *Dactylorhiza foliosa*

DAPHNE (THYMELAEACEAE)
93 T *arbuscula* (H4)
93 T × *burkwoodii* (H4)
93 T *cneorum* **'Eximia'** (H4)
93 T × *napolitana* (H4)
      retusa   ~ see *Daphne tangutica*
                        Retusa Group
93 T *tangutica* (H4)
93 T — **Retusa Group** (H4)

DIANTHUS (CARYOPHYLLACEAE)

(p)	Pink

93 H *alpinus* (H4)
93 H — **'Joan's Blood'** (H4)
93 H × *arvernensis* (p) (H4)
      'Auvergne'
            ~ see *Dianthus* × *arvernensis*
      'Bourboule'
            ~ see *Dianthus* 'La Bourboule'
      caesius   ~ see *Dianthus*
                        gratianopolitanus
      Cheddar pink   ~ see *Dianthus*
                        gratianopolitanus
93 H *deltoides* (H4)
93 H *gratianopolitanus* (H4)
93 H **'Inshriach Dazzler'** (p)
            (H4)
      'Joan's Blood' ~ see *Dianthus alpinus*
                        'Joan's Blood'
93 H **'La Bourboule'** (p) (H4)
      neglectus   ~ see *Dianthus pavonius*
93 H *pavonius* (H4)
93 H **'Pike's Pink'** (p) (H4)
93 H **'Whitehill'** (p) (H4)

DIASCIA (SCROPHULARIACEAE)
93 H *barberae* **'Ruby Field'** (H3-4)
      'Ruby Field'   ~ see *Diascia barberae*
                        'Ruby Field'

DICENTRA (PAPAVERACEAE)
      'Boothman's Variety'   ~ see *Dicentra*
                        'Stuart Boothman'
93 H **'Stuart Boothman'** (H4)

DODECATHEON (PRIMULACEAE)
    amethystinum   ~ see *Dodecatheon*
                         pulchellum
94 H *dentatum* (H4)
93 H *hendersonii* (H4)
    integrifolium   ~ see *Dodecatheon*
                         hendersonii
93 H *meadia* (H4)
93 H — **f.** *album* (H4)
    pauciflorum (Dur.) E.Greene
              ~ see *Dodecatheon meadia*
    — hort.   ~ see *Dodecatheon*
                         pulchellum
93 H *pulchellum* (H4)
    — *radicatum*   ~ see *Dodecatheon*
                         pulchellum
    radicatum   ~ see *Dodecatheon*
                         pulchellum

DRYAS (ROSACEAE)
93 T *octopetala* (H4)
93 T — **'Minor'** (H4)
93 T x *suendermannii* (H4)

EDRAIANTHUS (CAMPANULACEAE)
93 H *pumilio* (H4)

EPIMEDIUM (BERBERIDACEAE)
93 H *grandiflorum* (H4)
93 H — **'Nanum'** (H4)
93 H — **'Rose Queen'** (H4)
93 H — **'White Queen'** (H4)
    macranthum   ~ see *Epimedium*
                       grandiflorum
93 H x *youngianum* **'Niveum'** (H4)

ERANTHIS (RANUNCULACEAE)
93 H *hyemalis* (H4)
93 H — **'Guinea Gold' (Tubergenii Group)**
        (H4)

ERIGERON (ASTERACEAE)
94 H *aureus* **'Canary Bird'**
        (H4)

ERINACEA (PAPILIONACEAE)
93 T *anthyllis* (H4)
    pungens   ~ see *Erinacea anthyllis*

ERINUS (SCROPHULARIACEAE)
93 H *alpinus* (H4)

ERODIUM (GERANIACEAE)
    chamaedryoides **'Roseum'** hort.
        ~ see *Erodium* x *variabile*
                         'Roseum'
93 H *glandulosum* (H4)
    macradenum   ~ see *Erodium*
                         glandulosum
    petraeum subsp. *glandulosum*
        ~ see *Erodium glandulosum*
93 H x *variabile* **'Roseum'** (H4)

ERYTHRONIUM (LILIACEAE)
94 B *californicum* (H4)
93 B — **'White Beauty'** (H4)
93 B *dens-canis* (H4)
93 B **'Pagoda'** (H4)
93 B *revolutum* (H4)
    — **'White Beauty'** ~ see *Erythronium*
              californicum 'White Beauty'
93 B *tuolumnense* (H4)

EUPHORBIA (EUPHORBIACEAE)
93 H *myrsinites* (H4)

EURYOPS (ASTERACEAE)
93 T *acraeus* (H4)
    evansii   ~ see *Euryops acraeus*

FESTUCA (POACEAE)
93 H *glauca* **'Blaufuchs'** (H4)
    — **BLUE FOX** ~ see *Festuca glauca*
                       'Blaufuchs'

FRITILLARIA (LILIACEAE)
93 B *acmopetala* (H4)
97 B *hermonis* subsp. *amana* **'Cambridge'**
        (H4)
93 B *meleagris* var. *unicolor* subvar. *alba*
        (H4)
    nigra hort.
        ~ see *Fritillaria pyrenaica*
93 B *pallidiflora* (H4)
96 B *persica* **'Adiyaman'** (H4)
93 B *pyrenaica* (H4)

GALANTHUS (AMARYLLIDACEAE)
93 B **'Atkinsii'** (H4)
    caucasicus hort. (H4)   see *Galanthus*
              elwesii var. *monostictus*
93 B *elwesii* (H4)
93 B — var. *monostictus* (H4)
    graecus Orph. ex Boiss.
        ~ see *Galanthus elwesii*

93 B **'Magnet'** (H4)
93 B *nivalis* (H4)
93 B — f. *pleniflorus* **'Flore Pleno'** (d) (H4)
93 B *plicatus* (H4)   ~ *including both*
                              subsp. plicatus *and*
                              subsp. byzantinus
02 B *reginae-olgae* **subsp.** *reginae-olgae*
                              (H2-4)
93 B **'S. Arnott'** (H4)
02 B *woronowii* (H4)

GAULTHERIA (ERICACEAE)
93 T *cuneata* (H4)
93 T *procumbens* (H4)

GENISTA (PAPILIONACEAE)
     delphinensis   ~ see *Genista sagittalis*
                              subsp. *delphinensis*
93 T *lydia* (H4)
93 T *sagittalis* **subsp.** *delphinensis* (H4)
     sagittalis minor   ~ see *Genista*
                 sagittalis subsp. *delphinensis*

GENTIANA (GENTIANACEAE)
93 H *acaulis* (H4)
     angulosa hort.   ~ see *Gentiana verna*
                                    'Angulosa'
93 H *asclepiadea* (H4)
93 H **'Inverleith'** (H4)
     kochiana   ~ see *Gentiana acaulis*
     lagodechiana   ~ see *Gentiana*
               septemfida var. *lagodechiana*
93 H × *macaulayi* (H4)
93 H — **'Edinburgh'** (H4)
93 H *septemfida* (H4)
93 H — **var.** *lagodechiana* (H4)
93 H *sino-ornata* (H4)
93 H × *stevenagensis* (H4)
94 H **'Strathmore'** (H4)
     verna **subsp.** *angulosa* hort.
          ~ see *Gentiana verna* 'Angulosa'
02 H — **'Angulosa'** hort. (H4)

GERANIUM (GERANIACEAE)
93 H **'Ballerina'** (Cinereum Group) (H4)
93 H *cinereum* **subsp.** *subcaulescens*
               var. *subcaulescens* (H4)
                    ~ *previously listed as* G.
               cinereum *var.* subcaulescens
93 H *dalmaticum* (H4)
93 H *renardii* (H4)
93 H × *riversleaianum* **'Russell Prichard'**
                              (H4)

93 H *sanguineum* **'Album'** (H4)
     — **var.** *lancastrense*   ~ see *Geranium*
               sanguineum var. *striatum*
     — **var.** *prostratum* (Cav.) Pers.
          ~ see *Geranium sanguineum*
                              var. *striatum*
93 H — **'Shepherd's Warning'** (H4)
93 H — **var.** *striatum* (H4)
93 H *subcaulescens* **'Splendens'** (H4)
     ~ *previously listed as* G.cinereum *var.* sub-
                    caulescens *'Splendens'*

GEUM (ROSACEAE)
     alpinum   ~ see *Geum montanum*
93 H *montanum* (H4)

GLAUCIDIUM (GLAUCIDIACEAE)
93 H *palmatum* (H4)

GLOBULARIA (GLOBULARIACEAE)
93 T *cordifolia* (H4)

GYMNOCARPIUM (WOODSIACEAE)
93 F *dryopteris* (H4)

GYPSOPHILA (CARYOPHYLLACEAE)
93 H *repens* (H4)

HABERLEA (GESNERIACEAE)
93 H *rhodopensis* (H4)

HACQUETIA (APIACEAE)
93 H *epipactis* (H4)

HEBE (SCROPHULARIACEAE)
93 T *albicans* (H4)
     — **'Pewter Dome'**   ~ see *Hebe*
                              'Pewter Dome'
     'Emerald Gem'   ~ see *Hebe*
                              'Emerald Green'
93 T **'Emerald Green'** (H3)
     'Green Globe'   ~ see *Hebe* 'Emerald
                                    Green'
     'James Stirling'   ~ see *Hebe ochracea*
                              'James Stirling'
     mackenii ~ see *Hebe* 'Emerald Green'
93 T *macrantha* (H3)
     'Milmont Emerald'   ~ see *Hebe*
                              'Emerald Green'
93 T *ochracea* **'James Stirling'** (H4)
     perfoliata   ~ see *Parahebe perfoliata*
93 T **'Pewter Dome'** (H4)
93 T *pimeleoides* **'Quicksilver'** (H4)

93 T *pinguifolia* 'Pagei' (H4)
    'Porlock Purple'   ~ see *Parahebe*
                       catarractae 'Delight'
93 T *recurva* 'Boughton Silver' (H3)

HELIANTHEMUM (CISTACEAE)
93 T 'Amy Baring' (H4)
93 T 'Fire Dragon' (H4)
    'Fireball'   ~ see *Helianthemum*
                       'Mrs C.W. Earle'
93 T 'Henfield Brilliant' (H4)
93 T 'Jubilee' (d) (H4)
93 T 'Mrs C.W. Earle' (d) (H4)
    'Mrs Clay'   ~ see *Helianthemum*
                       'Fire Dragon'
93 T 'Rhodanthe Carneum' (H4)
    'Snow Queen'   ~ see *Helianthemum*
                       'The Bride'
93 T 'The Bride' (H4)
    'Wisley Pink'   ~ see *Helianthemum*
                       'Rhodanthe Carneum'
93 T 'Wisley Primrose' (H4)

HEPATICA (RANUNCULACEAE)
    angulosa   ~ see *Hepatica*
                       transsilvanica
93 H *nobilis* (H4)
93 H *transsilvanica* (H4)
    triloba   ~ see *Hepatica nobilis*

HYACINTHUS (HYACINTHACEAE)
    azureus   ~ see *Muscari azureum*

HYPERICUM (CLUSIACEAE)
93 T *olympicum* (H4)
93 T — f. *uniflorum* 'Citrinum' (H4)

IBERIS (BRASSICACEAE)
    commutata   ~ see *Iberis sempervirens*
93 T *sempervirens* (H4)
93 T — 'Schneeflocke' (H4)
    — **SNOWFLAKE**
     ~ see *Iberis sempervirens* 'Schneeflocke'

IPHEION (ALLIACEAE)
93 H *uniflorum* 'Froyle Mill' (H4)
93 H — 'Wisley Blue' (H4)

IRIS (IRIDACEAE)
94 B *bucharica* Foster (H3-4)
    chamaeiris   ~ see *Iris lutescens*
94 B *cristata* (H4)
94 B *lacustris* (H4)

94 B *lutescens* (H4)
94 B *magnifica* (H3-4)
    orchioides hort.   ~ see *Iris bucharica*
93 B *reticulata* (H4)
94 B *winogradowii* (H4)

KALMIA (ERICACEAE)
93 T *angustifolia* (H4)

KALMIOPSIS (ERICACEAE)
93 T *leachiana* (H4)

LATHYRUS (PAPILIONACEAE)
    cyaneus hort.   ~ see *Lathyrus vernus*
93 H *vernus* (H4)
97 H — 'Alboroseus' (H4)

x LEDODENDRON (ERICACEAE)
93 T 'Arctic Tern' (H4)

LEIOPHYLLUM (ERICACEAE)
93 T *buxifolium* (H4)

LEPTOSPERMUM (MYRTACEAE)
93 T *scoparium* 'Kiwi' (Nanum Group)
        (H3)

LEUCANTHEMOPSIS (ASTERACEAE)
    hosmariensis
     ~ see *Rhodanthemum hosmariense*

LEUCANTHEMUM (ASTERACEAE)
    hosmariense
     ~ see *Rhodanthemum hosmariense*

LEUCOJUM (AMARYLLIDACEAE)
93 B *autumnale* (H4)
93 B *vernum* (H4)

LEWISIA (PORTULACACEAE)
93 H *cotyledon* (H4)
93 H — var. *heckneri* (H4)
93 H — **Sunset Group** (H4)

LINUM (LINACEAE)
93 T *arboreum* (H4)
93 T 'Gemmell's Hybrid' (H4)

LITHODORA (BORAGINACEAE)
93 T *diffusa* 'Grace Ward' (H4)
93 T — 'Heavenly Blue' (H4)
    x *intermedia*
     ~ see *Moltkia* x *intermedia*

93 T *oleifolia* (H4)

LITHOSPERMUM (BORAGINACEAE)
  'Grace Ward' ~ see *Lithodora diffusa*
                      'Grace Ward'
  'Heavenly Blue'   ~ see *Lithodora*
                    diffusa 'Heavenly Blue'
  oleifolium   ~ see *Lithodora oleifolia*

LYCHNIS (CARYOPHYLLACEAE)
02 H *flos-jovis* (H4)
93 H *viscaria* **'Splendens Plena'** (d) (H4)

LYSIMACHIA (PRIMULACEAE)
93 H *nummularia* **'Aurea'** (H4)

MECONOPSIS (PAPAVERACEAE)
93 H **'Slieve Donard' (Infertile Blue
        Group)** (H4)
93 H *quintuplinervia* (H4)

MIMULUS (SCROPHULARIACEAE)
  'Andean Nymph'
        ~ see *Mimulus naiandinus*
93 H *cupreus* **'Whitecroft Scarlet'** (H4)
93 H **'Highland Red'** (H4)
93 H *naiandinus* (H3)
  ~ previously listed as M. 'Andean Nymph'

MOLTKIA (BORAGINACEAE)
93 T × *intermedia* (H4)

MUSCARI (HYACINTHACEAE)
93 B *armeniacum* (H4)
93 B *aucheri* (H4)
93 B *azureum* (H4)
  chalusicum
        ~ see *Muscari pseudomuscari*
93 B *pseudomuscari* (H4)

NARCISSUS (AMARYLLIDACEAE)
*Miniature and smaller daffodils are marked *.*

94 B *asturiensis* (13) (H3-4)
        ~ miniature yellow trumpet
daffodil, hugging the ground; requiring
acid soil and flowering from
late winter to early spring*
94 B *bulbocodium* (13) (H3-4)
        ~ hoop petticoat; miniature
yellow flowers with narrow petals
and large corona; best in a
wet position on acid soil*

(1)	Trumpet
(2)	Large-cupped
(3)	Small-cupped
(4)	Double
(5)	Triandrus
(6)	Cyclamineus
(7)	Jonquilla and Apodanthus
(8)	Tazetta
(9)	Poeticus
(10)	Bulbocodium
(11a)	Split-corona: Collar
(11b)	Split-corona: Papillon
(12)	Miscellaneous
(13)	Species

93 B *cyclamineus* (13) (H4)
        ~ miniature yellow trumpet
daffodil with strongly reflexed petals;
flowering in early spring
in a wet position on acid
soil; very durable*
94 B *jonquilla* (13) (H4)
        ~ jonquil; up to six strongly
scented yellow flowers
on a round stem*
  minimus hort.
        ~ see *Narcissus asturiensis*
94 B *minor* (13) (H4)
        ~ small yellow trumpet
daffodil with forward-facing petals*
94 B *pseudonarcissus* (13) (H4)
        ~ Lent lily; medium-size
trumpet daffodil with
downward-facing flowers,
straw coloured forward-facing petals
and a darker yellow corona
with little flange
93 B **'Tête-à-tête'** (12) (H4)
        ~ a magnificent free-
flowering little daffodil for
pots, rock garden or naturalising*
94 B *triandrus* (13) (H3)
        ~ Angel's tears; two to six
small white pendent flowers per stem,
with sharply reflexed petals;
flowering on acid soil*

OENOTHERA (ONAGRACEAE)
93 H *macrocarpa* (H4)
  missouriensis
        ~ see *Oenothera macrocarpa*

OLSYNIUM (IRIDACEAE)
93 H *douglasii* (H4)

OMPHALODES (BORAGINACEAE)
93 H *cappadocica* (H4)
96 H — **'Cherry Ingram'** (H4)

ONOSMA (BORAGINACEAE)
93 H *taurica* (H4)

OPHIOPOGON (CONVALLARIACEAE)
     'Black Dragon'   ~ see *Ophiopogon*
                  planiscapus 'Nigrescens'
93 H *planiscapus* **'Nigrescens'** (H4)
            ~ *also valued as a pot plant*
                       under glass

ORCHIS (ORCHIDACEAE)
     elata   ~ see *Dactylorhiza elata*
     foliosa   ~ see *Dactylorhiza foliosa*
     maderensis   ~ see *Dactylorhiza foliosa*

ORIGANUM (LAMIACEAE)
93 H *rotundifolium* (H4)

OURISIA (SCROPHULARIACEAE)
93 H **'Snowflake'** (H4)

OXALIS (OXALIDACEAE)
93 B *adenophylla* (H4)
93 B *enneaphylla* (H4)
93 B **'Ione Hecker'** (H4)

PAEONIA (PAEONIACEAE)
93 H *obovata* (H4)
93 H — var. *alba* (H4)

PARADISEA (ASPHODELACEAE)
93 B *liliastrum* (H4)

PARAHEBE (SCROPHULARIACEAE)
93 T *catarractae* **'Delight'** (H3)
     — **'Porlock Purple'**   ~ see *Parahebe*
                  catarractae 'Delight'
     'Greencourt'   ~ see *Parahebe*
                  catarractae 'Delight'
93 H *perfoliata* (H3-4)

PENSTEMON (SCROPHULARIACEAE)
93 T *davidsonii* var. *menziesii* (H4)
93 T *fruticosus* var. *scouleri* (H4)
93 T — — f. *albus* (H4)
     menziesii   ~ see *Penstemon davidsonii*
                      var. *menziesii*
93 T *newberryi* (H4)
93 T *pinifolius* (H4)

98 T — **'Wisley Flame'** (H4)
97 T *procerus* **'Roy Davidson'** (H4)
93 T *rupicola* (H4)
     scouleri   ~ see *Penstemon fruticosus*
                      var. *scouleri*

PERSICARIA (POLYGONACEAE)
93 H *affinis* **'Darjeeling Red'** (H4)
     — **'Dimity'**   ~ see *Persicaria affinis*
                      'Superba'
93 H — **'Donald Lowndes'** (H4)
93 H — **'Superba'** (H4)
93 H *vacciniifolia* (H4)

PETRORHAGIA (CARYOPHYLLACEAE)
93 H *saxifraga* (H4)

PHLOX (POLEMONIACEAE)
93 H *adsurgens* (H4)
     canadensis   ~ see *Phlox divaricata*
     'Chattahoochee'   ~ see *Phlox*
               divaricata subsp. *laphamii*
                      'Chattahoochee'
     'Daniel's Cushion'
             ~ see *Phlox subulata*
                   'McDaniel's Cushion'
93 H *divaricata* (H4)
93 H — subsp. *laphamii* **'Chattahoochee'**
     (H4)
93 H *douglasii* **'Boothman's Variety'** (H4)
93 H — **'Crackerjack'** (H4)
93 H — **'Iceberg'** (H4)
93 H — **'Red Admiral'** (H4)
93 H **'Kelly's Eye'** (H4)
93 H x *procumbens* **'Millstream'** (H4)
93 H *stolonifera* **'Blue Ridge'** (H4)
93 H *subulata* **'McDaniel's Cushion'** (H4)
93 H — **'Red Wings'** (H4)

× **PHYLLIOPSIS (ERICACEAE)**
98 T **'Coppelia'** (H4)

PHYLLODOCE (ERICACEAE)
93 T *caerulea* (H4)
     — *japonica*
            ~ see *Phyllodoce nipponica*
93 T *nipponica* (H4)

PLATYCODON (CAMPANULACEAE)
93 H *grandiflorus* (H4)
93 H — **'Apoyama'** (H4)
93 H — **'Mariesii'** (H4)

POLYGALA (POLYGALACEAE)
93 H *calcarea* 'Lillet' (H4)
93 T *chamaebuxus* (H4)
93 T — var. *grandiflora* (H4)
— 'Purpurea' ~ see *Polygala chamaebuxus* var. *grandiflora*
— 'Rhodoptera' ~ see *Polygala chamaebuxus* var. *grandiflora*

POLYGONUM (POLYGONACEAE)
affine 'Darjeeling Red'
~ see *Persicaria affinis* 'Darjeeling Red'
— 'Donald Lowndes'
~ see *Persicaria affinis* 'Donald Lowndes'
— 'Superbum' ~ see *Persicaria affinis* 'Superba'
vacciniifolium
~ see *Persicaria vacciniifolia*

POTENTILLA (ROSACEAE)
ambigua ~ see *Potentilla cuneata*
93 H *cuneata* (H4)
fragariiformis
~ see *Potentilla megalantha*
93 H *megalantha* (H4)
93 H × *tonguei* (H4)

PRIMULA (PRIMULACEAE)

(2)	Auricula
(4)	Candelabra
(7)	Cortusoides
(9)	Denticulata
(11)	Farinosae
(17)	Muscarioides
(30)	Vernales
(Poly)	Polyanthus
(Prim)	Primrose

× *arctotis* ~ see *Primula* × *pubescens*
93 H *auricula* L. (2) (H4)
93 H *denticulata* (9) (H4)
93 H *elatior* (30) (H4)
93 H *frondosa* (11) (H4)
'Garryard Guinevere'
~ see *Primula* 'Guinevere'
93 H 'Guinevere' (Poly)(30) (H4)
93 H 'Inverewe' (4) (H4)
93 H 'Lady Greer' (Poly)(30) (H4)
littoniana ~ see *Primula vialii*
93 H *marginata* (2) (H4)

98 H — 'Beamish' (2) (H4)
~ a hardy plant, but in the south of England recommended for cultivation in alpine house conditions
93 H — 'Linda Pope' (2) (H4)
98 H — 'Prichard's Variety' (2) (H4)
~ a hardy plant, but in the south of England recommended for cultivation in alpine house conditions
93 H × *pubescens* (2) (H4)
'Ravenglass Vermilion'
~ see *Primula* 'Inverewe'
93 H *rosea* (11) (H4)
sibthorpii ~ see *Primula vulgaris* subsp. *sibthorpii*
93 H *sieboldii* (7) (H4)
93 H *veris* (30) (H4)
93 H *vialii* (17) (H4)
93 H *vulgaris* subsp. *sibthorpii* (Prim)(30) (H4)
93 H — subsp. *vulgaris* (Prim)(30) (H4)
93 H 'Wanda' (Prim)(30) (H4)

PSEUDOMUSCARI (HYACINTHACEAE)
azureum ~ see *Muscari azureum*

PTILOTRICHUM (BRASSICACEAE)
spinosum 'Roseum'
~ see *Alyssum spinosum* 'Roseum'

PULSATILLA (RANUNCULACEAE)
93 H *alpina* subsp. *apiifolia* (H4)
— subsp. *sulphurea* ~ see *Pulsatilla alpina* subsp. *apiifolia*
93 H *halleri* (H4)
93 H — subsp. *slavica* (H4)
lutea ~ see *Pulsatilla alpina* subsp. *apiifolia*
93 H *vulgaris* (H4)
93 H — 'Alba' (H4)

PYRETHROPSIS (ASTERACEAE)
hosmariense
~ see *Rhodanthemum hosmariense*

RAMONDA (GESNERIACEAE)
93 H *myconi* (H4)
93 H *nathaliae* (H4)
pyrenaica ~ see *Ramonda myconi*

RANUNCULUS (RANUNCULACEAE)
93 H *gramineus* (H4)
93 H *montanus* 'Molten Gold' (H4)

RHODANTHEMUM (ASTERACEAE)
93 H *hosmariense* (H4)

RHODODENDRON (ERICACEAE)

(EA)	Evergreen azalea

    'Arctic Tern'   ~ see × *Ledodendron*
                      'Arctic Tern'
93 T *calostrotum* 'Gigha' (H4)
       ~ suitable for small gardens
93 T — subsp. *keleticum* (H4)
       ~ suitable for small gardens
93 T 'Cilpinense' (H3-4)
       ~ i.e. the FCC clone;
       suitable for small gardens
93 T 'Curlew' (H4)
       ~ suitable for small gardens;
       prefers cooler conditions
93 T 'Egret' (H4)
       ~ suitable for small gardens
93 T 'Ginny Gee' (H4)
       ~ suitable for small gardens
93 T 'Hinomayo' (EA) (H3-4)
       ~ suitable for small gardens
    impeditum 'Moerheim'
       ~ see *Rhododendron* 'Moerheim'
93 T *keiskei* var. *ozawae* 'Yaku Fairy' (H4)
       ~ suitable for small gardens
    keleticum
       ~ see *Rhododendron calostrotum*
       subsp. *keleticum*
93 T *kiusianum* (EA) (H4)
       ~ shows great variation but
       generally excellent; suitable
       for small gardens
93 T 'Merganser' (H4)
       ~ suitable for small gardens
93 T 'Moerheim' (H4)
       ~ suitable for small gardens
93 T *polycladum* 'Policy' (Scintillans
       Group) (H4)
       ~ i.e. the FCC clone of the Scintillans
       Group; suitable for small gardens
93 T 'Ptarmigan' (H3-4)
       ~ suitable for small gardens
93 T 'Ramapo' (H4)
       ~ suitable for small gardens
93 T *russatum* (H4)
       ~ suitable for small gardens

93 T 'Saint Merryn' (H4)
       ~ suitable for small gardens
93 T 'Sarled' (H4)
       ~ i.e. the AM clone; suitable
       for small gardens
93 T 'Scarlet Wonder' (H4)
       ~ suitable for small gardens

RHODOHYPOXIS (HYPOXIDACEAE)
93 H *baurii* (H4)

ROSCOEA (ZINGIBERACEAE)
93 H *cautleyoides* (H4)
93 H *humeana* (H4)
       ~ name often misapplied

SALIX (SALICACEAE)
93 T 'Boydii' (f) (H4)
93 T *helvetica* (H4)
93 T *lanata* (H4)
93 T *reticulata* (H4)

SANGUINARIA (PAPAVERACEAE)
93 H *canadensis* f. *multiplex* 'Plena'
       (d) (H4)

SANTOLINA (ASTERACEAE)
    chamaecyparissus var. *corsica*
       ~ see *Santolina chamaecyparissus*
       var. *nana*
93 T — var. *nana* (H4)

SAPONARIA (CARYOPHYLLACEAE)
93 H 'Bressingham' (H4)
93 H *ocymoides* (H4)
93 H — 'Rubra Compacta' (H4)
93 H × *olivana* (H4)

SATUREJA (LAMIACEAE)
93 T *coerulea* (H4)
    montana 'Coerulea'
       ~ see *Satureja coerulea*

SAXIFRAGA (SAXIFRAGACEAE)

(5)	Irregulares
(7)	Porphyrion
(8)	Ligulatae
(11)	Gymnopera
(15)	Saxifraga

    × *apiculata* sensu stricto hort.
       ~ see *Saxifraga*
       'Gregor Mendel'
93 H *callosa* (8) (H4)

— var. *bellardii*
    ~ see *Saxifraga callosa*
— *lingulata*   ~ see *Saxifraga callosa*
93 H 'Clarence Elliott' (*umbrosa*) (11) (H4)
cortusifolia var. *fortunei*
    ~ see *Saxifraga fortunei*
93 H 'Cranbourne' (x *anglica*) (7) (H4)
'Crimson Rose' (*paniculata*)
    ~ see *Saxifraga* 'Rosea'
98 H 'Cumulus' (*iranica* hybrid) (7) (H4)
96 H 'Duncan Lowe' (*andersonii*) (7) (H4)
93 H 'Faldonside' (x *boydii*) (7) (H4)
93 H *ferdinandi-coburgi* (7) (H4)
'Flavescens' misapplied
    ~ see *Saxifraga* 'Lutea'
florulenta Schott, Nyman & Kotschy
    ~ see *Saxifraga callosa*
93 H *fortunei* (5) (H4)
93 H 'Gloria' (*burseriana*) (7) (H4)
93 H 'Gregor Mendel' (x *apiculata*) (7)
    (H4)
93 H 'Jenkinsiae' (x *irvingii*) (7) (H4)
93 H 'Kathleen Pinsent' (8) (H4)
lingulata   ~ see *Saxifraga callosa*
'Lutea' (*aizoon*)
    ~ see *Saxifraga* 'Lutea'
    (*paniculata*)
93 H 'Lutea' (*paniculata*) (8) (H4)
93 H 'Luteola' (x *boydii*) (7) (H4)
93 H 'Major' (*cochlearis*) (8) (H4)
'Major Lutea'
    ~ see *Saxifraga* 'Luteola'
93 H 'Minor' (*cochlearis*) (8) (H4)
94 H 'Peter Burrow' (x *poluanglica*) (7)
    (H4)
primuloides
    ~ see *Saxifraga* 'Primuloides'
93 H 'Primuloides' (*umbrosa*) (11) (H4)
    ~ previously listed as
Saxifraga umbrosa var. primuloides
93 H 'Rosea' (*paniculata*) (8) (H4)
'Rubra' (*aizoon*)
    ~ see *Saxifraga* 'Rosea'
93 H 'Sanguinea Superba' (x *arendsii*)
    (15) (H4)
93 H 'Southside Seedling' (8) (H4)
93 H 'Splendens' (*oppositifolia*) (7)
    (H4)
93 H 'Theoden' (*oppositifolia*) (7) (H4)
93 H 'Tumbling Waters' (8) (H4)
umbrosa var. *primuloides*
    ~ see *Saxifraga* 'Primuloides'
93 H x *urbium* (11) (H4)

urbium primuloides 'Elliott's Variety'
    ~ see *Saxifraga* 'Clarence Elliott'
'Valborg'
    ~ see *Saxifraga* 'Cranbourne'
'Valentine'
    ~ see *Saxifraga* 'Cranbourne'

SCILLA (HYACINTHACEAE)
93 B *bifolia* (H4)
93 B *mischtschenkoana* 'Tubergeniana'
    (H4)
93 B *siberica* (H4)

SEDUM (CRASSULACEAE)
93 H *cauticola* (H4)
ellacombeanum
    ~ see *Sedum kamtschaticum*
    var. *ellacombeanum*
floriferum   ~ see *Sedum*
    kamtschaticum
93 H *kamtschaticum* (H4)
93 H — var. *ellacombeanum* (H4)
93 H — var. *kamtschaticum* 'Variegatum'
    (v) (H4)
93 H 'Ruby Glow' (H4)
93 H *spathulifolium* 'Cape Blanco' (H4)
93 H — 'Purpureum' (H4)
spurium DRAGON'S BLOOD
    ~ see *Sedum spurium* 'Schorbuser Blut'
93 H — 'Schorbuser Blut' (H4)
93 H 'Vera Jameson' (H4)

SEMPERVIVUM (CRASSULACEAE)
93 H *arachnoideum* (H4)
93 H — 'Laggeri'   ~ see *Sempervivum*
    arachnoideum
    subsp. *tomentosum*
93 H — subsp. *tomentosum* (H4)
arvernense
    ~ see *Sempervivum tectorum*
93 H *ciliosum* (H4)
93 H 'Commander Hay' (H4)
densum
    ~ see *Sempervivum tectorum*
93 H *tectorum* (H4)
webbianum   ~ see *Sempervivum*
    arachnoideum
    subsp. *tomentosum*

SILENE (CARYOPHYLLACEAE)
93 H *alpestris* 'Flore Pleno' (d) (H4)
93 H *schafta* (H4)

SISYRINCHIUM (IRIDACEAE)
    douglasii   ~ see *Olsynium douglasii*
    grandiflorum
           ~ see *Olsynium douglasii*
02 H *idahoense* **'Album'** (H4)
    'May Snow'   ~ see *Sisyrinchium*
                 idahoense 'Album'

SORBUS (ROSACEAE)
93 T *reducta* (H4)

SPIRAEA (ROSACEAE)
    japonica **'Alpina'**   ~ see *Spiraea*
                   japonica 'Nana'
93 T — **'Nana'** (H4)
93 T — **'Nyewoods'** ~ see *Spiraea japonica*
                         'Nana'

THYMUS (LAMIACEAE)
    'Anderson's Gold'
           ~ see *Thymus pulegioides*
                  'Bertram Anderson'
    x *citriodorus* 'Aureus'
      ~ see *Thymus pulegioides* 'Aureus'
    — **'Bertram Anderson'**
           ~ see *Thymus pulegioides*
                  'Bertram Anderson'
    — **'Golden Lemon'** misapplied
      ~ see *Thymus pulegioides* 'Aureus'
93 T — **'Silver Queen'** (v) (H4)
93 T **'Coccineus'** (H4)
                ~ *sometimes listed*
                  incorrectly under
                  T. serpyllum
    'E.B. Anderson'
           ~ see *Thymus pulegioides*
                  'Bertram Anderson'
93 T *polytrichus* **subsp. *britannicus***
           'Thomas's White' (H4)
         ~ *sometimes listed incorrect-*
         ly under T. serpyllum; *previously*
         listed as T. polytrichus
         subsp. britannicus *'Albus'*
93 T *pulegioides* **'Aureus'** (H4)
                  ~ *awarded as*
         T. × citriodorus *'Aureus'*
93 T — **'Bertram Anderson'** (H4)
         ~ *awarded as* T. × citriodorus
               'Bertram Anderson'
93 T *serpyllum* **'Pink Chintz'** (H4)

TIARELLA (SAXIFRAGACEAE)
    collina   ~ see *Tiarella wherryi*

93 H *cordifolia* (H4)
93 H *wherryi* (H4)

TRILLIUM (TRILLIACEAE)
93 B *chloropetalum* **var. *giganteum*** (H4)
    — **var. *rubrum***   ~ see *Trillium*
           chloropetalum var. *giganteum*
93 B *erectum* (H4)
93 B *grandiflorum* (H4)
93 B — **'Flore Pleno'** (d) (H4)
93 B *luteum* (H4)
93 B *rivale* (H3)
    sessile **var. *luteum***
           ~ see *Trillium luteum*
    — **'Rubrum'**   ~ see *Trillium*
           chloropetalum var.
           giganteum

TULIPA (LILIACEAE)

(15)	Miscellaneous

93 B *aucheriana* (15) (H4)
    batalinii   ~ see *Tulipa linifolia*
           Batalinii Group
93 B *clusiana* **var. *chrysantha*** (15) (H4)
93 B *linifolia* (15) (H4)
93 B — **Batalinii Group** (15) (H4)
93 B *tarda* (15) (H4)
93 B *turkestanica* (15) (H4)
93 B *urumiensis* (15) (H4)

UVULARIA (CONVALLARIACEAE)
93 B *grandiflora* (H4)

VACCINIUM (ERICACEAE)
93 T *vitis-idaea* **Koralle Group** (H4)

VERBASCUM (SCROPHULARIACEAE)
93 T **'Letitia'** (H3)

VERONICA (SCROPHULARIACEAE)
    austriaca **var. *dubia***
           ~ see *Veronica prostrata*
93 H *cinerea* (H4)
    perfoliata   ~ see *Parahebe perfoliata*
93 H *prostrata* (H4)
97 H — **'Spode Blue'** (H4)
    rupestris   ~ see *Veronica prostrata*

VIOLA (VIOLACEAE)

(Va)	Viola

93 H *cornuta* (H4)

93 H — **Alba Group** (H4)
93 H — **'Minor'** (H4)
93 H *cucullata* (H4)
93 H **'Jackanapes'** (Va) (H4)
93 H **'Molly Sanderson'** (Va) (H4)
    obliqua   ~ see *Viola cucullata*

WAHLENBERGIA (CAMPANULACEAE)
    pumilio   ~ see *Edraianthus pumilio*

ZAUSCHNERIA (ONAGRACEAE)
93 T *californica* **'Dublin'** (H3)
    — **'Glasnevin'**   ~ see *Zauschneria californica* 'Dublin'

PLANTS FOR GLASS

Heated Glass Protection

*Requiring heated glass protection (**H1**) or intermediate requirements between heated and unheated glass protection (**H1-2**)*

General

ABROMEITIELLA (BROMELIACEAE)
93 H *brevifolia* (H1) ~ *min. 2C*

ACALYPHA (EUPHORBIACEAE)
02 H *hispaniolae* (H1) ~ *min. 15C*
93 T *hispida* (H1) ~ *min. 15C*
02 T *wilkesiana* 'Hoffmannii' (H1) ~ *min. 15C*
02 T — 'Marginata' (H1) ~ *min. 15C*
02 T — 'Musaica' (H1) ~ *min. 15C*

X **ACHIMENANTHA (GESNERIACEAE)**
02 H 'Inferno' (H1) ~ *min. 10C*

ACHIMENES (GESNERIACEAE)
02 H 'Ambroise Verschaffelt' (H1) ~ *min. 10C*
02 H 'Hilda Michelssen' (H1) ~ *min. 10C*
02 H 'Paul Arnold' (H1) ~ *min. 10C*
02 H 'Stan's Delight' (d) (H1) ~ *min. 10C*

ADIANTUM (ADIANTACEAE)
93 F *raddianum* 'Kensington Gem' (H1) ~ *min. 10C*
02 F *tenerum* 'Farleyense' (H1) ~ *min. 10C*

AECHMEA (BROMELIACEAE)
93 H *chantinii* (H1) ~ *min. 10C*
93 H *fasciata* (H1) ~ *min. 10C*
93 H Foster's Favorite Group (H1) ~ *min. 10C*
93 H *fulgens* var. *discolor* (H1) ~ *min. 10C*
93 H *nudicaulis* (H1) ~ *min. 10C*
93 H *orlandiana* (H1) ~ *min. 10C*
93 H *racinae* (H1) ~ *min. 10C*
93 H 'Royal Wine' (H1) ~ *min. 10C*

AESCHYNANTHUS (GESNERIACEAE)
lobbianus ~ see *Aeschynanthus radicans*

93 T *longicaulis* (H1) ~ *min. 15C*
marmoratus
~ see *Aeschynanthus longicaulis*
parvifolius
~ see *Aeschynanthus radicans*
93 T *pulcher* (H1) ~ *min. 15C*
02 T *radicans* (H1) ~ *min. 15C*
— *lobbianus*
~ see *Aeschynanthus radicans*
93 T *speciosus* (H1) ~ *min. 15C*

AGAPANTHUS (ALLIACEAE)
93 B *africanus* (H1) ~ *min. 2C*
93 B — 'Albus' (H1) ~ *min. 2C*
93 B *caulescens* (H1) ~ *min. 2C*
93 B *praecox* subsp. *praecox* 'Variegatus'
(v) (H1) ~ *min. 2C*
umbellatus L'Hérit.
~ see *Agapanthus africanus*

AGAPETES (ERICACEAE)
02 T 'Ludgvan Cross' (H1-2) ~ *min. 2C*
93 T *serpens* (H1) ~ *min. 2C*

AGLAONEMA (ARACEAE)
02 H *costatum* f. *immaculatum* (H1) ~ *min. 15C*
93 H *modestum* (H1) ~ *min. 15C*
93 H 'Silver Queen' (H1) ~ *min. 15C*

ALBIZIA (MIMOSACEAE)
distachya ~ see *Paraserianthes lophantha*
lophantha ~ see *Paraserianthes lophantha*

ALLAMANDA (APOCYNACEAE)
neriifolia ~ see *Allamanda schottii*
93 T *schottii* (H1) ~ *min. 10C*

ALOCASIA (ARACEAE)
93 H × *amazonica* (H1)   *~ min. 15C*
02 H *macrorrhiza* 'Variegata' (v) (H1)
                                  ~ min. 15C

ANANAS (BROMELIACEAE)
93 H *bracteatus* var. *tricolor* (H1)
                                  ~ min. 10C

ANIGOZANTHOS (HAEMODORACEAE)
93 H *humilis* (H1)   *~ min. 2C*
93 H *manglesii* (H1)   *~ min. 2C*

ANTHURIUM (ARACEAE)
02 H *andreanum* (H1)   *~ min. 15C*
02 H *crystallinum* (H1)   *~ min. 15C*
02 H *scherzerianum* (H1)   *~ min. 15C*

APHELANDRA (ACANTHACEAE)
93 T *squarrosa* 'Louisae' (H1) *~ min. 10C*

ARAUCARIA (ARAUCARIACEAE)
   excelsa hort.   *~* see *Araucaria
                                   heterophylla*
93 T *heterophylla* (H1)   *~ min. 2C*

ARCHONTOPHOENIX (ARECACEAE)
93 T *cunninghamiana* (H1)   *~ min. 2C*

ARDISIA (MYRSINACEAE)
93 T *crispa* (H1)   *~ min. 2C*

ASPARAGUS (ASPARAGACEAE)
93 H *densiflorus* 'Myersii' (H1) *~ min. 2C*
93 H — **Sprengeri Group** (H1)   *~ min. 2C*

ASPIDISTRA (CONVALLARIACEAE)
93 H *elatior* (H1)   *~ min. 2C*
93 H — 'Variegata' (v) (H1)   *~ min. 2C*

ASPLENIUM (ASPLENIACEAE)
93 F *bulbiferum* (H1-2)
93 F *nidus* (H1)   *~ min. 15C*

ASYSTASIA (ACANTHACEAE)
   bella   *~* see *Mackaya bella*

BABIANA (IRIDACEAE)
02 B *stricta* (H1-2)   *~ min. 2C*

BEGONIA (BEGONIACEAE)
94 H 'Alto Scharff' (H1)
                      ~ min. 15C; shrub-like

(C)	Cane
(R)	Rex
(S)	Semperflorens Cultorum
(T)	x tuberhybrida (Tuberous)

94 H 'Burle Marx' (H1)   *~ min. 15C*
94 H 'Cleopatra' (H1)   *~ min. 15C;*
                                  rhizomatous
02 H *dregei* (T) (H1)   *~ min. 15C*
94 H 'Esther Albertine' (C) (H1)
                                  ~ min. 15C
93 H *fuchsioides* (H1)   *~ min. 10C*
   glaucophylla
                   ~ see *Begonia radicans*
   incarnata 'Metallica'
                   ~ see *Begonia metallica*
94 H 'Irene Nuss' (C) (H1)   *~ min. 15C*
   limmingheana
                   ~ see *Begonia radicans*
94 H *listada* (H1)   *~ min. 15C*
02 H 'Little Brother Montgomery' (H1)
                                  ~ min. 15C
94 H *maculata* (H1)   *~ min. 15C*
02 H 'Marmaduke' (H1)   *~ min. 15C*
93 H *masoniana* (H1)   *~ min. 15C*
93 H 'Merry Christmas' (R) (H1)
                                  ~ min. 15C
94 H *metallica* (H1)   *~ min. 15C*
94 H 'Mirage' (H1)   *~ min. 15C*
94 H 'Munchkin' (H1)   *~ min. 15C;*
                                  rhizomatous
94 H 'Orange Rubra' (C) (H1)   *~ min. 15C*
94 H 'Pinafore' (C) (H1)   *~ min. 15C*
   procumbens   *~* see *Begonia radicans*
94 H *radicans* (H1)   *~ min. 15C*
94 H 'Raspberry Swirl' (R) (H1)
                                  ~ min.15C
94 H 'Raymond George Nelson' (H1)
                      ~ min. 15C; shrub-like
94 H 'Ricky Minter' (H1)   *~ min. 15C;*
                                  rhizomatous
93 H 'Silver Queen' (R) (H1)   *~ min. 15C*
02 H 'Snowcap' (C) (H1)   *~ min. 15C*
94 H *solananthera* (H1)   *~ min. 15C*
94 H 'Sophie Cecile' (C) (H1)   *~ min. 15C*
93 H *sutherlandii* (H1)   *~ min. 2C*
94 H 'Thurstonii' (H1)   *~ min. 15C;*
                                  shrub-like
94 H 'Tiger Paws' (H1)   *~ min. 15C;*
                                  rhizomatous

BELOPERONE (ACANTHACEAE)
   guttata   *~* see *Justicia brandegeeana*

BILLBERGIA (BROMELIACEAE)
93 H × *gireaudiana* (H1)   ~ *min. 10C*
93 H **'Muriel Waterman'** (H1)   ~ *min. 10C*
93 H *pyramidalis* (H1)   ~ *min. 10C*
93 H *vittata* (H1)   ~ *min. 10C*
93 H × *windii* (H1)   ~ *min. 10C*

BLECHNUM (BLECHNACEAE)
02 F *brasiliense* (H1) ~ *min. 15C*
93 F *tabulare* (Thunb.) Kuhn (H1)
                   ~ *rare in cultivation; most ferns*
         grown under this name are B. chilense

BRUGMANSIA (SOLANACEAE)
93 T *arborea* **'Knightii'** (d) (H1)   ~ *min. 2C*
93 T × *candida* **'Grand Marnier'** (H1)
                                   ~ *min. 2C*
— **'Plena'**   ~ see *Brugmansia*
                        arborea 'Knightii'
93 T *suaveolens* (H1)   ~ *min. 2C*

BRUNFELSIA (SOLANACEAE)
     calycina   ~ see *Brunfelsia pauciflora*
93 T *pauciflora* (H1)   ~ *min. 10C*

BUDDLEJA (BUDDLEJACEAE)
02 T *madagascariensis* (H1)   ~ *min. 2C*
     nicodemia   ~ see *Buddleja*
                             madagascariensis

CALATHEA (MARANTACEAE)
02 H *crocata* (H1)   ~ *min. 15C*
93 H *lancifolia* (H1)   ~ *min. 15C*
02 H *majestica* (H1)   ~ *min. 15C*
93 H *makoyana* (H1)   ~ *min. 15C*
02 H *mediopicta* (H1)   ~ *min. 15C*
     ornata   ~ see *Calathea majestica*
02 H *picturata* (H1)   ~ *min. 15C*
02 H — **'Argentea'** (H1)   ~ *min. 15C*
02 H *roseopicta* (H1)   ~ *min. 15C*
93 H *zebrina* (H1)   ~ *min. 15C*

CALLISIA (COMMELINACEAE)
93 H *elegans* (H1)   ~ *min. 10C*

CANARINA (CAMPANULACEAE)
93 T *canariensis* (H1)   ~ *min. 2C*

CARYOTA (ARECACEAE)
02 T *mitis* (H1)   ~ *min. 15C*

CATHARANTHUS (APOCYNACEAE)
93 H *roseus* (H1)   ~ *min. 10C*

93 H — **'Albus'** (H1)   ~ *min. 10C*

CHAMAEDOREA (ARECACEAE)
93 T *elegans* (H1)   ~ *min. 10C*
     erumpens ~ see *Chamaedorea seifrizii*
93 T *metallica* Cook (H1)   ~ *min. 10C*
93 T *seifrizii* (H1)   ~ *min. 10C; the true*
     plant - many sold under this name are C.
     microspadix; *awarded as* C. erumpens

CHAMAEROPS (ARECACEAE)
     excelsa Thunb.   ~ see *Rhapis excelsa*

CHIRITA (GESNERIACEAE)
02 A *lavandulacea* (H1) ~ *min. 10C; annual*
93 H *sinensis* (H1)   ~ *min. 10C*

CHORIZEMA (PAPILIONACEAE)
93 T *cordatum* (H1)   ~ *min. 2C*

CHRYSALIDOCARPUS (ARECACEAE)
     lutescens   ~ see *Dypsis lutescens*

CHRYSOTHEMIS (GESNERIACEAE)
93 H *pulchella* (H1)   ~ *min. 10C*

× CITROFORTUNELLA (RUTACEAE)
93 T *microcarpa* (F) (H1)   ~ *min. 10C*
02 T — **'Tiger'** (v/F) (H1)   ~ *min. 10C*
     — **'Variegata'**
     ~ see × *Citrofortunella microcarpa* 'Tiger'

CITRUS (RUTACEAE)
     calamondin
          ~ see × *Citrofortunella microcarpa*
02 T *limon* **'Variegata'** (F/v) (H1)
                                   ~ *min. 10C*
02 T × *meyeri* **'Meyer'** (F) (H1)   ~ *min. 2C*
     microcarpa Philippine lime
          ~ see × *Citrofortunella microcarpa*
     mitis
          ~ see × *Citrofortunella microcarpa*

CLERODENDRUM (VERBENACEAE)
02 T *chinense* **'Pleniflorum'** (d) (H1)
                                   ~ *min. 15C*
     fragrans var. *pleniflorum*
          ~ see *Clerodendrum chinense*
                            'Pleniflorum'
02 T *myricoides* **'Ugandense'** (H1)
                                   ~ *min. 15C*
     philippinum   ~ see *Clerodendrum*
                        chinense 'Pleniflorum'

CLIVIA (AMARYLLIDACEAE)
93 H *miniata* (H1)   ~ *min. 2C*
93 H — 'Aurea' (H1)   ~ *min. 2C*
02 H — var. *citrina* (H1)   ~ *min. 2C*
02 H *nobilis* (H1)   ~ *min. 2C*

COCOS (ARECACEAE)
  weddelliana
          ~ see *Lytocaryum weddellianum*

COLOCASIA (ARACEAE)
  antiquorum ~ see *Colocasia esculenta*
93 B *esculenta* (H1)   ~ *min. 15C*

COLUMNEA (GESNERIACEAE)
02 T   *banksii* (H1)   ~ *min. 15C*
93 H 'Chanticleer' (H1)   ~ *min. 10C*
02 T *gloriosa* 'Superba' (H1)   ~ *min. 15C*
93 T *hirta* (H1)   ~ *min. 10C*
93 T 'Kewensis Variegata' (v) (H1)
                                                    ~ *min. 10C*
93 T 'Stavanger' (H1)   ~ *min. 10C*

COPROSMA (RUBIACEAE)
02 T *repens* 'Marble Queen' (m/v) (H1-2)
                                                    ~ *min. 2C*
02 T — 'Picturata' (m/v) (H1-2) ~ *min. 2C*

CORDYLINE (AGAVACEAE)
02 T *fruticosa* 'Amabilis' (H1) ~ *min. 10C*
02 T — 'Baptistii' (H1)   ~ *min. 10C*
02 T — 'Firebrand' (H1)   ~ *min. 10C*
02 T — 'Guilfoylei' (H1)   ~ *min. 10C*
02 T — 'Red Edge' (H1)   ~ *min. 10C*

CROSSANDRA (ACANTHACEAE)
02 T *infundibuliformis* (H1)   ~ *min. 15C*

CRYPTANTHUS (BROMELIACEAE)
93 H *bivittatus* (H1)   ~ *min. 10C*
93 H — 'Pink Starlight' (v) (H1)
                                                    ~ *min. 10C*
93 H *bromelioides* var. *tricolor* (v) (H1)
                                                    ~ *min. 10C*
93 H *fosterianus* (H1)   ~ *min. 10C*
93 H 'It' (v) (H1)   ~ *min. 10C*
93 H *zonatus* (H1)   ~ *min. 10C*

CTENANTHE (MARANTACEAE)
93 H *amabilis* (H1)   ~ *min. 15C*
93 H *lubbersiana* (H1)   ~ *min. 15C*
93 H *oppenheimiana* 'Tricolor' (H1)
                                                    ~ *min. 15C*

CUPHEA (LYTHRACEAE)
93 T *hyssopifolia* (H1)   ~ *min. 2C*
93 T *ignea* (H1)   ~ *min. 2C*
  platycentra   ~ see *Cuphea ignea*

CYCAS (CYCADACEAE)
93 T *revoluta* (H1)   ~ *min. 2C*

CYCLAMEN (PRIMULACEAE)
95 B 'Concerto Apollo' (H1)
                             ~ *from seed; min. 2C*
95 B *persicum* 'Halios Bright Fuchsia'
          (H1)   ~ *from seed; min. 2C*
95 B — 'Halios Scarlet Red' (H1)
                             ~ *from seed; min. 2C*
95 B — 'Halios Violet' (H1)   ~ *from seed;*
                             min. 2C; awarded as
                  C. 'Halios Cattleya Violet'
95 B — 'Halios White' (H1)
                             ~ *from seed; min. 2C*
95 B 'Sierra Fuchsia' (H1)
                             ~ *from seed; min. 2C*
95 B 'Sierra Light Purple' (H1)
                             ~ *from seed; min. 2C*
95 B 'Sierra Pink With Eye' (H1)
                             ~ *from seed; min. 2C*
95 B 'Sierra Scarlet' (H1)
                             ~ *from seed; min. 2C*
95 B 'Sierra White With Eye' (H1)
                             ~ *from seed; min. 2C*

CYPERUS (CYPERACEAE)
  alternifolius hort.
          ~ see *Cyperus involucratus*
  haspan hort.
          ~ see *Cyperus papyrus* 'Nanus'
93 H *involucratus* (H1)   *min. 5C*

CYRTANTHUS (AMARYLLIDACEAE)
93 B *elatus* (H1)   ~ *min. 10C*
02 B *falcatus* (H1)   ~ *min. 2C*
  purpureus   ~ see *Cyrtanthus elatus*
  speciosus   ~ see *Cyrtanthus elatus*

CYTISUS (PAPILIONACEAE)
  racemosus hort.
          ~ see *Genista × spachiana*
  × *spachianus*
          ~ see *Genista × spachiana*

DARLINGTONIA (SARRACENIACEAE)
93 H *californica* (H1)   ~ *min. 2C*

DASYLIRION (AGAVACEAE)
02 T *wheeleri* (H1)   ~ *min. 2C*

DATURA (SOLANACEAE)
suaveolens
                    ~ see *Brugmansia suaveolens*
versicolor **'Grand Marnier'**
                    ~ see *Brugmansia* × *candida*
                                    'Grand Marnier'

DAVALLIA (DAVALLIACEAE)
93 F *canariensis* (H1)   ~ *min. 10C*

DELOSPERMA (AIZOACEAE)
02 T *aberdeenense* (H1)   ~ *min. 2C*

DIANTHUS (CARYOPHYLLACEAE)

(pf)	Perpetual-flowering Carnation

97 H **'Ann Franklin'** (pf) (H1)   ~ *min. 2C*
96 H **'Ann Unitt'** (pf) (H1)   ~ *min. 2C*
96 H **'Dark Pierrot'** (pf) (H1)   ~ *min. 2C*
93 H **'Dunkirk Spirit'** (pf) (H1)   ~ *min. 2C*
93 H **'Fragrant Ann'** (pf) (H1)   ~ *min. 2C*
98 H **'Incas'** (pf) (H1)   ~ *min. 2C*
95 H **'Indios'** (pf) (H1)   ~ *min. 2C*
93 H **'Jacqueline Ann'** (pf) (H1)   ~ *min. 2C*
93 H **'John Faulkner'** (pf) (H1)   ~ *min. 2C*
96 H **'Malaga'** (pf) (H1)   ~ *min. 2C*
98 H **'Maureen Lambert'** (pf) (H1)

                                    ~ *min. 2C*
95 H **'Royal Scot'** (pf) (H1)   ~ *min. 2C*
98 H **'Tempo'** (pf) (H1)   ~ *min. 2C*
97 H **'V.E. Jubilation'** (pf) (H1) ~ *min. 2C*

DIEFFENBACHIA (ARACEAE)
02 H × *bausei* (v) (H1)   ~ *min. 15C*
02 H **'Camille'** (v) (H1)   ~ *min. 15C*
02 H **'Exotica'** (v) (H1)   ~ *min. 15C*
02 H **'Tropic Snow'** (v) (H1)   ~ *min. 15C*

DIOON (ZAMIACEAE)
02 T *edule* (H1)   ~ *min. 5C*

DIOSCOREA (DIOSCOREACEAE)
02 B *batatas* **'Rudolph Rhoers'** (H1)
                                    ~ *min. 5C*

DIZYGOTHECA (ARALIACEAE)
elegantissima
                    ~ see *Schefflera elegantissima*

DRACAENA (AGAVACEAE)
02 T *draco* (H1)   ~ *min. 10C*
02 T *fragrans* **(Deremensis Group)**
            'Lemon Lime' (v) (H1)
                                    ~ *min. 15C*
93 T — — **'Warneckei'** (v) (H1)
                                    ~ *min. 15C*
02 T — — **'Yellow Stripe'** (v) (H1)
                                    ~ *min. 15C*
93 T — **'Massangeana'** (v) (H1)
                                    ~ *min. 15C*
93 T *marginata* (v) (H1)   ~ *min. 15C*
02 T — **'Tricolor'** (v) (H1)   ~ *min. 15C*
02 T — **'Variegata'** (v) (H1)   ~ *min. 15C*
93 T *reflexa* **'Variegata'** (v) (H1)
                                    ~ *min. 15C*
93 T *sanderiana* (v) (H1)   ~ *min. 15C*
02 T *surculosa* **'Florida Beauty'** (v) (H1)
                                    ~ *min. 15C*

DYPSIS (ARECACEAE)
93 T *lutescens* (H1)   ~ *min. 10C; awarded*
                as Chrysalidocarpus lutescens

ELATOSTEMA (URTICACEAE)
93 H *repens* (H1)   ~ *min. 10C; previously*
                listed as E. repens *var.* repens
95 H — *var. pulchrum* (H1)   ~ *min. 15C;*
                awarded as E. pulchra

ERANTHEMUM (ACANTHACEAE)
02 T *pulchellum* (H1)   ~ *min. 10C*

EUCHARIS (AMARYLLIDACEAE)
02 B *amazonica* (H1)   ~ *min. 10C*
grandiflora hort.
                    ~ see *Eucharis amazonica*

EUPHORBIA (EUPHORBIACEAE)
02 T *fulgens* (H1)   ~ *min. 15C*
93 T *milii* (H1)   ~ *min. 10C*
02 T — *var. splendens* (H1)   ~ *min. 10C*

FARFUGIUM (ASTERACEAE)
93 H *japonicum* **'Aureomaculatum'** (v)
            (H1)   ~ *min. 2C*
tussilagineum **'Aureomaculatum'**
                    ~ see *Farfugium japonicum*
                                    'Aureomaculatum'

FICUS (MORACEAE)
93 T *benjamina* (H1)   ~ *min. 10C*
02 T — **'Starlight'** (v) (H1)   ~ *min. 15C*

93 T *binnendijkii* (H1) ~ *min. 10C*
93 T *deltoidea* (H1) ~ *min. 10C*
93 T *elastica* 'Black Knight' (H1)
  ~ *min. 10C*
93 T — 'Decora' (H1) ~ *min. 10C*
93 T — 'Doescheri' (v) (H1) ~ *min. 10C*
93 T — 'Schrijveriana' (v) (H1)
  ~ *min. 10C*
93 T — 'Tricolor' (H1) ~ *min. 10C*
  longifolia hort.
  ~ see *Ficus binnendijkii*
93 T *lyrata* (H1) ~ *min. 10C*
93 T *rubiginosa* (H1) ~ *min. 10C*
02 T — 'Variegata' (v) (H1) ~ *min. 15C*

FITTONIA (ACANTHACEAE)
93 H *albivenis* **Argyroneura Group** (H1)
  ~ *min. 15C; awarded as* F. verschaffeltii
  var. argyroneura
93 H — **Verschaffeltii Group** (H1)
  ~ *min. 15C; awarded as*
  F. verschaffeltii
  verschaffeltii ~ see *Fittonia albivenis*
  Verschaffeltii Group

FORTUNELLA (RUTACEAE)
02 T × *crassifolia* 'Meiwa' (F) (H1)
  ~ *min. 10C*
02 T 'Fukushu' (F) (H1) ~ *min. 10C*

GARDENIA (RUBIACEAE)
  augusta ~ see *Gardenia jasminoides*
  florida L. ~ see *Gardenia jasminoides*
  grandiflora
  ~ see *Gardenia jasminoides*
02 T *jasminoides* (H1) ~ *min. 15C*

GENISTA (PAPILIONACEAE)
93 T × *spachiana* (H1) ~ *min. 2C*

GUZMANIA (BROMELIACEAE)
93 H *lingulata* (H1) ~ *min. 15C*
93 H — var. *minor* (H1) ~ *min. 15C*
93 H *monostachya* (H1) ~ *min. 15C*
93 H *musaica* (H1) ~ *min. 15C*
93 H *sanguinea* (H1) ~ *min. 15C*

GYNURA (ASTERACEAE)
93 H *aurantiaca* 'Purple Passion' (H1)
  ~ *min. 15C*
  sarmentosa hort.
  ~ see *Gynura aurantiaca* 'Purple Passion'

HABRANTHUS (AMARYLLIDACEAE)
  andersonii ~ see *Habranthus tubispathus*
02 B *robustus* (H1) ~ *min. 5C*
02 B *tubispathus* (H1) ~ *min. 5C*

HAEMANTHUS (AMARYLLIDACEAE)
02 B *albiflos* (H1) ~ *min. 5C*
02 B *coccineus* (H1) ~ *min. 5C*
  kalbreyeri ~ see *Scadoxus multiflorus*
  subsp. *multiflorus*
  katherinae ~ see *Scadoxus multiflorus*
  subsp. *katherinae*

HEDYCHIUM (ZINGIBERACEAE)
93 H *coccineum* (H1) ~ *min. 2C*
93 H *gardnerianum* (H1) ~ *min. 2C*

HELIOTROPIUM (BORAGINACEAE)
94 T 'Chatsworth' (H1) ~ *min. 2C;*
  suitable for bedding
94 T 'Princess Marina' (H1) ~ *min. 2C;*
  suitable for bedding

HIBISCUS (MALVACEAE)
02 T *rosa-sinensis* 'Cooperi' (v) (H1)
  ~ *min. 15C*
93 T *schizopetalus* (H1) ~ *min. 10C*

HIPPEASTRUM (AMARYLLIDACEAE)
93 B 'Belinda' (H1) ~ *min. 2C*
93 B 'Bestseller' (H1) ~ *min. 2C*
93 B 'Orange Souvereign' (H1) ~ *min. 2C*
02 B *papilio* (H1) ~ *min. 10C*
93 B 'Star of Holland' (H1) ~ *min. 2C*

HOWEA (ARECACEAE)
02 T *belmoreana* (H1) ~ *min. 10C*
93 T *forsteriana* (H1) ~ *min. 10C*

HOYA (ASCLEPIADACEAE)
  bella ~ see *Hoya lanceolata* subsp. *bella*
93 T *lanceolata* subsp. *bella* (H1)
  ~ *min. 10C*

HYMENOCALLIS (AMARYLLIDACEAE)
02 B × *festalis* (H1) ~ *min. 10C*
93 B × *macrostephana* (H1) ~ *min. 2C*
02 B 'Sulphur Queen' (H1) ~ *min. 10C*

HYPOESTES (ACANTHACEAE)
93 H *phyllostachya* (v) (H1)
  ~ *often grown as* H. sanguinolenta;
  min. 10C

sanguinolenta misapplied
~ see *Hypoestes phyllostachya*

IMPATIENS (BALSAMINACEAE)
02 H *marianae* (H1)   ~ *min. 10C*
93 H *repens* (H1)   ~ *min. 10C*

IRESINE (AMARANTHACEAE)
93 H *lindenii* (H1)   ~ *min. 10C*

JUSTICIA (ACANTHACEAE)
93 H *brandegeeana* (H1)   ~ *min. 10C*
      floribunda   ~ see *Justicia rizzinii*
      guttata   ~ see *Justicia brandegeeana*
      pauciflora   ~ see *Justicia rizzinii*
93 H *rizzinii* (H1)   ~ *min. 10C*

KENTIA (ARECACEAE)
      belmoreana
              ~ see *Howea belmoreana*
      forsteriana   ~ see *Howea forsteriana*

KOHLERIA (GESNERIACEAE)
93 H *eriantha* (H1)   ~ *min. 10C*
02 H 'Jester' (H1)   ~ *min. 15C*
93 H 'Strawberry Fields' (H1)   ~ *min. 10C*
93 H 'Tane' (H1)   ~ *min. 10C*
93 H *warscewiczii* (H1)   ~ *min. 10C*

LACHENALIA (HYACINTHACEAE)
93 B *aloides* var. *aurea* (H1)   ~ *min. 2C*
93 B — var. *quadricolor* (H1)   ~ *min. 2C*
02 B — var. *vanzyliae* (H1)   ~ *min. 2C*
02 B *bulbifera* (H1)   ~ *min. 2C*
02 B — 'George' (H1)   ~ *min. 2C*
02 B *contaminata* (H1)   ~ *min. 2C*
02 B *orchioides* (H1)   ~ *min. 2C*
      pendula   ~ see *Lachenalia bulbifera*
02 B *pustulata* (H1)   ~ *min. 2C*
02 B *viridiflora* (H1)   ~ *min. 2C*

LAGERSTROEMIA (LYTHRACEAE)
93 T *indica* (H1)   ~ *min. 2C*

LAMPRANTHUS (AIZOACEAE)
      aberdeenensis
              ~ see *Delosperma aberdeenense*

LEUCOCORYNE (ALLIACEAE)
02 B *purpurea* (H1)   ~ *min. 5C*

LIGULARIA (ASTERACEAE)
      tussilaginea 'Aureo-maculata'
              ~ see *Farfugium japonicum* 'Aureomaculatum'

LIVISTONA (ARECACEAE)
93 T *chinensis* (H1)   ~ *min. 2C*

LUCULIA (RUBIACEAE)
93 T *gratissima* (H1-2)

LYTOCARYUM (ARECACEAE)
93 T *weddellianum* (H1)   ~ *min. 10C*

MACKAYA (ACANTHACEAE)
93 T *bella* (H1)   ~ *min. 2C*

MARANTA (MARANTACEAE)
02 H *leuconeura* var. *erythroneura* (H1)
                                     ~ *min. 15C*
93 H — var. *kerchoveana* (H1)   ~ *min. 15C*

MATTHIOLA (BRASSICACEAE)
93 P Cinderella Series (H1)
                          ~ *sold as a mixture*

MEDINILLA (MELASTOMATACEAE)
02 T *magnifica* (H1)   ~ *min. 15C*

MICROCOELUM (ARECACEAE)
      weddelianum   ~ see *Lytocaryum weddellianum*

MUSA (MUSACEAE)
93 T *acuminata* 'Dwarf Cavendish' (F)
           (H1)   ~ *AAA Group; min. 10C*
      cavendishii   ~ see *Musa acuminata* 'Dwarf Cavendish'
93 T *coccinea* (H1)   ~ *min. 10C*
93 T *ornata* (H1)   ~ *min. 10C*
      uranoscopus ~ see *Musa coccinea*

NEMATANTHUS (GESNERIACEAE)
02 T *gregarius* (H1)   ~ *min. 15C*
      radicans ~ see *Nematanthus gregarius*
93 T 'Tropicana' (H1)   ~ *min. 10C*

NEOREGELIA (BROMELIACEAE)
93 H *carolinae* f. *tricolor* (v) (H1) ~ *min. 10C*
93 H *marmorata* (H1)   ~ *min. 10C*
93 H *spectabilis* (H1)   ~ *min. 10C*

NEPHROLEPIS (OLEANDRACEAE)
02 F *exaltata* **'Elegantissima'** (H1)
        ~ *min. 5C*
02 F — **'Fluffy Ruffles'** (H1) ~ *min. 5C*
02 F — **'Hillii'** (H1)   ~ *min. 5C*

NIDULARIUM (BROMELIACEAE)
02 H *fulgens* (H1)   ~ *min. 15C*

NIEREMBERGIA (SOLANACEAE)
   caerulea (H1)
    ~ see *Nierembergia linariifolia*
   hippomanica
    ~ see *Nierembergia linariifolia*
93 H *linariifolia* (H1)   ~ *min. 2C*

NOLINA (AGAVACEAE)
93 T *recurvata* (H1)   ~ *min. 2C*

OPLISMENUS (POACEAE)
93 H *africanus* **'Variegatus'** (v) (H1)
        ~ *min. 10C*
   hirtellus **'Variegatus'**
   ~ see *Oplismenus africanus* 'Variegatus'

ORNITHOGALUM (HYACINTHACEAE)
02 B *dubium* (H1)   ~ *min.5C*
02 B *thyrsoides* (H1)   ~ *min.5C*

OXALIS (OXALIDACEAE)
   regnellii ~ see *Oxalis triangularis*
       subsp. *papilionacea*
02 B *triangularis* subsp. *papilionacea* (H1)
        ~ *min. 2C*
02 B *versicolor* (H1)   ~ *min. 2C*

PACHYSTACHYS (ACANTHACEAE)
93 T *lutea* (H1)   ~ *min. 10C*

PANDANUS (PANDANACEAE)
93 T *tectorius* **'Laevis'** (H1) ~ *min. 10C*
93 T — **'Veitchii'** (H1)   ~ *min. 10C*

PARASERIANTHES (MIMOSACEAE)
   distachya
    ~ see *Paraserianthes lophantha*
93 T *lophantha* (H1)   ~ *min. 2C*

PAVONIA (MALVACEAE)
02 T *multiflora* Jussieu (H1) ~ *min. 15C*

PEPEROMIA (PIPERACEAE)
93 H *argyreia* (H1)   ~ *min. 10C*

93 H *caperata* **'Emerald Ripple'** (H1)
        ~ *min. 10C*
93 H — **'Little Fantasy'** (H1) ~ *min. 10C*
02 H — **'Luna Red'** (H1)   ~ *min. 15C*
93 H — **'Variegata'** (v) (H1) ~ *min. 10C*
02 H *griseoargentea* (H1)   ~ *min. 15C*
93 H *obtusifolia* (H1)   ~ *min. 10C*
02 H — **'USA'** (**Magnoliifolia Group**) (H1)
        ~ *min. 15C*
   sandersii ~ see *Peperomia argyreia*
93 H *scandens* (H1)   ~ *min. 10C*
02 H *velutina* (H1)   ~ *min. 15C*

PHILODENDRON (ARACEAE)
93 T *bipinnatifidum* (H1)   ~ *min. 10C*

PHLEBODIUM (POLYPODIACEAE)
   aureum   see *Polypodium aureum*

PILEA (URTICACEAE)
93 H *cadierei* (H1)   ~ *min. 10C*
93 H — **'Minima'** (H1)   ~ *min. 10C*
93 H *involucrata* **'Moon Valley'** (H1)
        ~ *min. 15C*
93 H — **'Norfolk'** (H1)   ~ *min. 15C*
93 H *peperomioides* (H1)   ~ *min. 10C*

PLATYCERIUM (POLYPODIACEAE)
   alcicorne hort. ~ see *Platycerium bifurcatum*
93 F *bifurcatum* (H1)   ~ *min. 15C*
   grande hort.   ~ see *Platycerium*
        superbum
93 F *superbum* (H1) ~ *min. 15C; awarded*
       as P. grande *hort.*
93 F *eitchii* (H1)   ~ *min. 10C*

PLECTRANTHUS (LAMIACEAE)
93 H *oertendahlii* (H1)   ~ *min. 2C*

PLEOMELE (AGAVACEAE)
   reflexa **'Variegata'** ~ see *Dracaena*
       reflexa 'Variegata'

PLUMBAGO (PLUMBAGINACEAE)
93 T *auriculata* (H1-2)
02 T — var. *alba* (H1-2)   ~ *min. 5C*
   capensis   ~ see *Plumbago*
        auriculata
02 T *indica* (H1)   ~ *min. 15C*
   — *rosea*   ~ see *Plumbago indica*

PLUMERIA (APOCYNACEAE)
02 T *rubra* (H1)   ~ *min. 10C*

POLIANTHES (AGAVACEAE)
93 H *tuberosa* (H1-2)

POLYGALA (POLYGALACEAE)
93 T × *dalmaisiana* (H1) ~ *min. 2C*
myrtifolia 'Grandiflora' ~ see
Polygala × *dalmaisiana*

POLYPODIUM (POLYPODIACEAE)
93 F *aureum* (H1) ~ *min. 10C.*

POLYSCIAS (ARALIACEAE)
balfouriana ~ see *Polyscias*
scutellaria
02 T *guilfoylei* (H1) ~ *min. 15C*
02 T — 'Victoriae' (H1) ~ *min. 15C*
02 T *scutellaria* 'Marginata' (H1) ~ *min. 15C*

PRIMULA (PRIMULACEAE)

(30)	Vernales
(Prim)	Primrose

02 P **Charisma Series** (Prim) (H1)
~ *sold as a mixture; min. 2C; for
pot and container culture*
93 P **'Danova Purple, White Edge'
(Danova Series)** (Prim)(30) (H1)
~ *min. 2C*
93 P **'Danova Rose' (Danova Series)**
(Prim)(30) (H1) ~ *min. 2C*
02 P **Danova Series** (Prim) (H1)
~ *sold as a mixture; min. 2C; for
pot and container culture*
98 H *obconica* 'Libre Magenta' (H1)
~ *min. 2C; from seed, under glass*
98 H — 'Libre White' (H1) ~ *min. 2C;
from seed, under glass*

PSEUDOPANAX (ARALIACEAE)
93 T **'Cyril Watson' (Adiantifolius Group)**
(H1) ~ *min. 2C*
93 T *lessonii* 'Gold Splash' (v) (H1)
~ *min. 2C*
93 T **'Purpureus'** (H1) ~ *min. 2C*

PTERIS (PTERIDACEAE)
93 F *cretica* var. *albolineata* (H1)
~ *min. 2C*

RADERMACHERA (BIGNONIACEAE)
93 T *sinica* (H1) ~ *min. 10C*

RHAPIS (ARECACEAE)
93 T *excelsa* (H1) ~ *including* R. humilis;
min. 2C

RHOEO (COMMELINACEAE)
spathacea 'Variegata'
~ see *Tradescantia
spathacea* 'Vittata'

RUELLIA (ACANTHACEAE)
93 H *makoyana* (H1) ~ *min. 10C*

RUMOHRA (DAVALLIACEAE)
93 F *adiantiformis* (H1) ~ *min. 10C*

RUSSELIA (SCROPHULARIACEAE)
93 H *equisetiformis* (H1) ~ *min. 10C*
juncea ~ see *Russelia equisetiformis*

SALVIA (LAMIACEAE)
93 H *discolor* (H1) ~ *min. 2C*
93 H *leucantha* (H1) ~ *min. 2C*

SANSEVIERIA (AGAVACEAE)
93 H *trifasciata* 'Bantel's Sensation' (H1)
~ *min. 10C*
93 H — 'Craigii' (H1) ~ *min. 10C*
93 H — 'Golden Hahnii' (v) (H1)
~ *min. 10C*
93 H — 'Hahnii' (H1) ~ *min. 10C*
93 H — 'Laurentii' (v) (H1) ~ *min. 10C*
93 H — 'Moonshine' (H1) ~ *min. 10C*

SARRACENIA (SARRACENIACEAE)
93 H × *catesbyi* (H1) ~ *min. 2C*
93 H × *chelsonii* (H1) ~ *min. 2C*
93 H × *excellens* (H1) ~ *min. 2C*
93 H *flava* (H1) ~ *min. 2C*
93 H *leucophylla* (H1) ~ *min. 2C*
93 H × *mitchelliana* (H1) ~ *min. 2C*
93 H × *wrigleyana* (H1) ~ *min. 2C*

SCADOXUS (AMARYLLIDACEAE)
93 B *multiflorus* subsp. *katherinae* (H1)
~ *min. 2C*
02 B — subsp. *multiflorus* (H1) ~ *min. 5C*

SCHEFFLERA (ARALIACEAE)
93 T *actinophylla* (H1) ~ *min. 10C*
93 T *arboricola* (H1) ~ *min. 10C*
93 T — 'Gold Capella' (H1) ~ *min. 10C*
93 T *elegantissima* (H1) ~ *min. 10C*

SELAGINELLA (SELAGINELLACEAE)
93 H *kraussiana* (H1) ~ *min. 2C*
93 H — 'Brownii' (H1) ~ *min. 2C*
93 H — 'Variegata' (v) (H1) ~ *min. 2C*
93 H *martensii* (H1) ~ *min. 10C*
93 H *uncinata* (H1) ~ *min. 10C*

SENNA (CAESALPINIACEAE)
93 T *artemisioides* (H1) ~ *min. 2C*

SINNINGIA (GESNERIACEAE)
93 H *canescens* (H1) ~ *min. 10C*
98 P 'Empress Purple Spotted' (H1)
~ *min. 5C, from seed, under glass*
98 P 'Empress Red' (H1) ~ *min. 5C,*
from seed, under glass
02 P Empress Series (H1) ~ *min. 5C; sold*
as a mixture

SOLENOSTEMON (LAMIACEAE)
94 T 'Buttermilk' (v) (H1) ~ *min. 2C*
94 T 'Crimson Ruffles' (v) (H1) ~ *min. 2C*
94 T 'Firebrand' (v) (H1) ~ *min. 2C*
94 T 'Glory of Luxembourg' (v) (H1)
~ *min. 2C*
94 T 'Lord Falmouth' (H1) ~ *min. 2C*
94 T 'Paisley Shawl' (v) (H1) ~ *min. 2C*
94 T 'Picturatus' (v) (H1) ~ *min. 2C*
94 T 'Pineapple Beauty' (v) (H1) ~ *min. 2C*
94 T 'Pineapplette' (H1) ~ *min. 2C*
94 T 'Royal Scot' (v) (H1) ~ *min. 2C*
94 T 'Walter Turner' (v) (H1) ~ *min. 2C*
94 T 'Wisley Tapestry' (v) (H1) ~ *min. 2C*

SONERILA (MELASTOMATACEAE)
93 H *margaritacea* (H1) ~ *min. 15C*

SPARRMANNIA (TILIACEAE)
93 T *africana* (H1) ~ *min. 2C*

SPATHIPHYLLUM (ARACEAE)
93 H 'Mauna Loa' (H1) ~ *min. 15C*

STENOTAPHRUM (POACEAE)
93 H *secundatum* 'Variegatum' (v) (H1)
~ *min. 10C*

STRELITZIA (STRELITZIACEAE)
93 H *reginae* (H1) ~ *min. 10C*

STREPTOCARPUS (GESNERIACEAE)
93 H 'Albatross' (H1) ~ *min. 10C*
02 H 'Amanda' Dibley (H1)

02 H 'Bethan' (H1) ~ *min. 10C*
02 H 'Carys' (H1) ~ *min. 10C*
02 H 'Catrin' (H1) ~ *min. 10C*
02 H 'Chorus Line' (H1) ~ *min. 10C*
02 H 'Crystal Ice' PBR (H1) ~ *min. 10C*
93 H 'Cynthia' (H1) ~ *min. 10C*
02 H 'Daphne' (H1) ~ *min. 10C*
93 H 'Falling Stars' (H1) ~ *min. 10C*
02 H *glandulosissimus* (H1) ~ *min. 10C*
93 H 'Gloria' (H1) ~ *min. 10C*
02 H 'Happy Snappy' (H1) ~ *min. 10C*
93 H 'Heidi' (H1) ~ *min. 10C*
93 H 'Helen' (H1) ~ *min. 10C*
02 H 'Jennifer' (H1) ~ *min. 10C*
93 H 'Kim' (H1) ~ *min. 10C*
02 H 'Laura' (H1) ~ *min. 10C*
93 H 'Lisa' (H1) ~ *min. 10C*
02 H 'Maassen's White' (H1) ~ *min. 10C*
02 H 'Melanie' (H1) ~ *min. 10C*
93 H 'Paula' (H1) ~ *min. 10C*
93 H 'Ruby' (H1) ~ *min. 10C*
93 H *saxorum* (H1) ~ *min. 10C*
93 H 'Snow White' (H1) ~ *min. 10C*
93 H 'Stella' (H1) ~ *min. 10C*
93 H 'Susan' (H1) ~ *min. 10C*
93 H 'Tina' (H1) ~ *min. 10C*

STREPTOSOLEN (SOLANACEAE)
93 T *jamesonii* (H1) ~ *min. 2C*

STROBILANTHES (ACANTHACEAE)
93 T *dyeriana* (v) (H1) ~ *min. 10C*

STROMANTHE (MARANTACEAE)
amabilis ~ see *Ctenanthe amabilis*
93 H *sanguinea* var. *spectabilis* (H1)
~ *min. 15C*

SYAGRUS (ARECACEAE)
weddeliana ~ see *Lytocaryum*
weddellianum

TECOMA (BIGNONIACEAE)
93 T *capensis* (H1) ~ *min. 10C*

TETRANEMA (SCROPHULARIACEAE)
93 H *roseum* (H1) ~ *min. 2C*

TIBOUCHINA (MELASTOMATACEAE)
semidecandra hort. ~ see *Tibouchina*
urvilleana
93 T *urvilleana* (H1) ~ *min. 10C*

TILLANDSIA (BROMELIACEAE)
02 H *argentea* (H1)   *~ min. 15C*
02 H *cyanea* (H1)   *~ min. 15C*
93 H *lindenii* (H1)   *~ min. 15C*

TRACHELIUM (CAMPANULACEAE)
93 H *caeruleum* (H1)   *~ min. 2C*

TRADESCANTIA (COMMELINACEAE)
      blossfeldiana 'Variegata'   *~ see*
         Tradescantia cerinthoides 'Variegata'
93 H **cerinthoides 'Variegata'** (v) (H1)
                                   ~ min. 2C
93 H ***fluminensis* 'Aurea'** (H1) *~ min. 2C*
93 H — **'Quicksilver'** (v) (H1) *~ min. 2C*
93 H — **'Tricolor Minima'** (H1) *~ min. 2C*
      — **'Variegata'**   *~ see Tradescantia*
                          fluminensis 'Aurea'
      pendula *~ see Tradescantia zebrina*
93 H **sillamontana** (H1)   *~ min. 2C*
93 H **spathacea 'Vittata'** (H1) *~ min. 10C*
      tricolor *~ see Tradescantia zebrina*
93 H **zebrina** (H1)   *~ min. 2C*
      — *pendula* *~ see Tradescantia zebrina*
93 H — **'Purpusii'** (H1)   *~ min. 2C*
93 H — **'Quadricolor'** (v) (H1) *~ min. 2C*

VELTHEIMIA (HYACINTHACEAE)
93 B *bracteata* (H1)   *~ min. 2C*
93 B *capensis* (H1)   *~ min. 10C*
      viridifolia hort.   *~ see Veltheimia*
                                  capensis

— Jacq.   *~ see Veltheimia bracteata*

VESTIA (SOLANACEAE)
93 T *foetida* (H1)   *~ min. 2C*
      lycioides   *~ see Vestia foetida*

VRIESEA (BROMELIACEAE)
93 H *duvaliana* (H1)   *~ min. 15C*
93 H *fosteriana* (H1)   *~ min. 15C*
93 H *psittacina* (H1)   *~ min. 10C*
93 H *saundersii* (H1)   *~ min. 15C*
93 H *splendens* (H1)   *~ min. 15C*

WASHINGTONIA (ARECACEAE)
93 T *filifera* (H1)   *~ min. 2C*

WESTRINGIA (LAMIACEAE)
93 T *fruticosa* (H1)   *~ min. 10C*
      rosmariniformis   *~ see Westringia*
                                  fruticosa

YUCCA (AGAVACEAE)
93 T *elephantipes* (H1)   *~ min. 2C*
      guatemalensis   *~ see Yucca*
                                  elephantipes

ZANTEDESCHIA (ARACEAE)
93 B *elliottiana* (H1)   *~ min. 2C*
93 B *rehmannii* (H1)   *~ min. 2C*

ZEPHYRANTHES (AMARYLLIDACEAE)
      robusta   *~ see Habranthus robustus*

Cacti & Succulents

ADENIUM (APOCYNACEAE)
02   **obesum** (H1)   *~ min. 10C; shrubby*

AEONIUM (CRASSULACEAE)
93   **arboreum** (H1)   *~ min. 2C*
93   — **'Atropurpureum'** (H1) *~ min. 2C*
93   **haworthii** (H1)   *~ min. 2C*
93   **tabuliforme** (H1)   *~ min. 2C*
93   **undulatum** (H1)   *~ min. 2C*
93   **'Zwartkop'** (H1)   *~ min. 2C;*
                          previously listed as
                    A. arboreum *'Schwartzkopf'*

AGAVE (AGAVACEAE)
94   **americana** (H1)   *~ min. 2C*

94   — **'Mediopicta'** (v) (H1)   *~ min. 2C;*
                 leaves with a yellow centre stripe
94   — **'Mediopicta Alba'** (v) (H1)
                          ~ min. 2C; leaves with a
                                   white centre stripe
      — **'Mediopicta'** misapplied
      ~ see Agave americana 'Mediopicta Alba'
94   — **'Variegata'** (v) (H1)   *~ min. 2C;*
                   leaves with a yellow edge
94   **filifera** (H1)   *~ min. 2C*
94   **parviflora** (H1)   *~ min. 2C*
94   **potatorum** (H1)   *~ min. 2C*
94   **stricta** (H1)   *~ min. 2C*
02   **utahensis** (H1)   *~ min. 0C*
94   **victoriae-reginae** (H1) *~ min. 2C*

AICHRYSON (CRASSULACEAE)
93 × *domesticum* 'Variegatum' (v) (H1)
~ *min. 10C*

ALOE (ALOACEAE)
02 *arborescens* 'Variegata' (v) (H1)
~ *min. 5C; shrubby*
94 *aristata* (H1) ~ *min. 2C*
94 *bakeri* (H1) ~ *min. 2C*
barbadensis ~ see *Aloe vera*
02 *brevifolia* (H1) ~ *min. 5C*
02 *descoingsii* (H1) ~ *min. 10C*
02 *haworthioides* (H1) ~ *min. 10C*
94 *melanacantha* (H1) ~ *min. 2C*
94 *rauhii* (H1) ~ *min. 2C*
94 *somaliensis* (H1) ~ *min. 2C*
93 *variegata* (v) (H1) ~ *min. 2C*
93 *vera* (H1) ~ *min. 2C*

APOROCACTUS (CACTACEAE)
02 *flagelliformis* (H1) ~ *min. 2C*

APTENIA (AIZOACEAE)
02 *cordifolia* (H1-2) ~ *min. 2C; short-lived perennial*

ASTROPHYTUM (CACTACEAE)
93 *myriostigma* (H1) ~ *min. 2-10C*

CARRUANTHUS (AIZOACEAE)
02 *caninus* (H1) ~ *min. 2C*

CEROPEGIA (ASCLEPIADACEAE)
93 *linearis* subsp. *woodii* (H1) ~ *min. 10C*
02 *sandersonii* (H1) ~ *min. 2C*
93 *stapeliiformis* (H1) ~ *min. 2C*
woodii ~ see *Ceropegia linearis* subsp. *woodii*

CHEIRIDOPSIS (AIZOACEAE)
02 *denticulata* (H1) ~ *min. 2C*
02 *peculiaris* (H1) ~ *min. 2C*

CLEISTOCACTUS (CACTACEAE)
93 *ritteri* (H1) ~ *min. 2-10C*
93 *strausii* (H1) ~ *min. 2-10C*

CONOPHYTUM (AIZOACEAE)
02 *bilobum* (H1) ~ *min. 2C*
02 *flavum* (H1) ~ *min. 2C*
02 *gratum* (H1) ~ *min. 2C*
02 *longum* (H1) ~ *min. 2C*
02 *minimum* (H1) ~ *min. 2C*

02 *obcordellum* (H1) ~ *min. 2C*
02 *pellucidum* (H1) ~ *min. 2C*
02 *truncatum* (H1) ~ *min. 2C*

COPIAPOA (CACTACEAE)
93 *hypogaea* (H1) ~ *min. 2-10C*

CORYPHANTHA (CACTACEAE)
93 *andreae* (H1) ~ *min. 2-10C*
93 *pallida* (H1) ~ *min. 2-10C*

COTYLEDON (CRASSULACEAE)
gibbiflora var. *metallica*
~ see *Echeveria gibbiflora* var. *metallica*

CRASSULA (CRASSULACEAE)
argentea ~ see *Crassula ovata*
93 *falcata* (H1) ~ *min. 10C*
93 *ovata* (H1) ~ *min. 10C*
93 — 'Hummel's Sunset' (v) (H1)
~ *min. 10C*
portulacea ~ see *Crassula ovata*
93 *pyramidalis* (H1) ~ *min. 10C*
93 *rupestris* (H1) ~ *min. 10C*

CYANOTIS (COMMELINACEAE)
93 *kewensis* (H1) ~ *min. 10C*
93 *somaliensis* (H1) ~ *min. 10C*

DISOCACTUS (CACTACEAE)
93 *nelsonii* (H1) ~ *min. 2-10C*

ECHEVERIA (CRASSULACEAE)
93 *agavoides* (H1) ~ *min. 2C*
93 'Bittersweet' (H1) ~ *min. 2C*
93 × *derosa* 'Worfield Wonder' (H1)
~ *min. 2C*
93 *derenbergii* (H1) ~ *min. 2C*
93 *elegans* (H1) ~ *min. 2C*
93 'Frank Reinelt' (H1) ~ *min. 2C*
93 *gibbiflora* var. *metallica* (H1)
~ *min. 2C*
93 × *gilva* 'Blue Surprise' (H1)
~ *min. 2C*
93 — 'Red' (H1) ~ *min. 2C*
glauca Bak. ~ see *Echeveria secunda* var. *glauca*
93 *harmsii* (H1) ~ *min. 2C*
93 *leucotricha* (H1) ~ *min. 2C*
93 'Perle von Nürnberg' (H1) ~ *min. 2C*
93 *pulidonis* (H1) ~ *min. 2C*
93 *pulvinata* (H1) ~ *min. 2C*

02   *secunda* **var.** *glauca* (H1)   ~ *min. 2C;*
                                    suitable for bedding
93   *setosa* (H1)   ~ *min. 2C*
93   **'Victor Reiter'** (H1)   ~ *min. 2C*

ECHINOCEREUS (CACTACEAE)
93   *berlandieri* (H1)   ~ *min. 2-10C*
93   *reichenbachii* (H1)   ~ *min. 2-10C*
93   *subinermis* (H1)   ~ *min. 2-10C*

ECHINOPSIS (CACTACEAE)
93   *ancistrophora* (H1)   ~ *min. 2-10C*
02   *chamaecereus* (H1)   ~ *min. 2C*
      cinnabarina   ~ see *Lobivia*
                                    cinnabarina
93   *eyriesii* (H1)   ~ *min. 2-10C*
      kermesina ~ see *Echinopsis mamillosa*
                                    var. *kermesina*
93   *mamillosa* **var.** *kermesina* (H1)
                                    ~ *min. 2-10C*

ESCOBARIA (CACTACEAE)
93   *roseana* (H1)   ~ *min. 2-10C*

ESPOSTOA (CACTACEAE)
93   *nana* (H1)   ~ *min. 2-10C*

EUPHORBIA (EUPHORBIACEAE)
02   *horrida* (H1)   ~ *min. 5C; shrubby*
02   *meloformis* (H1)   ~ *min. 5C*
02   *obesa* (H1)   ~ *min. 5C*
02   *viguieri* (H1)   ~ *min. 10C; shrubby*

FAUCARIA (AIZOACEAE)
93   *candida* (H1)   ~ *min. 2-10C*
02   *tigrina* (H1)   ~ *min. 2C*
02   *tuberculosa* (H1)   ~ *min. 2C*

FENESTRARIA (AIZOACEAE)
02   *aurantiaca* (H1)   ~ *min. 2C*

FEROCACTUS (CACTACEAE)
93   *fordii* (H1)   ~ *min. 2-10C*
93   *glaucescens* (H1)   ~ *min. 2-10C*
93   *viridescens* (H1)   ~ *min. 2-10C*

FRITHIA (AIZOACEAE)
02   *pulchra* (H1)   ~ *min. 2C*

GASTERIA (LILIACEAE)
02   *batesiana* (H1)   ~ *min. 2C*
02   *nitida* **var.** *armstrongii* (H1)
                                    ~ *min. 2C*

GRAPTOPETALUM (CRASSULACEAE)
02   *bellum* (H1)   ~ *min. 2C*

GYMNOCALYCIUM (CACTACEAE)
93   *andreae* (H1)   ~ *min. 2-10C*
93   *baldianum* (H1)   ~ *min. 2-10C*
93   *quehlianum* (H1)   ~ *min. 2-10C*
93   *tillianum* (H1)   ~ *min. 2-10C*
93   *uruguayense* (H1)   ~ *min. 2-10C*

HAMATOCACTUS (CACTACEAE)
      setispinus ~ see *Thelocactus setispinus*

HATIORA (CACTACEAE)
93   *gaertneri* (H1)   ~ *min. 10C*
93   *rosea* (H1)   ~ *min. 10C*
93   *salicornioides* (H1)   ~ *min. 2-10C*

HAWORTHIA (ALOACEAE)
93   *attenuata* **f.** *caespitosa* (H1)
                                    ~ *min. 2-10C*
02   *pumila* (H1)   ~ *min. 2C*
02   *reinwardtii* (H1)   ~ *min. 2C*
02   *retusa* (H1)   ~ *min. 2C*
      tesselata   ~ see *Haworthia venosa*
                                    subsp. *tesselata*
02   *truncata* (H1)   ~ *min. 2C*
93   *venosa* **subsp.** *tesselata* (H1)
                                    ~ *min. 2-10C*

HELIOCEREUS (CACTACEAE)
93   *speciosus* (H1)   ~ *min. 2-10C*

HILDEWINTERA (CACTACEAE)
93   *aureispina* (H1)   ~ *min. 2-10C*

JATROPHA (EUPHORBIACEAE)
02   *podagrica* (H1)   ~ *min. 10C; shrubby*

KALANCHOE (CRASSULACEAE)
02   *beharensis* (H1)   ~ *min. 10C; shrubby*
02   *manginii* (H1)   ~ *min. 10C*
02   **'Mariko'** (H1)   ~ *min. 10C*
02   *marmorata* (H1)   ~ *min. 10C*
02   *millotii* (H1)   ~ *min. 10C*
93   *pumila* (H1)   ~ *min. 2C*
93   **'Tessa'** (H1)   ~ *min. 10C*
93   *tomentosa* (H1)   ~ *min. 10C*
93   **'Wendy'** (H1)   ~ *min. 10C*

KLEINIA (ASTERACEAE)
02   *stapeliiformis* (H1)   ~ *min. 10C;*
                                    shrubby

LAMPRANTHUS (AIZOACEAE)
 deltoides ~ see *Oscularia deltoides*
 oscularis ~ see *Oscularia deltoides*

LEPISMIUM (CACTACEAE)
93 *houlletianum* (H1)   ~ *min. 2-10C*

LITHOPS (AIZOACEAE)
02 *aucampiae* (H1)   ~ *min. 2C*
02 *bromfieldii* (H1)   ~ *min. 2C*
02 *hallii* (H1)   ~ *min. 2C*
02 *hookeri* (H1)   ~ *min. 2C*
02 *karasmontana* (H1)   ~ *min. 2C*
02 *lesliei* (H1)   ~ *min. 2C*
02 *olivacea* (H1)   ~ *min. 2C*
02 *pseudotruncatella* (H1) ~ *min. 2C*
02 *salicola* (H1)   ~ *min. 2C*
02 *schwantesii* (H1)   ~ *min. 2C*

LOBIVIA (CACTACEAE)
93 *aurea* (H1)   ~ *min. 2-10C*
93 *cinnabarina* (H1)   ~ *min. 2-10C*
93 *jajoiana* (H1)   ~ *min. 2-10C*
93 *winteriana* (H1)   ~ *min. 2-10C*
93 *wrightiana* (H1)   ~ *min. 2-10C*

MAMMILLARIA (CACTACEAE)
93 *baumii* (H1)   ~ *min. 2-10C*
93 *bocasana* (H1)   ~ *min. 2-10C*
93 *bombycina* (H1)   ~ *min. 2-10C*
93 *candida* (H1)   ~ *min. 2-10C*
93 *carmenae* (H1)   ~ *min. 2-10C*
93 *elongata* (H1)   ~ *min. 2-10C*
93 *geminispina* (H1)   ~ *min. 2-10C*
93 *hahniana* (H1)   ~ *min. 2-10C*
93 *parkinsonii* (H1)   ~ *min. 2-10C*
93 *plumosa* (H1)   ~ *min. 2-10C*
93 *pringlei* (H1)   ~ *min. 2-10C*
93 *prolifera* (H1)   ~ *min. 2-10C*
93 *sphaerica* (H1)   ~ *min. 2-10C*
93 *spinosissima* (H1)   ~ *min. 2-10C*
93 *zeilmanniana* (H1)   ~ *min. 2-10C*

MATUCANA (CACTACEAE)
93 *aurantiaca* (H1)   ~ *min. 2-10C*
93 *intertexta* (H1)   ~ *min. 2-10C*

NEOCHILENIA (CACTACEAE)
 mitis   ~ see *Neoporteria napina*
                             f. mitis
 paucicostata   ~ see *Neoporteria*
                          paucicostata

NEOHENRICIA (AIZOACEAE)
93 *sibbettii* (H1)   ~ *min. 2-10C*

NEOPORTERIA (CACTACEAE)
93 *multicolor* (H1)   ~ *min. 2-10C*
93 *napina* f. *mitis* (H1) ~ *min. 2-10C*
93 *paucicostata* (H1)   ~ *min. 2-10C*
93 *wagenknechtii* (H1)   ~ *min. 2-10C*

NOPALXOCHIA (CACTACEAE)
93 *phyllanthoides* (H1)   ~ *min. 2-10C*

NOTOCACTUS (CACTACEAE)
93 *apricus* (H1)   ~ *min. 2-10C*
93 *crassigibbus* (H1)   ~ *min. 2-10C*
93 *magnificus* (H1)   ~ *min. 2-10C*
93 *mammulosus* (H1)   ~ *min. 2-10C*
93 *scopa* (H1)   ~ *min. 2-10C*
93 *uebelmannianus* (H1)   ~ *min. 2-10C*

OPUNTIA (CACTACEAE)
93 *microdasys* 'Albata' (H1)
                             ~ *min. 2-10C*
 — 'Angel's Wings'   ~ see *Opuntia*
                       microdasys 'Albata'
02 *rufida* (H1)   ~ *min.2C*

ORBEA (ASCLEPIADACEAE)
93 *variegata* (v) (H1)   ~ *min. 2C*

OREOCEREUS (CACTACEAE)
93 *hendriksenianus* var. *densilanatus*
     (H1)   ~ *min. 2-10C*

OSCULARIA (AIZOACEAE)
02 *deltoides* (H1-2)   ~ *min. 2C*

PACHYPODIUM (APOCYNACEAE)
02 *geayi* (H1)   ~ *min. 10C; shrubby*
02 *lamerei* (H1)   ~ *min. 10C; shrubby*

PARODIA (CACTACEAE)
93 *mairanana* (H1)   ~ *min. 2-10C*
 mammulosa   ~ see *Notocactus*
                          mammulosus
93 *penicillata* (H1)   ~ *min. 2-10C*
93 *schwebsiana* (H1)   ~ *min. 2-10C*
 scopa   ~ see *Notocactus scopa*
93 *subterranea* (H1)   ~ *min. 2-10C*

PEDILANTHUS (EUPHORBIACEAE)
02 *tithymaloides* 'Variegatus' (v) (H1)
                       ~ *min. 5C; shrubby*

PLEIOSPILOS (AIZOACEAE)
93 *bolusii* (H1)   ~ *min. 2-10C*
02 *compactus* (H1)   ~ *min. 2C*
02 *nelii* (H1)   ~ *min. 2C*

REBUTIA (CACTACEAE)
    arenacea   ~ see *Sulcorebutia*
                               arenacea
93 *aureiflora* (H1)   ~ *min. 2-10C*
    candiae   ~ see *Sulcorebutia candiae*
    canigueralii   ~ see *Sulcorebutia*
                               canigueralii
93 *deminuta* (H1)   ~ *min. 2-10C*
93 *donaldiana* (H1)   ~ *min. 2-10C*
    glomeriseta   ~ see *Sulcorebutia*
                               glomeriseta
93 *haagei* (H1)   ~ *min. 2-10C*
93 *kupperiana* (H1)   ~ *min. 2-10C*
93 *marsoneri* (H1)   ~ *min. 2-10C*
    mentosa   ~ see *Sulcorebutia*
                               mentosa
93 *muscula* (H1)   ~ *min. 2-10C*
93 *narvaecensis* (H1)   ~ *min. 2-10C*
    neocumingii   ~ see *Weingartia*
                               neocumingii
    pseudominuscula   ~ see *Rebutia*
                               deminuta
93 *senilis* var. *kesselringiana* (H1)
                           ~ *min. 2-10C*
    steinbachii   ~ see *Sulcorebutia*
                               steinbachii
93 *violaciflora* (H1)   ~ *min. 2-10C*

RHIPSALIDOPSIS (CACTACEAE)
    gaertneri   ~ see *Hatiora gaertneri*

RHIPSALIS (CACTACEAE)
    houlletiana   ~ see *Lepismium*
                               houlletianum
93 *monacantha* (H1)   ~ *min. 2-10C*
93 *pilocarpa* (H1)   ~ *min. 2-10C*

RHOMBOPHYLLUM (AIZOACEAE)
02 *rhomboideum* (H1)   ~ *min. 2C*

SCHLUMBERGERA (CACTACEAE)
93 × *buckleyi* (H1)   ~ *min. 10C*

SEDUM (CRASSULACEAE)
93 *morganianum* (H1)   ~ *min. 2C*

SENECIO (ASTERACEAE)
02 *haworthii* (H1)   ~ *min. 2C*

STAPELIA (ASCLEPIADACEAE)
93 *gigantea* (H1)   ~ *min. 2C*
    variegata   ~ see *Orbea variegata*

STOMATIUM (AIZOACEAE)
02 *meyeri* (H1)   ~ *min. 2C*
02 *niveum* (H1)   ~ *min. 2C*

SULCOREBUTIA (CACTACEAE)
93 *arenacea* (H1)   ~ *min. 2-10C*
93 *candiae* (H1)   ~ *min. 2-10C*
93 *canigueralii* (H1)   ~ *min. 2-10C*
93 *crispata* (H1)   ~ *min. 2-10C*
93 *flavissima* (H1)   ~ *min. 2-10C*
93 *glomeriseta* (H1)   ~ *min 2-10C*
93 *mentosa* (H1)   ~ *min. 2-10C*
93 *mizquensis* (H1)   ~ *min. 2-10C*
93 *steinbachii* (H1)   ~ *min. 2-10C*
93 *tunariensis* (H1)   ~ *min. 2-10C*

THELOCACTUS (CACTACEAE)
93 *bicolor* (H1)   ~ *min. 2-10C*
93 *setispinus* (H1)   ~ *min. 2-10C*

TITANOPSIS (AIZOACEAE)
02 *calcarea* (H1)   ~ *min. 2C*

TRICHODIADEMA (AIZOACEAE)
02 *densum* (H1)   ~ *min. 2C*
02 *stellatum* (H1)   ~ *min. 2C*

WEINGARTIA (CACTACEAE)
93 *multispina* (H1)   ~ *min. 2-10C*
93 *neocumingii* (H1)   ~ *min. 2-10C*
93 *pilcomayensis* (H1)   ~ *min. 2-10C*
93 *pulquinensis* (H1)   ~ *min. 2-10C*

Climbers

ALLAMANDA (APOCYNACEAE)
93 *cathartica* 'Hendersonii' (H1)
~ *min. 15C*

ARISTOLOCHIA (ARISTOLOCHIACEAE)
elegans ~ see *Aristolochia littoralis*
93 *littoralis* (H1) ~ *min. 10C*

ASPARAGUS (ASPARAGACEAE)
93 *asparagoides* (H1) ~ *min. 2C*
plumosus ~ see *Asparagus setaceus*
93 *setaceus* (H1) ~ *min. 10C*
02 — 'Pyramidalis' (H1) ~ *min. 2C*

BOMAREA (ALSTROEMERIACEAE)
93 *caldasii* (H1) ~ *min. 2C*

BOUGAINVILLEA (NYCTAGINACEAE)
93 × *buttiana* 'Killie Campbell' (H1)
~ *min. 10C*
93 — 'Mrs Butt' (H1) ~ *min. 10C*
93 — 'Poulton's Special' (H1)
~ *min. 10C*
'Crimson Lake' misapplied
~ see *Bougainvillea* × *buttiana* 'Mrs Butt'
93 *glabra* (H1) ~ *min. 10C*
'Mrs Butt' ~ see *Bougainvillea* × *buttiana* 'Mrs Butt'
'Poultonii Special' ~ see *Bougainvillea* × *buttiana* 'Poulton's Special'
93 *spectabilis* 'Margaret Bacon' (H1)
~ *min. 10C*

CISSUS (VITACEAE)
93 *antarctica* (H1) ~ *min. 2C*
93 *rhombifolia* (H1) ~ *min. 10C*
93 — 'Ellen Danica' (H1) ~ *min. 10C*

CLERODENDRUM (VERBENACEAE)
93 *splendens* (H1) ~ *min. 15C*
93 *thomsoniae* (H1) ~ *min. 15C*

DIOSCOREA (DIOSCOREACEAE)
02 *elephantipes* (H1) ~ *min. 5C*

EPIPREMNUM (ARACEAE)
93 *aureum* (H1) ~ *min. 10C*

pinnatum 'Aureum'
~ see *Epipremnum aureum*
93 — 'Aztec' (H1) ~ *min. 10C*

FICUS (MORACEAE)
93 *pumila* (H1)

GELSEMIUM (LOGANIACEAE)
93 *sempervirens* (H1-2)

GLORIOSA (COLCHICACEAE)
93 *superba* (H1) ~ *min. 10C*

HARDENBERGIA (PAPILIONACEAE)
93 *comptoniana* (H1) ~ *min. 2C*
93 *violacea* (H1) ~ *min. 2C*

HIBBERTIA (DILLENIACEAE)
93 *scandens* (H1) ~ *min. 2C*
volubilis ~ see *Hibbertia scandens*

HOYA (ASCLEPIADACEAE)
93 *carnosa* (H1) ~ *min. 2C*
93 — 'Exotica' (H1) ~ *min. 10C*

IPOMOEA (CONVOLVULACEAE)
acuminata ~ see *Ipomoea indica*
93 *horsfalliae* (H1) ~ *min. 2C*
93 *indica* (H1) ~ *min. 2C*
learii ~ see *Ipomoea indica*

JASMINUM (OLEACEAE)
02 *angulare* (H1) ~ *min. 5C*
93 *azoricum* (H1) ~ *min. 2C*
blinii ~ see *Jasminum polyanthum*
02 *grandiflorum* 'De Grasse' (H1)
~ *min. 5C*
93 *polyanthum* (H1-2)
02 *sambac* (H1) ~ *min. 5C*
02 — 'Maid of Orleans' (d) (H1)
~ *min. 5C*

MANDEVILLA (APOCYNACEAE)
93 × *amabilis* 'Alice du Pont' (H1)
~ *min. 10C; previously listed under M. × amoena*
02 *boliviensis* (H1) ~ *min. 10C*
02 *splendens* (H1) ~ *min. 10C*

MONSTERA (ARACEAE)
93 *deliciosa* (F) (H1)   ~ *min. 10C*
93 — **'Variegata'** (v) (H1)   ~ *min. 10C*

PANDOREA (BIGNONIACEAE)
93 *jasminoides* **'Rosea Superba'** (H1)
                              ~ *min. 10C*

PASSIFLORA (PASSIFLORACEAE)
93 *alata* (F) (H1)   ~ *min. 10C*
93 **'Amethyst'** (H1)   ~ *min. 2C;*
                    not P. amethystina Mikan,
                    though has been distributed
                    under the name
    amethystina misapplied
                    ~ see *Passiflora* 'Amethyst'
93 × *exoniensis* (H1)   ~ *min. 2C*
93 **'Incense'** (F) (H1)   ~ *min. 2C*
93 *mollissima* (F) (H1)   ~ *min. 2C*
93 *quadrangularis* L. (F) (H1)   ~ *min. 10C*
93 × *violacea* (H1)   ~ *min. 2C*

PHILODENDRON (ARACEAE)
93 *angustisectum* (H1)   ~ *min. 15C*
    elegans   ~ see *Philodendron*
                              angustisectum
93 *erubescens* (H1)   ~ *min. 15C*
93 — **'Burgundy'** (H1)   ~ *min. 15C*
93 *scandens* (H1)   ~ *min. 10C*

RHODOCHITON (SCROPHULARIACEAE)
93 R *atrosanguineus* (H1-2)
    volubilis
        ~ see *Rhodochiton atrosanguineus*

RHOICISSUS (VITACEAE)
93 *capensis* (H1)   ~ *min. 2C*

SCINDAPSUS (ARACEAE)
    aureus   ~ see *Epipremnum aureum*
93 *pictus* **'Argyraeus'** (H1)   ~ *min. 10C*

SENECIO (ASTERACEAE)
93 *macroglossus* **'Variegatus'** (v) (H1)
                              ~ *min. 2C*

SOLLYA (PITTOSPORACEAE)
    fusiformis   ~ see *Sollya*
                              heterophylla
93 *heterophylla* (H1)   ~ *min. 2C*

STEPHANOTIS (ASCLEPIADACEAE)
93 *floribunda* (H1)   ~ *min. 10C*

SYNGONIUM (ARACEAE)
93 *podophyllum* (H1)   ~ *min. 10C*

TETRASTIGMA (VITACEAE)
93 *voinierianum* (H1)   ~ *min. 15C*

THUNBERGIA (ACANTHACEAE)
93 *grandiflora* (H1)   ~ *min. 10C*
93 *mysorensis* (H1)   ~ *min. 15C*

TROPAEOLUM (TROPAEOLACEAE)
93 *ciliatum* (H1)   ~ *min. 2C*
93 *tricolor* (H1)   ~ *min. 2C*

Heated Glass, Summer Display

Perennials for over-wintering under heated glass, placed outside for summer display

General

ARCTOTIS (ASTERACEAE)
98 H × *hybrida* 'Flame' (H1+3)   ~ *min. 2C*
98 H — 'Mahogany' (H1+3)   ~ *min. 2C*

ARGYRANTHEMUM (ASTERACEAE)
02 H 'Butterfly' (H1+3)   ~ *min. 2C*
canariense hort.
    ~ see *Argyranthemum
    frutescens* subsp. *canariae*
93 H 'Cornish Gold' (H1+3)   ~ *min. 2C*
93 H 'Donington Hero' (H1+3)   ~ *min. 2C*
foeniculaceum hort. (pink)
    ~ see *Argyranthemum* 'Petite Pink'
93 H *foeniculaceum* (Willd.) Webb & Sch.Bip.
    'Royal Haze' (H1+3)
        ~ *valued especially as a
        foliage plant; min. 2C*
93 H *frutescens* subsp. *canariae* (H1+3)
        ~ *min. 2C*
02 H — 'Sugar Button' PBR (d) (H1+3)
        ~ *min. 2C*
93 H *gracile* 'Chelsea Girl' (H1+3)
        ~ *min. 2C; valued as a foliage plant*
93 H 'Jamaica Primrose' (H1+3)
        ~ *min. 2C*
'Jamaica Snowstorm'
    ~ see *Argyranthemum* 'Snow Storm'
93 H 'Levada Cream' (H1+3)   ~ *min. 2C*
93 H *maderense* (H1+3)   ~ *min. 2C*
93 H 'Mary Cheek' (d) (H1+3)   ~ *min. 2C*
'Nevada Cream'
        ~ see *Argyranthemum
        'Levada Cream'*
ochroleucum
    ~ see *Argyranthemum maderense*
93 H 'Petite Pink' (H1+3)   ~ *min. 2C*
'Pink Delight'   ~ see *Argyranthemum
    'Petite Pink'*
93 H 'Qinta White' (d) (H1+3)   ~ *min. 2C*
'Royal Haze'   ~ see *Argyranthemum
    foeniculaceum* 'Royal Haze'
93 H 'Snow Storm' (H1+3)   ~ *min. 2C*
93 H 'Vancouver' (d) (H1+3)   ~ *min. 2C*
93 H 'Whiteknights' (H1+3)   ~ *min. 2C*

BEGONIA (BEGONIACEAE)
02 **DRAGON WING RED 'Bepared'** PBR
    (H1+3)   ~ *min. 10C*

BIDENS (ASTERACEAE)
93 H *ferulifolia* (H1+3)   ~ *min. 2C*

CHLOROPHYTUM (ANTHERICACEAE)
93 H *comosum* 'Variegatum' (v) (H1+3)
        ~ *min. 2C*
93 H — 'Vittatum' (v) (H1+3)   ~ *min. 2C*

ENSETE (MUSACEAE)
02 T *ventricosum* (H1+3)   ~ *min. 5C*

EXACUM (GENTIANACEAE)
02 A *affine* (H1+3)   ~ *min. 10C;
        annual/biennial*

FUCHSIA (ONAGRACEAE)
02 T 'Alison Sweetman' (H1+3)   ~ *min. 5C*
02 T 'Autumnale' (H1+3)   ~ *min. 5C*
02 T 'Ballet Girl' (d) (H1+3)   ~ *min. 5C*
02 T 'Bella Forbes' (d) (H1+3)   ~ *min. 5C*
93 T 'Billy Green' (H1+3)   ~ *min. 10C*
boliviana 'Alba'   ~ see *Fuchsia
    boliviana* var. *alba*
93 T *boliviana* var. *alba* (H1+3)   ~ *min. 10C*
— var. *luxurians*   ~ see *Fuchsia
    boliviana* var. *alba*
— — 'Alba'   ~ see *Fuchsia boliviana*
        var. *alba*
02 T 'Carla Johnston' (H1+3)   ~ *min. 5C*
02 T 'Chang' (H1+3)   ~ *min. 5C*
cordifolia hort. ~ see *Fuchsia splendens*
corymbiflora alba   ~ see *Fuchsia
    boliviana* var. *alba*
02 T 'Dancing Flame' (d) (H1+3) ~ *min. 5C*
93 T *fulgens* (H1+3)   ~ *min. 10C*
93 T 'Gartenmeister Bonstedt' (H1+3)
        ~ *min. 10C*
02 T 'Lottie Hobby' (H1+3)   ~ *min. 5C*
02 T 'Love's Reward' (H1+3)   ~ *min. 5C*
02 T 'Lye's Unique' (H1+3)   ~ *min. 5C*
93 T 'Mary' (H1+3)   ~ *min. 10C*
02 T 'Micky Goult' (H1+3)   ~ *min. 5C*
02 T 'Mieke Meursing' (H1+3)   ~ *min. 5C*
02 T *paniculata* (H1+3)   ~ *min. 5C*

02 T **'Pink Marshmallow'** (d) (H1+3)
~ *min. 5C*
02 T **'Preston Guild'** (H1+3)   ~ *min. 5C*
93 T *splendens* (H1+3)   ~ *min. 10C*
93 T **'Thalia'** (H1+3)   ~ *min. 10C*
02 T **'Whiteknights Pearl'** (H1+3)
~ *min. 5C*

GAZANIA (ASTERACEAE)
93 H **'Aztec'** (H1+3)   ~ *min. 2C*
93 H **'Cookei'** (H1+3)   ~ *min. 2C*
96 H **'Dorothy'** (H1+3)   ~ *min. 2C*
96 H **'Michael'** (H1+3)   ~ *min. 2C*
96 H **'Northbourne'** (H1+3)   ~ *min. 2C*
96 H *rigens* var. *uniflora* (H1+3) ~ *min. 2C*
93 H — **'Variegata'** (v) (H1+3)   ~ *min. 2C*

GREVILLEA (PROTEACEAE)
93 T *robusta* (H1+3)   ~ *min. 2C*

LOBELIA (CAMPANULACEAE)
96 P *richardsonii* (H1+3)   ~ *min. 10C*

LOTUS (PAPILIONACEAE)
02 T *berthelotii* deep red (H1+3)   ~ *min. 2C*
02 T — × *maculatus* (H1+3)   ~ *min. 2C*

MUSA (MUSACEAE)
02 T *acuminata* **'Zebrina'** (H1+3) ~ *min. 10C*
        ensete   ~ see *Ensete ventricosum*
02 T *velutina* (H1+3)   ~ *min. 10C*

NERIUM (APOCYNACEAE)
02 T *Oleander* **'Variegatum'** (v) (H1+3)
~ *min. 5C*

OSTEOSPERMUM (ASTERACEAE)
93 H **'Buttermilk'** (H1+3)   ~ *min. 2C*
93 H **'Pink Whirls'** (H1+3)   ~ *min. 2C*
93 H **'Silver Sparkler'** (v) (H1+3) ~ *min. 2C*
        'Tauranga'   ~ see *Osteospermum*
'Whirlygig'
93 H **'Whirlygig'** (H1+3)   ~ *min. 2C*

PELARGONIUM (GERANIACEAE)
        'A Happy Thought'
~ see *Pelargonium* 'Happy Thought'
93 H **'Alice Crousse'** (I/d) (H1+3) ~ *min. 2C*
93 H AMETHYST **'Fisdel'** PBR (I/d) (H1+3)
~ *min. 2C*
94 H **'Ann Hoystead'** (R) (H1+3)
~ *min. 2C*

(A)	Angel
(C)	Coloured Foliage (in combination)
(d)	Double (in combination)
(Dec)	Decorative
(Dw)	Dwarf
(Fr)	Frutetorum
(I)	Ivy-leaved
(Min)	Miniature
(R)	Regal
(Sc)	Scented-leaved
(St)	Stellar (in combination)
(U)	Unique
(Z)	Zonal
(v)	variegated (in combination)

99 H ANTIK ORANGE **'Tikorg'** PBR (Antik
Series) (Z) (H1+3)
~ *min. 2C; single; recommended for*
cultivation under glass
93 H **'Apache'** (Z/d) (H1+3)   ~ *min. 2C*
93 H **'Apple Blossom Rosebud'** (Z/d)
(H1+3)   ~ *min. 2C*
93 H **'Ashfield Monarch'** (Z/d) (H1+3)
~ *min. 2C*
93 H **'Ashfield Serenade'** (Z) (H1+3)
~ *min. 2C*
94 H **'Askham Fringed Aztec'** (R) (H1+3)
~ *min. 2C*
93 H **'Attar of Roses'** (Sc) (H1+3) ~ *min. 2C*
93 H **'Aztec'** (R) (H1+3)   ~ *min. 2C*
        BALCON IMPERIAL   ~ see *Pelargonium*
'Roi des Balcons Impérial'
        'Balcon Lilas'   ~ see *Pelargonium*
'Roi des Balcons Lilas'
        'Balcon Rouge'   ~ see *Pelargonium*
'Roi des Balcons Impérial'
        'Balcon Royale'   ~ see *Pelargonium*
'Roi des Balcons Impérial'
        'Ballerina'   ~ see *Pelargonium*
'Carisbrooke'
93 H **'Belinda Adams'** (Min/d) (H1+3)
~ *min. 2C*
99 H BELLINZONA **'Klebelli'** PBR (Z) (H1+3)
~ *min. 2C; single*
93 H   **'Ben Franklin'** (Z/d/v) (H1+3) ~ *min. 2C*
93 H   **'Bird Dancer'** (Dw/St) (H1+3) ~ *min. 2C*
02 H **'Black Magic Rose'** (Z) (H1+3) ~ *min. 2C*
02 H **'Black Magic Scarlet'** (H1+3) ~ *min. 2C*
94 H **'Bodey's Picotee'** (R) (H1+3) ~ *min. 2C*
96 H **'Bolero'** (U) (H1+3)   ~ *min. 2C*
93 H **'Brackenwood'** (Dw/d) (H1+3)
~ *min. 2C*
93 H **'Bredon'** (R) (H1+3)   ~ *min. 2C*
93 H **'Bridal Veil'** (Min/C) (H1+3) ~ *min. 2C*
94 H **'Bushfire'** (R) (H1+3)   ~ *min. 2C*

99 H **'Cardinalis'** (Z) (H1+3)   ~ *min. 2C; single*

93 H **'Cariboo Gold'** (Min/C) (H1+3)
    ~ *min. 2C*

94 H **'Carisbrooke'** (R) (H1+3)   ~ *min. 2C*

CASCADE LILAC   ~ see *Pelargonium* 'Roi des Balcons Lilas'

CASCADE RED   ~ see *Pelargonium* 'Red Cascade'

94 H **'Catford Belle'** (A) (H1+3)   ~ *min. 2C*

96 H **'Charity'** (Sc) (H1+3)

93 H **'Chelsea Gem'** (Z/d/v) (H1+3)
    ~ *min. 2C*

96 H **'Citriodorum'** (Sc) (H1+3)

99 H **'Claire'** (Z) (H1+3) ~ *min. 2C; single; recommended for cultivation under glass*

93 H **'Copthorne'** (Sc) (H1+3)   ~ *min. 2C*

93 H **'Corsair'** (Z/d) (H1+3)   ~ *min. 2C*

93 H **'Crimson Unique'** (U) (H1+3)
    ~ *min. 2C*

93 H *crispum* **'Variegatum'** (Sc/v) (H1+3)
    ~ *min. 2C*

93 H **'Dame Anna Neagle'** (Dw/d) (H1+3)
    ~ *min. 2C*

94 H **'Darmsden'** (A) (H1+3)   ~ *min. 2C*

93 H **'Dolly Varden'** (Z/v) (H1+3)
    ~ *min. 2C*

93 H **'Earl of Chester'** (Min/d) (H1+3)
    ~ *min. 2C*

94 H **'Eileen Postle'** (R) (H1+3)   ~ *min. 2C*

93 H **'Fantasia' white** (Dw/d) (H1+3)
    ~ *min. 2C*

94 H **'Fareham'** (R) (H1+3)   ~ *min. 2C*

93 H **'Flakey'** (I/d/v) (H1+3)   ~ *min 2C; valued especially for its foliage effect*

99 H **'Flamenca'** (Z) (H1+3)   ~ *single*

93 H **'Flower of Spring'** (Z/v) (H1+3)
    ~ *min. 2C*

93 H **'Francis Parrett'** (Min/d) (H1+3)
    ~ *min. 2C*

93 H **'Frank Headley'** (Z/v) (H1+3)
    ~ *min. 2C*

94 H **'Fringed Aztec'** (R) (H1+3)
    ~ *min. 2C*

93 H **'Galilee'** (I/d) (H1+3)   ~ *min. 2C*

93 H **'Galway Star'** (Sc/v) (H1+3)
    ~ *min. 2C*

94 H **'Gemma Jewel'** (R) (H1+3)
    ~ *min. 2C*

96 H **'Gemstone'** (Sc) (H1+3)   ~ *min. 2C*

94 H **'Georgina Blythe'** (R) (H1+3)
    ~ *min. 2C*

02 H **'Golden Harry Hieover'** (Z/C) (H1+3)
    ~ *min. 2C; suitable for bedding*

96 H **'Grace Thomas'** (Sc) (H1+3)
    ~ *min. 2C*

93 H **'Grenadier'** (Z/St/d) (H1+3) ~ *min. 2C*

93 H **'Happy Thought'** (Z/v) (H1+3)
    ~ *min. 2C*

93 H **'Hope Valley'** (Dw/C/d) (H1+3)
    ~ *min. 2C*

93 H INGRES **'Guicerdan'** [PBR] (I/d) (H1+3)
    ~ *min. 2C*

93 H **'Irene'** (Z/d) (H1+3)   ~ *min. 2C*

93 H **'Irene Cal'** (Z/d) (H1+3)   ~ *min. 2C*

93 H **'Irene Toyon'** (Z) (H1+3)   ~ *min. 2C*

93 H **'Isidel'** (I/d) (H1+3)   ~ *min. 2C*

94 H **'Joy'** (R) (H1+3)   ~ *min. 2C*

94 H **'Julia'** (R) (H1+3)   ~ *min. 2C*

99 H **'Juve'** (Z) (H1+3)   ~ *min. 2C; single*

94 H **'Kettlebaston'** (A) (H1+3) ~ *min. 2C*

93 H **'La France'** (I/d) (H1+3)   ~ *min. 2C*

93 H **'Lady Plymouth'** (Sc/v) (H1+3)
    ~ *min. 2C*

96 H **'Lara Candy Dancer'** (Sc) (H1+3)

94 H **'Lara Maid'** (A) (H1+3)   ~ *min. 2C*

96 H **'Lara Starshine'** (Sc) (H1+3) ~ *min. 2C*

94 H **'Lavender Grand Slam'** (R) (H1+3)
    ~ *min. 2C*

93 H **'L'Elégante'** (I/v) (H1+3)   ~ *min. 2C; valued especially for its foliage effect*

LILAC CASCADE   ~ see *Pelargonium* 'Roi des Balcons Lilas'

93 H **'Little Alice'** (Dw/d) (H1+3) ~ *min. 2C*

93 H **'Lord Bute'** (R) (H1+3)   ~ *min. 2C*

'Lord de Ramsey' ~ see *Pelargonium* 'Tip Top Duet'

93 H **'Mabel Grey'** (Sc) (H1+3) ~ *min. 2C*

93 H **'Madame Crousse'** (I/d) (H1+3)
    ~ *min. 2C*

93 H **'Madame Salleron'** (Min/v) (H1+3)
    ~ *min. 2C*

94 H **'Margaret Soley'** (R) (H1+3) ~ *min. 2C*

02 H **'Maverick Scarlet'** (H1+3)   ~ *min. 2C*

93 H **'Morval'** (Dw/C/d) (H1+3) ~ *min. 2C*

02 H **'Moulin Rouge'** (H1+3)   ~ *min. 2C*

93 H **'Mr Henry Cox'** (Z/v) (H1+3)
    ~ *min. 2C*

93 H **'Mrs J.C. Mappin'** (Z/v) (H1+3)
    ~ *min. 2C*

02 H **'Mrs Quilter'** (Z/C) (H1+3)
    ~ *min. 2C; suitable for bedding*

02 P   **Multibloom Series** (Z) (H1+3)
        ~ sold as a mixture
96 H   **'Mystery'** (U) (H1+3)   *~ min. 2C*
96 H   **'Nervous Mabel'** (Sc) (H1+3)
                                        ~ min. 2C
02 H   **'Orange Appeal'** (H1+3)   *~ min. 2C*
96 H   **'Orsett'** (Sc) (H1+3)   *~ min. 2C*
93 H   **'Paton's Unique'** (U/Sc) (H1+3)
                                        ~ min. 2C
93 H   **'Pavilion'** (Min) (H1+3)   *~ min. 2C*
96 H   **'Peter's Luck'** (Sc) (H1+3)   *~ min. 2C*
96 H   **'Princeanum'** (Sc) (H1+3)   *~ min. 2C*
        'Princess of Balcon' ~ see *Pelargonium*
                'Roi des Balcons Lilas'
02 H   **'Pulsar Deep Rose'** (H1+3)   *~ min. 2C*
96 H   **'Radula'** (Sc) (H1+3)   *~ min. 2C*
93 H   **'Red Cascade'** (I) (H1+3)   *~ min. 2C*
93 H   **'Renee Ross'** (I/d) (H1+3)   *~ min. 2C*
93 H   **'Rodomont'** (I) (H1+3)   *~ min. 2C*
93 H   **'Roi des Balcons Impérial'** (I) (H1+3)
                                        ~ min. 2C
93 H   **'Roi des Balcons Lilas'** (I) (H1+3)
                                        ~ min. 2C
96 H   **'Roller's Satinique'** (U) (H1+3)
                                        ~ min. 2C
93 H   **ROSAIS** (I/d) (H1+3)   *~ min. 2C*
93 H   **'Rosita'** (Dw/d) (H1+3)   *~ min. 2C*
96 H   **'Royal Oak'** (Sc) (H1+3)   *~ min. 2C*
94 H   **'Royal Princess'** (R) (H1+3) *~ min. 2C*
94 H   **'Sancho Panza'** (Dec) (H1+3)
                                        ~ min. 2C
94 H   **'Sefton'** (R) (H1+3)   *~ min. 2C*
02 H   **'Sensation Scarlet'** (H1+3)   *~ min. 2C*
93 H   **SOLIDOR** (I/d) (H1+3)   *~ min. 2C*
93 H   **'South American Bronze'** (R) (H1+3)
                                        ~ min. 2C
94 H   **'Spanish Angel'** (A) (H1+3) *~ min. 2C*
94 H   **'Splendour'** (R) (H1+3)   *~ min. 2C*
94 H   **'Starlight Magic'** (A) (H1+3) *~ min. 2C*
        'Stellar Grenadier'
                ~ see *Pelargonium* 'Grenadier'
96 H   **'Sweet Mimosa'** (Sc) (H1+3) *~ min. 2C*
94 H   **'The Barle'** (A) (H1+3)   *~ min. 2C*
93 H   **'The Boar'** (Fr) (H1+3)   *~ min. 2C*
94 H   **'The Tone'** (A) (H1+3)   *~ min. 2C*
94 H   **'Tip Top Duet'** (A) (H1+3)   *~ min. 2C*
93 H   **tomentosum** (Sc) (H1+3)   *~ min. 2C*
99 H   **'United'** (Z) (H1+3) *~ min. 2C; single*
93 H   **'Vancouver Centennial'** (Dw/St/C)
        (H1+3)   *~ min. 2C*
94 H   **'Variegated Madame Layal'** (A/v)
        (H1+3)   *~ min. 2C*
94 H   **'Velvet Duet'** (A) (H1+3)   *~ min. 2C*

93 P   **Video Series** (Dw) (H1+3)
                        ~ sold as a mixture
02 H   **'Vogue Carmine Red'** (H1+3) *~ min. 2C*
02 H   **'Vogue Red'** (H1+3)   *~ min. 2C*
96 H   **'Voodoo'** (U) (H1+3)   *~ min. 2C*
94 H   **'Wayward Angel'** (A) (H1+3)
                                        ~ min. 2C
94 H   **'White Glory'** (R) (H1+3)   *~ min. 2C*
93 H   **'Yale'** (I/d) (H1+3)   *~ min. 2C*

PHOENIX (ARECACEAE)
93 T   *canariensis* (H1+3)   *~ min. 2C*
93 T   *roebelenii* (H1+3)   *~ min. 10C*

PTERIS (PTERIDACEAE)
93 F   *cretica* (H1+3)   *~ min. 2C*

SALVIA (LAMIACEAE)
        bacheriana   ~ see *Salvia buchananii*
93 H   *buchananii* (H1+3)   *~ min. 2C*
93 H   *cacaliifolia* (H1+3)   *~ min. 2C*
93 H   *oppositiflora* (H1+3)   *~ min. 2C*

THUNBERGIA (ACANTHACEAE)
02 H   *gregorii* (H1+3)   *~ min. 5C*

ZINNIA (ASTERACEAE)
02 H   **'Benary's Giant Lilac'** (Benary's
                Giants Series) (H1+3)   *~ min. 2C*
02 H   **'Dasher Orange'** (Dasher Series)
                (H1+3)   *~ min. 2C*
02 H   **'Dasher Pink'** (Dasher Series)
                (H1+3)   *~ min. 2C*
02 H   **'Dreamland Mixed'** (Dreamland
                Series) (H1+3)   *~ min. 2C*
02 H   **'Dreamland Rose'** (Dreamland
                Series) (H1+3)   *~ min. 2C*
02 H   **'Dreamland Scarlet'** (Dreamland
                Series) (H1+3)   *~ min. 2C*
02 H   **'Dreamland Yellow'**(Dreamland
                Series) (H1+3)   *~ min. 2C*
02 H   **'Oklahoma Mixed'** (Oklahoma
                Series) (H1+3)   *~ min. 2C*
02 H   **'Peter Pan Gold'** (Peter Pan Series)
                (H1+3)   *~ min. 2C*
02 H   **'Profusion Orange'** PBR (Profusion
                Series) (H1+3)   *~ min. 2C*
02 H   **'Profusion White'** (Profusion Series)
                (H1+3)   *~ min. 2C*
02 H   **'Short Stuff Orange'** (Short Stuff
                Series) (H1+3)   *~ min. 2C*
02 H   **'Starbright Orange'** (Starbright
                Series) (H1+3)   *~ min. 2C*

Unheated Glass Protection

Requiring unheated glass protection (H2); may be grown outside in some circumstances (H2-3)

General

ABUTILON (MALVACEAE)
93 T **'Canary Bird'** (H2)
93 T **'Cannington Carol'** (v) (H2)
93 T **'Cannington Peter'** (v) (H2)
× *hybridum* **'Savitzii'**
~ see *Abutilon* 'Savitzii'
93 T **'Kentish Belle'** (H2-3)
99 T **'Linda Vista Peach'** (H2)
~ *as a pot plant for the glasshouse*
99 T **'Marion'** (H2)
93 T × *milleri* (H2)
93 T **'Nabob'** (H2)
93 T **'Orange Glow'** (v) (H2)
~ *foliage mottled*
99 T **'Savitzii'** (v) (H2) ~ *as a foliage plant for summer bedding and cultivation under glass*
93 T **'Souvenir de Bonn'** (v) (H2)

ACACIA (MIMOSACEAE)
armata ~ see *Acacia paradoxa*
93 T *baileyana* (H2)
93 T — **'Purpurea'** (H2)
93 T *dealbata* (H2)
02 T *paradoxa* (H2)
02 T *pravissima* (H2-3)
93 T *retinodes* (H2)

ADIANTUM (ADIANTACEAE)
cuneatum ~ see *Adiantum raddianum*
97 F *raddianum* (H2)
97 F — **'Brilliantelse'** (H2)
97 F — **'Fritz Lüthi'** (H2)

ALBIZIA (MIMOSACEAE)
93 T *julibrissin* f. *rosea* (H2-3)

ALOYSIA (VERBENACEAE)
citriodora ~ see *Aloysia triphylla*
94 T *triphylla* (H2)

ALSTROEMERIA (ALSTROEMERIACEAE)
94 B **H.R.H. PRINCESS ALEXANDRA 'Zelblanca'** (H2)
~ *for cultivation under unheated glass*

94 B **H.R.H. PRINCESS ALICE 'Staverpi'** PBR (H2) ~ *recommended for cultivation under unheated glass; previously listed as A. FIONA*

AMARYLLIS (AMARYLLIDACEAE)
02 B *belladonna* (H2-3)

ANOMATHECA (IRIDACEAE)
cruenta ~ see *Anomatheca laxa*
02 B *laxa* (H2-3)
02 B — var. *alba* (H2-3)

AQUILEGIA (RANUNCULACEAE)
02 H **'Blue Bird'** (Songbird Series) (H2)
02 H **'Bunting'** (Songbird Series) (H2)
02 H **'Dove'** (Songbird Series) (H2)
02 H **'Florida'**(State Series) (H2)
02 H **'Louisiana'** (State Series) (H2)
02 H **'Origami Red and White'** (Butterfly Series) (H2) ~ *may be sold as* RED ADMIRAL
02 H **'Origami Rose and White'** (Butterfly Series) (H2) ~ *may be sold as* CRENISE ROSA

ARALIA (ARALIACEAE)
papyrifera ~ see *Tetrapanax papyrifer*

ASARINA (SCROPHULARIACEAE)
erubescens ~ see *Lophospermum erubescens*
lophantha ~ see *Lophospermum erubescens*
lophospermum ~ see *Lophospermum erubescens*

BRUNSVIGIA (AMARYLLIDACEAE)
rosea **'Minor'** ~ see *Amaryllis belladonna*

BUDDLEJA (BUDDLEJACEAE)
93 T *asiatica* (H2)
02 T *officinalis* (H2)

CALCEOLARIA (SCROPHULARIACEAE)
93 P *integrifolia* **'Sunshine'** (H2-3)

CAMELLIA (THEACEAE)
93 T **'Doctor Clifford Parks'** (*reticulata*
        × *japonica*) (H2)
93 T *japonica* **'Drama Girl'** (H2)
93 T — **'Grand Slam'** (H2)

CAMPANULA (CAMPANULACEAE)
93 H *isophylla* (H2)
93 H — **'Alba'** (H2)
93 H — **'Mayi'** (H2)

CESTRUM (SOLANACEAE)
93 T **'Newellii'** (H2)

CHRYSANTHEMUM (ASTERACEAE)

(3a)	Indoor Incurved: Large-flowered
(3b)	Indoor Incurved: Medium-flowered
(3c)	Indoor Incurved: Small-flowered
(4a)	Indoor Reflexed: Large-flowered
(4b)	Indoor Reflexed: Medium-flowered
(4c)	Indoor Reflexed: Small-flowered
(5a)	Indoor Intermediate: Large-flowered
(5b)	Indoor Intermediate: Medium-flowered
(5c)	Indoor Intermediate: Small-flowered
(6a)	Indoor Anemone: Large-flowered
(6b)	Indoor Anemone: Medium-flowered
(6c)	Indoor Anemone: Small-flowered
(9a)	Indoor Spray: Anemone
(9b)	Indoor Spray: Pompon
(9c)	Indoor Spray: Reflexed
(9d)	Indoor Spray: Single
(9e)	Indoor Spray: Intermediate
(9f)	Indoor Spray: Spider, Quill, Spoon or Any Other Type
(15b)	October-flowering Intermediate: Medium-flowered

94 H **'Apricot Shoesmith Salmon'** (4a) (H2)
        ~ *disbudded, under glass*
94 H **'Bagley Rose'** (15b) (H2)
        ~ *disbudded, under glass*
94 H **'Bagley Tang'** (15b) (H2)
        ~ *disbudded, under glass*
94 H **'Beacon'** (5a) (H2)
        ~ *disbudded, under glass*
93 H **'Blush Shoesmith Salmon'** (H2)
        ~ *disbudded, under glass*
94 H **'Bronze Cassandra'** (5b) (H2)
        ~ *disbudded, under glass*
93 H **'Bronze Mayford Perfection'** (5a) (H2)
        ~ *disbudded, under glass*
93 H **'Bronze Nurosemary'** (9d) (H2)
        ~ *spray, under glass*

01 H **'Cassandra'** (5b) (H2)
        ~ *disbudded; late-flowering*
01 H **'Cerise Mundial'** (H2)
        ~ *spray; late-flowering*
93 H **'Cerise Shoesmith Salmon'** (4a) (H2)
        ~ *disbudded, under glass*
93 H **'Crimson Shoesmith Salmon'** (4b) (H2)
        ~ *disbudded, under glass*
94 H **'Dark Red Mayford Perfection'** (4b)
        (H2)   ~ *disbudded, under glass*
94 H **'Deane Dainty'** (9f) (H2)
        ~ *spray, under glass*
94 H **'Fiji'** (9c) (H2)   ~ *spray, under glass*
93 H **'Galaxy'** (9d) (H2)~ *spray, under glass*
01 H **'Gold Mundial'** (H2)
        ~ *spray; late-flowering*
94 H **'Golden Cassandra'** (5b) (H2)
        ~ *disbudded, under glass*
93 H **'Golden Mayford Perfection'** (5a) (H2)
        ~ *disbudded, under glass*
93 H **'Golden Shoesmith Salmon'** (4a) (H2)
        ~ *disbudded, under glass*
96 H **'Golden Snowdon'** (3b) (H2)
        ~ *late flowering*
93 H **'Long Island Beauty'** (6b) (H2)
        ~ *spray, under glass*
96 H **'May Shoesmith'** (5a) (H2)
        ~ *late flowering*
93 H **'Mayford Perfection'** (5a) (H2)
        ~ *disbudded, under glass*
93 H **'Nurosemary'** (9d) (H2)
        ~ *spray, under glass*
93 H **'Orange Shoesmith Salmon'** (4b)
        (H2)   ~ *disbudded, under glass*
94 H **'Peach Fiji'** (9c) (H2) ~ *spray, under glass*
96 H **'Pink Deane Joy'** (9a) (H2)
        ~ *late flowering*
94 H **'Pink Frill'** (9f) (H2)
        ~ *spray, under glass*
94 H **'Pink Gin'** (9c) (H2)
        ~ *spray, under glass*
93 H **'Pink Nurosemary'** (9d) (H2)
        ~ *spray,under glass*
93 H **'Primrose Mayford Perfection'** (5a)
        (H2)   ~ *disbudded, under glass*
01 H **'Princess Anne'** (H2)
        ~ *disbudded; late-flowering*
93 H **'Purple Shoesmith Salmon'** (4a) (H2)
        ~ *disbudded, under glass*
94 H **'Red Bagley Tang'** (15b) (H2)
        ~ *disbudded, under glass*
93 H **'Red Medallion'** (H2)
        ~ *spray, under glass*

96 H **'Red Resilient'** (4b) (H2)
~ late flowering
94 H **'Resilient'** (4b) (H2)
~ disbudded, under glass
94 H **'Robeam'** (9c) (H2)
~ spray, under glass
96 H **'Ropure'** (9c) (H2)   *~ late flowering*
93 H **'Rose Mayford Perfection'** (5a) (H2)
~ disbudded, under glass
94 H **'Roy Coopland'** (5b) (H2)
~ disbudded, under glass
94 H **'Royal Fiji'** (9c) (H2)
~ spray, under glass
94 H **'Rynoon'** (9d) (H2)
~ spray, under glass
93 H **'Rystar'** (9d) (H2) *~ spray, under glass*
94 H **'Salmon Cassandra'** (5b) (H2)
~ disbudded, under glass
93 H **'Salmon Nurosemary'** (9d) (H2)
~ spray, under glass
94 H **'Satin Pink Gin'** [PBR] (9c) (H2)
~ spray, under glass
93 H **'Shoesmith Salmon'** (4a) (H2)
~ disbudded, under glass
94 H **'Snowdon'** (5b/9c) (H2)
~ disbudded, under glass
96 H **'Sputnik'** (9f) (H2)   *~ late flowering*
01 H **'Stockton'** (3b) (H2)
~ disbudded; late-flowering
93 H **'Superbronze Shoesmith Salmon'** (H2)
~ disbudded, under glass
94 H **'Tricia'** (9d) (H2)   *~ spray, under glass*
93 H **'Vibrant'** (9c) (H2) *~ spray, under glass*
94 H **'Victor Rowe'** (5b) (H2)
~ disbudded, under glass
96 H **'White Rynoon'** (9d) (H2)
~ late flowering
94 H **'White Sands'** (9a) (H2)
~ spray, under glass
94 H **'Yellow American Beauty'** (5b) (H2)
~ disbudded, under glass
93 H **'Yellow Galaxy'** (9d) (H2)
~ spray, under glass
94 H **'Yellow John Hughes'** (3b) (H2)
~ disbudded, under glass
93 H **'Yellow Long Island Beauty'** (6a)
(H2)   *~ spray, under glass*
93 H **'Yellow Mayford Perfection'** (5a)
(H2)   *~ disbudded, under glass*
93 H **'Yellow Nurosemary'** (9d) (H2)
~ spray, under glass
94 H **'Yellow Resilient'** (5b) (H2)
~ disbudded, under glass

93 H **'Yellow Shoesmith Salmon'** (4a) (H2)
~ disbudded, under glass

CLIANTHUS (PAPILIONACEAE)
93 T ***puniceus*** (H2)
93 T — **'Albus'** (H2)
— **'Red Admiral'**
~ see Clianthus puniceus
— **'Red Cardinal'**
~ see Clianthus puniceus
— **'White Heron'**
~ see Clianthus puniceus 'Albus'

CORREA (RUTACEAE)
02 T ***alba*** **'Pinkie'** (H2)
93 T ***backhouseana*** (H2)
02 T **'Dusky Bells'** (H2)
'Harrisii'   *~ see Correa* 'Mannii'
93 T **'Mannii'** (H2)
02 T **'Marian's Marvel'** (H2)
02 T ***pulchella*** (H2)
02 T ***reflexa*** (H2)
speciosa   *~ see Correa reflexa*

CUPRESSUS (CUPRESSACEAE)
93   ***cashmeriana*** (H2)   *~ previously listed*
as C. torulosa *'Cashmeriana'*

CYCLAMEN (PRIMULACEAE)
96 B **'Laser Rose'** (H2)
~ intermediate type
96 B **'Laser Salmon with Eye'** (H2)
~ intermediate type
96 B **'Laser Scarlet'** (H2)
~ intermediate type
96 B **'Laser White'** (H2)
~ intermediate type
96 B **'Miracle Deep Rose'** (H2)
~ miniature
96 B **'Miracle Deep Salmon'** (H2)
~ miniature
96 B **'Miracle Scarlet'** (H2)   *~ miniature*
96 B **'Miracle White'** (H2)   *~ miniature*

DICKSONIA (DICKSONIACEAE)
97 F ***squarrosa*** (H2)

ECHIUM (BORAGINACEAE)
02 T ***candicans*** (H2-3)
fastuosum   *~ see Echium candicans*
02 H ***pininana*** (H2-3)   *~ monocarpic*
pinnifolium   *~ see Echium pininana*
02 T ***wildpretii*** (H2-3)

EUCOMIS (HYACINTHACEAE)
02 B *autumnalis* (H2-3)
02 B *bicolor* (H2-3)
    undulata   ~ see *Eucomis autumnalis*

EURYOPS (ASTERACEAE)
93 T *pectinatus* (H2)

FATSIA (ARALIACEAE)
    papyrifera   ~ see *Tetrapanax papyrifer*

GERANIUM (GERANIACEAE)
93 H *maderense* (H2)

HEBE (SCROPHULARIACEAE)
    elliptica 'Variegata'
      ~ see *Hebe* × *franciscana* 'Variegata'
93 T × *franciscana* 'Variegata' (v) (H2)

HELICHRYSUM (ASTERACEAE)
93 T *petiolare* (H2)   ~ *min. 2C; suitable for bedding*
    — 'Aureum'   ~ see *Helichrysum petiolare* 'Limelight'
02 T — 'Goring Silver' (H2-3)
    ~ *min. 2C; suitable for bedding*
96 T — 'Limelight' (H2)
    ~ *min. 2C; suitable for bedding*
93 T — 'Variegatum' (v) (H2)   ~ *min. 2C; suitable for bedding*
    petiolatum   ~ see *Helichrysum petiolare*

LAPEIROUSIA (IRIDACEAE)
    cruenta   ~ see *Anomatheca laxa*
    laxa   ~ see *Anomatheca laxa*

LAVATERA (MALVACEAE)
    bicolor   ~ see *Lavatera maritima*
93 T *maritima* (H2-3)
    maritima bicolor
      ~ see *Lavatera maritima*

LILIUM (LILIACEAE)

> (IX)   All species and their varieties and forms

93 B *longiflorum* (IX) (H2-3)

LIPPIA (VERBENACEAE)
    citriodora   ~ see *Aloysia triphylla*

LOPHOSPERMUM (SCROPHULARIACEAE)
93 P *erubescens* (H2-3)

MALVA (MALVACEAE)
    bicolor   ~ see *Lavatera maritima*

MAURANDYA (SCROPHULARIACEAE)
    erubescens
      ~ see *Lophospermum erubescens*

MIMULUS (SCROPHULARIACEAE)
93 T *aurantiacus* (H2-3)
    glutinosus
      ~ see *Mimulus aurantiacus*
    — *luteus*   ~ see *Mimulus aurantiacus*

NEPHROLEPIS (OLEANDRACEAE)
97 F *exaltata* (H2)

NERINE (AMARYLLIDACEAE)
02 B *sarniensis* (H2-3)

OXYPETALUM (ASCLEPIADACEAE)
    caeruleum   ~ see *Tweedia caerulea*

PAROCHETUS (PAPILIONACEAE)
93 H *africanus* (H2)

PELLAEA (ADIANTACEAE)
93 F *rotundifolia* (H2)

PERILLA (LAMIACEAE)
93 A *frutescens* var. *crispa* (H2)
    — var. *nankinensis*
      ~ see *Perilla frutescens* var. *crispa*

PINUS (PINACEAE)
93   *patula* (H2-3)

PITTOSPORUM (PITTOSPORACEAE)
    'Nanum Variegatum'
      ~ see *Pittosporum tobira* 'Variegatum'
93 T *tobira* 'Variegatum' (v) (H2-3)

PLECTRANTHUS (LAMIACEAE)
98 H *argentatus* (H2)

PRIMULA (PRIMULACEAE)
93 H *kewensis* (12) (H2)

PROSTANTHERA (LAMIACEAE)
02 T *ovalifolia* (H2)
93 T *rotundifolia* (H2)
    — 'Chelsea Girl'   ~ see *Prostanthera rotundifolia* 'Rosea'
02 T — 'Rosea' (H2)

REHMANNIA (SCROPHULARIACEAE)
angulata hort.   ~ see *Rehmannia elata*
02 H *elata* (H2)

RHAPHIOLEPIS (ROSACEAE)
93 T *umbellata* (H2-3)   ~ *valued in particular for cultivation under glass*

RHODODENDRON (ERICACEAE)
bullatum
   ~ see *Rhododendron edgeworthii*
93 T **'Countess of Haddington'** (H2)
93 T *edgeworthii* (H2-3)
93 T **'Fragrantissimum'** (H2-3)
93 T **'Lady Alice Fitzwilliam'** (H2-3)

SAXIFRAGA (SAXIFRAGACEAE)

(5)   Irregulares

sarmentosa
   ~ see *Saxifraga stolonifera*
93 H *stolonifera* (5) (H2)
93 H **'Tricolor'** (*stolonifera*) (5) (H2)

SEDUM (CRASSULACEAE)
93 H *sieboldii* **'Mediovariegatum'** (v) (H2-3)

SPARAXIS (IRIDACEAE)
02 B *grandiflora* (H2-3)

STYLIDIUM (STYLIDIACEAE)
93 H *crassifolium* (H2)   ~ *min. 2C*

TETRAPANAX (ARALIACEAE)
93 T *papyrifer* (H2-3)   ~ *min. 2C*

TRADESCANTIA (COMMELINACEAE)
02 H *pallida* (H2-3)
93 H — **'Purpurea'** (H2-3)   ~ *awarded as* T. pallida *'Purple Heart'*
purpurea
   ~ see *Tradescantia pallida* 'Purpurea'

TRITONIA (IRIDACEAE)
02 B *crocata* (H2-3)

TROPAEOLUM (TROPAEOLACEAE)
93 H *majus* **'Hermine Grashoff'** (d) (H2-3)   ~ *min. 2C*

TWEEDIA (ASCLEPIADACEAE)
93 H *caerulea* (H2)

VERBENA (VERBENACEAE)
93 H **'Sissinghurst'** (H2-3)
'Tenerife'   ~ see *Verbena* 'Sissinghurst'

ZEPHYRANTHES (AMARYLLIDACEAE)
02 B *grandiflora* (H2-3)

Climbers

JASMINUM (OLEACEAE)
93   *mesnyi* (H2-3)
primulinum   ~ see *Jasminum mesnyi*

MANDEVILLA (APOCYNACEAE)
02   *laxa* (H2)
suaveolens   ~ see *Mandevilla laxa*

PASSIFLORA (PASSIFLORACEAE)
93   *antioquiensis* Karst (H2)

93   *racemosa* (H2)
93   **'Star of Bristol'** (H2)

TRACHELOSPERMUM (APOCYNACEAE)
93   *asiaticum* (H2-3)
93   *jasminoides* (H2-3)
93   — **'Variegatum'** (v) (H2-3)
majus Nakai   ~ see *Trachelospermum asiaticum*

Plants for the Alpine House

ANEMONE (RANUNCULACEAE)
  vernalis   ~ see *Pulsatilla vernalis*

ASPERULA (RUBIACEAE)
  aristata subsp. *thessala*
              ~ see *Asperula sintenisii*
  nitida subsp. *puberula*
              ~ see *Asperula sintenisii*
93 H *sintenisii* (H2-3)

CAMPANULA (CAMPANULACEAE)
93 H *formanekiana* (H2-3)
93 H **'Joe Elliott'** (H2-3)

CLEMATIS (RANUNCULACEAE)

(Fo)   Forsteri group

93 T *marmoraria* (Fo) (H2-3)

CORYDALIS (PAPAVERACEAE)
00 H *schanginii* subsp. *ainii* (H2)

CYCLAMEN (PRIMULACEAE)
93 B *mirabile* (H2-3)
93 B *peloponnesiacum* (H2-3)
93 B *pseudibericum* (H2-3)
  repandum subsp. *peloponnesiacum*
              ~ see *Cyclamen peloponnesiacum*

DIONYSIA (PRIMULACEAE)
93 H *aretioides* (H2)

DRABA (BRASSICACEAE)
93 H *longisiliqua* (H2)

FRITILLARIA (LILIACEAE)
93 B *michailovskyi* (H2)

HELICHRYSUM (ASTERACEAE)
  coralloides
              ~ see *Ozothamnus coralloides*
  marginatum hort.
              ~ see *Helichrysum milfordiae*
93 H *milfordiae* (H2-3)

HELLEBORUS (RANUNCULACEAE)
93 H *lividus* (H2-3)

IPHEION (ALLIACEAE)
93 H **'Rolf Fiedler'** (H2-3)

IRIS (IRIDACEAE)
94 B *aucheri* (H2)
  sindjarensis   ~ see *Iris aucheri*

LEPTOSPERMUM (MYRTACEAE)
93 T *scoparium* **'Nichollsii Nanum'** (H2-3)

LEUCOJUM (AMARYLLIDACEAE)
93 B *nicaeense* (H2-3)

LEWISIA (PORTULACACEAE)
93 H *brachycalyx* (H2)
93 H *tweedyi* (H2)

NARCISSUS (AMARYLLIDACEAE)
Miniature and smaller daffodils are marked *.

(13)   Species

94 B *cantabricus* subsp. *cantabricus* var.
        cantabricus (13) (H2)
              ~ *icy white hoop petticoat flowers*
        *on short stems; flowering in early spring**
94 B — subsp. *cantabricus* var. *foliosus*
        (13) (H2)
              ~ *milk-white hoop petticoat*
        *daffodils flowering in late autumn**
  marvieri
  ~ see *Narcissus rupicola* subsp. *marvieri*
94 B *romieuxii* (13) (H2-3)
              ~ *pale primrose hoop petticoat*
                flowers on short stems;
                *flowering in late winter**
94 B *rupicola* subsp. *marvieri* (13) (H2)
              ~ *solitary yellow flowers on short*
              stems; narrow spreading petals
              *and a conical corona with lobed rim**
94 B — subsp. *rupicola* (13) (H2-3)
              ~ *solitary yellow flowers on short*
              stems, the petals spreading and usually
              *broad, the corona deeply lobed**

ORIGANUM (LAMIACEAE)
93 H *amanum* (H2-3)

OZOTHAMNUS (ASTERACEAE)
93 T *coralloides* (H2-3)

PAEONIA (PAEONIACEAE)
93 H *cambessedesii* (H2-3)

PHYSOPLEXIS (CAMPANULACEAE)
93 H *comosa* (H2-3)

PHYTEUMA (CAMPANULACEAE)
   comosum ~ see *Physoplexis comosa*

PLEIONE (ORCHIDACEAE)
   bulbocodioides **Limprichtii Group**
        ~ see *Pleione limprichtii*
93 H *formosana* (H2)
93 H *limprichtii* (H2)
93 H **Shantung g. 'Muriel Harberd'** (H2)
93 H **Versailles g. 'Bucklebury'** (H2)

PRIMULA (PRIMULACEAE)

(2)	Auricula

02 H *allionii* (2) (H2)
   glutinosa All. ~ see *Primula allionii*

PULSATILLA (RANUNCULACEAE)
93 H *vernalis* (H2)

RANUNCULUS (RANUNCULACEAE)
93 H *calandrinioides* (H2-3)

SARMIENTA (GESNERIACEAE)
93 H *repens* (H2)

SAXIFRAGA (SAXIFRAGACEAE)

(7)	Porphyrion
(15)	Saxifraga

93 H *cebennensis* (15) (H2)
93 H *federici-augusti* subsp. *grisebachii* (7)
      (H2-3)
   grisebachii
     ~ see *Saxifraga federici-augusti*
          subsp. *grisebachii*
93 H **'Wisley'** (*federici-augusti* subsp.
   grisebachii) (7) (H2-3)

SISYRINCHIUM (IRIDACEAE)
93 H *macrocarpon* (H2-3)

TECOPHILAEA (TECOPHILAEACEAE)
93 B *cyanocrocus* (H2)
93 B — **'Leichtlinii'** (H2)

VERBASCUM (SCROPHULARIACEAE)
93 T *dumulosum* (H2-3)
93 T **'Golden Wings'** (H2-3)

HARDY & HALF-HARDY ANNUALS

Annuals for the Garden

AGERATUM (ASTERACEAE)
95   'Blue Danube' (H3)
95   'Blue Horizon' (H3)
93   'Blue Lagoon' (H3)
02   *houstonianum* 'Hawaii White' (H3)
02   — 'Pacific Plus' (H3)
93   'Pacific' (H3)

AMARANTHUS (AMARANTHACEAE)
93   *hypochondriacus* 'Green Thumb' (H3)
93   — 'Pygmy Torch' (H3)

AMMOBIUM (ASTERACEAE)
02 P   *alatum* 'Bikini' (H3)

ANAGALLIS (PRIMULACEAE)
93 P   *monellii* (H4)
02 P   — 'Gentian Blue' (H4)

ANTIRRHINUM (SCROPHULARIACEAE)
94 P   'Bronze Chimes' (H3)
93 P   Coronette Series (H3)
         ~ sold as a mixture
93 P   Floral Carpet Series (H3)
         ~ sold as a mixture
02 P   Kim Series (H3)   *~ sold as a mixture*
94 P   'Pink Bells' (H3)
02 P   Sonnet Series (H3)
         ~ sold as a mixture
94 P   'Yellow Bells' (H3)

AQUILEGIA (RANUNCULACEAE)
93 P   Music Series (H4)
         ~ sold as a mixture

ARABIS (BRASSICACEAE)
93 P   *alpina* subsp. *caucasica* 'Schneehaube' (H4)
93 P   *blepharophylla* 'Frühlingszauber' (H4)
     — SPRING CHARM
         ~ see Arabis blepharophylla 'Frühlingszauber'
   SNOW CAP   *~ see Arabis alpina* subsp. *caucasica* 'Schneehaube'

BEGONIA (BEGONIACEAE)

(S)	Semperflorens Cultorum

97 P   'Ambassador Rose' (Ambassador Series) (S) (H3)
97 P   'Expresso Rose' (Expresso Series) (S) (H3)
97 P   'Expresso Scarlet' (Expresso Series) (S) (H3)
97 P   'Olympia Starlet' (Olympia Series) (S) (H3)
97 P   'Olympia White' (Olympia Series) (S) (H3)
02 P   Party Series (H3)
         ~ sold as a mixture
02 P   'Super Olympia Light Pink' (Super Olympia Series) (H3)

BELLIS (ASTERACEAE)
02 P   *perennis* Tasso Series (H4)
         ~ sold as a mixture

BRACTEANTHA (ASTERACEAE)
93   *bracteata* 'Bright Bikini Mixed' (H3)
02   — Chico Series (H3)
         ~ sold as a mixture

BRUGMANSIA (SOLANACEAE)
   meteloides   *~ see Datura inoxia*

CALENDULA (ASTERACEAE)
93   *officinalis* 'Fiesta Gitana' (H4)

CALLISTEPHUS (ASTERACEAE)
02   *chinensis* Milady Series (H3)
         ~ sold as a mixture

CENTAUREA (ASTERACEAE)
93 P   *cineraria* subsp. *cineraria* (H3)

CHRYSANTHEMUM (ASTERACEAE)
   segetum 'Court Jester'   *~ see Ismelia versicolor* 'Court Jesters Mixed'

CLEOME (CAPPARACEAE)
93   *hassleriana* 'Helen Campbell' (H3)

COBAEA (COBAEACEAE)
93 P *scandens* (H3)
93 P — f. *alba* (H3)

CONVOLVULUS (CONVOLVULACEAE)
93   *tricolor* 'Blue Ensign' (H4)

COREOPSIS (ASTERACEAE)
93   *tinctoria* 'Sunrise' (H4)

COSMOS (ASTERACEAE)
99   *bipinnatus* 'Sensation Pinkie' (H4)
93   — Sonata Series (H4)
                    ~ *sold as a mixture*

CYNOGLOSSUM (BORAGINACEAE)
93   *amabile* (H4)

DAHLIA (ASTERACEAE)
02 P Figaro Series (H3)
                    ~ *sold as a mixture*

DATURA (SOLANACEAE)
02 P *inoxia* (H3)
              ~ *can be annual or perennial*
       meteloides   ~ *see Datura inoxia*

DIANTHUS (CARYOPHYLLACEAE)
93 P *barbatus* 'Auricula-Eyed Mixed'
              (H4)
93 P — Nigrescens Group (H4)

DIGITALIS (SCROPHULARIACEAE)
       apricot hybrids   ~ *see Digitalis*
                    purpurea 'Sutton's Apricot'
       purpurea 'Alba' (Thompson &
              Morgan)   ~ *see Digitalis*
                    purpurea f. *albiflora*
93   — f. *albiflora* (Thompson & Morgan)
              (H4)
93   — Excelsior Group (Suttons;
              Unwins) (H4)
93   — 'Sutton's Apricot' (H4)
93   — 'The Shirley' (Gloxinioides
              Group) (H4)

DOROTHEANTHUS (AIZOACEAE)
02   *bellidiformis* (H3)

ERYNGIUM (APIACEAE)
93   *giganteum* (H4)
99   — 'Silver Ghost' (H4)
       Miss Willmott's ghost
                    ~ *see Eryngium giganteum*

ERYSIMUM (BRASSICACEAE)
       allionii
                    ~ *see Erysimum × marshallii*
93 P *cheiri* 'Persian Carpet'
              (H4)
93 P × *marshallii* (H4)
                    ~ *previously listed*
                    as E. *allionii*

ESCHSCHOLZIA (PAPAVERACEAE)
93   *caespitosa* (H4)
93   *californica* (H4)
93   — 'Dali' (H4)

GAILLARDIA (ASTERACEAE)
93   'Dazzler' (H4)

GAZANIA (ASTERACEAE)
93 P 'Chansonette' (H3)
96 P 'Daybreak Bright Orange'
              (Daybreak Series) (H3)
                    ~ *bedding type*
96 P 'Daybreak Garden Sun' (Daybreak
              Series) (H3)   ~ *bedding type*
02 P Talent Series (H3)
                    ~ *sold as a mixture*

HELIANTHUS (ASTERACEAE)
00   *annuus* 'Claret' (H3)
00   — 'Pastiche' (H3)
00   — 'Valentine' (H3)

IMPATIENS (BALSAMINACEAE)
93 P *walleriana* Accent Series (H3)
                    ~ *sold as a mixture*
02 P — Super Elfin Series (H3)
                    ~ *sold as a mixture*
02 P — Tempo Series (H3)
                    ~ *sold as a mixture*

IPOMOEA (CONVOLVULACEAE)
93   'Heavenly Blue' (H3)

ISMELIA (ASTERACEAE)
93   *versicolor* 'Court Jesters Mixed' (H3)
                    ~ *awarded as Chrysanthemum*
                    segetum 'Court Jester'

LATHYRUS (PAPILIONACEAE)
00   *odoratus* **'Alaska Blue'** (H4)
                   ~ tall, Spencer
95   — **'America'** (H4) *~ tall, old-fashioned*
97   — **'Aunt Jane'** (H4)   *~ tall, Spencer*
97   — **'Bert Boucher'** (H4) *~ tall, Spencer*
94   — **'Bishop Rock'** (H4)   *~ tall, Spencer*
00   — **'Bobby's Girl'** (H4)   *~ tall, Spencer*
99   — **'Bristol'** (H4)   *~ tall, Spencer*
93   — **'Charlie's Angel'** (H4)
                   ~ tall, Spencer
94   — **'Colin Unwin'** (H4)   *~ tall, Spencer*
97   — **'Dave Thomas'** (H4) *~ tall, Spencer*
97   — **'Dawn Chorus'** (H4)
            ~ medium height, Spencer
95   — **'Dorothy Eckford'** (H4)
            ~ tall, old-fashioned
96   — **'Evening Glow'** (H4) *~ tall, Spencer*
95   — **'Flora Norton'** (H4)
            ~ tall, old-fashioned
99   — **'Florencecourt'** (H4) *~ tall, Spencer*
98   — **'Gwendoline'** (H4)   *~ tall, Spencer*
96   — **'Hannah's Harmony'** (H4)
          ~ medium height, Spencer
01   — **'Heartbeat'** (H4)   *~ tall, Spencer*
01   — **'Isabella Cochrane'** (H4)
                   ~ tall, Spencer
95   — **'Janet Scott'** (H4)
            ~ tall, old-fashioned
94   — **'Jayne Amanda'** (H4) *~ tall, Spencer*
94   — **'Jilly'** (H4)   *~ tall, Spencer*
95   — **'King Edward VII'** (H4)
            ~ tall, old-fashioned
97   — **'Kiri Te Kanawa'** (H4) *~ tall, Spencer*
01   — **'Linda C'** (H4)   *~ tall, Spencer*
99   — **'Lizbeth'** (H4)   *~ tall, Spencer;*
         previously listed as 'Lisbeth'
97   — **'Margaret Joyce'** (H4) *~ tall, Spencer*
96   — **'Marie's Melody'** (H4)
          ~ medium height, Spencer
97   — **'Millennium'** (H4)   *~ tall, Spencer*
94   — **'Mrs Bernard Jones'** (H4)
                ~ tall, Spencer
94   — **'Noel Sutton'** (H4)   *~ tall, Spencer*
00   — **'Oklahoma'** (H4)
97   — **'Oban Bay'** (H4)   *~ tall, Spencer*
01   — **'Oxford Blue'** (H4) *~ tall, Spencer*
99   — **'Patricia Anne'** (H4) *~ tall, Spencer*
97   — **'Phoebe'** (H4)   *~ tall, Spencer*
95   — **'Pink Cupid'** (H4)
            ~ dwarf, old-fashioned
99   — **'Pinocchio'** (H4)   *~ dwarf, Spencer*
96   — **'Pocahontas'** (H4)   *~ tall, Spencer*

99   — **'Ron Entwistle'** (H4) *~ tall, Spencer*
94   — **'Royal Flush'** (H4)   *~ tall, Spencer*
95   — **'Sicilian Pink'** (H4)   *~ tall, Spencer*
96   — **'Solway Fanfare'** (H4)
               ~ medium, Spencer
94   — **'Southbourne'** (H4)   *~ tall, Spencer*
00   — **'Starlight Sonata'** (H4)
                   ~ tall, Spencer
02   — **'Sunset'** (H4)   *~ tall, Spencer*
96   — **'Tahiti Sunrise'** (H4) *~ tall, Spencer*
96   — **'Teresa Maureen'** (H4)
            ~ tall, old-fashioned
94   — **'Toby Robinson'** (H4)
                   ~ tall, Spencer
01   — **'Valerie Harrod'** (H4)
                   ~ tall, Spencer
99   — **'Virgo'** (H4)
      ~ tall, Spencer; available from
         Kings Seeds as part of their
         'Signs of the Zodiac' series
01   — **'Wedding Day'** (H4)
                   ~ tall, Spencer
94   — **'White Supreme'** (H4)
                   ~ tall, Spencer

LAVATERA (MALVACEAE)
96   **'Pink Beauty'** (H3)
96   **'Salmon Beauty'** (H3)
96   **'Silver Cup'** (H3)
02   *trimestris* **Beauty Series** (H3)
               ~ sold as a mixture
96   **'White Beauty'** (H3)

LIMNANTHES (LIMNANTHACEAE)
93   *douglasii* (H4)

LIMONIUM (PLUMBAGINACEAE)
93 P   *bonduellii* **'Forever Gold'** (H3)

LINUM (LINACEAE)
93   *grandiflorum* (H3)

LOBELIA (CAMPANULACEAE)
     'Cinnabar Deep Red'
         ~ see Lobelia 'Fan Tiefrot'
     'Cinnabar Rose'
       ~ see Lobelia 'Fan Zinnoberrosa'
     COMPLIMENT SCARLET   *~ see Lobelia*
         'Kompliment Scharlach'
93 P   *erinus* **'Cambridge Blue'** (H3)
02 P   — **Cascade Series** (H3)
               ~ sold as a mixture
93 P   — **'Colour Cascade'** (H3)

93 P — **'Crystal Palace'** (H3)
~ *award confirmed, for N.L.*
Chrestensen selection only,
in 1998 after trial as a cultivar
suitable for growing
in the open ground

93 P — **'Mrs Clibran'** (H3)

98 P — **'Regatta Midnight Blue'** (H3)
~ *as a cultivar suitable for*
growing in the open ground
and trailing in hanging pots

98 P — **'Regatta Sky Blue'** (H3)
~ *as a trailing cultivar suitable*
for growing in hanging pots

98 P — **'Riviera Blue Eyes'** (H3)
~ *as a cultivar suitable for*
growing in the open ground

98 P — **'String of Pearls'** (H3)
~ *as a cultivar suitable for*
growing in the open ground;
award applies to S.E. Marshall's
selection

FAN DEEP RED
~ see *Lobelia* 'Fan Tiefrot'

'Fan Deep Rose'
~ see *Lobelia* 'Fan Orchidrosa'

97 P **'Fan Orchidrosa'** (H3-4)
~ *previously listed as*
L. FAN ORCHID ROSE

97 P **'Fan Scharlach'** (H3-4)

97 P **'Fan Tiefrot'** (H3-4)

97 P **'Fan Zinnoberrosa'** (H3-4)

93 P **'Kompliment Scharlach'** (H3-4)

'Zinnoberrosa'   ~ see *Lobelia* 'Fan
Zinnoberrosa'

LOBULARIA (BRASSICACEAE)

02   *maritima* **Easter Bonnet Series**
(H3)   ~ *sold as a mixture*

02   — **Golf Series** (H3)
~ *sold as a mixture*

98   — **'Rosie O'Day'** (H3)

98   — **'Snowdrift'** (H3)

98   — **'Violet Queen'** (H3)

8   — **'Wonderland White'** (H3)

LUNARIA (BRASSICACEAE)

93   *annua* var. *albiflora* (H4)

LUPINUS (PAPILIONACEAE)

93 P **Band of Nobles Series** (H4)

MESEMBRYANTHEMUM
bellidiformis   ~ see *Dorotheanthus*
bellidiformis
criniflorum   ~ see *Dorotheanthus*
bellidiformis

MIMULUS (SCROPHULARIACEAE)

93 P **'Calypso'** (H3)

93 P *cardinalis* (H3)

93 P *lewisii* (H3)

02 P **Magic Series** (H4)   ~ *sold as a mixture*

MYOSOTIS (BORAGINACEAE)

93   **'Blue Ball'** (H4)

93   **'Ultramarine'** (H4)

NICOTIANA (SOLANACEAE)

93   **Domino Series** (H3)

93   *langsdorffii* (H3)

93   **'Lime Green'** (H3)

93 P *sylvestris* (H3)

NIGELLA (RANUNCULACEAE)

93   *damascena* **'Miss Jekyll'**
(H4)

93   — **'Miss Jekyll Alba'** (H4)

OMPHALODES (BORAGINACEAE)

93   *linifolia* (H4)

linifolia alba
~ see *Omphalodes linifolia*

PAPAVER (PAPAVERACEAE)

93   *commutatum* (H4)

02   — **'Ladybird'** (H4)

PETUNIA (SOLANACEAE)

02 P **CASCADIAS YELLOW EYE 'Dancaseye'**
(Cascadias Series) PBR (H3)

02 P **'Charlie's Angels Champagne'**
(Charlie's Angels Series) (H3)

02 P **'Charlie's Angels Charlie'**
(Charlie's Angels Series) (H3)

02 P **CONCHITA BLUEBERRY FROST**
'Conblue' (Conchita Series) (H3)

02 P **CONCHITA CRANBERRY FROST**
'Concran' (Conchita Series) (H3)

02 P **CONCHITA EVENING GLOW**
'Conglow' (Conchita Series) (H3)

02 P **CONCHITA STRAWBERRY FROST**
'Constraw' (Conchita Series) (H3)

02 P **HAPPY DREAM 'Danpethap'**
(Petitunia Series) (H3)

93 P × *hybrida* Carpet Series (H3)
~ *sold as a mixture*
02 P — Duo Series (H3) ~ *sold as a mixture*
93 P — Mirage Series (H3) ~ *sold as a mixture*
99 P — 'Storm Lavender' (H3)
~ *Grandiflora type*
99 P — 'Storm Pink' (H3)
~ *Grandiflora type*
99 P — 'Storm Salmon' (H3)
~ *Grandiflora type*
multiflora Carpet Series
~ see *Petunia* × *hybrida* Carpet Series
— Mirage Series
~ see *Petunia* × *hybrida* Mirage Series
02 P SURFINIA PINK VEIN 'Suntosol' PBR (H3)
02 P SURFINIA PURPLE 'Shihi Brilliant' (H3)
02 P SURFINIA PURPLE VEIN
'Sunpurve' PBR (H3)
02 P SURFINIA SKY BLUE 'Keilavbu' PBR (H3)

PHLOX (POLEMONIACEAE)
02 *drummondii* Buttons Series (H3)
~ *sold as a mixture*
97 — 'Phlox of Sheep' (H3)

PRIMULA (PRIMULACEAE)
02 P Husky Series (Prim) (H4)
~ *sold as a mixture*

RICINUS (EUPHORBIACEAE)
93 P *communis* 'Carmencita' (H3)

RUDBECKIA (ASTERACEAE)
00 *amplexicaulis* (H3)
00 P *hirta* 'Indian Summer' (H3)
00 P — 'Toto' (H3)

SALPIGLOSSIS (SOLANACEAE)
02 Royale Series (H3) ~ *sold as a mixture*

SALVIA (LAMIACEAE)
93 P *argentea* (H3)
93 P *coccinea* 'Lady in Red' (H3)
93 P *farinacea* 'Victoria' (H3)
94 P *splendens* 'Phoenix Mixed' (H3)
94 P — 'Red Arrow' (H3)
93 P — 'Vanguard' (H3)

SCABIOSA (DIPSACACEAE)
93 *stellata* 'Drumstick' (H3)

SCHIZANTHUS (SOLANACEAE)
02 *pinnatus* 'Hit Parade' (H3)

SENECIO (ASTERACEAE)
02 P *cineraria* 'Cirrus' (H3)
93 P — 'Silver Dust' (H3)

TAGETES (ASTERACEAE)
93 'Aurora Light Yellow' (H3)
~ *dwarf French marigold*
93 'Dainty Marietta' (H3)
~ *dwarf French marigold*
93 'Disco Orange' (H3)
~ *dwarf French marigold*
93 'Disco Yellow' (H3)
~ *dwarf French marigold*
93 'Discovery' (H3) ~ *African marigold*
01 Gold Coins Series (H3)
~ *African marigold; sold as a mixture*
93 'Hero Orange' (H3)
~ *dwarf French marigold*
93 'Honeycomb' (H3)
~ *dwarf French marigold*
01 'Inca Orange' (Inca Series) (H3)
93 'Perfection' (H3)
~ *African marigold*
93 'Queen Sophia' (H3)
~ *dwarf French marigold*
93 'Safari Mixture' (H3)
~ *dwarf French marigold*
93 'Safari Scarlet' (H3)
~ *dwarf French marigold*
93 'Safari Tangerine' (H3)
~ *dwarf French marigold*
93 'Tiger Eyes' (King; Marshall) (H3)
~ *dwarf French marigold*
93 'Zenith Lemon Yellow' (H3)
~ *dwarf French marigold*

TROPAEOLUM (TROPAEOLACEAE)
93 *majus* Alaska Series (v) (H3)
~ *sold as a mixture*
93 Whirlybird Series (H3)
~ *sold as a mixture*

VERBENA (VERBENACEAE)
01 P *canadensis* 'Toronto' (H3)
01 P 'Moon River' (H3)
01 P 'Peaches and Cream'
(H3)
01 P Quartz Series (H3) ~ *awarded to the
mixture sold as 'Bunting'*
93 P *rigida* (H3) ~ *re-confirmed after trial 2001*
93 P Sandy Series (H3) ~ *sold as a mixture;
re-confirmed after trial 2001*
venosa ~ see *Verbena rigida*

VIOLA (VIOLACEAE)

(P)	Pansy

93 P   **Joker Series** (P) (H4)
~ *sold as a mixture*
99 P   **'Juliette Blue, Pale Wings'** (H4)
~ *small flowered*
93 P   **Princess Series** (H4) ~ *sold as a mixture*
99 P   **'Sorbet Blueberry Cream' (Sorbet**
Series) (H4)   ~ *small flowered*
99 P   **'Sorbet Yellow Delight' (Sorbet**
Series) (H4) ~ *small flowered*
99 P   **'Sorbet Yellow Frost' (Sorbet Series)**
(H4)   ~ *small flowered*

99 P   **'Splendid Blue and Yellow'** (H4)
~ *small flowered*
02 P   **Universal Plus Series** (H4)
~ *sold as a mixture*
99 P   **'Velour Purple and White' (Velour**
Series) (H4)   ~ *small flowered*

XANTHOPHTHALMUM (ASTERACEAE)
segetum **'Court Jester'**
~ *see* Ismelia versicolor
'Court Jesters Mixed'

Annual grasses for drying

AIRA (POACEAE)
95   *elegantissima* (H3)

LAGURUS (POACEAE)
95   *ovatus* (H3)

PENNISETUM (POACEAE)
rueppellii   ~ see *Pennisetum setaceum*
95   *setaceum* (H3) ~ *awarded as* P. rueppelii

SETARIA (POACEAE)
95   *macrostachya* (H3)

FRUIT AND VEGETABLES

The Vegetable Garden

Award vegetables that have been deleted from the EC Common Catalogue *are not included in this list.*

ASPARAGUS (*Asparagus officinalis*)
01 **'Backlim'** (H4)
~ *F1 hybrid; consistently high yield of large spears*
93 **'Connover's Colossal'** (H4)
~ *Sore's selection only. Early; heavy yield of good quality spears. Reconfirmed after trial 2001*
01 **'Gijnlim'** (H4)
~ *F1 hybrid; early. Consistently high yield of mid green spears with purple tips*
93 **'Lucullus'** (H4)
~ *F1 hybrid; later cropping. Good yield of medium-sized spears*

AUBERGINE (*Solanum melongena*)
95 **'Adona'** (H2)
~ *F1 hybrid. High yield of large shiny purple fruit*
95 **'Bonica'** (H2)
~ *F1 hybrid. Very large, bulbous, shiny purple fruit. Excellent cropper*
93 **'Galine'** (H2)
~ *F1 hybrid. Very large, round, shiny fruit*
95 **'Mohican'** (H2)
~ *F1 hybrid. Compact habit with bulbous white shiny fruit*
93 **'Rima'** (H2)
~ *F1 hybrid. High yield of large, typically bulbous, shiny purple fruit*
95 **'Vernal'** (H2)
~ *F1 hybrid. Long, bulbous, shiny fruit*

BEANS
Broad bean, November sown (*Vicia faba*)
95 **'Aquadulce'** (H4)
~ *ideal for November sowing*

93 **'Aquadulce Claudia'** (H4)
~ *not too tall; a good compact plant. An early crop when spring sown. Reconfirmed after trial 1999*
95 **'Aquadulce Loretta'** (H4)
~ *ideal for November sowing*

Broad bean, spring sown (*Vicia faba*)
93 **'Aquadulce Claudia'** (H4)
~ *not too tall; a good compact plant. An early crop when spring sown. Reconfirmed after trial 1999*
93 **'Express'** (H3-4)
~ *quick maturing, with well filled pods*
93 **'Imperial Green Longpod'** (H3-4)
~ *good green colour and flavour; particularly good for freezing. Reconfirmed after trial 1999*
99 **'Jubilee Hysor'** (H3-4)
~ *good yield; uniform, well filled pods*
99 **'Masterpiece Green Longpod'** (H3-4)
~ *slender, well filled pods; good green colour; good flavour*
99 **'Medes'** (H3-4)
~ *high yield of uniform, good-sized pods*
93 **'Meteor'** (H3-4)
~ *an early crop with well filled, even pods; good flavour. Reconfirmed after trial 1999*
93 **'The Sutton'** (H3-4)
~ *dwarf compact plants, with nice flavour; ideal for smaller gardens and windy situations. Reconfirmed after trial 1999*
93 **'Topic'** (H3-4)
~ *early maturing with a good yield. Reconfirmed after trial 1999*
93 **'Witkiem Major'** (H3-4)
~ *a good early yield, with uniform pods; plants not too tall. Reconfirmed after trial 1999*
99 **'Witkiem Manita'** (H3-4)
~ *a good early yield, with uniform pods*
93 **'Witkiem Vroma'** (H3-4)
~ *early cropping with medium length, well filled pods*

Climbing French bean (*Phaseolus vulgaris*)

93 **'Algarve' (flat)** (H3)
~ high yield; uniform mid green stringless pods. Reconfirmed after trial 2000

00 **'Cobra' (round)** (H3)
~ very high early yield; long, fleshy; very attractive

93 **'Cunera' (round)** (H3)
~ mid green stringless pods

93 **'Diamant' (round)** (H3)
~ stringless pods

00 **'Emerite' (round)** (H3)
~ a medium to high yield of uniform, medium to long, slightly curved, fleshy, attractive beans

93 **'Eva' (round)** (H3)
~ very early. Long straight fleshy pods, wider podded than other round varieties. Reconfirmed after trial 2000

93 **'Hunter' (flat)** (H3)
~ attractive long stringless pods. Slow to show seed development. Reconfirmed after trial 2000

00 **'Kingston Gold' (flat)** (H3)
~ attractive smooth, yellow pod; uniform, slow maturing, green podded beans

93 **'Kwintus' (flat)** (H3)
~ high yield with long stringless pods

93 **'Musica' (flat)** (H3)
~ quick maturing, with long stringless pods

00 **'Sultana' (round)** (H3)
~ early, attractive, French bean type. Medium to high yield of very uniform, medium to long, mid green, reasonably fleshy beans. Does not seed too quickly

Dwarf French bean (*Phaseolus vulgaris*)

93 **'Annabel'** (H3)
~ slightly curved green pods, held high in the plant; upright habit. Reconfirmed after trial 1996

96 **'Artigo'** (H3)   ~ strong growing with high yield of large long green pods

02 **'Berggold' (wax podded)** (H3)
~ attractive, clear golden, medium to long beans with slightly curved and flattened pods

01 **'Cantare'** PBR (H3)
~ medium length, fleshy, good taste

93 **'Cropper Teepee'** (H3)
~ upright habit. Mid green large pods, held high in the plant. Reconfirmed after trial 1996

93 **'Delinel'** (H3)
~ strong growing with long, dark green pods. Reconfirmed after trial 2001

96 **'Ferrari'** (H3)
~ high yield; compact habit with straight, shortish, dark green pods

01 **'Filao'** (H3)
~ a short, fine, good quality bean

02 **'Golddukat' (wax podded)** (H3)
~ very early; high yield of pale yellow beans with some greening. Slightly curved and flattened pods

96 **'Irago'** (H3)
~ very early; high yield. Upright habit, with long, straight, mid green pods held high in the plant. Reconfirmed after trial 2001

01 **'Jessica'** (H3)
~ medium length, fleshy, attractive beans with a good flavour. Potential high yield

01 **'Maja'** (H3)
~ long, fat, good for slicing; the highest yield in the trial

01 **'Maradonna'** (H3)
~ medium to short, mid green, flattish pods

01 **'Marona'** (H3)
~ late; medium length, dark green, fat pods; good potential yield

01 **'Nomad'** (H3)
~ medium to short, fairly pale, uniform, straight, slightly flattened pods. High yield

02 **'Orinoco' (wax podded)** (H3)
~ medium yield of medium to long, rounded, straight, slim, greenish-yellow pods

01 **'Safari'** (H3)
~ short, slim, mid green, round, attractive pods. Low yields

02 **'Sonesta' (wax podded)** (H3)
~ early. High yield of bright yellow, fairly long, straight, slightly flattened pods. A compact plant

93 **'Sprite'** (H3)   ~ heavy yield, with long dark green pods

96 **'The Prince'** (H3)
~ Suttons maintenance only. Excellent yield; straight pale green pods

Runner bean (*Phaseolus coccineus*)

93 **'Achievement'** (H3)
~ maincrop with long, smooth, slender pods

99 **'Achievement Merit'** (H3)
~ *very long, straight, slender, smooth pods*
99 **'Desiree'** (H3)
~ *stringless pods with thick fleshy walls*
99 **'Enorma'** (H3)
~ *late; long, smooth, slender pods*
99 **'Flare'** (H3)
~ *attractive slender pods; high yield*
99 **'Lady Di'** (H3)
~ *attractive, blemish-free, long, slender pods*
93 **'Liberty'** (H3)
~ *very long pods; a popular show variety*
99 **'Red Rum'** (H3)
~ *good early and late yield; slim, straight, stringless pods, of medium length*
99 **'Rotblühende'** (H3)
~ *broad pods, fairly straight and smooth; good yield*
99 **'Titan'** (H3)
~ *long, straight, slender pods; good yield*
99 **'White Apollo'** (H3)
~ *long, smooth, fleshy pods; excellent early and late yield*
99 **'White Emergo'** (H3)
~ *late; smooth, tender, uniform pods, with good colour*
99 **'White Lady'** PBR (H3)
~ *late; very fleshy pods*
99 **'Wisley Magic'** (H3)
~ *very long pods; very high early and late yield; previously listed as 'Pulsar'*

BEETROOT (*Beta vulgaris*)
Beetroot varieties with long red root
93 **'Cheltenham Green Top'** (H4)
~ *good flesh colour*
93 **'Forono'** (H4)
~ *very good flesh colour*

Beetroot varieties with round red root
93 **'Action'** (H4)
~ *F1 hybrid; uniform roots with good flesh colour and freedom from rings. Appears to have good bolting resistance. Reconfirmed after trial 2001*
93 **'Bikores'** (H4)
~ *good flesh colour and freedom from internal rings. Good bolting resistance. Reconfirmed after trial 2001*

93 **'Boltardy'** (H4)
~ *good bolting resistance*
93 **'Bonel'** (H4)
~ *good flesh colour and freedom from internal rings. Reconfirmed after trial 2001*
01 **'Monodet'** (H4)
~ *monogerm*; uniform roots with smooth skins and good flesh colour*
93 **'Monogram'** (H4)
~ *monogerm* with good flesh colour and smooth skins*
93 **'Pablo'** (H4)
~ *F1 hybrid; good flesh colour and very good freedom from internal rings. Appears to have good bolting resistance. Reconfirmed after trial 2001*
01 **'Pronto'** (H4)
~ *very uniform, with smooth skins and high yield potential*
01 **'Red Ace'** (H4)
~ *F1 hybrid; uniform roots, with good flesh colour and no rings*
93 **'Regala'** (H4)
~ *very good flesh colour and good bolting resistance. Reconfirmed after trial 2001*
93 **'Wodan'** (H4)
~ *F1 hybrid with good flesh colour*

BORECOLE or CURLY KALE
(*Brassica oleracea* Acephala Group)

> * *The seed of beetroot, called a cluster, is the dried seedhead of the plant, which may contain as many as three true seeds. Monogerm varieties are bred to produce one seed per cluster.*

00 **'Afro'** (H4)
~ *medium height; mid green leaves, curled to the edge. Winters well*
93 **'Bornick'** (H4)
~ *F1 hybrid; finely curled pale to mid green leaves. For early cropping*
93 **'Fribor'** (H4)
~ *F1 hybrid; mid to dark green well curled leaves. Winters well*
99 **'Redbor'** (H4)
~ *F1 hybrid. Tall plants with open habit; strongly curled purple-green leaves. Winters well*
99 **'Reflex'** (H4)
~ *F1 hybrid. Tall plants with very finely curled blue-green leaves. Winters well*

93 **'Winterbor'** (H4)
~ F1 hybrid. Tall plants with
finely curled blue-green leaves.
Winters well. Reconfirmed after
trial 1999

BROCCOLI, SPROUTING
(*Brassica oleracea* **Italica Group**)
Purple sprouting broccoli
95 **'Claret'** (H4)
~ F1 hybrid. Very tall; heavy yield of dark
purple spears from March through April
95 **'Early Purple Sprouting Improved'** (H4)
~ very tall; steady crop from March to
April
95 **'Late Purple Sprouting'** (H4)
~ tall; a modest yield from late March
through April
95 **'Red Arrow'** (H4)
~ tall; a heavy crop from February
through April
95 **'Red Spear'** (H4)
~ medium height plants; a heavy crop
from early February to April
95 **'Redhead'** (H4)
~ very tall plants; a good crop of
large spears of good purple colour
from early March through April

White sprouting broccoli
95 **'White Eye'** (H4)
~ tight white buds; early white spears
for picking in March
95 **'White Star'** (H4)
~ good weight; late white spears for
cutting in April

BRUSSELS SPROUTS
(*Brassica oleracea* **Gemmifera Group**)
– all F1 hybrids
99 **'Bosworth'** (H4)
~ late. Oval, mid to dark green, solid,
closely spaced sprouts. Easy to pick;
plants stand well. Quality still
good in February
99 **'Cascade'** (H4)
~ late. Smooth, clean, well spaced,
fairly round sprouts. Uniform plants
which stand and yield well
93 **'Cavalier'** (H4)
~ midseason. Dark green, well spaced
sprouts. Plants produce high yields
of good quality

99 **'Clodius'** (H4)
~ midseason. Good quality, round,
smooth, solid, sweet sprouts. Plants
stand and yield well
99 **'Diablo'** (H4)
~ early midseason. Good quality, clean,
smooth, round sprouts of good flavour.
The medium to tall plants have a pale
green cabbage-like head
93 **'Icarus'** (H4)
~ early. Large, smooth, solid sprouts.
Plants stand well. Susceptible to white
blister and ringspot
93 **'Igor'** (H4)
~ midseason to late. Small, smooth
sprouts which tend to become loose if
not picked in time
99 **'Lunet'** (H4)
~ midseason. Tall plants producing a
very high yield of large, oval, fairly
sweet sprouts which are easy to pick
and have good resistance to ringspot.
Plants can lodge (lean over)
93 **'Patent'** (H4)
~ midseason. Large, round, smooth,
dark green, solid sprouts
99 **'Revenge'** (H4)
~ late. Very uniform plants producing a
good yield of solid, round, clean, mid
green sprouts. Can be hard to pick
93 **'Roger'** (H4)
~ midseason. Large, smooth,
good quality, pale green
sprouts. Plants stand well
99 **'Romulus'** PBR (H4)
~ late. Well spaced, smooth, round,
solid sprouts with a sweet taste.
Plants stand and yield well
00 **'Wellington'** (H4)
~ late. Very good quality smooth, dark
green, round, solid sprouts

CABBAGE (*Brassica oleracea* Capitata Group)
Spring cabbage (all pointed)
93 **'Duncan'** (H4)
~ F1 hybrid. Mid to dark green
uniform heads with well closed
bases. A good early yield;
plants heart slowly to produce
small, solid heads. Reconfirmed
after trial 2001 as spring greens
and hearted cabbage

93 **'First Early Market 218'** (H4)
~ *mid green, fairly compact heads of good colour and uniformity. Plants heart slowly to produce large, rather loose heads. Also as hearted greens*

01 **'First Early Market 218 - Early Market'** (H4)
~ *as hearted greens. Quick maturing, good quality heads*

01 **'First Early Market 218 - Mastercut'** (H4) ~ *as spring greens; attractive dark green outer leaves; well filled hearts*

94 **'Jason'** (H4)
~ *F1 hybrid; a vigorous variety producing heavy heads*

93 **'Offenham 1 Myatt's Offenham Compacta'** (H4)
~ *mid to dark green, attractive heads; medium to large, fairly solid hearts. Reconfirmed after trial 2001 as a hearted cabbage*

01 **'Offenham 3 - Mastergreen'** (H4)
~ *as spring greens; very uniform heads with tidy leaf bases; light green leaves; well filled hearts*

93 **'Pixie'** (H4)
~ *mid green with good basal quality, producing small well hearted heads. Reconfirmed after trial 2001 as a very early hearted cabbage*

94 **'Pyramid'** (H4)
~ *F1 hybrid. Very uniform, medium-sized, solid, pointed heads; quite slow to mature; reconfirmed after trial 2001 as a hearted cabbage, and after trial 2002 as a summer cabbage*

01 **'Sparkel'** (H4)
~ *F1 hybrid. Late; attractive dark green leaves*

Summer cabbage (season June to August)
98 **'Augustor'** (H3)
~ *F1 hybrid; midseason. Bright green compact plants; uniform, medium-sized, solid, round heads with a short core*

02 **'Cape Horn'** (H3)
~ *F1 hybrid; midseason to late; pointed. A larger, smooth-leaved cabbage*

98 **'Charmant'** (H3)
~ *F1 hybrid; late. Round, bright green uniform heads with short cores*

93 **'Derby Day'** (H3)
~ *early. Bright, round, mid green, well filled heads. Reconfirmed after trial 1998*

98 **'Elisa'** PBR (H3)
~ *F1 hybrid; early. Compact round heads with bright green glossy leaves*

02 **'Excel'** (H3)
~ *F1 hybrid; midseason to late; pointed. Uniform, tidy cabbage with a good colour and well filled head*

93 **'First of June'** (H3)
~ *early. Round, mid green, with fairly long internal core*

98 **'Golden Cross'** (H3)
~ *F1 hybrid; early. Very uniform, small, round, solid, bright green cabbage*

98 **'Gonzales'** (H3)
~ *F1 hybrid. A compact round cabbage with small, dense heads and attractive pale green leaves*

98 **'Green Express'** (H3)
~ *F1 hybrid; midseason. Round, medium to large, dark green heads, well filled with short cores*

93 **'Grenadier'** (H3)
~ *F1 hybrid; midseason. Rather large, round, uniform, mid green heads*

02 **'Greyhound'** (H3)
~ *early maturing; pointed; pale to mid green; medium to large frame*

98 **'Hermes'** (H3)
~ *F1 hybrid; early midseason. Compact, round, solid, mid green heads with short cores*

02 **'Hispi'** (H3)
~ *F1 hybrid; early. Smooth, pointed, dark green outer leaves, with good uniformity and well filled heart*

02 **'Marshall's Kingspi'** (H3)
~ *F1 hybrid; early; pointed. Small frame with a well filled head*

98 **'Metino'** (H3)
~ *F1 hybrid; late. Flat to round, smooth heads with dark green leaves and very short cores*

98 **'Nordri'** (H3)
~ *F1 hybrid; early-midseason. Round, solid, blue-green heads with short cores*

98 **'Patron'** (H3)
~ *F1 hybrid; midseason. Round, solid, bright green heads with erect outer protecting leaves and short cores*

94 **'Pyramid'** (H4)
~ F1 hybrid. Very uniform, medium-sized, solid, pointed heads; quite slow to mature; reconfirmed after trial 2001 as a hearted cabbage, and after trial 2002 as a summer cabbage

02 **'Spitfire'** (H3)
~ F1 hybrid; midseason; pointed. Quite large, with smooth, dark green outer leaves; good habit

93 **'Stonehead'** (H3)
~ F1 hybrid; late. Uniform, round, mid green heads. Also useful for cropping into the autumn from later planting

Early red cabbage (non-storing; season September to October)

93 **'Langedijker Red Early'** (H3)
~ round to oval, solid heads; less uniform than the hybrids

96 **'Rodeo'** (H3)
~ F1 hybrid. Good colour, short core; uniform

96 **'Rondy'** (H3)
~ F1 hybrid; early. Oval, smooth, uniform, solid heads

96 **'Rookie'** (H3)
~ F1 hybrid; early. Round to slightly flat heads

93 **'Ruby Ball'** (H3)
~ F1 hybrid; early. Uniform, round heads

Winter white cabbage (for storage)

93 **'Marathon'** (H3)
~ F1 hybrid; to harvest and store before frosts (stores well). Round to flat, solid heads

Savoy cabbage (season September to March) – all F1 hybrids

00 **'Alaska'** (H4)
~ midseason to late. Dark green, well blistered leaves; small to medium heads

95 **'Clarissa'** (H3)
~ early. Flattened round heads, with dark green leaves; solid. Good peppery flavour

00 **'Denver'** PBR (H4)
~ early to midseason. Dark outer leaves with fine blister; heads dense, paler green, small to medium size

01 **'Endeavour'** (H4)
~ late. Attractive, mid green, well blistered, medium-sized heads with good internal quality and sweet taste. Long stems

95 **'Famosa'** (H3)
~ very early. Bright mid green leaves with reddish veins. Plants uniform

93 **'Julius'** (H3)
~ very early. Bright green, attractive, large, round heads. Reconfirmed after trial 1995

95 **'Midvoy'** (H3)
~ F1 hybrid. Dark green blistered outer leaves with mid green, solid, round hearts

00 **'Primavoy'** (H3)
~ early. Round, solid heads which do not stand well

95 **'Protovoy'** (H3)
~ very early. Dark green, well blistered outer leaves; pale green, round, solid hearts

93 **'Taler'** (H4)
~ midseason. Round to flat round, grey-green heads with good uniformity

93 **'Tarvoy'** (H4)
~ midseason to late. Mid to dark grey-green, small, round, solid heads. Will stand for a long period after maturity. Reconfirmed after trial 2000

01 **'Tundra'** (H4)
~ dark green, slightly blistered leaf; heads solid and attractive. Sweet-tasting; overwinters well

01 **'Wintessa'** (H4)
~ late. Dark green well blistered leaves, with uniform well filled heads of good quality and flavour. Plants stand well

00 **'Wivoy'** (H4)
~ late. Tidy, dark green well blistered leaves; slightly flattened, round, well filled heads

Winter hybrid cabbage (season November to March)

98 **'Beretta'** (H4)
~ dark green, blistered, Savoy-like leaves with dense heads of good flavour

98 **'Celtic'** (H4)
~ large leafy plants with bright green leaves and good, solid, uniform heads. Reconfirmed after trial 2000

98   **'Colt'** PBR (H4)
~ a medium-sized, dense, good quality
cabbage with good flavour
98   **'Embassy'** (H4)
~ lightly blistered, bright green leaves;
well-filled and sweet-tasting
98   **'Renton'** (H4)
~ early maturing
98   **'Roulette'** (H4)
~ small, well filled heads; suitable for
the smaller garden
98   **'Winchester'** PBR (H4)
~ small, good quality heads; suitable
for the smaller garden

**January King cabbage (season November
to March) – all F1 hybrids**
98   **'Flagship'** (H4)
~ relatively early. Uniform, flat, round
heads with pronounced purple colour.
Plants stand well
98   **'Holly'** (H4)
~ flat, round, heads; dark green leaves
with good purple colouring. Winters well
93   **'Marabel'** (H4)
~ mid green leaves with good,
deep red colour; round heads
with good standing ability.
Reconfirmed after trial 2000
01   **'Robin'** (H4)
~ dark green leaves with good purple
colour; very sweet tasting. Heads
small and solid; plants have long
stems which lean. Winter hardy

**CALABRESE (Brassica oleracea
Italica Group) – all F1 hybrids**
95   **'Arcadia'** (H3)
~ May sown. Late, small, mid to dark
green buds, medium to heavy yields
95   **'Corvet'** (H3)
~ May sown. Large heads with
small buds, medium maturity
(84 days from sowing); holds
well, heads easy to see
95   **'Fiesta'** (H3)
~ May sown. Medium-size heads with
small buds set deep in the leaf, late
maturing (92 days from sowing)
95   **'Flash'** (H3)
~ May sown. Crops over a long period;
large heads with small to medium bud
size hold well (80-90 days from sowing)

95   **'Lord'** (H3)
~ May sown. Medium maturing, large
heads set down within leaves (85 days
from sowing)
95   **'Skiff'** (H3)
~ May sown. Medium to large heads
crop over a long period and hold well
(80-90 days from sowing)
95   **'Tiara'** (H3)
~ May sown. Early, medium-sized heads
95   **'Trixie'** (H3)
~ May sown. Medium maturing, large
heavy heads, small bud size, holding
well at maturity (84 days from sowing)
95   **'Viking'** (H3)
~ May sown. Early, small heads. Does
not stand well. Concentrated maturity
(80 days from sowing)

CARROT (Daucus carota)
99   **'Adelaide'** (H3)
~ F1 hybrid; very early. Quickly forms
stump-ended roots; almost coreless; fine
tops. Ideal for successional sowings and
early sowing in frames
95   **'Autumn King 2'** (H3)
~ maincrop. Large, tapering stump roots;
strong tops; bold shoulders. Ideal for storing
93   **'Bangor'** (H3)
~ F1 hybrid. Smooth cylindrical roots with
excellent core colour. Bulks up quickly for
heavy yields. Can be stored over winter
95   **'Barcelona'** (H3)
~ F1 hybrid; maincrop. Long, smooth,
cylindrical, deep orange roots. Strong
healthy tops; shows mildew tolerance.
Ideal for winter storage
95   **'Berjo'** (H3)
~ maincrop. Heavy yields of smooth
cylindrical roots with bright orange
flesh. Suitable for storing
95   **'Bertan'** (H3)
~ F1 hybrid; maincrop. Very sweet
orange-fleshed cylindrical roots that
resist splitting. Ideal for storing
93   **'Bolero'** PBR (H3)
~ F1 hybrid. Later-maturing maincrop,
long, slender, cylindrical roots of good
uniformity and colour; can be stored
from later sowings
93   **'Camberley'** (H3)
~ maincrop. Long roots with deep
orange flesh

93 **'Campestra'** (H3)
~ *a shorter-rooted 'Autumn King' with smooth, cylindrical, stump-ended roots of excellent flesh colour and flavour. Heavy yields*

93 **'Cleopatra'** (H3)
~ *F1 hybrid; 'Autumn King' hybrid. Heavy, smooth, long, well coloured roots of good flavour. Excellent storage variety*

94 **'Evora'** (H3)
~ *F1 hybrid; a long, slender-rooted hybrid, excellent as a bunching carrot. Ideal for successional sowings and for early sowing in frames*

99 **'Flyaway'** (H3)
~ *F1 hybrid. Maincrop; medium length, stump-ended hybrid with sweet orange flesh. Partial resistance (i.e. lack of attraction) to carrot flies*

93 **'Ingot'** (H3)
~ *F1 hybrid. Maincrop; almost coreless, long, cylindrical roots; sweet deep orange flesh with claimed high vitamin C content*

95 **'Kamaran'** (H3)
~ *'Autumn King' F1 hybrid for later sowing to lift and store over winter. Strong tops; high yields of smooth, heavy, tapering roots*

95 **'Kazan'** (H3)
~ *'Autumn King' F1 hybrid for later sowing for winter storage. Very good colour and flavour for a late carrot. Strong tops. Heavy yields*

95 **'Kingston'** (H3)
~ *'Autumn King' hybrid for later sowing for winter storage. One of the best for colour, taste, yield and uniformity. Strong tops*

99 **'Maestro'** PBR (H3)
~ *F1 hybrid; maincrop. Strong tops, with long, smooth, almost cylindrical, stump-ended roots. Good all-round disease tolerance*

93 **'Mokum'** (H3)
~ *F1 hybrid. Slightly tapering roots, well coloured to the tip; good sweetness; almost coreless. Good for bunching*

99 **'Nairobi'** (H3)
~ *F1 hybrid; second early/early maincrop. Strong tops, with uniform, broader shouldered, cylindrical, stump-ended roots. Heavy yields*

93 **'Nantucket'** (H3)
~ *F1 hybrid; early maturing maincrop. Smooth, deep orange, blunt-ended, good quality roots. Ideal for successional sowings and early sowing in frames. Reconfirmed after trial 1999*

93 **'Napoli'** (H3)
~ *F1 hybrid, very early maturing. Strong tops for easy pulling; quick to bulk up. Ideal for successional sowings and early sowing in frames*

94 **'Natan'** (H3)
~ *F1 hybrid; early maturing. Strong tops for easy pulling; quick to bulk up. Ideal for successional sowings or early sowing in frames*

93 **'Newmarket'** (H3)
~ *maincrop; longer-rooted F1 hybrid. Heavy yields of broader shouldered, smooth, tapering roots of sweet taste and good colour*

93 **'Panther'** (H3)
~ *F1 hybrid; early maturing. Smooth, cylindrical, stump-ended, coreless roots. Ideal for successional sowings or early sowing in frames*

93 **'Parabell'** (round) (H3)
~ *early maturing, round-rooted, smooth 'Paris Market' type of good flavour. Ideal for successional sowings and early sowing in frames. Reconfirmed after trial 1999*

93 **'Parano'** (H3)
~ *F1 hybrid. Smooth-skinned, cylindrical, almost coreless, blunt-ended roots with deep orange flesh. Ideal for successional sowings and early sowing in frames*

93 **'Parmex'** (round) (H3)
~ *early maturing, round-rooted 'Paris Market' type; good uniformity and core colour. Ideal for successional sowings*

94 **'Sytan'** (H3)
~ *maincrop; smooth, broader-shouldered, tapering roots of good colour and sweet taste; shows partial resistance (i.e. lack of attraction) to carrot fly. Reconfirmed after trial 1999*

99 **'Tempo'** (H3)
~ *F1 hybrid. Smooth, medium length stump-ended roots of good colour and taste; quick to bulk up. Ideal for successional sowings and early sowing in frames*

99   **'Yukon'** (H3)
~ *F1 hybrid; bulks up quickly to produce cylindrical stump-ended roots of good colour and flavour. Ideal for successional sowings and early sowing in frames*

CAULIFLOWER
(*Brassica oleracea* Botrytis Group)
Winter cauliflower for spring heading
(maturing from March to May)
97   **'Admirable'** (H4)
~ *F1 hybrid; early-midseason. Good quality, medium-sized heads*
97   **'Christingle'** (H4)
~ *late. Deep white curds of an excellent quality*
97   **'Colombo'** (H4)
~ *F1 hybrid; very early. Deep white curds*
97   **'Dalton'** (H4)
~ *F1 hybrid; early. Very good quality, medium to large curds*
97   **'Galleon'** (H4)
~ *early midseason. Medium to large, good quality curds, with very good leaf protection*
97   **'Jerome'** (H4)
~ *F1 hybrid; early midseason. Medium to large, very good quality curds*
97   **'Martian'** PBR (H4)
~ *F1 hybrid; early midseason. Large, solid, good quality curds*
97   **'Mayfair'** PBR (H4)
~ *F1 hybrid; midseason. Good quality, medium-sized, solid curds*
97   **'Nomad'** (H4)
~ *F1 hybrid; midseason. Good quality, medium-sized curds*
97   **'Prestige'** (H4)
~ *F1 hybrid; midseason to late. Good quality, large to medium-sized, well protected heads*
97   **'Walcheren Winter - Armado May'** (H4)
~ *early midseason. Good quality, medium to large curds*
97   **'Walcheren Winter 3 - Armado'** (H4)
~ *early with a long cutting season. Good quality curds*

Summer heading cauliflower (season June to mid July)
97   **'Amsterdam'** (H3)
~ *F1 hybrid. Well protected deep, white, solid curds*

97   **'Asterix'** (H3)
~ *F1 hybrid; midseason. Vigorous plants with long leaves and medium-sized, white, solid, well protected curds*
93   **'Aubade'** (H3)
~ *early to midseason. Not very vigorous plants with semi-erect leaves and smooth curds*
97   **'Barcelona'** (H3)
~ *F1 hybrid; midseason. Deep, round, solid, well protected curds*
97   **'Beauty'** (H3)
~ *F1 hybrid; midseason to late. Fairly vigorous plants with deep, white, solid curds*
97   **'Fargo'** (H3)
~ *F1 hybrid; late. Deep, white, well protected curds*
97   **'Fastman'** (H3)
~ *early to midseason. Plants with rather spreading leaves and solid heads*
97   **'Mayflower'** (H3)
~ *F1 hybrid; very early. Medium-sized curds*
97   **'Nautilus'** (H3)
~ *F1 hybrid; late. Vigorous plants with deep, white, well protected curds of excellent quality*
93   **'Perfection'** (H3)
~ *very early. Large curds, tending to be flat*
93   **'Plana'** (H3)
~ *F1 hybrid; midseason. Uniform, vigorous plants with large creamy white curds*
97   **'Predominant'** (H3)
~ *early midseason. Medium-sized, solid, deep curds*
93   **'White Rock'** (H3)
~ *late. Deep, white, well protected curds*

Autumn heading cauliflower (season September to November)
94   ***'Alverda' (H3)***
~ *early to midseason. Smooth, green curds of good depth with some bracting. When cooked, the contrast between the green surface of the curd and its white centre is very attractive*
02   **'Autumn Glory'** (H3)
~ *early, crops over a longer period; smaller, creamy curds; good depth*

02 **'Aviso'** (H3)
~ *F1 hybrid; early cropping, with a short cropping period; high proportion of first class, smooth, white curds*

93 **'Belot'** (H3)
~ *F1 hybrid; very late. Large, compact, deep, solid, very white curds. Extremely well protected*

93 **'Castlegrant'** (H3)
~ *F1 hybrid; midseason. Well protected, smooth, solid curds which can be flattish and show some looseness*

94 **'Esmeraldo'** (H3)
~ *F1 hybrid. Smooth green curds of good depth. Attractive when cooked*

93 **'Kestel'** (H3)
~ *early midseason. Smooth curds, tending to yellow*

93 **'Lindon'** (H3)
~ *F1 hybrid; midseason. Well protected, good quality, deep curds*

94 **'Marmalade'** (H3)
~ *F1 hybrid; very early; deep, orange curds*

94 **'Minaret'** (H3)
~ *early. Green curd formed of a spiral of pyramidal pinnacles. Can become loose*

02 **'Minneapolis'** (H3)
~ *F1 hybrid; midseason to late maturity, cropping over a long period; deep, smooth, firm curds*

02 **'Moby Dick'** (H3)
~ *F1 hybrid; early with a short cropping period; uniform, very deep, heavy curds*

02 **'Pavilion'** PBR (H3)
~ *F1 hybrid; early with a short cropping period; very uniform; good white colour, size and depth*

02 **'Regata'** (H3)
~ *F1 hybrid; midseason with a long cropping period; deep, solid curds*

94 **'Red Lion'** (H3)
~ *very late. Small, attractive, purple heads*

02 **'Skywalker'** (H3)
~ *F1 hybrid; early with a short cropping period; very good white colour; good size and depth*

94 **'Talbot'** (H3)
~ *late with a long cropping period. Good size and depth; creamy colour. Reconfirmed after trial 2002*

93 **'Vidoke'** (H3)
~ *F1 hybrid; late. Medium-sized, solid, deep, white curds*

94 **'Violet Queen'** (H3)
~ *very early. Purple, medium-sized curds of good depth*

94 **'Violetta Italia'** (H3)
~ *very early. Purple, medium to large curds of good depth*

02 **'White Excel'** (H3)
~ *F1 hybrid; early with a short cropping period. Very uniform; bright white colour; good size and depth. High proportion of superb, firm, first class curds*

CELERIAC
(*Apium graveolens* var. *rapaceum*)

00 **'Diamant'** (H3)
~ *clean, white, medium-sized*

00 **'Ibis'** (H3)
~ *neat round ball, very uniform, fairly small*

00 **'Kojak'** (H3)
~ *flattened ball shape, clean and white, very smooth*

93 **'Monarch'** (H3)
~ *white-skinned, bold and smooth*

00 **'Prinz'** (H3)
~ *smooth, small to medium, flattened and round*

CELERY
(*Apium graveolens* var. *dulce*)

93 **'Celebrity'** PBR (H3)
~ *self-blanching, fairly short plants, with ribbed petioles and good flavour. Reconfirmed after trial 2001*

94 **'Crystal'** (H3)
~ *F1 hybrid; self-blanching, fairly tall, with smooth petioles and attractive, upright habit*

93 **'Giant Pink - Mammoth Pink'** (H3)
~ *pink-tinged, green variety for blanching or earthing up; solid stems*

93 **'Ivory Tower'** (H3)
~ *self-blanching; tall with smooth petioles and good flavour*

93 **'Lathom Self Blanching'** (H3)
~ *self-blanching, with short ribbed petioles and good flavour. Vigorous habit. Reconfirmed after trial 2001*

94   **'Lathom Self Blanching Galaxy'** (H3)
~ *self blanching, medium length petioles, ribbed, bold plants*

94   **'Loret'** (H3)
~ *self blanching short plants, rather ribby*

01   **'Moonbeam'** (H3)
~ *good length of smooth petioles, good weight*

94   **'Octavius'** (H3)
~ *F1 hybrid. Green type, with mid green, smooth petioles and good flavour*

01   **'Tango'** (H3)
~ *very straight petioles, with a strong flavour*

94   **'Victoria'** (H3)
~ *F1 hybrid. Green type, with tall smooth succulent petioles and good flavour. Well shaped plants*

CHARD
(*Beta vulgaris* subsp. *cicla* var. *flavescens*) – see also spinach beet

00   **'Bright Lights'** (H3)
~ *good colourful mix, including reds, yellows and whites; very ornamental and decorative*

00   **'Bright Yellow'** (H3)
~ *bright golden yellow petioles and mid green puckered leaf*

00   **'Charlotte'** (H3)
~ *striking red colour, nice upright leaf, neat plant habit*

00   **'Fordhook Giant'** (H3)
~ *attractive shiny green, puckered leaf with long succulent white petioles*

00   **'Lucullus'** (H3)
~ *plenty of tender, light green leaf with long succulent white petioles*

00   **'Rhubarb Chard'** (H3)
~ *good red colour, uniform*

CHICORY – LEAFY TYPES
(*Cichorium intybus*)
Radicchio

02   **'Indigo'** (H3)
~ *dense round heads; very uniform with dark green outer leaves and red hearts*

02   **'Leonardo'** (H3)
~ *well developed heart; good internal red colour*

02   **'Palla Rossa'** (H3)
~ *medium to large heads, well filled red hearts, fairly uniform; no bolting*

Sugar loaf

02   **'Pan di Zucchero'** (H3)
~ *uniform plants with medium to large frames and dark green outer leaves. Hearts blanch well*

02   **'Zuckerhut'** (H3)
~ *medium-sized plants with dark green outer leaves and well developed, well blanched hearts*

CHINESE CABBAGE
(*Brassica rapa* Chinensis Group)

93   **'Kingdom 65'** (H3)
~ *F1 hybrid; medium, green barrel-shaped heads*

93   **'Mariko'** (H3)
~ *F1 hybrid. Small, barrel-shaped heads; good bolting resistance*

93   **'Nerva'** (H3)
~ *F1 hybrid; early, dense, barrel-shaped heads*

CORNSALAD (*Valerianella locusta*)

94   **'Baval'** (H3)
~ *mid green, medium leaved; good flavour. Made good growth and remained free of disease under frames*

94   **'Cavallo'** (H3)
~ *long-leaved traditional type; gives a good yield under frames*

94   **'Medaillon'** (H3)
~ *slow growing, short, thick-leaved under frames*

COURGETTE (*Cucurbita pepo*)

93   **'Acceste'** (H3)
~ *F1 hybrid. Very high yield of heavy, medium to long, lightly speckled fruits*

93   **'Astoria'** (H3)
~ *F1 hybrid. High yield of heavy, medium length fruits*

98   **'Bambino'** (H3)
~ *F1 hybrid. Bush type; a high yield of dark green fruits*

98   **'Blackjack'** (H3)
~ *F1 hybrid. Bush type; a high yield of slender, very dark green fruits*

98 **'Consul'** (H3)
~ *F1 hybrid. Bush type; a very high yield of slender, mid green fruits*

93 **'Defender'** (H3)
~ *F1 hybrid. A high yield of medium-sized, slender, very lightly flecked fruits*

93 **'Early Gem'** (H3)
~ *F1 hybrid; a high yield of slender, lightly speckled fruits. Easy to see on the plant*

98 **'El Greco'** (H3)
~ *F1 hybrid. Bush type; plant of open habit with mid green fruits*

98 **'Jemmer'** (H3)
~ *F1 hybrid. Bush type; high yield of slim yellow fruits*

93 **'President'** (H3)
~ *F1 hybrid. A high yield of medium-sized, medium speckled fruits*

98 **'Raven'** (H3)
~ *F1 hybrid. Bush type; a good yield of dark green fruits*

93 **'Supremo'** (H3)
~ *F1 hybrid. A very high yield of heavy, dark green fruits*

98 **'Valiant'** (H3)
~ *F1 hybrid. A bush type; a good yield of dark green fruits*

98 **'Venus'** (H3)
~ *F1 hybrid. Bush type; smooth, spine-free stems with dark green glossy fruits*

CUCUMBER (*Cucumis sativus*)

02 **'Athene'** (H1-2)
~ *F1 hybrid. High yield of medium length, slim, bright, dark green fruits with slightly bulbous end; slightly ribbed*

02 **'Birgit' (smooth-skinned)** (H1-2)
~ *F1 hybrid. High yield of medium length, smooth fruits; good for exhibition*

95 **'Bush Champion' (ridge)** (H3)
~ *F1 hybrid. High yield of short dark green fruit*

02 **'Carmen'** (H1-2)
~ *F1 hybrid; high yield of standard length, dark green, slightly ribbed fruits*

93 **'Danimas'** (H1-2)
~ *F1 hybrid. Very short-fruited variety, producing many well proportioned fruits per plant*

93 **'Femdan'** (H1-2)
~ *F1 hybrid. Traditional long cucumber with nice neck and very dark prolific fruiting*

95 **'Fortos' (gherkin)** (H3)
~ *attractive uniform fruit*

02 **'Macao'** (H1-2)
~ *F1 hybrid; high yield of very attractive, glossy, straight, dark green fruits; very uniform*

95 **'Marketmore' (ridge)** (H3)
~ *good yield of short, attractive, dark green fruits. Grown in the open garden. Reconfirmed after trial 2001*

01 **'Masterpiece'** (H3)
~ *fairly short, slender, smooth-skinned, dark green cucumber, nice and straight, with good flavour and healthy foliage. Grown in the open garden*

93 **'Monique'** (H1-2)
~ *F1 hybrid. Traditional long cucumber; long-necked but very straight. Moderate yield*

01 **'Prima Top'** (H3)
~ *F1 hybrid; medium length, dark green, long, smooth-skinned cucumber with good flesh colour and healthy foliage. Grown in the open garden*

02 **'Teide'** (H1-2)
~ *F1 hybrid; medium to long, mid green, slightly ribbed fruits*

01 **'Tokyo Slicer'** (H3)
~ *F1 hybrid; long, smooth-skinned, dark green, uniform fruits. Grown in the open garden*

02 **'Tyria'** (H1-2)
~ *F1 hybrid; attractive, dark green, slightly ribbed fruits*

02 **'Zeina'** (H1-2)
~ *F1 hybrid; very high yield of short, very uniform, bright fruits with a slight handle. A very strong growing plant*

ENDIVE (*Cichorium endivia*)

96 **'Atria' (curled)** [PBR] (H3)
~ *very fine-cut leaf. Well blanched and solid hearted*

02 **'Frisée Glory'** (H3)
~ *frisée endive with small frame and uniform, deeply, finely cut leaf. An attractive addition to a salad*

96 **'Golda' (Batavian)** (H3)
~ *short-leaf Batavian type. Well hearted*

96   **'Jeti' (curled)** (H3)
~ *a broad-leaved endive with uniform mid green heads of good quality. Reconfirmed after trial 2002*

02   **'Lassie'** PBR (H3)
~ *a frisée endive with high yield of very deeply cut leaf; medium frames; good flavour*

96   **'Pancalieri' (curled)** (H3)
~ *very strong cut-leaf type. Does not blanch well*

96   **'Sally' (curled)** (H3)
~ *extra fine-cut leaf. Small size and flat-growing*

02   **'Wallone'** (H3)
~ *frisée endive, very vigorous, with a large frame. High yield of mid to dark green, finely cut leaf. Suits 'cut and come again' cropping*

FENNEL, FLORENCE
(*Foeniculum vulgare* var. *azoricum*)

96   **'Atos' (bulb)** (H3)
~ *quick maturing with uniform, medium to large round bulbs*

96   **'Carmo' (bulb)** (H3)
~ *F1 hybrid. Quick maturing with medium-sized, round, fine quality bulbs*

96   **'Dover' (bulb)** (H3)
~ *early with large roundish bulbs. Moderate uniformity*

96   **'Heracles' (bulb)** (H3)
~ *quick maturing. Medium large, slightly flattened bulbs of excellent quality*

96   **'Zefa Fino' (bulb)** (H3)
~ *quick maturing. Medium large, round, very uniform bulbs of excellent quality*

KALE, CURLY – see borecole

KOHLRABI
(*Brassica oleracea* Gongylodes Group)

97   **'Adriana'** (H3)
~ *good quality, flattened globe shape; uniform, green, small to medium size. For an open pollination type, quick maturing*

93   **'Domino'** (H3)
~ *early, for cultivation under frames*

97   **'Kongo'** (H3)
~ *F1 hybrid. Exceptional quality; green, very rapid grower, very sweet and moist, with high yield and attractive short leaves*

97   **'Quickstar'** (H3)
~ *F1 hybrid. Very uniform and early; green, medium to large, with short tops; pleasant strong flavour*

97   **'Rapidstar'** (H3)
~ *F1 hybrid. Very uniform; green; medium to large and flattened*

LEEK (*Allium porrum*)
Early maturing leek

00   **'Autumn Giant 2 - Porvite'** (H4)
~ *dark green erect flags; uniform, solid, long shafts; slight bulbing, high yield, low levels of rust*

00   **'Autumn Mammoth 3 - Firena'** (H4)
~ *dark green erect plants, with a good yield of well blanched leeks. Some bolters from early sowing; little bulbing and low levels of rust*

00   **'Brecon'** (H4)
~ *F1 hybrid. Uniform, dark green, erect, with long smooth shafts and no bulbing*

00   **'Carlton'** PBR (H4)
~ *F1 hybrid. Plants with mid to dark green flags and good uniformity. Above average bolting*

00   **'King Richard'** (H4)
~ *very long shafts with pale green flags; high yields with low levels of bolting*

00   **'Mammoth Blanch'** (H4)
~ *a show variety suitable for December sowing. Early maturing, with high yields of well shaped leeks with pale green flags, long, heavy shafts and no bolters*

00   **'Pancho'** (H4)
~ *good early yield of medium long, mid green, solid shafts with only slight bulbing. Little rust*

00   **'Swiss Giant - Prelina'** (H4)
~ *pale flags with a good yield; some rust*

00   **'Swiss Giant - Tilina'** (H4)
~ *very high yield of medium to long, slightly bulby leeks with slight bolting*

00   **'Upton'** PBR (H4)
~ *F1 hybrid. Uniform, very dark green flags with no bulbing and very little bolting and rust*

Maincrop leek

02   **'Apollo'** (H4)
~ *F1 hybrid; smooth, with slightly pale green leaves; high December yield*

93 **'Autumn Mammoth 3 - Cobra'** (H4)
~ *midseason to late. Short to medium with dark green flags, but below average uniformity*

93 **'Autumn Mammoth 3 - Enak'** (H4)
~ *early to midseason. Medium long, well blanched, with mid to dark green, erect flags*

93 **'Blauwgroene Herfst - Profina'** (H4)
~ *early to midseason. Medium to long, erect, slim shafts with dark green flags and some bulbing*

93 **'Blauwgroene Herfst - Verina'** (H4)
~ *early. Medium length with mid green flags and little bulbing*

02 **'Blue Green Autumn - Conora'** (H4)
~ *medium length; smooth straight shanks with mid green leaves*

02 **'Blue Green Winter - Laura'** (H4)
~ *medium length; well blanched and slightly bulby*

93 **'Giant Winter - Catalina'** (H4)
~ *midseason to late. Uniform short shafts with dark green flags*

02 **'Kajak'** (H4)
~ *quite short shanks; uniform, well-blanched, dark green leaves*

93 **'Longbow'** (H4)
~ *midseason. Uniform, medium length, slightly bulby leeks*

02 **'Mammoth Pot'** (H4)
~ *uniform, with whole stem blanched and light green flag. High December yield. A good short garden plant*

00 **'Swiss Giant - Jolant'** (H4)
~ *for December cropping, high yield; medium to dark green flags; long, solid shafts with little bulbing and very few bolters. Low levels of rust infection (reconfirmed after trial 2002)*

02 **'Toledo'** (H4)
~ *late. Uniform, medium to long smooth shanks, with dark green flags*

93 **'Winterreuzen - Granada'** (H4)
~ *late. Uniform, with dark green flags; tends to split*

LETTUCE (*Lactuca sativa*)
Butterhead, for spring cropping under protection
97 **'Beverley'** PBR (H3)
~ *produces small, solid, mid green heads with rapid growth*

00 **'Cynthia'** (H3)
~ *well hearted, mid green, uniform, good shape*

00 **'Oskar'** (H3)
~ *very good quality; heavy heads; very clean, very uniform, medium to large frame, dark green, attractive, well hearted, thick leaved*

00 **'Ravel'** (H3)
~ *early, well hearted, thick leaved variety, medium dark green, fairly erect leaf*

00 **'Ricardo'** (H3)   ~ *firm hearted*

00 **'Tzigane'** (H3)
~ *nice open hearted, uniform, medium to large frame, dark green, clean base*

Butterhead, for summer cropping in the open garden
02 **'Cassandra'** (H3)
~ *slower to mature; large, tidy frame, with short internal stem and pale to mid green leaves*

97 **'Clarion'** (H3)
~ *open heads, with pale to mid green leaves. Reconfirmed after trial 2002*

02 **'Diana'** (H3)
~ *slower to mature; large frame, with short internal stem and leafy, uniform, mid to dark green heads*

02 **'Enya'** (H3)
~ *uniform, dense, well hearted, tidy heads. Good garden variety*

02 **'Fatima'** (H3)
~ *large frame; uniform, dense, pale to mid green, well hearted heads*

93 **'Lilian'** (H3)
~ *round, well filled heads, with smooth mid green leaves. Reconfirmed after trial 1997 and 2002*

02 **'Plenty'** PBR (H3)
~ *uniform, pale to mid green, with tidy, well filled hearts*

02 **'Roxy'** (H3)
~ *uniform heads; mid to dark green with deep red tinge; slow to mature*

02 **'Sangria'** (H3)
~ *pale to mid green leaves with a bright reddish tinge; good uniform hearts. Slower to mature*

97 **'Sunny'** (H3)
~ *a good-sized lettuce; very early and quick maturing. Reconfirmed after trial 2002*

02   **'Titan'** PBR (H3)
      ~ *mid green, well hearted, tidy heads;*
      slower to mature. Good garden variety

Butterhead, for autumn cropping under protection

97   **'Avondefiance'** (H3)
      ~ *medium to large mid green heads*
97   **'Beverley'** PBR (H3)
      ~ *produces small, solid, mid green*
      heads with rapid growth
97   **'Clarion'** (H3)
      ~ *open heads, with pale to mid green*
      leaves. Reconfirmed after trial 2002
00   **'Ricardo'** (H3)
      ~ *firm hearted*
97   **'Sunny'** PBR (H3)
      ~ *a good-sized lettuce; very early and*
      quick maturing

Cos lettuce

99   **'Attico'** (H3)
      ~ *early. Mid to dark green 'Little Gem'*
      type with dense heads
99   **'Bubbles'** (H3)
      ~ *small heads with dark green crinkly*
      leaves
93   **'Corsair'** (H3)
      ~ *vigorous large frame with mid to pale*
      green slightly blistered leaves
99   **'Cosmic'** (H3)
      ~ *medium size with pale to mid green*
      slightly blistered leaves
99   **'Crisp Mint'** (H3)
      ~ *very fast growing; crinkly leaf and*
      well filled heart
99   **'Darkland Cos'** (H3)
      ~ *not too blistered; good standing; uni-*
      form, nice medium dark green even colour
00   **'Density'** (H3)
      ~ *semi-Cos with leafy, erect habit; dark*
      green, very uniform
93   **'Jewel'** (H3)
      ~ *larger than 'Little Gem' with slightly*
      more blistered leaves. Reconfirmed after
      trial 1999
99   **'Kendo'** PBR (H3)
      ~ *a red-leaved 'Little Gem' type.*
      Reconfirmed after trial 2000
93   **'Little Gem'** (H3)
      ~ *small solid heads with mid green,*
      medium blistered leaves. Reconfirmed
      after trial 1999

99   **'Little Gem Pearl'** (H3)
      ~ *'Little Gem' type but with paler green,*
      more blistered leaves
99   **'Little Leprechaun'** (H3)
      ~ *semi-Cos with dark red leaves*
93   **'Lobjoit's Green Cos'** (H3)
      ~ *large, rather open heads, with*
      relatively smooth mid green leaves.
      Reconfirmed after trial 1999
99   **'Parris Island'** (H3)
      ~ *vigorous with pale green uniform heads*
99   **'Pinokkio'** (H3)
      ~ *medium-sized, dark green*
99   **'Romany'** (H3)
      ~ *early to mature. A round-edged, well*
      turned leaf; some mildew resistance
99   **'Verte Maraichere'** (H3)
      ~ *a very old variety; erect, medium to*
      pale leaves with slight blistering

Crisphead lettuce

94   **'Beatrice'** (H3)
      ~ *small to medium-sized mid green leafy*
      heads; early to mature
01   **'Blush'** (H3)
      ~ *a baby iceberg with slight red blush*
      on grey green outer leaves
01   **'Challenge'** PBR (H3)
      ~ *very large solid hearts, mid to dark*
      green leaves
01   **'Court'** (H3)
      ~ *compact and early*
01   **'Dickinson'** (H3)
      ~ *medium to large frame, solid well*
      filled heads; early
94   **'Kelvin'** PBR (H3)
      ~ *greyish-green solid hearts which are*
      early to mature
93   **'Lakeland'** (H3)
      ~ *large frame with well-hearted heads*
      and bright green leaves; later to mature
94   **'Leopard'** (H3)
      ~ *large frame with well filled heads*
94   **'Malika'** (H3)
      ~ *early. Small framed, dark green well*
      filled heads
94   **'Minigreen'** (H3)
      ~ *early. Uniform, attractive heads with*
      well formed hearts. Reconfirmed after
      trial 2001
01   **'Robinson'** PBR (H3)
      ~ *medium to large frame, good quality*
      solid hearts

94   **'Roxette'** PBR (H3)
~ *shorter-leaved type with tidy, solid hearts*

01   **'Set'** PBR (H3)
~ *medium to large size; an early, solid,
heavy lettuce*

Leafy lettuce

95   **'Black-seeded Simpson Improved'** (H3)
~ *yellow-green leaves with frilled
edges. Cos-like in growth*

95   **'Catalogna'** (H3)
~ *strong growing oak leaf type. Light
green slightly blistered leaves*

95   **'Cocarde'** (H3)
~ *large oak leaf type, with bronze green-
tinged leaves*

95   **'Cordoba'** (H3)
~ *a darker 'Lollo Rossa' type.
Tightly frilled*

95   **'Ferrari'** (H3)
~ *an oak leaf type. Frilled with
heavily bronzed outer leaves*

95   **'Frillice'** PBR (H3)
~ *small growing plants with heavily
serrated dark green leaves*

95   **'Frisby'** (H3)
~ *compact growth with mid green tightly
frilled leaves*

95   **'Ibis'** (H3)
~ *large with shiny bronze frilled leaves*

95   **'Impuls'** (H3)
~ *'Lollo Rossa' type with tightly frilled
bronzed and red leaves*

95   **'Krizet'** (H3)
~ *'Salad Bowl' type with light green
frilled leaves*

95   **'Lollo Rossa'** (H3)
~ *Fothergill's and Marshall mainte-
nances only. Round, medium-sized
plants with green centred leaves and
bronzed frilled outer leaves*

95   **'Loros'** (H3)
~ *a slightly smaller growing 'Lollo
Rossa' type*

95   **'New Red Fire'** (H3)
~ *large, with puckered light bronze
outer leaves*

95   **'Raisa'** (H3)
~ *compact oak leaf type with bronze
and frilled out leaves*

95   **'Red Ruffles'** (H3)
~ *large oak leaf type, open
hearted with bronze
blistered leaves*

95   **'Red Salad Bowl'** (H3)
~ *large oak leaf type. Green leaves
flushed with red on the edge*

95   **'Salad Bowl'** (H3)
~ *large open hearted plants with light
green frilled leaves*

95   **'Sesam'** PBR (H3)
~ *a smaller growing darker leaved
'Lollo Rossa' type*

95   **'Sunburst'** (H3)
~ *a medium-sized cabbage lettuce with
deep red/bronze outer leaves*

MANGETOUT – see pea, mangetout

MARROW (*Cucurbita pepo*)

97   **'Badger Cross'** (H3)
~ *F1 hybrid. Later bush variety; small,
good shape with dark striped fruits.
Claimed CMV tolerance*

97   **'Clarita'** (H3)
~ *F1 hybrid; early cropping. High yield
of pear-shaped, green-white fruits.
Needs cutting when small*

97   **'Minipak'** (H3)
~ *later bush variety, with small dark
striped fruits*

97   **'Tiger Cross'** (H3)
~ *F1 hybrid. High yield of pale striped
fruits. Claimed CMV tolerance*

MELON (*Cucumis melo*)

93   **'Amber Nectar'** (H2)
~ *oval fruit of good size. Ripe fruit flesh
is orange with very good flavour*

99   **'Durandal'** (H2)
~ *F1 hybrid; early to mid
season. Flattened globe-shaped
fruit with faint grooves and heavy
cork netting; flesh orange
when ripe*

99   **'Early Dawn'** (H2)
~ *F1 hybrid; early ripening. Oval fruit
with dark green grooves and heavy cork
netting; flesh orange when ripe*

99   **'Edonis'** (H2)
~ *F1 hybrid; early ripening. Oval to
globular fruit with dark green grooves
and heavy cork netting; flesh orange
when ripe*

93   **'Ogen'** (H2)
~ *oval-round fruit with yellow-green
flesh*

93   'Sweetheart' (H2)
        ~ early ripening; globular, medium-
        sized, cream-coloured fruit with orange
                                            flesh

ONION (*Allium cepa* unless otherwise stated)

Salad onion – non bulbing with strong flavour (*A. fistulosum* and hybrids)

96   'Beltsville Bunching' (H3)
        ~ tall stems with a good length of
                                            blanch
96   'Emerald Isle' (H3)
        ~ medium strong stems; very uniform
96   'Feast' (H3)
        ~ F1 hybrid. Good quality, uniform,
                                            long-stemmed
96   'Ishiko' (H3)
        ~ strong growing, mid to dark green
                        leaves with a good yield
96   'Ishikura' (H3)
        ~ strong growing; long-stemmed
96   'Laser' (H3)
        ~ very strong tall stems; high yield
96   'Savel' (H3)
        ~ long stems with a good length of
                                            blanch
96   'White Spear' (H3)
        ~ long slender stems with dark green
                                            leaves

Salad onion – traditional; winter hardy; mild flavour

96   'Ramrod' (H4)
        ~ strong growing; long stems; dark
                green leaves. Very uniform
93   'White Lisbon' (H4)
        ~ mid green leaves with high yields.
                Good for successional sowing.
                        Overwinters well
93   'Winter Over' (H4)
        ~ dark green leaves, with high yields;
                may become bulby. Overwinters well
93   'Winter White Bunching' (H4)
        ~ strong growing with dark green
                leaves. Overwinters well

Maincrop bulb onion

93   'Golden Bear' (H3)
        ~ F1 hybrid; early. Thin-skinned, high-
                shouldered bulbs; do not store well
95   'Goldito' (H3)
        ~ F1 hybrid. Dark straw-coloured bulbs
                with thick skins; store well

93   'Hygro' (H3)
        ~ F1 hybrid. Good yields of
        thick-skinned straw-coloured bulbs;
                                            store well
95   'Hyton' (H3)
        ~ F1 hybrid. Good yields of dark straw-
                        coloured bulbs; store well
95   'Marco' (H3)
        ~ F1 hybrid. Flattened globe-shaped
                        bulbs; store well
95   'Rijnsburger 5 Balstora' (H3)
        ~ thick-skinned, dark straw-coloured
                        bulbs; store well
95   'Unwins Exhibition' (H3)
        ~ an exhibition onion suitable for
        January sowing under heated conditions

Overwintered bulb onion, grown from seed

93   'Buffalo' (H4)
        ~ F1 hybrid. Good yields of flattened
                globe-shaped bulbs with thin skins
93   'Imai Early Yellow' (H4)
        ~ slightly flattened globe-shaped bulbs;
        dark straw-coloured, with fairly thick skins

Bulb onions grown from sets

02   'Autumn Gold Improved' (H3)
        ~ uniform, excellent size, with good skin
                        and colour; good yield
93   'Centurion' (H3)
        ~ F1 hybrid. Flattened globe-shaped
        bulbs with straw-coloured skins of good
        thickness. Reconfirmed after trial 2002
02   'Hercules' (H3)
        ~ F1 hybrid; slightly elongated bulbs
                with good skin. No bolters
93   'Jagro' (H3)
        ~ F1 hybrid. Good yield of globe-
        shaped bulbs, with good skin; later
        ripening. No bolters. Reconfirmed after
                                            trial 2002
93   'Jetset' (H3)
        ~ F1 hybrid; early. Uniform, flattened
        globe-shaped bulbs with thick, yellow-
                                            brown skins
02   'Setton' (H3)
        ~ F1 hybrid. Good yield, with good
                                            dark skin
93   'Sturon' (H3)
        ~ very good yield of globe-shaped,
        slightly high-shouldered bulbs, with
        good yellow-brown skins. Reconfirmed
                                            after trial 2002

93 **'Turbo'** (H3)
~ *globe-shaped to slightly conical bulbs with brown skins. Some skin splitting*

Shallot
93 **'Atlantic'** (H3)
~ *medium to large bulbs with thin, straw-yellow skins. Reconfirmed after trial 2001*
01 **'Delvad'** (H3)
~ *uniform bulbs with thick reddish brown skins*
93 **'Giant Yellow Improved'** (H3)
~ *uniform, large bulbs with bright, pale brownish skins. Very good yield*
01 **'Golden Gourmet'** (H3)
~ *well shaped, good size; high yield*
01 **'Jermor'** (H3)
~ *good skin, uniform shape and size; suitable for exhibition*
01 **'Longor'** PBR (H3)
~ *good yield and shape; also suitable for exhibition*
01 **'Matador'** (H3)
~ *F1 hybrid; thick skins, and good yield*
93 **'Pikant'** (H3)
~ *bulbs well protected by many layers of reddish brown skins. Reconfirmed after trial 2001*
93 **'Santé'** (H3)
~ *attractive, reddish brown, uniform bulbs with smooth skins. Plant a month later than others to avoid bolting*
93 **'Success'** (H3)
~ *reddish brown bulbs with good skins*

PARSLEY (*Petroselinum crispum*)
97 **'Bravour'** (H4)
~ *a reliable cropper, good stalks, well curled*
97 **'Curlina'** (H4)
~ *compact and uniform; tightly curled*
97 **'Decora'** (H4)
~ *uniform; dark green curled*
97 **'Envy'** (H4)
~ *uniform; mid green curled*
97 **'Favorit'** (H4)
~ *very even; dark green and nicely curled*
97 **'Garland'** (H4)
~ *good vigorous growth; mid green curled*

93 **'Moss Curled'** (H4)
~ *well curled*
93 **'Moss Curled 4 - Afro'** (H4)
~ *well curled, dark green*

PARSNIP (*Pastinaca sativa*)
93 **'Cobham Improved Marrow'** (H4)
~ *wedge- and bayonet-shaped roots with smooth skins; good canker resistance. Reconfirmed after trial 2001*
01 **'Countess'** (H4)
~ *F1 hybrid; smooth skin, shallow crowns, pale cream colour*
01 **'Dagger'** (H4)
~ *F1 hybrid; a smooth parsnip with a shallow crown, very uniform*
01 **'Excalibur'** (H4)
~ *F1 hybrid. A long cream-coloured parsnip with a smooth skin; uniform shape*
01 **'Gladiator'** (H4)
~ *F1 hybrid; very smooth skin, good potential yield, uniform shape, shallow lenticels*
93 **'Javelin'** (H4)
~ *F1 hybrid. Wedge-shaped; yields well. Good canker resistance*
93 **'Tender and True'** (H4)
~ *long roots of mixed size*
01 **'White Spear'** (H4)
~ *uniform shape, shallow lenticels, smooth skin, good white colour*

PEA (*Pisum sativum*)
98 **'Ambassador'** (H3)
~ *maincrop; medium-sized twin pods, easy to pod; good yield with even distribution*
97 **'Bayard'** (H3)
~ *early; a good crop with an average of 8 peas per pod; plants semi-leafless and therefore easy to pick*
93 **'Cavalier'** (H3)
~ *Tozers maintenance only; maincrop; long straight pods, mostly paired; variable maturity therefore good for garden use. Reconfirmed after trial 1998*
98 **'Cockpit'** (H3)
~ *maincrop; semi-leafless with very long pod; well filled with a good colour*
93 **'Early Onward'** (H3)
~ *early; high yield of blunt-ended pods borne in pairs*

98 **'Griffin'** (H3)
~ *maincrop; dark green, with small to medium pods in twos or threes; good flavour*

97 **'Holiday'** (H3)
~ *early; a good cropper; long pods with 8 very sweet peas per pod; easy to pick*

97 **'Hunter'** (H3)
~ *early; a heavy cropper with pods over the whole of the plant; an average of 8 peas per pod*

93 **'Hurst Greenshaft'** (H3)
~ *maincrop; heavy yield of dark green long pointed pods. Reconfirmed after trial 1998*

97 **'Kelvedon Wonder'** (H3)
~ *early; large mid to dark green pods, with an average of 7-8 peas per pod*

97 **'Little Marvel'** (H3)
~ *early; early maturing, good flavoured pea, easily shelled with an average of 7 peas per pod*

98 **'Oasis'** PBR (H3)
~ *maincrop; a later maturing variety. Cropped well, blunt-ended pods*

98 **'Onward'** (H3)
~ *first of the main crop with a high yield and good flavour*

98 **'Oregon Trail'** (H3)
~ *maincrop; good habit; short pods. Good yield over a long picking period*

98 **'Rondo'** (H3)
~ *maincrop; large, broad, straight, pointed pods*

98 **'Saturn'** (H3)
~ *maincrop; a heavy cropper, not too tall, with dark green foliage; a long picking period*

98 **'Show Perfection'** (H3)
~ *maincrop; an 'exhibition' pea, very tall with long dark green pods. A high yield over a long period*

Mangetout pea
00 **'Delikata'** (H3)
~ *tall, with similar pods to 'Oregon Sugar Pod'. A shade earlier and carries a heavy crop. Pods soon form strings if not picked regularly. Mildew and fusarium resistant*

93 **'Edula'** (H3)
~ *fairly dwarf habit with a good crop of curved fleshy pods*

00 **'Norli'** (syn. SUGAR DWARF SWEET GREEN) (H3)
~ *medium height. About the earliest maturing and a heavy cropper but over a short period and so requires successional sowing. Stronger flavour than 'Oregon Sugar Pod'*

93 **'Oregon Sugar Pod'** (H3)
~ *Bakker maintenance only; medium length, with flushes of broad, flat pods over an extended picking period. Must be picked whilst young and stringless. Reconfirmed after trial 2000*

93 **'Reuzensuiker'** (H3)
~ *medium height, pods larger, broader and more fleshy than 'Oregon Sugar Pod' with a concentrated set high on the plant*

00 **'Snow Wind'** PBR (H3)
~ *semi-leafless type producing dark green, sweet pods. Good crop over a long picking season. Would be self supporting if grown in a block instead of rows*

SUGAR DWARF SWEET GREEN see 'Norli'

Sugarsnap pea
00 **'Cascadia'** (H3)
~ *dwarf habit producing very fleshy, crisp, sweet pods, which remain tender and sweet over a longer period than many snaps. Heavy crops over a long picking season*

00 **'Delikett'** (H3)
~ *dwarf habit. Young, dark green pods stringless but soon form strings; become fleshier and sweeter with age. Very well cropped and a long season of picking*

00 **'Sugar Ann'** (H3)
~ *medium height. Very early maturing with a huge crop of pale green pods of succulent, sweet taste*

00 **'Sugar Lord'** (H3)
~ *very tall vigorous plant; extremely high yield of uniform good-coloured pods*

POTATO (*Solanum tuberosum*)
Potato (1st early)
98 **'Accent'** PBR (H3)
~ *a super-tasting new potato, with pale creamy-yellow waxy flesh. Eelworm and common scab resistance*

93 **'Concorde'** (H3)
~ *long oval yellow tubers with waxy yellow flesh. Eelworm resistant. Reconfirmed after trial 1998*

98 **'Foremost'** (H3)
~ *Originally 'Suttons Foremost'. Ever popular 'new potato' with slightly waxy, firm, white, good flavoured flesh that does not discolour or disintegrate on cooking*

98 **'Red Duke of York'** (H3)
~ *oval red sport of 'Duke of York' with moist pale yellow flesh of superb flavour. Excellent roasted but a good all-rounder as tubers bulk up quickly if left to mature as a late Second Early*

98 **'Winston'** PBR (H3)
~ *bulks up quickly to produce large, even-shaped tubers. Creamy moist flesh of excellent flavour which does not discolour on cooking*

Potato (2nd early)

98 **'British Queen'** (H3)
~ *heavy and uniform crop of white-skinned and floury textured tubers of delicious flavour for all cooking purposes*

98 **'Charlotte'** (H3)
~ *long oval variety producing yellow skinned and waxy tubers with creamy yellow flesh of first class flavour either hot or cold*

98 **'Dark Red Norland'** (H3)
~ *dark red skinned oval tubers and pure white flesh. Heavy cropping. Good flavour for boiling and roasting*

98 **'Kondor'** PBR (H3)
~ *large pale red-skinned oval tubers with tasty, almost waxy, yellow flesh. Very high yields. Excellent for baking*

98 **'Lady Christl'** PBR (H3)
~ *bulks up very quickly and is almost a First Early. Long oval, shallow-eyed, pale yellow-skinned and creamy flesh which remains firm on cooking. Eelworm resistant*

98 **'Nadine'** PBR (H3)
~ *exceptionally smooth skin and shallow eyes. Cream flesh with a moist, waxy texture that does not discolour on cooking. Heavy uniform yields. An exhibitor's favourite*

93 **'Stroma'** PBR (H3)
~ *long oval orange red-skinned tubers with firm yellow waxy flesh with a mild flavour; can be left as an early maincrop*

Potato (early maincrop)

93 **'Avalanche'** (H3)
~ *'Maris Piper' as a parent gives guaranteed yields and flavour. Creamy, quite floury flesh for mash, chips and baking*

93 **'Maxine'** PBR (H3)
~ *large, smooth, pale red-skinned tubers with white waxy flesh. Uniform tubers so also recommended for exhibitors. Eelworm resistant. Reconfirmed after trial 1998*

93 **'Navan'** PBR (H3)
~ *heavy crop of oval, white-skinned and creamy white-fleshed tubers. Ideal for chips and roasting. Eelworm resistant*

93 **'Picasso'** PBR (H3)
~ *one of the heaviest croppers with creamy skin and striking bright red eyes. Waxy fine-flavoured flesh, particularly when boiled. Eelworm resistant and good resistance to common scab. Reconfirmed after trial 1998*

98 **'Roseval'** (H3)
~ *vivid carmine skin contrasting with yellow waxy flesh of superb flavour as a salad, hot or cold*

RADICCHIO – see chicory

RADISH (*Raphanus sativus*)

96 **'Cherry Belle'** (H3)
~ *medium-sized leaf. Round red roots of good size*

96 **'Cyros'** (H3)
~ *F1 hybrid. Small leaf; round red roots of excellent colour. Reconfirmed after trial 2002*

02 **'Flamboyant'** (H3)
~ *cylindrical type; red with small white tip. Uniform, medium-sized tops*

96 **'Flamboyant Sabina'** (H3)
~ *quick maturing red roots with small white tip*

96 **'French Breakfast 2'** (H3)
~ *uniform crimson roots with white tip*

96 **'French Breakfast 3'** (H3)
~ *crimson roots with one-third white tip*

00   **'Gandar'** (H3)
*~ uniform; cylindrical shape; good
red colour with small white tip;
attractive bunch*

00   **'Isar'** (H3)
*~ F1 hybrid; excellent size and form;
round shape with erect short tops*

00   **'Juwasprint'** (H3)
*~ very uniform; globe shape; bright red
colour with short tops*

96   **'Marabelle'** (H3)
*~ small leaf. Early with round red
smallish roots. Reconfirmed after
trial 2000 and 2002*

00   **'Mirabeau'** (H3)
*~ F1 hybrid. A widely grown variety
with short tops; globe shape; bright red.
Reconfirmed after trial 2002*

00   **'Printo'** (H3)
*~ F1 hybrid; excellent colour; nice
round shape; medium tops*

93   **'Ribella'** (H3)
*~ small leaf. Round bright red roots.
Reconfirmed after trial 1996*

93   **'Rondar'** (H3)
*~ round bright attractive uniform roots.
Reconfirmed after trial 1996*

00   **'Rougette'** (H3)
*~ a very quick grower with very short
tops; uniform and of good colour; round
shape. Reconfirmed after trial 2002*

02   **'Rudi'** ᴾᴮᴿ (H3)
*~ round type; uniform, with good red
colour; very short tops*

02   **'Saxa'** (H3)
*~ round type; large root, maturing
early; bright red, medium length tops*

96   **'Scarlet Globe'** (H3)
~ round medium to large red roots

93   **'Short Top Forcing'** (H3)
*~ small leaf. Deep round roots of excel-
lent colour. Reconfirmed after trial 2000*

96   **'Sparkler'** (H3)
*~ Unwin's maintenance only; slightly flat-
tened round red roots with a white base*

96   **'Summer Crunch'** (H3)
*~ 'French Breakfast' type with small
white tip*

02   **'Sunto'** (H3)
*~ F1 hybrid; round type; good colour,
early, very short tops*

96   **'Tinto'** (H3)
~ small leaf with large round red roots

SHALLOT – see onion

SPINACH (*Spinacia oleracea*)

96   **'Atlanta'** (H3)
*~ mid green large round leaves.
Good cropper*

02   **'Campania'** (H3)
*~ F1 hybrid. Quick maturing, with mid
to dark green leaves; large frame.
Bulks up quickly*

02   **'Emilia'** (H3)
*~ F1 hybrid. Mid to dark green, slightly
blistered (semi-Savoy) leaves. Prostrate,
slower developing plants*

02   **'Grodane'** (H3)
*~ F1 hybrid. Smooth, bright, mid to
dark green leaves with slight blistering.
Vigorous plants producing a bulky crop*

96   **'Mazurka'** (H3)
*~ F1 hybrid. Round, dark green leaf.
Useful crop; stands well before bolting.
Reconfirmed after trial 2000*

00   **'Medania'** (H3)
*~ slightly blistered, large round leaves.
Bulked well*

96   **'Monnopa'** (H3)
*~ upright leaf habit. Round, pale green
leaves; a good crop*

00   **'Palco'** (H3)
~ late; mid green, upright leaf

02   **'Scenic'** (H3)
*~ F1 hybrid. Large, prostrate, bright
mid green leaves. High yielding, with
midseason maturity. Suitable for 'cut
and come again'*

96   **'Space'** (H3)
*~ F1 hybrid. Round, yellow-green,
slightly puckered leaf. Later maturing
and stands well*

02   **'Spartacus'** (H3)
*~ F1 hybrid. Attractive, very dark
green, blistered leaf. Tight hearts;
good vigour. Fairly slow to mature.
Would suit 'cut and come again'
cropping*

96   **'Spokane'** (H3)
*~ F1 hybrid. Round, dark green, leaf;
smaller growing. Later maturing and
stands well. Reconfirmed after trial
2000 and 2002*

00   **'Tetona'** (H3)
*~ F1 hybrid. Very upright, smooth,
rounded leaf; slow growing*

93 **'Triathlon'** (H3-4)
~ *F1 hybrid; early. Large, pointed, yellow-green leaves; strong growing. An excellent crop*

02 **'Trinidad'** (H3)
~ *F1 hybrid. Upright, vigorous, dark green, shiny leaf. Slightly blistered. Later to mature; well suited to autumn cropping*

02 **'Toscane'** (H3)
~ *F1 hybrid. Very uniform; quite smooth, with green petioles and attractive, mid to dark green leaves. Later maturing crop*

SPINACH BEET (*Beta vulgaris* subsp. *cicla* var. *cicla*) – see also chard
00 **'Perpetual Spinach'** (H3)
~ *mid to pale green with fairly soft texture, medium vigour*

SUGARSNAP – see pea, sugarsnap

SWEDE (*Brassica napus* Napobrassica Group)
02 **'Brora'** ᴾᴮᴿ (H4)
~ *uniform crop; very good smooth shape and colour*

02 **'Magres'** (H4)
~ *fairly round; good size. Yellow flesh contrasts with purple skin*

02 **'Ruby'** ᴾᴮᴿ (H4)
~ *good colour skin, good yellow flesh; elongated shape with a long handle*

SWEET CORN (*Zea mays*)
96 **'Dickson'** (supersweet) (H3)
~ *early to mature; tall plants, with good length cobs. Some colour variation*

96 **'Dynasty'** (supersweet) (H3)
~ *mid season maturity. Tall plants, with long, well filled cobs*

96 **'Golden Sweet'** (supersweet) (H3)
~ *mid season variety. Very tall plants, with medium length cobs*

96 **'Gourmet'** (supersweet) (H3)
~ *early to mature. Tall plants with long, very well filled cobs*

96 **'Northern Extra Sweet'** (supersweet) (H3)
~ *early to mature. Plants of medium height; good length cobs with large kernels*

96 **'Ovation'** (supersweet) (H3)
~ *early maturing. Tall plants with long cobs*

96 **'Start Up'** (supersweet) (H3)
~ *quick maturing. Plants of medium height, with medium length cobs of fine quality*

93 **'Sundance'** (H3)
~ *early to midseason. Short plants, with short well filled cobs*

SWEET PEPPER (*Capsicum annuum* var. *annuum* Grossum Group)
98 **'Ace'** (H2)
~ *F1 hybrid. Uniform bright fruits of a good medium size on compact, short plants*

98 **'Ariane'** (H2)
~ *F1 hybrid. Thick-fleshed, with a good orange colour*

93 **'Bell Boy'** (H2)
~ *F1 hybrid. Good-shaped fruits on compact plants. Reconfirmed after trial 1998*

98 **'Bendigo'** (H2)
~ *F1 hybrid; an early variety. Bright shiny fruits with thick flesh*

93 **'Canape'** (H2)
~ *F1 hybrid. Good shape, with bright red fruits. Reconfirmed after trial 1998*

98 **'Cuneo Giallo'** (H2)
~ *very large fruits; good for stuffing*

93 **'Gypsy'** (H2)
~ *F1 hybrid; very early. Thin-fleshed, pointed, bright red fruits; a prolific cropper. Reconfirmed after trial 1998*

98 **'Unicorn'** (H2)
~ *F1 hybrid. Nice tapering shape; good colour and yield*

98 **'Vidi'** (H2)
~ *F1 hybrid. Compact plants, with a high yield of thick-fleshed, good-coloured fruits*

TOMATO (*Lycopersicon esculentum*)
97 **'Alicante'** (H2)
~ *good shape; heavy crop of attractive fruits which ripen well*

97 **'Arasta'** (H2)
~ *F1 hybrid. Good shape and flavour; very bright juicy flesh*

97   **'Cristal'** (H2)
~ *F1 hybrid. Good shape and flavour; very high yield of large, attractive fruits with glossy skin and dark flesh*

97   **'Golden Sunrise'** (H2)
~ *later maturing; small yellow fruits*

93   **'Outdoor Girl'** (H2)
~ *early. Indeterminate, round red fruits with good flavour*

97   **'Pannovy'** (H2)
~ *F1 hybrid. Thick skin; very high yield*

97   **'Piranto'** (H2)
~ *F1 hybrid. Good shape and colour; high yield of large fruits with good succulent flesh. Small calyx, average flavour*

93   **'Shirley'** (H2)
~ *F1 hybrid; fairly early. Uniform trusses; nice round red fruit of medium size and average flavour. Reconfirmed after trial 1997*

97   **'Spectra'** (H2)
~ *F1 hybrid; a later variety. Good quality; uniform and attractive green back free fruits*

97   **'Tangella'** (H2)
~ *small fruits, of an attractive orange colour; fairly low yield but early*

93   **'Tigerella'** (H2)
~ *interesting attractive striped fruit with quite good flavour. Reconfirmed after trial 1997*

93   **'Tornado'** (H2)
~ *F1 hybrid; early. Bush plants, with thin-skinned juicy fruits*

97   **'Vanessa'** (H2)
~ *F1 hybrid. High yield of green back free, succulent fruits with very nice flavour*

93   **'Yellow Perfection'** (H2)
~ *indeterminate, uniform, round, pale, yellow fruit*

Cherry tomato
93   **'Gardener's Delight'** (H2)
~ *indeterminate plants, producing long trusses of fruits of good flavour under glass or outside. Reconfirmed after trial 1998*

93   **'Gold Nugget'** (H2)
~ *early. Compact plants, with golden yellow, oval fruits. Reconfirmed after trial 1998*

98   **'Jenny'** (H3)
~ *F1 hybrid. A tall variety; good trusses of bright orange fruits*

98   **'Nectar'** (H3)
~ *F1 hybrid; early. Good shape, with trusses of bright red fruits*

98   **'Ruby'** (H3)
~ *F1 hybrid; early. Vigorous habit; a prolific crop of even-sized, bright red fruits on long single trusses*

98   **'Sun Baby'** (H3)
~ *good trusses of uniform, attractive, yellow fruits*

98   **'Sunset'** (H3)
~ *F1 hybrid. Good yield of bright orange fruits*

98   **'Sweet Million'** (H3)
~ *F1 hybrid. Long trusses of sweet, round, bright red fruits; good yield*

98   **'Yellow Debut'** (H3)
~ *F1 hybrid. Good flavoured, medium-sized fruits on long, strong, branched trusses*

TURNIP (*Brassica rapa* Rapifera Group)
97   **'Atlantic'** (H3)
~ *attractive flattened round roots with a purple top; very quick maturing*

97   **'Ivory'** (H3)
~ *uniform, attractive, long cylindrical roots, white and smooth, with a sweet flavour*

97   **'Market Express'** (H3)
~ *F1 hybrid. Uniform, medium size, smooth, round, pure white, shiny roots*

93   **'Tokyo Cross'** (H3)
~ *F1 hybrid. Uniform, medium size, smooth, round, pure white, shiny roots. Reconfirmed after trial 1997*

97   **'Tokyo Top'** (H3)
~ *F1 hybrid. Uniform size; small, white, shiny, round roots*

The Fruit Garden

APPLE (*Malus domestica*)
98 'Alkmene' (D) (H4)
93 'Arthur Turner' (C) (H4)
93 'Ashmead's Kernel' (D) (H4)
93 'Belle de Boskoop' (C/D) (H4)
93 'Blenheim Orange' (C/D) (H4)
93 'Bramley's Seedling' (C) (H4)
93 'Charles Ross' (C/D) (H4)
93 'Claygate Pearmain' (D) (H4)
98 DELBARESTIVALE 'Delcorf' (D) (H4)
93 'Discovery' (D) (H4)
93 'Dummellor's Seedling' (C) (H4)
            ~ *previously listed as Apple*
                        'Dumelow's Seedling'
93 'Edward VII' (C) (H4)
93 'Egremont Russet' (D) (H4)
93 'Ellison's Orange' (D) (H4)
93 'Elstar' (D) (H4)
93 'Emneth Early' (C) (H4)
93 'Falstaff' PBR (D) (H4)
93 'Fiesta' PBR (D) (H4)
93 'George Neal' (C) (H4)
93 'Golden Delicious' (D) (H4)
93 'Golden Noble' (C) (H4)
93 'Greensleeves' PBR (D) (H4)
93 'Grenadier' (C) (H4)
93 'Idared' (D) (H4)
93 'James Grieve' (D) (H4)
93 'Jonagold' (D) (H4)
93 'Jupiter' PBR (D) (H4)
93 'Kidd's Orange Red' (D) (H4)
93 'King of the Pippins' (D) (H4)
93 'King Russet' (D) (H4)
93 'Lane's Prince Albert' (C) (H4)
93 'Laxton's Epicure' (D) (H4)
            ~ *awarded as apple 'Epicure'*
93 'Laxton's Fortune' (D) (H4)
            ~ *awarded as apple 'Fortune'*
93 'Lord Lambourne' (D) (H4)
93 'Merton Charm' (D) (H4)
93 'Mother' (D) (H4)
93 'Newton Wonder' (D/C) (H4)
93 'Peasgood's Nonsuch' (C) (H4)
93 'Pixie' (D) (H4)
93 'Ribston Pippin' (D) (H4)
93 'Rosemary Russet' (D) (H4)
93 'Royal Gala' (D) (H4)
93 'Saint Edmund's Pippin' (D) (H4)
93 'Sunset' (D) (H4)

93 'Suntan' (D) (H4)
93 'Warner's King' (C) (H4)
93 'Winston' (D) (H4)
93 'Worcester Pearmain' (D) (H4)

APRICOT (*Prunus armeniaca*)
98 'Moorpark' (F) (H3)
            ~ *'Early Moorpark' often sold*
                        under this name

BLACKBERRY (*Rubus fruticosa* agg.)
93 'Fantasia' PBR (F) (H4)
93 'Loch Ness' PBR (F) (H4)

BLACKCURRANT (*Ribes nigrum*)
95 'Ben Connan' PBR (B) (H4)
93 'Ben Lomond' PBR (B) (H4)
93 'Ben Sarek' PBR (B) (H4)

CHERRY, MORELLO (*Prunus cerasus*)
93 'Morello' (F) (H4)

CHERRY, SWEET (*Prunus avium*)
95 'Merchant' (F) (H4)
93 'Stella' (sweet) (F) (H4)

DAMSON (*Prunus insititia*)
00 'Farleigh Damson' (C) (H4)
98 'Prune Damson' (C) (H4)

FIG (*Ficus carica*)
93 'Brown Turkey' (F) (H3)

GOOSEBERRY (*Ribes uva-crispa*
var. *reclinatum*)
93 'Careless' (C) (H4)
94 'Greenfinch' PBR (F) (H4)
93 'Invicta' PBR (C) (H4)
93 'Leveller' (C/D) (H4)
93 'Whinham's Industry' (C/D) (H4)

GREENGAGE (*Prunus domestica*)
98 'Cambridge Gage' (D) (H4)

LOGANBERRY (*Rubus* x *loganobaccus*)
93 'LY 59' (F) (H4)
93 'LY 654' (F) (H4)

NECTARINE (*Prunus persica*
var. *nectarina*)
98   'Early Rivers' (F) (H3)
98   'Lord Napier' (F) (H3)

PEACH (*Prunus persica*)
98   'Duke of York' (F) (H3)
98   'Peregrine' (F) (H3)
98   'Rochester' (F) (H3)

PEAR (*Pyrus communis*)
93   'Beth' (D) (H4)
93   'Beurré Hardy' (D) (H4)
93   'Catillac' (C) (H4)
93   'Concorde' PBR (D) (H4)
93   'Conference' (D) (H4)
93   'Doyenné du Comice' (D) (H4)
93   'Joséphine de Malines' (D) (H4)
93   'Onward' (D) (H4)
93   'Pitmaston Duchess' (C/D) (H4)
93   'Williams' Bon Chrétien' (D/C) (H4)

PLUM (*Prunus domestica*)
00   'Blue Rock' **(C/D)** (C/D) (H4)
95   'Blue Tit' (C/D) (H4)
93   'Czar' (C) (H4)
93   'Early Laxton' (C/D) (H4)
94   'Edwards' (C/D) (H4)
93   'Imperial Gage' (C/D) (H4)
94   'Jefferson' (D) (H4)
95   'Laxton's Delight' (D) (H4)
00   'Mallard' **(D)** (D) (H4)
93   'Marjorie's Seedling' (C) (H4)
95   'Opal' (D) (H4)
93   'Ouillins Gage' (C/D) (H4)
93   'Pershore' (C) (H4)
95   'Reeves' (C) (H4)

93   'Sanctus Hubertus' (D) (H4)
95   'Valor' (C/D) (H4)
93   'Victoria' (C/D) (H4)

RASPBERRY (*Rubus idaeus*)
93   'Autumn Bliss' PBR (F) (H4)
00   'Glen Ample' PBR (F) (H4)
93   'Glen Moy' PBR (F) (H4)
93   'Glen Prosen' PBR (F) (H4)
93   'Leo' PBR (F) (H4)
93   'Malling Admiral' (F) (H4)
94   'Malling Delight' (F) (H4)
93   'Malling Jewel' (F) (H4)

REDCURRANT (*Ribes rubrum*)
93   'Jonkheer van Tets' (R) (H4)
93   'Red Lake' (R) (H4)
93   'Stanza' (R) (H4)

SILVANBERRY (*Rubus*)
94   'Silvan' (F) (H4)

STRAWBERRY (*Fragaria* spp.)
93   'Aromel' (F) (H4)
93   'Cambridge Favourite' (F) (H4)
94   'Hapil' PBR (F) (H4)
93   'Honeoye' (F) (H4)
94   'Pegasus' PBR (F) (H4)
94   'Rhapsody' PBR (F) (H4)
95   'Symphony' PBR (F) (H4)

TAYBERRY (*Rubus* Tayberry Group)
93   Tayberry Group (F) (H4)

WHITECURRANT (*Ribes rubrum*)
93   'White Grape' (W) (H4

NEW TRIALS IN 2003

These trials are held to compare and assess plants for the Award of Garden Merit; to show the range of plants within each group; to demonstrate their cultivation; to describe, photograph and check their names.

The following trials will take place at RHS Garden Wisley and are open to the public unless otherwise stated.
**   parallel trials at Harlow Carr and Wisley gardens
***   parallel trials at Rosemoor, Harlow Carr and Wisley gardens

Floral trials from seed
> *Agastache*
> *Cosmos*
> *Echinacea*
> Annual *Papaveraceae* (to include *Argemone, Eschscholzia, Hunnemannia,*
>   *Papaver commutatum, P. somniferum* and *P. rhoeas*)
> *Myosotis* (2003-2004)
> Wallflowers, bedding (2003-2004)**

Floral trials from plugs
> *Calibrachoa* in pots and hanging baskets

Floral trials from plants
> *Actaea* (including *Cimicifuga*)
> *Agastache***
> *Eupatorium* (hardy herbaceous)
> *Geranium*, hardy, Stage 2 (including *G. psilostemon, G. sanguineum*
>   and *G.* × *oxonianum* and related species and cultivars)
> *Sedum* (*Hylotelephium* types), excluding alpines

Under glass
> *Bougainvillea*, suitable for growing in pots

Vegetable trials from seed
> Calabrese to include tender stemmed
> Chinese cabbage for autumn
> Garlic (November planting) for judging 2004***
> Lettuce, coloured leaf types***
> Salad Potato***
> Sweetcorn (excluding normal sugar types)

In unheated plastic tunnel
> Tomato, beefsteak

Fruit trials
> Late season Strawberry (2002-2004)

TRIALS ALREADY UNDERGOING ASSESSMENT IN 2003

Floral trials
Cordyline in containers (2002 and 2003)
Echinacea (2001-2003)
Geranium, hardy, (including *G. clarkei*, *G. himalayense*, *G. pratense*, *G. cinereum*
and related species and cultivars) (2003-2005)
Miscanthus, short cultivars (2001-2003)

Flowers from seed
Aquilegia (2002-2003)
Aubrieta (2002-2004)
Echinacea (2002-2003)

Rock Garden plant trials
Geranium, for the rock garden (2003-2006)
Saxifraga, silver-leaved types (2001-2003)
Hyacinthaceae, hardy small blue bulbs (2001-2003)

Woody trials
near Pinetum
Clematis - *C. alpina* and *C. macropetala* (2001-2003/4)
Rhododendron yakushimanum hybrids (1996-2005)
on adjacent site not normally open to the public
Fuchsia, hardy (2002-2004)
Skimmia (2001-2005)

Vegetables
Broccoli, purple sprouting, to crop from Jan 2003

Long-term trials under way in 2002
Daffodil 2002-2003
Daffodil 2003-2004
Chrysanthemum, garden – sprays and disbuds
Chrysanthemum, garden – 'cushion mums'**
Chrysanthemum, late flowering – under glass
Dahlia
Delphinium 2002-2003
Delphinium 2003-2004
Iris, bearded - 2nd year of 3 year trial
Iris, Pacific Coast - last year of 3 year trial
Iris, tall bearded - last year of 3 year trial
Iris (moisture-loving) 1st year of 3 year trial
Iris sibirica - 1st year of 3 year trial
Iris spuria - 1st year of 4 year trial
Miniature and dwarf pinks
Garden pinks
Border carnations
Perpetual flowering carnations - under glass
Sweet peas**
Tulips in grass

INDEX TO ORNAMENTAL GENERA

Abelia 9
Abies
  dwarf 46
  large/medium 44
Abromeitiella 106
Abutilon
  for unheated glass 127
  hardy shrubs 9
Acacia 127
Acaena
  as rock plants 91
  hardy perennials 48
Acalypha 106
Acanthus 48
Acer 9
Achillea
  as rock plants 91
  hardy perennials 48
X *Achimenantha* 106
Achimenes 106
Aconitum
  as rock plants 91
  hardy perennials 48
Actaea 48
Actinidia 39
Adenium 116
Adiantum
  as rock plants 91
  for heated glass 106
  for unheated glass 127
  hardy perennials 89
Aechmea 106
Aeonium 116
Aeschynanthus 106
Aesculus 9
Aethionema
  as rock plants 91
  hardy shrubs 9
Agapanthus
  for heated glass 106
  hardy perennials 74
Agapetes 106
Agave 116
Ageratum 134
Aglaonema 106
Agrostemma see *Lychnis*
Aichryson 117
Aira 139
Ajuga 48
Albizia
  for heated glass 106
  for unheated glass 127

Alchemilla
  as rock plants 91
  hardy perennials 48
Allamanda
  for heated glass 106
  for heated glass (climbing) 121
Allium
  as rock plants 91
  bulbous perennials 74
Alnus 9
Alocasia 107
Aloe 117
Aloysia 127
Alstroemeria
  for unheated glass 127
  tuberous perennials 74
Alyssum
  as rock plants 91
  hardy perennials see *Aurinia*
  hardy shrubs 9
Amaranthus 134
Amaryllis 127
Amelanchier 9
Ammobium 134
Ampelopsis see *Parthenocissus*
Anagallis
  annuals 134
Ananas 107
Anaphalis 48
Anchusa
  hardy perennials 48
Andromeda
  as rock plants 91
  hardy shrubs 10
Androsace
  as rock plants 91
  hardy perennials 48
Anemone
  as rock plants 92
  for the alpine house 132
  hardy perennials 49
Anigozanthos 107
Anomatheca 127
Antennaria
  as rock plants 92
  hardy perennials 49
Anthemis
  as rock plants 92
  hardy perennials 49

Anthericum
  as rock plants 92
  rhizomatous perennials 74
Anthurium 107
Anthyllis
  as rock plants 92
  hardy perennials 49
Antirrhinum 134
Aphelandra 107
Aporocactus 117
Aptenia 117
Aquilegia
  annuals 134
  as rock plants 92
  hardy perennials 49
Arabis
  annuals 134
  as rock plants 92
  hardy perennials 49
Aralia
  for under glass see *Tetrapanax*
  hardy shrubs 10
Araucaria 107
Arbutus 10
Archontophoenix 107
Arctotis 123
Ardisia 107
Arenaria
  as rock plants 92
  hardy perennials 50
Argyranthemum 123
Arisaema
  as rock plants 92
  tuberous perennials 74
Aristolochia 121
Armeria
  as rock plants 92
  hardy perennials 50
Artemisia
  as rock plants 92
  hardy perennials 50
  hardy shrubs 10
Arum 74
Aruncus 50
Arundinaria see *Fargesia, Pleioblastus, Pseudosasa,* or *Semiarundinaria*
Asarina see *Lophospermum*
Asparagus
  climbing 121
  for heated glass 107

Asperula
  as rock plants 92
  for the alpine house 132
  hardy perennials 50
Aspidistra 107
Asplenium
  as rock plants 92
  for heated glass 107
  hardy perennials 89
Astelia 50
Aster
  as rock plants 92
  hardy perennials 50
Astilbe
  as rock plants 93
  hardy perennials 50
Astrantia 51
Astrophytum 117
Asystasia see *Macleaya*
Athyrium 89
Aubrieta
  as rock plants 93
  hardy perennials 51
Aucuba 10
Aurinia
  as rock plants 93
  hardy perennials 51
Avena see *Helictotrichon*
Asystasia see *Mackaya*
Azara 10
Babiana 107
Ballota 10
Baptisia 50
Beaucarnea see *Nolina*
Begonia
  annuals 134
  for heated glass 107, 123
  tuberous perennials 74
Bellis
  annuals 134
Beloperone see *Justicia*
Berberis
  hardy perennials 93
  hardy shrubs 10
Bergenia 51
Beschorneria 51
Betula 10
Bidens 123
Billardiera 51
Billbergia 108
Blechnum
  as rock plants 93
  for heated glass 108
  hardy perennials 89
Bocconia see *Macleaya*
Bomarea 121
Bougainvillea 121
Brachyglottis 11
Bracteantha 134

Brugmansia
  annuals 134
  for heated glass 108
Brunfelsia 108
Brunnera 51
Brunsvigia see *Amaryllis*
Buddleja
  for heated glass 108
  for unheated glass 127
  hardy shrubs 11
Butomus 51
Buxus 11
Calathea 108
Calceolaria
  for unheated glass 127
  hardy shrubs 11
Calendula 134
Calla see *Zantedeschia*
Callicarpa 11
Callisia 108
Callistemon 11
Callistephus 134
Calluna 11
Calocedrus 44
Caltha 51
Camassia 74
Camellia
  for unheated glass 127
  hardy shrubs 11
Campanula
  as rock plants 93
  for the alpine house
    132
  for unheated glass
    127
  hardy perennials 51
Campsis 39
Canarina 108
Canna 52
Cardamine
  as rock plants 93
  hardy perennials 52
Carex 52
Carpenteria 13
Carpinus 13
Carruanthus 117
Caryopteris 13
Caryota 108
Cassiope
  as rock plants 93
  hardy shrubs 13
Castanea 13
Catalpa 13
Catananche 52
Catharanthus 108
Ceanothus 13
Cedrus 44
Celastrus 39
Centaurea 134

Ceratostigma
  hardy perennials 52
  hardy shrubs 13
Cercidiphyllum 13
Cercis 13
Ceropegia 117
Cestrum
  for unheated glass 127
  hardy shrubs 13
Chaenomeles 13
Chamaecyparis
  dwarf 46
  large/medium 44
Chamaecytisus 13
Chamaedorea 108
Chamaerops
  for heated glass 108
  hardy shrubs 13
Cheiranthus see *Erysimum*
Cheiridopsis 117
Chiastophyllum
  as rock plants 93
  hardy perennials 52
Chimonanthus 14
Chionodoxa
  as rock plants 93
  bulbous perennials 74
Chirita 108
Chlorophytum 123
Choisya 14
Chorizema 108
Chrysalidocarpus see *Dypsis*
Chrysanthemopsis see
    Rhodanthemum
Chrysanthemum
  annuals 134
  as rock plants 93
  for unheated glass 128
  hardy perennials 52
Chrysothemis 108
Chusquea 47
Cimicifuga see *Actaea*
Cissus 121
Cistus 14
X *Citrofortunella* 108
Citrus 108
Cleistocactus 117
Clematis
  as rock plants 93
  climbing 39
  for the alpine house 132
  hardy perennials 55
  hardy shrubs 14
Cleome 135
Clerodendrum
  for heated glass 108
  for heated glass (climbing)
    121
  hardy shrubs 14

Clethra 14
Clianthus 129
Clivia 109
Cobaea 135
Cocos see Lytocaryum
Codonopsis
  as rock plants 93
  climbing 41
Colchicum
  as rock plants 94
  cormous perennials 75
Colocasia 109
Columnea 109
Conophytum 117
Convallaria 75
Convolvulus
  annuals 135
  as rock plants 94
  hardy perennials 55
  hardy shrubs 14
Copiapoa 117
Coprosma 109
Cordyline
  for heated glass 109
  hardy shrub 14
Coreopsis
  annuals 135
  hardy perennials 56
Cornus
  as rock plants 94
  hardy perennials 56
  hardy shrubs 14
Coronilla 15
Correa 129
Cortaderia 73
Corydalis
  as rock plants 94
  for the alpine house
    132
  hardy perennials 56
Corylopsis 15
Corylus 15
Coryphantha 117
Cosmos 134
Cotinus 15
Cotoneaster
  as rock plants 94
  hardy shrubs 15
Cotyledon see Chiastophyllum
    or Echeveria
Crambe 56
Crassula 117
Crataegus 15
Crepis
  as rock plants 94
  hardy perennials 56
Crinodendron 15
Crinum 56
Crocosmia 75

Crocus
  as rock plants 94
  cormous perennials 75
Crossandra 109
Cryptanthus 109
Cryptomeria
  dwarf 46
  large/medium 44
Ctenanthe 109
Cuphea 109
X Cupressocyparis 44
Cupressus
  for unheated glass 129
  large/medium 44
Cyananthus
  as rock plants 95
  hardy perennials 56
Cyanotis 117
Cycas 109
Cyclamen
  as rock plants 95
  for heated glass 109
  for the alpine house 132
  for unheated glass 129
  tuberous perennials 75
Cydonia 15
Cynara 56
Cynoglossum 135
Cyperus 109
Cyrtanthus 109
Cyrtomium 89
Cytisus
  as rock plants 95
  for heated glass see Genista
  hardy shrubs 15
Daboecia 15
Dactylorhiza
  as rock plants 95
  hardy perennials 56
Dahlia
  annuals 135
  hardy perennials 56
Daphne
  as rock plants 95
  hardy shrubs 16
Darlingtonia 109
Darmera 57
Dasylirion 110
Datura
  annuals 135
  for heated glass see
    Brugmansia
Davallia
  for heated glass 110
  hardy 89
Davidia 16
Delosperma 110
Delphinium
  hardy perennials 57

Desfontainia 16
Desmodium 16
Deutzia 16
Dianthus
  as annuals 135
  as rock plants 95
  for heated glass 110
  hardy perennials 58
Diascia
  as rock plants 95
  hardy perennials 59
Dicentra
  as rock plants 95
  hardy perennials 59
Dicksonia
  for unheated glass
    129
  hardy 89
Dictamnus 59
Dieffenbachia 110
Digitalis
  annuals 135
  hardy perennials 59
Dionysia 132
Dioon 110
Dioscorea
  for heated glass 110
  for heated glass (climbing)
    121
Dipelta 16
Disanthus 16
Disocactus 117
Dizygotheca
  see Schefflera
Dodecatheon
  as rock plants 96
  hardy perennials 59
Doronicum 60
Dorotheanthus 135
Draba 132
Dracaena 110
Drimys 16
Dryas
  as rock plants 96
  hardy shrubs 16
Dryopteris 89
Dypsis 110
Echeveria 117
Echinocereus 118
Echinops 60
Echinopsis 118
Echium 129
Edraianthus
  as rock plants 96
  hardy perennials 60
Elaeagnus 16
Elatostema 110
Embothrium 16
Enkianthus 16

Ensete 123
Epimedium
  as rock plants 96
  hardy perennials 60
Epipremnum 121
Eranthemum 110
Eranthis
  as rock plants 96
  hardy perennials 60
Eremurus 60
Erica 16
Erigeron
  as rock plants 96
  hardy perennials 60
Erinacea
  as rock plants 96
  hardy shrubs 17
Erinus
  as rock plants 96
  hardy perennials 60
Eriobotrya 17
Erodium
  as rock plants 96
  hardy perennials 60
Eryngium
  annuals 135
  hardy perennials 60
Erysimum
  annuals 135
  hardy perennials 60
Erythronium
  as rock plants 96
  bulbous perennials 76
Escallonia 17
Eschscholzia 135
Escobaria 118
Espostoa 118
Eucalyptus 17
Eucharis 110
Eucomis 76, 130
Eucryphia 17
Euonymus 17
Eupatorium 60
Euphorbia
  as rock plants 96
  for heated glass 110,
    118
  hardy perennials 60
  hardy shrubs 18
Euryops
  as rock plants 96
  for unheated glass 130
  hardy shrubs 18
Exacum 123
Exochorda 18
Fabiana 18
Fagus 18
Farfugium 110
Fargesia 47

X *Fatshedera* 18
Fatsia
  hardy shrubs 18
  under glass see
    Tetrapanax
Faucaria 118
Felicia 18
Fenestraria 118
Ferocactus 118
Festuca
  as rock plants 96
  hardy perennials 73
Ficus
  climbing 121
  for heated glass 110
Filipendula 61
Fittonia 111
Forsythia 18
Fortunella 111
Fothergilla 18
Fraxinus 18
Fremontodendron 18
Frithia 118
Fritillaria
  as rock plants 96
  for the alpine house 132
  bulbous perennials 76
Fuchsia
  for heated glass 123
  hardy shrubs 18
Gaillardia 135
Galanthus
  as rock plants 96
  bulbous perennials 76
Galega 61
Galtonia 76
Gardenia 111
Garrya 19
Gasteria 118
Gaultheria
  as rock plants 97
  hardy shrubs 19
Gaura 61
Gazania
  annuals 135
  for heated glass 124
Gelsemium
  climbing 121
Genista
  as rock plants 97
  for heated glass 111
  hardy shrubs 19
Gentiana
  as rock plants 97
  hardy perennials 61
Geranium
  as rock plants 97
  for unheated glass 130
  hardy perennials 61

Geum
  as rock plants 97
  hardy perennials 62
Gillenia 62
Ginkgo 45
Gladiolus 76
Glaucidium
  as rock plants 97
  hardy perennials 62
Gleditsia 19
Globularia
  as rock plants 97
  hardy shrubs 19
Gloriosa 121
Graptopetalum 118
Grevillea
  for heated glass 124
  hardy shrubs 19
Griselinia 19
Gunnera 62
Guzmania 111
Gymnocalycium 118
Gymnocarpium
  as rock plants 97
  hardy perennials 89
Gynura 111
Gypsophila
  as rock plants 97
  hardy perennnials 62
Haberlea
  as rock plants 97
  hardy perennials 62
Habranthus 111
Hacquetia
  as rock plants 97
  hardy perennials 62
Haemanthus 111
Hakonechloa 73
Halesia 19
X *Halimiocistus* 19
Halimium 19
Hamamelis 19
Hamatocactus see
  Thelocactus
Hardenbergia 121
Hatiora 118
Haworthia 118
Hebe
  as rock plants 97
  for unheated glass 130
  hardy shrubs 19
Hedera 41
Hedychium
  for heated glass 111
  hardy perennials 62
Helenium 62
Helianthemum
  as rock plants 98
  hardy shrubs 20

Helianthus
  annuals 135
  hardy perennials 62
Helichrysum
  for unheated glass 130
  for the alpine house
    132
  hardy shrubs 20
Helictotrichon 73
Heliocereus 118
Heliopsis 62
Heliotropium 111
Helleborus
  for the alpine house
    132
  hardy perennials 62
Hemerocallis 76
Hepatica
  as rock plants 98
  hardy perennials 62
Heuchera 62
X *Heucherella* 63
X *Hibanobambusa* 47
Hibbertia 121
Hibiscus
  for heated glass 111
  hardy shrubs 20
Hildewintera 118
Hippeastrum 111
Hippophae 20
Hoheria 21
Hosta 63
Howea 111
Hoya
  climbing 121
  for heated glass 111
Humulus 42
Hyacinthus
  as rock plants 98
  bulbous perennials
    76
Hydrangea
  climbing 42
  hardy shrubs 21
Hymenocallis 111
Hypericum
  as rock plants 98
  hardy shrubs 21
Hypoestes 111
Iberis
  as rock plants 98
  hardy shrubs 21
Ilex 21
Impatiens
  annuals 135
  for heated glass 112
Indigofera 22
Indocalamus 47
Inula 63

Ipheion
  as rock plants 98
  for the alpine house 132
  hardy perennials 63
Ipomoea
  annuals 135
  climbing 121
Iresine 112
Iris
  as rock plants 98
  bulbous or rhizomatous
    perennials 76
  for the alpine house 132
Ismelia 135
Itea 21
Jasminum
  climbing 42
  for heated glass (climbing)
    121
  for unheated glass
    (climbing) 131
  hardy shrubs 22
Jatropha 118
Jovellana 22
Juglans 22
Juniperus
  dwarf 46
  large/medium 45
Justicia 112
Kalanchoe 118
Kalmia
  as rock plants 98
  hardy shrubs 22
Kalmiopsis
  as rock plants 98
  hardy shrubs 22
Kentia see *Howea*
Kerria 22
Kirengeshoma 63
Kleinia 118
Kniphofia 80
Koelreuteria 22
Kohleria 112
Kolkwitzia 22
Laburnum 22
Lachenalia 112
Lagerstroemia 112
Lagurus 139
Lamium 63
Lampranthus see *Delosperma*
  or *Oscularia*
Lapageria 42
Lapeirousia see *Anomatheca*
Larix 45
Lathyrus
  annuals 136
  as rock plants 98
  climbing 42
  hardy perennials 64

Laurus 22
Lavandula 22
Lavatera
  annuals 136
  for unheated glass 130
  hardy shrubs 23
X *Ledodendron*
  as rock plants 98
  hardy shrubs 23
Leiophyllum
  as rock plants 98
  hardy shrubs 23
Lepismium 119
Leptospermum
  as rock plants 98
  for the alpine house 132
  hardy shrubs 23
Lespedeza 23
Leucanthemella 64
Leucanthemopsis see
  Rhodanthemum
Leucanthemum
  for rock plants see
    Rhodanthemum
  hardy perennials 64
Leucocoryne 112
Leucojum
  as rock plants 98
  bulbous perennials 80
  for the alpine house 132
Leucothoe 23
Lewisia
  as rock plants 98
  for the alpine house 132
  hardy perennials 64
Leycesteria 23
Libertia 64
Libocedrus see *Calocedrus*
Ligularia
  for heated glass 112
  hardy perennials 64
Ligustrum 23
Lilium
  bulbous perennials 80
  for unheated glass 130
Limnanthes 136
Limonium 136
Lindera 23
Linum
  annuals 136
  as rock plants 98
  hardy shrubs 23
Lippia see *Aloysia*
Liquidambar 23
Liriodendron 23
Liriope 80
Lithodora
  as rock plants 98
  hardy shrubs 23

Lithops 119
Lithospermum see *Lithodora*
Livistona 112
Lobelia
    annuals 136
    hardy perennials 64
    heated glass 124
Lobivia 119
Lobularia 137
Lonicera
    climbing 42
    hardy shrubs 23
Lophospermum 130
Lotus
    for heated glass 124
    hardy shrub 23
Luculia 112
Luma 23
Lunaria 137
Lupinus
    annuals 137
    hardy shrubs 23
Lychnis
    as rock plants 99
    hardy perennials 64
Lysichiton 64
Lysimachia
    as rock plants 99
    hardy perennials 64
Lythrum 64
Lytocaryum 112
Mackaya 112
Macleaya 64
Magnolia 24
Mahonia 24
Maianthemum see *Smilacina*
Malus 24
Malva
    for unheated glass see
      Lavatera
    hardy perennials 64
Mammillaria
    for heated glass 119
Mandevilla
    for heated glass 121
    for unheated glass
      (climbing) 131
Maranta 112
Matteuccia 89
Matthiola 112
Matucana 119
Maurandya see
    Lophospermum
Meconopsis
    as rock plants 99
    hardy perennials 64
Medinilla 112
Melianthus 24
Mertensia 64

Mesembryanthemum see
    Dorotheanthus
Metasequoia 45
Microbiota 47
Microcoelum
    see *Lytocaryum*
Milium 73
Mimulus
    annuals 137
    as rock plants 99
    for unheated glass 130
    hardy perennials 64
Miscanthus 73
Molinia 73
Moltkia
    as rock plants 99
    hardy shrubs 24
Monarda 64
Monstera 122
Morus 24
Musa
    for heated glass 112, 124
    hardy shrubs 24
Muscari
    as rock plants 99
    bulbous perennials 80
Myosotis 137
Myrtus 24
Nandina 24
Narcissus
    as rock plants 99
    bulbous perennials 80
    for the alpine house 132
Nematanthus 112
Nemesia 65
Neochilenia see *Neoporteria*
Neohenricia 119
Neoporteria 119
Neoregelia 112
Nepeta 65
Nephrolepis
    for heated glass 113
    for unheated glass 130
Nerine
    bulbous perennials 86
    for unheated glass 130
Nerium 124
Nicotiana 137
Nidularium 113
Nierembergia 113
Nigella 137
Nolina 113
Nopalxochia 119
Notocactus 119
Nymphaea 65
Nyssa 24
Oenothera
    as rock plants 99
    hardy perennials 65

Olearia 24
Olsynium
    as rock plants 99
    hardy perennials 65
Omphalodes
    annuals 137
    as rock plants 100
    hardy perennials 65
Onoclea 90
Onopordum 65
Onosma
    as rock plants 100
    hardy perennials 65
Ophiopogon
    as rock plants 100
    for bulbous species see
      Liriope
    hardy perennials 65
Oplismenus
    for heated glass 113
Opuntia 119
Orbea 119
Orchis see *Dactylorhiza*
Oreocereus 119
Origanum
    as rock plants 100
    for the alpine house 132
    hardy perennials 65
Ornithogalum
    bulbous perennials 86
    for heated glass 113
Oscularia 119
Osmanthus 25
Osmarea see *Osmanthus*
Osmunda 90
Osteospermum
    for heated glass 124
    hardy perennials 65
Ourisia
    as rock plants 100
    hardy perennials 66
Oxalis
    as rock plants 100
    for heated glass 113
    hardy perennials 86
Oxypetalum see *Tweedia*
Ozothamnus
    for the alpine house 132
    hardy shrubs 25
Pachypodium 119
Pachysandra 25
Pachystachys 113
Paeonia
    as rock plants 100
    for the alpine house 132
    hardy perennials 66
    hardy shrubs 25
Pandanus 113
Pandorea 122

Papaver
  annuals 137
  hardy perennials 66
Paradisea
  as rock plants 100
  rhizomatous perennials
    86
Parahebe
  as rock plants 100
  hardy perennials 66
  hardy shrubs 25
Paraserianthes 113
Parochetus 130
Parodia 119
Parrotia 25
Parthenocissus 42
Passiflora
  climbing 42
  for heated glass (climbing)
    122
  for unheated glass
    (climbing) 131
Paulownia 25
Pavonia 113
Pedilanthus 119
Pelargonium 124
Pellaea 130
Peltiphyllum see *Darmera*
Pennisetum
  annuals 139
  hardy perennials 73
Penstemon
  as rock plants 100
  hardy perennials 66
  hardy shrubs 25
Peperomia 113
Perilla 130
Pernettya see *Gaultheria*
Perovskia 25
Persicaria
  as rock plants 100
  hardy perennials 67
Petrorhagia
  as rock plants 100
  hardy perennials 67
Petunia 138
Phalaris 73
Phanerophlebia see
  Cyrtomium
Philadelphus 25
Philodendron
  for heated glass 113
  for heated glass (climbing)
    121
Phlebodium see
  Polypodium
Phlomis
  hardy perennials 67
  hardy shrubs 25

Phlox
  annuals 138
  as rock plants 100
  hardy perennials 67
Phoenix 126
Phormium 25
Photinia 25
Phygelius 26
X *Phylliopsis*
  as rock plants 100
  hardy shrub 26
Phyllitis see *Asplenium*
Phyllodoce
  as rock plants 100
  hardy shrubs 26
Phyllostachys 47
Physalis 67
Physocarpus 26
Physoplexis 133
Physostegia 67
Phyteuma see *Physoplexis*
Picea
  dwarf 47
  large/medium 45
Pieris 26
Pilea 113
Pileostegia 42
Pinus
  dwarf 47
  for unheated glass
    130
  large/medium 45
Pittosporum
  for unheated glass
    130
  hardy shrubs 26
Plagianthus see *Hoheria*
Platanus 26
Platycerium 113
Platycladus
  dwarf 47
  large/medium 45
Platycodon
  as rock plants 100
  hardy perennials 67
Plectranthus
  for heated glass 113
  for unheated glass
    130
Pleioblastus 47
Pleione 133
Pleiospilos 120
Pleomele see *Dracaena*
Plumbago
  for heated glass 113
  hardy perennials 67
Plumeria 113
Podocarpus 45
Polemonium 67

Polianthes 114
Poliothyrsis 26
Polygala
  as rock plants 101
  for heated glass 114
  hardy perennials 68
  hardy shrubs 26
Polygonatum 68
Polygonum see *Persicaria*
Polypodium
  for heated glass 114
  hardy perennials 90
Polyscias 114
Polystichum 90
Pontederia 68
Populus 26
Potentilla
  as rock plants 101
  hardy perennials 68
  hardy shrubs 27
Primula
  annuals 138
  as rock plants 101
  for the alpine house 133
  for heated glass 114
  for unheated glass 130
  hardy perennials 68
Prostanthera
  for unheated glass 130
  hardy shrubs 27
Prunella 69
Prunus 27
Pseudolarix 45
Pseudomuscari see *Muscari*
Pseudopanax 114
Pseudosasa 47
Pseudotsuga 45
Ptelea 27
Pteris
  for heated glass 114,
    126
Pterocarya 27
Pterostyrax 27
Ptilotrichum see *Alyssum*
Pulmonaria 69
Pulsatilla
  as rock plants 101
  for the alpine house 133
  hardy perennials 69
Punica 28
Pyracantha 28
Pyrethropsis see
  Rhodanthemum
Pyrus 28
Quercus 28
Radermachera 114
Ramonda
  as rock plants 101
  hardy perennials 69

Ranunculus
  as rock plants 102
  for the alpine house 133
  hardy perennials 69
Rebutia 120
Rehmannia
  for unheated glass 130
  hardy perennials 69
Rhamnus 28
Rhaphiolepis 131
Rhapis 114
Rhazya see *Amsonia*
Rheum 69
Rhipsalidopsis see *Hatiora*
Rhipsalis 120
Rhodanthemum
  as rock plants 102
  hardy perennials 69
Rhodochiton 122
Rhododendron
  as rock plants 102
  for unheated glass 131
  hardy shrubs 28
Rhodohypoxis
  as rock plants 102
  hardy perennials 69
Rhoeo see *Tradescantia*
Rhoicissus 122
Rhombophyllum 120
Rhus 32
Ribes 32
Ricinus 138
Robinia 32
Rodgersia 69
Romneya 69
Rosa
  climbing 42
  hardy shrubs 32
Roscoea
  as rock plants 102
  hardy perennials 69
Rosmarinus 36
Rubus 36
Rudbeckia
  annuals 138
  hardy perennials 69
Ruellia 114
Rumohra 114
Ruscus see *Danae*
Russelia 114
Salix
  as rock plants 102
  hardy shrubs 36
Salpiglossis 138
Salvia
  annuals 138
  for heated glass 114,126
  hardy perennials 70
  hardy shrubs 36

Sambucus 36
Sanguinaria
  as rock plants 102
  hardy perennials 70
Sansevieria 114
Santolina
  as rock plants 102
  hardy shrubs 36
Saponaria
  as rock plants 102
  hardy perennials 70
Sarcococca 36
Sarmienta 133
Sarracenia 114
Sasa see *Indocalamus*
Satureja
  as rock plants 102
  hardy shrubs 37
Saxifraga
  as rock plants 102
  for the alpine house 133
  for uheated glass 131
  hardy perennials 70
Scabiosa
  annuals 138
  hardy perennials 71
Scadoxus 114
Schefflera 114
Schizanthus 138
Schizophragma 43
Schizostylis 86
Schlumbergera 120
Sciadopitys 46
Scilla
  as rock plants 103
  bulbous perennials 86
Scindapsus 122
Sedum
  as rock plants 103
  for heated glass 120
  for unheated glass 131
  hardy perennials 71
Selaginella 114
Semiarundinaria 47
Sempervivum
  as rock plants 103
  hardy perennials 71
Senecio
  annuals 138
  for heated glass 120
  for heated glass (climbing) 122
  hardy perennials 71
  hardy shrubs 37
Senna 115
Sequoia 46
Sequoiadendron 46
Seriphidium 71
Setaria 139

Sidalcea 71
Silene
  as rock plants 103
  hardy perennials 71
Silphium 71
Sinarundinaria see
  Fargesia
Sinningia 115
Sisyrinchium
  as rock plants 104
  for alpine house 133
  for hardy perennials 71
Skimmia 37
Smilacina 86
Solanum 43
Solenostemon 115
Solidago 71
X *Solidaster* 71
Sollya 122
Sonerila 115
Sophora 37
Sorbaria 37
Sorbus
  as rock plants 104
  hardy shrubs 37
Sparaxis 131
Sparrmannia 115
Spartium 37
Spathiphyllum 115
Spiraea
  as rock plants 104
  hardy perennials 71
  hardy shrubs 37
Stachys 71
Stachyurus 37
Stapelia 120
Stenotaphrum 115
Stephanotis 122
Stewartia 37
Stipa 73
Stomatium 120
Strelitzia 115
Streptocarpus 115
Streptosolen 115
Strobilanthes 115
Stromanthe 115
Stylidium 131
Styrax 38
Sulcorebutia 120
Syagrus see *Lytocaryum*
Symphytum 71
Syngonium 122
Syringa 38
Tagetes 138
Tamarix 38
Tanacetum 72
Taxodium 46
Taxus 46
Tecoma 115

Tecophilaea 133
Tetranema 115
Tetrapanax 131
Tetrastigma 122
Teucrium 38
Thalictrum 72
Thamnocalamus see
    Fargesia
Thelocactus 120
Thuja
    dwarf 47
    large/medium 46
Thujopsis 46
Thunbergia 122, 126
Thymus
    as rock plants 104
    hardy shrubs 38
Tiarella
    as rock plants 104
    hardy perennials 72
Tibouchina 115
Tilia 38
Tillandsia 116
Titanopsis 120
Tolmiea 72
Trachelium 116
Trachelospermum 131
Trachycarpus 38
Tradescantia
    for heated glass 116
    for unheated glass 131
    hardy perennials 72
Trichodiadema 120
Tricyrtis 72
Trillium
    as rock plants 104
    rhizomatous perennials 86

Tristagma see *Ipheion*
Tritomia 131
Trollius 72
Tropaeolum
    annuals 138
    climbing 43
    for heated glass (climbing)
        122
    for unheated glass 131
Tsuga 46
Tulipa
    as rock plants 104
    bulbous perennials 86
Tweedia 131
Ulex 38
Uvularia
    as rock plants 104
    rhizomatous perennials 88
Vaccinium
    as rock plants 104
    hardy shrubs 38
Veltheimia 116
Veratrum 72
Verbascum
    as rock plants 104
    for the alpine house 133
    hardy perennials 72
    hardy shrubs 39
Verbena
    annuals 138
    for unheated glass 131
    hardy perennials 72
Veronica
    as rock plants 104
    hardy perennials 72
Vestia 116
Viburnum 39

Vinca 72
Viola
    annuals 139
    as rock plants 104
    hardy perennials 73
Vitis 43
Vriesea 116
Wahlenbergia see
    Edraianthus
Washingtonia 116
Weigela 39
Weingartia 120
Westringia 116
Wisteria 43
Woodsia 90
Woodwardia 90
Xanthoceras 39
Xanthophthalmum 139
Yucca
    for heated glass 116
    hardy perennials 39
Zantedeschia
    for heated glass 116
    rhizomatous perennials
        88
Zauschneria
    as rock plants 105
    hardy shrubs 39
Zelkova 39
Zephyranthes 116, 131
Zinnia 126